Corporation Nation

HANEY FOUNDATION SERIES

A volume in the Haney Foundation Series, established in 1961
with the generous support of Dr. John Louis Haney

Corporation Nation

Robert E. Wright

PENN

UNIVERSITY OF PENNSYLVANIA PRESS

PHILADELPHIA

Copyright © 2014 University of Pennsylvania Press

Published by
University of Pennsylvania Press
Philadelphia, Pennsylvania 19104-4112
www.upenn.edu/pennpress

Printed in the United States of America on acid-free paper
10 9 8 7 6 5 4 3 2 1

Library of Congress Cataloging-in-Publication Data
Wright, Rober E. (Robert Eric), 1969–
    Corporation nation / Robert E. Wright. — 1st ed.
        p. cm. — (Haney Foundation series)
    Includes bibliographical references and index.
    ISBN 978-0-8122-4564-6 (hardcover : alk. paper)
    1. Corporations—United States—History—19th century. 2. Corporate governance—United States—History—19th century. 3. Corporate governance—United States—History—21st century. 4. Big business—United States—History—21st century. I. Title. II. Series: Haney Foundation series.
HD2785.W75 2013
338.7'4097309034—dc23
                                                                                    2013020982

Nations, like man, rise, flourish, and decay.

—Ferris Pell, *Review of the Administration and Civil Police
of the State of New York* (1819)

Contents

Chapter 1

The Corporation Nation Emerges

If they were honestly and safely conducted, [corporations] would afford a safe and satisfactory investment for small sums and thus tend to equalize the wealth of the people.

—V. H. Lockwood, 1897[1]

The development of the for-profit business corporation over time has never been well understood, even in the nation most responsible for its economic ascendance, the United States. "American-style corporate capitalism," two business scholars recently proclaimed, "is an international juggernaut" (an overwhelmingly destructive force) and perhaps the single most important institutional feature of modern, developed economies the globe over.[2] Yet even leading scholars of the U.S. economy have underestimated the number, ubiquity, and economic importance of early corporations, creating the misapprehension that they were insignificant until after, or perhaps during, the Civil War.[3]

Two reporters for the generally astute economics weekly *The Economist* recently wrote a book that called the corporation "yet another quirky . . . invention" of "Victorian Britain."[4] Many contemporaries, however, believed that America, not the Mother Country, was responsible for raising corporations from vehicles of monopoly privilege to a widely used form of business. "In no other age or country," wrote Andrew Allison in 1884, "have private corporations entered so extensively into the business of the country, never so thoroughly into the details of everyday life, as with us."[5] Moreover, while Britain embraced the corporate form before most other nations did, the economies of both America and Britain were significantly corporatized well before Victoria's long reign began in 1837.

"By the time that [Supreme Court Chief Justice John] Marshall left the Court in 1836," legal historian Arthur Selwyn Miller noted in 1968, "the corporation . . . had become a key institution in American life."[6] As the new data presented in Chapter 4 show, Miller's intuition was right. In addition to setting the historical record straight, this book seeks to improve the internal governance and external regulation of corporations today. Business leaders as well as policymakers have forgotten the conditions under which corporations thrive and the circumstances in which they are likely to flail or fail. That memory lapse has caused Americans some serious consternation recently—in the form of Enron, Lehman Brothers, Comcast, Fannie Mae, Bernie Madoff, and others too numerous to mention—and, I fear, will cause even more serious trouble in the relatively near future. Until they relearn to govern themselves, corporations will continue to face two major risks: increased government regulation and the withdrawal of investor demand. Either outcome could injure the economy, while the occurrence of both—if investors widely believe that new regulations would burden corporate profits without improving governance—could prove economically devastating. Think dangerous drop in liquidity, withdrawal of foreign portfolio investment, stock market meltdown, and ultimately decreased incentive for entrepreneurs to innovate due to an anemic IPO market. Such a disaster scenario is not unrealistic. Money, it is said, "stays where it is well treated," and currently, it is regularly abused by the nation's regulators and its largest corporations. Currently, the public has more confidence in gas-station attendants than in bankers and more confidence in auto repairmen than in investment advisers.[7]

Corporate governance malfeasance has raised the cost of capital in the past and could do so again. After the Civil War, shady railroad managers frightened "legitimate investment," nearly killing "the goose which lays the golden egg" in the words of one critic.[8] "Worthy stock enterprises," complained another, "languish from public distrust in stock companies."[9] In the late nineteenth century, investment gurus regularly cautioned individuals not to buy common stocks because good information about corporate financials was lacking. Legal reforms aimed to change that; but in the wake of numerous scandals, their success appears doubtful.[10]

Despite all the disclosure laws passed since, financial information remains of dubious quality. According to Jonathan Macey, one of the world's leading experts on all things corporate, stockholders must "trust" that corporate executives will treat their money right because "shareholders have . . . virtually no contractual rights to corporate cash flows."[11] Most investors today don't know that, and they overestimate the power of regulators to monitor executives on their behalf. When investors realize that what they get in return for their hard-earned money is at the whim of overpaid corporate executives, not the rule of law, there will be economic hell to pay. "If the confidence of the public in great corporations is destroyed," noted one scholar during the Great Depression, "as it has been already sorely shaken in numerous recent instances of gross lapses from duty, the entire stability of our institutions will be thereby undermined."[12] Disgruntled investors today could also withdraw from the equities markets, some scholars warn. "The fundamental problem of the corporation," noted economists Charles Calomiris and Carlos Ramirez in the mid-1990s, "is to secure funding from people who are not directly in control of the use of those funds."[13] Without safeguards, managers can, and will, bilk investors to the point that "suppliers of funds may not find it worthwhile to transfer their savings to corporations." And because a majority of Americans now own stock, if only indirectly via their retirement accounts and other mutual fund holdings, the economic, political, and social risks of a "capital strike" are greater than ever. Even if such a strike were not widespread enough to result in economic meltdown, any sizable change in investor sentiments away from corporate securities would likely raise the cost of corporate capital and hence slow economic growth.[14]

Before the Civil War, investors in U.S. corporations enjoyed much more security than they do today. Many of the "glaring abuses" and "evils" of modern corporations, a Depression-era corporate critic argued, "are due to the transformation of small, closely held, personal business corporations of the type which existed in the earlier days of the Republic, into nationwide companies whose stock is widely held in many dispersed hands and which too often are characterized by loose, careless management and control."[15] The concomitant erosion of traditional governance checks and balances, this book will show, played perhaps an even larger role in the demise of investor security after the Civil War.[16]

Action is necessary because the corporation is too economically important to be allowed to wither. Within a few years of adoption of the Constitution, the corporation was ingrained in almost every aspect of Americans' economic lives, from finance to transportation, as Joshua Gilpin discovered when he set out from Philadelphia "to the Western parts of Pennsylvania" in 1809: "After crossing the Schuylkill permanent Bridge [a corporation], we took the Lancaster turnpike [another corporation]," used money issued by corporate banks, and even slept in a hotel owned by a corporation.[17] In 1835, a pundit noted that the great internal improvements of the period, "the roads, canals, tunnels, are the result of those laws which permit, and those systems of government which do not trammel, the association of wealth."[18] As another corporate booster put it that same year, "almost every instance of valuable public improvement that meets the eye, is to be traced directly or indirectly to the agency of that much-decried monster—Corporation!"[19] Still another, writing two years later, noted that if contemporaries looked in "different directions" they could not "but see their beneficial influences upon the condition of the country."[20] If anything, corporations are even more important to the nation's economic health today.

Miller claimed that history provided "no convincing answers" for why America became the consummate corporation nation before the Civil War (1861–65). This book shows that a generally effective system of internal governance allowed early corporations to raise (what were then) significant sums of equity capital *at start up* without the aid of investment banks or other intermediaries. Americans did not invent the for-profit business corporation, but they did perfect the form—and far earlier than most believe—in the first half of the nineteenth century, surpassing the British and other precedents (discussed in Chapter 2) quickly and completely, despite the misgivings expressed by corporate critics detailed in Chapter 3. As Chapter 4 shows, by the early nineteenth century, the young nation had chartered more corporations than any other country on earth and sustained its lead throughout the antebellum period. As shown in Chapter 5, corporations proliferated widely throughout the nation, north and south, east and west, because the benefits of creating them generally outweighed the costs. Corporate privileges like the ability to sue and be sued in its own name, perpetual succession, use of a corporate seal, limited liability, entity shielding, share transferability, and relatively clear laws concerning the operations and governance of joint-stock companies allowed corporations to grow much bigger, much faster than they could have as traditional partnerships or sole proprietorships. That, in turn, allowed them to achieve scale economies (lower production costs per unit produced), the most profitable (Coasean) degree of vertical integration, and market power (some degree of control over prices and quantities). As eighteenth-century British political economist Sir James Steuart correctly noted, "by uniting the stocks of several merchants together, an enterprise far beyond the force of any one, becomes practicable to the community."[21]

Incorporators had to pay postage, publishing, and other lobbying costs and were not assured of receiving a charter, but the expected direct costs of incorporation were typically minimal, especially after the passage of general incorporation acts in many states in the 1840s and 1850s. "The difference, in point of delay, trouble and expense, between forming a private corporation under a general law, and obtaining a special charter," a late nineteenth-century jurist claimed, "may be likened to that between modern traveling by railroad and the old fashioned stage coach."[22] But the chartering of more than 22,000 businesses by special act before 1861 suggests that the "stage-coach" approach to incorporation was more an inconvenience than a barrier to entrepreneurs.[23]

The indirect costs of incorporation and large size—the so-called agency costs of having numerous agents and employees complete important work tasks on behalf of the owners—were more substantial but could be mitigated by screening, employee incentives, and other governance principles, which are discussed in Chapter 6. A few early corporations survive to this day, but most eventually exited via bankruptcy, a deliberate winding down of their affairs, or merger (then typically called "amalgamation"). Most failed companies were driven out of business by more efficiently managed competitors, but a few were extinguished by corporate governance failures (various types of fraud), such as those detailed in Chapter 7. As described in Chapter 8, defalcations spawned regulatory responses that more or less prevented the exact repetition of earlier frauds but did little or nothing to prevent new types of expropriation from taking place. Chapter 9 takes up that theme by tracing the history of corporate governance and regulation from the Civil War to the present. The book concludes in Chapter 10 with the suggestion that a new approach to regulation is needed if the number and severity of corporate financial scandals are to be significantly reduced. Returning to the governance principles of our forebears is a good place to start.[24]

Restoring internal governance to a semblance of health and improving external regulation will not be easy; nothing of such crucial importance ever is. Retaining investor confidence in corporations is essential to the nation's continued material prosperity. Corporate precocity helped the early U.S. economy to grow and develop more rapidly than any other in the world. "The limited liability corporation," Columbia University president Nicholas Murray Butler argued in the late nineteenth century, "is the greatest single discovery of modern times," a sort of "technology" that unleashed more familiar technologies like steam and electricity.[25] Without corporations, reformer Henry Wood wrote in 1889, "science, invention, art, and production would fail to find wide and general expression, and material, commercial, and even intellectual progress would be turned backwards."[26] If anything, corporations are even more important today.

It simply is not true, as some earlier economic historians believed, that the U.S. economy did not "take off" until sometime after 1830. The best available evidence indicates that per-capita incomes began increasing soon after the ratification of the Constitution and have continued unabated, save for the undulations of the business cycle, until the present time. The same goes for industrial production. America grew wealthy because of the solidity of its institutions, not its great expanse, a point that nineteenth-century Americans well understood. "A broad land is not necessary to a great people," one noted in 1845. "An earnest industry, a bold enterprise, a comprehensive wisdom, have made" the nation "what it is, and are able to make it all it could wish to be."[27]

Nineteenth-century Americans realized that the business corporation was one of the most important of those growth-inducing institutions.[28] "The surprising influence of these institutions, in promoting the general Improvement of the Country," Massachusetts governor Levi Lincoln proclaimed, "may be witnessed wherever they are situated. Look but to the villages of Lowell and Ware, places where the very wastes of nature, as if by the magic of machinery, have suddenly converted into scenes of busy population, of useful industry, and of wealth."[29] "On a spot where a few years ago there was but two or three houses," aspiring pastor Ephraim Abbot noted in 1812, "there is a village of 64 families and 500 people in some way employed about the factory."[30] "By their [corporations'] aid," a committee of New York legislators noted in 1826, "the spirit of improvement has marched into the wilderness with a rapidity of advance that has astonished the world, and new commercial towns have sprung up amid the haunts of the savage as if by the work of magic, where the wants of trade have been called for and been gratified with new establishments."[31] Corporations, especially commercial banks, were believed to help farmers, a major contingent of the economy throughout the antebellum era, to bring "their lands into good order" and make them "very productive" by allowing them to erect "proper buildings," to use "clover and plaster" to restore tired lands, and to achieve economies of scale in livestock production.[32] Banks and networks of transportation corporations also helped farmers to receive good cash prices for their crops far from major markets.[33]

Corporations also lifted overall living standards. Railroads, for example, boasted that they could provide "ready and cheap access" to "beautiful rural district[s]" with their "healthful attractions to all who desire to seek them . . . to enjoy the invigorating air of the country . . . during the summer months."

Businessmen could even commute daily by taking "the cars in the evening and retire to some cool retreat in the country . . . returning by an early train the following morning. It is needless to say, that this would be a convenience and a luxury that would be appreciated by a large class of the community."[34] The Staten Island Railroad drew the "wealthy population" of Philadelphia and New York to the island "as a summer resort for sea-bathing" and served as the "center of delightful union between the refined and intelligent families of the two chief cities of this country."[35]

The poor also benefited, primarily when they purchased low-cost goods produced by corporations that did not possess undue market power. Manufacturers "reduced the price of cloth to the consumer," a contemporary claimed, "more than two-thirds" without yielding more than 6 percent profit on average. At the same time, nails dropped from fourteen cents to less than five cents per pound, and many other goods also became more affordable. Many low-income individuals also received wages from corporations, but that benefit must be balanced with the fact that corporations displaced many tradesmen and other small businesspersons.[36]

Corporations were not merely a convenient means of improving economic efficiency and living standards; they were often indispensable to those lofty goals because they provided unique ways for people to cooperate. As Butler claimed in 1911: "[C]ooperation . . . has come to stay as an economic fact. . . . It cannot be stopped. . . . This new movement of cooperation has manifested itself . . . in the limited liability corporation."[37] "Perhaps the primary feature of a corporation," another early corporate historian explained, "is that it exists to further certain purposes, particularly purposes which those persons who have associated themselves with it—usually voluntarily, would find it difficult or impossible to achieve merely as individuals."[38] "Large sums have in many instances been raised for carrying on private business, as well as improvements of great public utility," an anonymous author pointed out in 1829, "which could never probably have been carried through successfully without corporations."[39] "Extensive experience," another wrote in 1852, "as well as observation, establishes the fact, that combinations may accomplish what individual cannot; what one may fail to accomplish for himself, the many may accomplish for each other."[40]

In the early nineteenth century, private capital would go where even governments feared to tread. "The undertaking was deemed so hazardous that the State declined adventuring in it"[41] was then a common refrain in corporate histories and charter petitions. With the exception of the large state canal

systems, most of which ended disastrously,[42] governments allowed pioneer-
ing entrepreneurs, such as investors in the Schuylkill Navigation Company, to
bear the risk of spending too much on too little. "This, however," noted a
contemporary, "is the history of every new business, large or small."[43]

But people will invest only in enterprises that promise them a fair return,
something many corporations today have trouble doing because of the
shoddy ways in which they are governed. Pundits often claim that Americans
do not save enough, but they rarely trace the cause to an underlying distrust
of corporations—or rather, the individuals charged with managing them. As
argued in the final chapter of this book, business and policy leaders can improve corporate governance by understanding and building upon past governance arrangements and thus reinvigorate a sagging U.S. economy.[44]

Chapter 2

Before the Constitution

> Our national funds, our bank stock, the stock of our fire and marine
> insurance companies, turnpike stock, our active trading capital and real
> estate, compose the great mass of our country's wealth.
>
> —A Citizen, 1806[1]

Before describing the rise of corporations in America in detail, it is important
to define terms and to describe the early development of the corporate form.
The Western legal tradition countenanced three major types of corporations:
municipal (towns and cities); nonprofit (charities, churches, schools, various
societies); and for-profit (business). Each type was important in its own right;
indeed, the three types blurred together at first. Early Americans helped to
make the distinctions among the three types clearer but only for-profit corporations—to wit, businesses whose main purpose was to earn revenues that
exceeded their expenditures for the benefit of their owner or owners are discussed in detail herein.[2]

Business corporations can be distinguished from two other archetypical
forms of business organization: the sole proprietorship and the partnership.
In the former, an individual and a business were legally one entity. Typically,
entry and exit into business in that form were easy, and the business was small
and utterly dependent on the proprietor for its continuation. In the latter,
sometimes called a "general partnership," two or more individuals agreed to
combine their resources for the good of the group. Each partner remained
fully liable for all the business's debts, and the business had to dissolve when
any change in the partnership occurred, such as the death or withdrawal of
one of the partners. "When an individual, or a number of individuals, enter

into trade, either together or alone," one antebellum American explained, "they risk their all."[3] Both the liability and dissolution provisions kept the number of partners limited, generally to four or fewer, because the costs of monitoring other partners and reestablishing the business increased dramatically with each additional partner.[4]

Expropriation of fellow partners, while by no means common, did occur. "My partner in the vendue business, Mr. Yates," Archibald Campbell explained in his letter of resignation as president of the Baltimore branch of the Bank of the United States in 1800, "secretly and without my participation in any manner whatever has issued Notes to an unknown amount and discounted them it is supped [*sic*] at usurious rates—the proceeds of which he has applied to private purposes."[5] Campbell had to claim bankruptcy as a result. Around the same time, a partner in a small mercantile firm complained that he could not obtain credit because his partner was notoriously imprudent with money, expending large sums on horse races, "a whore in Philada," and a couple of servants.[6] Later, Abraham Lincoln suffered at the hands of a partner who drank more than he worked; but by paying off the partnership's debts in full, he earned the sobriquet "Honest Abe."[7]

Although usually larger than proprietorships, early American partnerships typically did not command large capitals. Nevertheless, the partnership form was ideal for many endeavors, especially mercantile and small manufacturing businesses.[8] By the Civil War, thirty-one states, including Connecticut, New Jersey, New York, and Louisiana, also allowed the creation of limited partnerships.[9] The form, which proved a popular adaptation of French and Dutch practices, allowed investors called "silent" or "special" partners to fund entrepreneurial activities without endangering their entire net worth, by turning over day-to-day control of the business to managing partners, who alone remained fully liable for the company's debts. Such partnerships could, and actually did, grow larger than the typical general partnership. Nevertheless, they could not grow as large as some lines of business demanded because limited partnerships, like general ones, had to dissolve if a single partner left. Moreover, the illiquidity of the stakes that special partners held in limited partnerships undoubtedly dampened the overall appeal of the limited partnership form. "The wealthy drone rests easy and secure," noted one contemporary, "but men in active business require what is easily convertible into coin or some other valuable commodity."[10]

Corporations rectified the weaknesses of both major forms of partnership. Most important, corporations enjoyed continuous or, as it was more often termed, perpetual succession. That did not mean that corporations were immortal, as some have erroneously claimed, but rather that stockholders' shares could be bought, sold, bequeathed, or otherwise transferred to new owners without triggering the dissolution of the business. "In the case of a corporation," by contrast, "the occurrence of such an event" was, in the words of one anonymous observer, "productive of no embarrassment."[11] The resulting liquidity of corporate shares (though not without certain legal nuances) allowed corporations to tap the savings of hundreds or even thousands of small investors without suffering the considerable costs of frequent reorganization. John Marshall, in his 1819 *Dartmouth College* decision, argued that corporations were invented "chiefly for the purpose of clothing bodies of men, in succession."[12] This is not to argue that family businesses could not survive a long time, even centuries, without the power of perpetual succession, but merely that the power made it easier to last longer and to grow larger.[13]

Another attraction for investors was limited liability, or the ability of stockholders to avoid claims on their personal assets in the event of the corporation's bankruptcy. In other words, stockholders protected by limited liability were not responsible for the corporation's debts, so the creditors of a failed corporation could not attach stockholders' property (or persons) any further than the par value of the stocks they owned at the time that the unpaid debt was incurred. (If a stockholder had yet to pay for all his or her stock, however, creditors were generally entitled to the balance due.) By the 1930s, if not earlier, most observers believed that the corporate feature that was "most renowned is that of limited liability."[14] The extent to which early U.S. shareholders actually enjoyed limited liability has been a matter of some controversy. Historians Oscar and Mary Handlin and, more recently, Pauline Maier and Colleen Dunlavy have argued strenuously that limited liability extended to very few early U.S. corporations. They pointed out, correctly, that few early charters explicitly granted limited liability to shareholders.[15] Their claim that in such cases, liability under common law remained unlimited, as in general partnerships, is, however, erroneous.[16] For starters, most experts, including early jurists, believed that the common law supported limited liability in the case of corporations.[17] Early America's two leading experts on corporate law, Joseph Angell and Samuel Ames, stated in 1832 that no rule of law was "better settled, than that, in general, the individual members of a private corporate body are not liable for the debts, either in their persons or in their property, beyond the amount of property which they have in the stock," an opinion widely held by their contemporaries.[18] The importance of that discrepancy is muddied by the fact that the role of the common law in U.S. corporate jurisprudence is unclear. "It has long been perceived," an anonymous writer noted in 1829, "that the common law of corporations was not adequate to govern these numerous institutions."[19]

The Handlins and their proponents have established beyond a reasonable doubt that liability rules were not uniform over time and space and that early on, limited liability was not legally ironclad. Nevertheless, they exaggerated the weaknesses of early limited liability. Although most American jurists were not generally cognizant of British precedents in the matter, many correctly intuited that limiting stockholders' liability to the sums they had invested (or promised to invest) made the most economic sense.[20] Justice Chapman of Connecticut, for example, questioned whether it could be "the intention of the legislature that a man should be in jeopardy all his lifetime if he should purchase a single share."[21] The balance of public opinion also held that corporate shareholders enjoyed limited liability unless their company's charter specifically stated otherwise.[22] Full liability, many realized, discouraged investment by rendering the stockholders' "risk . . . altogether disproportioned to his chance of profit. If the business is successful, he can scarcely expect to make more, at the utmost, than fifteen, twenty, or thirty per cent. a year on his investment of a hundred dollars, while he may hazard an ample fortune."[23]

Banking historian Bray Hammond claimed that exempting "stockholders from personal liability became established in subterranean fashion with almost no formal advocacy and with very little formal recognition—quite as if it were something men liked but were ashamed of."[24] He was right that the widespread adoption of limited liability was a quiet affair but quite wrong about it being something secretly foisted upon society. The issue was not tested in the courts early on because there were so few corporate failures before the 1810s.[25] When courts finally did rule, they upheld limited liability where charters remained silent on the issue, partly because the ability to transfer shares made it difficult, though not impossible, to enforce full liability on anyone other than directors.[26] The liquidity of shares, in other words, rendered it "quite impossible to know who the proprietors" had been when specific debts were contracted.[27]

Legislators could, and did, impose double, proportional, or unlimited liability when they saw fit—typically, in the words of one jurist, "to prevent reckless schemes" and to "be a check to wild corporate enterprises."[28] Several states mandated higher levels of liability, at least for specific types of corporations. They could do so, ostensibly, because corporate governance was strong enough that investors could still be found despite the potential higher liability. By virtue of acts passed in 1809, 1818, 1821, and 1827, stockholders in Massachusetts manufacturing companies were subject to full liability, although the precise nature of that liability remained in doubt because of ambiguous legal language in each act. Critics of the law abounded, partly because unlimited liability was thought "unjust and oppressive . . . because it imposes on stockholders a risk wholly disproportionate to any possible chance of profit."[29] Moreover, manufacturers in adjacent states, including Maine after it cleaved from the Bay State, attracted significant equity investment from Boston—some claimed that it was millions of dollars—by offering more liberal liability provisions. "No prudent man," a critic of the law argued, "will consent to pursue wealth, even in its most alluring paths, while these destructive statutes are hanging over his head and threatening his ruin."[30] Ultimately, Massachusetts allowed limited liability for manufacturers to staunch such capital flight. The reform also increased the overall level of investment by broadening participation in Massachusetts manufacturing corporations.[31]

Shareholders in insurance companies in Maryland were proportionally liable, as were bank shareholders in Georgia. In other words, if a shareholder owned 10 percent of an insolvent corporation's shares, he or she was responsible for up to 10 percent of any of its remaining debts after the corporation's assets had been liquidated. California also imposed proportional liability on stockholders in its corporations and gave up the rule only in 1931, as investors hard hit by the Depression complained of the high risks and decreased liquidity of the shares of California corporations. Shareholders in the Charleston Fire Insurance Company were under double liability and hence, in the event of the corporation's bankruptcy, were legally bound to pay to any unsatisfied creditors a sum equal to the par value of the shares they owned. Investors in some New Jersey manufacturers before 1824 were subject to double liability, as were stockholders in about half of the mining companies chartered in that state before 1835. Stockholders in note-issuing banks in New York were also subject to double liability after 1850.[32]

In 1831, former Treasury secretary Albert Gallatin noted that bank "stockholders are made personally responsible, in some of the states."[33] Rhode Island, for example, adopted unlimited liability for bank shareholders. The main result was to turn its banks into relatively undercapitalized, insider-lending institutions. Also, the directors of some banks and insurers in Maryland, Massachusetts, New Jersey, New York, Pennsylvania, and South Carolina were fully liable in their personal capacities if they engaged in illegal or fraudulent activities, such as knowingly issuing notes beyond a prescribed limit or continuing to sell policies or make loans after their corporation's net worth became negative. New York's Chancery Court, for example, threatened the directors of the failed Bank of Columbia with a $50,000 personal fine if they did not immediately "desist and refrain from issuing bills or notes . . . from receiving deposits . . . [and] from making discounts."[34] In many of its bank charters, New Jersey made directors personally liable for all notes not redeemed by the bank. Most attempts to enact higher levels of stockholder liability, however, foundered because it was widely believed that it "would deter capitalists and persons of limited means" from investing.[35]

So most, but by no means all, stockholders in corporations chartered in the United States before 1860 were protected by limited liability.[36] Modern experimental research shows that such protection increased investment because few people are willing to risk large sums even if the risk of loss is exceedingly low. Most people are willing to pay $1 for a one-in-a-million chance of winning $1 million; but, in what is called the Saint Petersburg Paradox, very few will receive $1 for a one-in-a-million chance of losing $1 million, although the two risks are mathematically equivalent.[37] The paradox is probably of ancient origin and was certainly as strong in the nineteenth century as today.[38] "No one," in the words of an anonymous contemporary, was "willing to put his whole estate in peril, however small that peril may be."[39] Many potential investors also found it anomalous that anyone should be liable for debts unknowingly contracted by a third party.[40]

Varieties of Business Corporations

> At the close of the middle ages the rule was judicially
> settled that only the king could make a corporation,
> but even the repetition of this rule did not effectively
> eradicate the popular notion, strong because it was
> very old, that substantially the same result could be
> obtained by free association.
>
> —*Julius Goebel, 1939*[41]

Early U.S. business corporations came in several varieties, the oddest of which was a "legal curiosity" known as the corporation sole, a sole proprietor that enjoyed corporate privileges. Although fairly numerous, they were so inconsequential that by the end of the nineteenth century, legal scholars claimed that they were "not known in U.S."[42] They have since been supplanted by forms such as the S corporation.[43]

Most early U.S. corporations were joint stock: they were owned by investors who purchased transferable equity shares in the corporation. Shares were sometimes called "actions" because jurists considered them personal property "in action" as opposed to "in possession"; they were claims on the net profits of the business and not claims on particular pieces of real property.[44]

A significant number of corporations, mostly insurers, savings banks, and cemeteries, were organized as mutuals: they were owned by their customers (policyholders, depositors, or plot owners). Although sometimes misidentified as nonprofit institutions by modern observers, mutual corporations were indeed for-profit ventures. "Persons insuring under the 'mutual' rates," explained actuary Harvey Tuckett in an 1850 treatise, "participate in the profits of the business of the Institution." He added that mutuals might not be as profitable as insurers owned by stockholders because they tended not to push as hard for new business.[45] Higher initial premiums, a lack of capital, weak incentives for managers, and low levels of policyholder monitoring of management were other disadvantages of the form. The strengths of mutuality were that any profits generated were shared by policyholders rather than by a distinct group of stockholders, and they were generally easier and cheaper to incorporate and get into operation. Taxes and regulations constant, mutuals tended to outperform joint-stock corporations in long-term businesses such as life insurance and savings banking.[46]

Some early entrepreneurs tried to leverage the relative advantages of the joint-stock and mutual forms by creating hybrid corporations that were a mix of both—that is, owned partially by stockholders and partially by policyholders. Policyholders in some mixed life insurers could choose a policy with a lower premium that did not participate in profits or one with a higher premium that could later be decreased via profit-sharing dividends.[47]

Most early U.S. corporations were chartered by the special act of a state legislature. The matter was largely a state affair because, despite the eloquent defense of the constitutionality of the Bank of the United States (1791–1811; 1816–36) by Alexander Hamilton and others, many early Americans questioned the federal government's power to charter businesses outside Washington, D.C. Only during the Civil War did the federal government finally firmly assert its power to charter banks and other businesses. By that time, many states had reduced the importance of, or had even outright banned, special incorporation in favor of so-called general incorporation laws that allowed all persons meeting specific criteria to incorporate their businesses through a bureaucratic mechanism—that is, without direct legislative approval. General incorporation was cheaper, faster, and ostensibly fairer than special incorporation but also considerably less flexible. Incorporators and other promoters of companies chartered under special laws liked to point potential investors to the "favorable act of incorporation" that they had received. Although poorly worded charters could cause considerable controversy and uncertainty, possession of relatively liberal charter terms was a selling point that companies chartered under general laws could not credibly claim.[48]

General incorporation laws largely grew out of two concerns: that special incorporation invited political corruption and dampened competition; and that the government could lose control of the chartering process entirely because of the possible proliferation of unincorporated joint-stock companies. Legislators also wanted to free up time for other business, as by the 1830s, "special grant after grant, and charters upon charters, have come to constitute nearly the whole mass of legislative enactments," or rather "nearly one-half of the time of the legislature," according to more careful contemporary observers and modern scholars.[49] Freedom of association had deep roots in Anglo, and later American, religious and political history, so it was natural for entrepreneurs to associate, if necessary, without explicit government sanction. Most early joint-stock land companies remained unincorporated but claimed corporate-like powers, although most contemporaries believed that corporations could "be created only by act of assembly." Several early banks that were formed with Alexander Hamilton's help, including the Bank of New York and the Merchants Bank of New York, began business without a charter. Before 1800, at least a dozen companies, ranging from banks to insurers to manufacturers, formed and began operations without receiving explicit legislative approval.[50]

While the government could always demand the formal incorporation of businesses that sought to exercise sovereign powers such as monopoly or eminent domain, other corporate powers, including perpetual succession and limited liability, could be replicated to some extent by private contract. The power of eminent domain was necessary for most transportation companies because although most property owners along desirable canal, rail, and turnpike routes sold "upon equitable terms," took stock in exchange for their land, or even donated the property because they understood "the advantages accruing to themselves and the public," others demanded "exorbitant" prices. Whether it was lawful, under some state constitutions, for the government to allow private for-profit corporations to exercise eminent domain was not always clear, but the practice generally continued, anyway.[51]

Like their British counterparts, unincorporated joint-stock companies in America claimed the other benefits of the corporate form. Despite doubts about the legality of their actions, their shares could be transferred without causing the dissolution of the company. They also held annual meetings, published annual reports, and so forth, just as duly chartered corporations did. The Providence Hat Manufacturing Company, for example, did not have a charter but advertised its annual election of directors as if it were lawfully incorporated. (Established sometime before July 1808, the company sold a variety of hats on liberal terms to wholesalers but for cash only to retail customers. The company apparently folded in early 1811, shortly after its sales agent quit for undisclosed reasons.)[52] Such examples prompted one scholar to claim that unincorporated joint-stock companies "at the end of the eighteenth century . . . were not modified partnerships, but had become corporations in all but the technical legal sense."[53] Indeed, many even asserted that their investors enjoyed limited liability by virtue of various expedients, including contracts between the company and its creditors. Such claims were considered tenuous, so many unchartered companies sought formal charters as soon as it was expedient to do so.[54]

"The unincorporated situation of the company, now that its operations were becoming more extensive," an early historian of the Lehigh Coal and Navigation Company explained, "caused uneasiness among the stockholders with regard to their personal liabilities, and necessarily operated as a check to the prosperous extension of the business."[55] Investors in other unchartered joint-stock associations evinced similar trepidation, and not without reason— legislators and judges wanted to maintain some control over large commercial enterprises and hence had difficulty perceiving the legitimacy of anything other than proprietorships, partnerships, limited partnerships (where allowed by law), and dutifully chartered corporations. Although the threat of drastic or draconian action against unchartered associations was relatively minor in a nation that fetishized property rights as much as early America did, many entrepreneurs sought the relative certainty of formal incorporation as soon as they could. The Merrimack Manufacturing Company, for example, began business without a charter in December 1821, but the first article of its association agreement stipulated that it would "petition the Legislature, as soon as may be."[56] A formal charter was indeed obtained soon thereafter, in February 1822.[57]

Other companies were content to leave well enough alone. In 1820, the stockholders of the unincorporated Newburyport Fishing Company decided to "continue the business another year."[58] Similarly, the Hollywood Cemetery in Richmond began operations without a charter in 1847 but issued stock certificates that indicated that the company "intended to be incorporated." When the legislature refused to charter the company, some subscribers motioned "in favor of selling the property and dividing the proceeds." The resolution failed "by a very large majority." Instead, the company drew up bylaws and articles of association that converted the concern into unincorporated mutual owned by the lot holders. Company leaders unhappy with that outcome later complained that several corporations "in the state in the neighborhood of other cities" had already received charters and wondered why theirs alone "should be refused." When "an unexpected and violent opposition . . . started in the House of Delegates" appeared "likely to defeat" the company's next charter application" on the grounds that the cemetery would "retard the growth of the city in that direction, . . . injuriously affect the health of the citizens," and possibly infect the water supply, the company countered point by point and began a strenuous lobbying effort. Yet in March 1850, the charter was again "rejected, finally, by an overwhelming vote," which made it difficult to sell lots even to the next of kin of the recently deceased. Again, the stakeholders voted to remain in business.[59]

Companies like the Hollywood Cemetery and the Newburyport Fishing Company filled the gap between partnerships and special corporations. After the widespread adoption of general incorporation laws after the Civil War, they slowly faded into extinction, as they no longer served the purpose of granting relatively easy access to most corporate advantages.[60]

Evolution of the Corporate Form

> Little law dealing strictly with business corporations
> had been developed in England before 1775, and
> what there was had hardly penetrated to the
> fastnesses of the new world. Consequently the legal
> principles which grew up, first in the Confederation
> and later in the United States, were largely a native
> product, molded primarily by the exigencies of the
> American scene.
>
> —*Charles C. Abbott, 1936*[61]

In addition to helping usher in general incorporation laws, unchartered joint-stock companies were important because they show that organizational forms between the general partnership and the full-blown corporation have existed, a point critical to understanding the evolution of the corporate form over the many centuries of its existence. Business entities with many corporate characteristics called *sreni* existed in India as early as 800 BC and were in widespread use before disappearing from the subcontinent around the time of the Muslim invasions in AD 1000. Muslims did not develop the corporate form, some scholars believe, because Islam lacked the concept of legal personhood. Business ventures therefore remained small and of short duration. The inability to form large, lasting, flexible enterprises arguably hampered the development of Muslim economies more severely than usury strictures did. In any event, not until the late nineteenth century did Muslim countries begin to adopt the corporate form in significant numbers, and they looked for guidance to Euro-American examples rather than to the ancient *sreni*. Similarly, China was home to factories so large that they put European ones to shame. They were, however, static, state-controlled entities that did not require private investors to pool their resources.[62]

Although remarkably similar to modern corporations in many ways, *sreni* had no clear connection to the development of Euro-American corporations, which some scholars have traced from Greek beginnings to Roman collegia, corpora, and *societates*. Critics counter that Roman institutions like the collegia are best characterized as quasi-corporations because they were temporary in nature, and only those servicing the state, such as tax collectors and military suppliers, provided limited liability protections for investors. Over time, the collegia lost their voluntary features and increasingly became organs of the Empire. Finally, no direct connection between Roman collegia and modern corporations has been discovered. Proponents counter that it was obvious that from "Roman ideas emerged common law corporations for municipal government, for eleemosynary institutions, for charities, religion and education," and, from this, it was not "difficult to apply the same principle to associations for business enterprises."[63]

Whatever its ultimate origins, the modern corporation emerged proximately from a stew of medieval and early modern European business forms such as the *commenda* and *societas*. The former was a limited liability partnership of limited duration; the latter a joint-stock form that offered share transferability but not limited liability. *Societas* could grow quite large but, unlike later joint-stock companies, were assessment-based. Rather than issue shares with fixed values, in other words, they could call upon investors for additional funds as necessary. Religious strictures on lending encouraged the development of both business forms by providing entrepreneurs with equity-based financing options.[64]

The Italian city-states were home to *compagnie*, proto-corporations or "super companies" that were large, semipermanent partnerships composed of hundreds of employees and numerous partners who controlled transferable shares. Although partially family-based, super companies such as Bardi and Peruzzi had many non-family-member partners and large numbers of unrelated employees. The enterprises were complex conglomerates but not formally incorporated. By the early fifteenth century, unincorporated joint-stock companies had formed in Italy, Austria, and Germany. In France and Germany, businesses called *Gewerkschaften* obtained some corporate qualities but, at least at first, lacked transferable shares.[65]

In 1602, a business that some consider the first modern corporation, the Dutch East India Company, received a charter that explicitly granted limited liability to investors. Other continental powers also began incorporating large trading companies in the seventeenth century. Before the eighteenth century, continental European nations had incorporated several score business firms, but most of them, even those granted monopoly rights, failed.[66]

In Britain, business corporations were an outgrowth of urban and economic development and the guilds, market towns, universities, and other forms of associative behavior that the development spurred. Although more akin to trade unions than corporations, guilds enjoyed perpetual succession, and their use of a common seal, a minor attribute of the corporate form, became more common over time. By the fifteenth century, some British jurists had already interpreted associations like guilds as distinct legal units instead of mere agglomerations of multiple individuals. That insight allowed for the evolution of quasi-corporations in mining and foreign trade, endeavors driven to grow larger by the expansion of international trade. Companies such as the Mines Royal, the Mineral and Battery Works, the Merchants of the Staple, and the Merchants Adventurers, so-called regulated companies, resulted. The regulated companies were not joint stock, and their members did not enjoy limited liability; but the companies did have market power, a charter, and a common name and seal. Members joined not by buying a share but by serving a long apprenticeship, which, of course, limited the size and effectiveness of the regulated companies. Although subject to the company's rules, each member otherwise employed his own capital as he wished.[67]

Permanent joint-stock companies arose when the costs of organizing as temporary joint ventures increased after it became necessary to acquire long-term fixed assets, such as foreign trading posts. The Muscovy or Russia Company, for instance, was established in the 1550s to facilitate trade with Russia, which, at that time, had no Baltic port and hence was accessible only via the far north passage to Archangel. Unlike earlier "companies," the Muscovy was created by British entrepreneurs to conduct large-scale, long-term trade. Hundreds of investors—who could sell out their shares to others without disrupting the company's business or legal existence—funded the enterprise. Another "company" that formed at about the same time to trade to Africa was a much more traditional enterprise. In 1581, the Levant Company (which changed its name to the Turkey Company when it reorganized in 1591) and the East India Company (chartered in 1600) were formed on plans similar to that of the Muscovy. Investors in those endeavors, like investors in most British corporations and joint-stock companies formed before the mid-nineteenth century, did not enjoy the protection of limited liability, even though the prospect of losing everything was known to discourage investment.[68]

By one count, 137 business corporations formed in Britain before 1695. Most of the earlier ones failed during the civil war and other upheavals of the seventeenth century, so there were only about fifteen still in operation when the Glorious Revolution occurred in 1688. While most shut down for mundane reasons, the formation of new business corporations was undoubtedly hindered by the relative lack of rule of law that prevailed in pre-Revolution Britain, as exemplified by the periodic purges of municipal corporations and revamping of their charters implemented at the behest of the Stuarts.[69]

About 100 business corporations formed in the aftermath of the Glorious

Revolution. Many of those soon ceased operations, but new ones continued to sprout up because of improved (less predatory) political governance. Enough took root to increase the percentage of total British wealth held in corporate form from about 1.3 percent in 1695 to 13 percent at the height of the South Sea Bubble a quarter of a century later. Little of that was employed directly in trade or production, as many of the companies operated primarily as government bond mutual funds.[70]

Moreover, British policymakers were intent on severely limiting use of the corporate form. By virtue of an act passed in 1708, England limited itself to just one chartered bank, the Bank of England. The rest of its banks, which numbered some 230 in 1797 after a massive die-off in 1793, were partnerships of not more than six people. Banks in Scotland, by contrast, were joint-stock associations, as political economist James Steuart put it, "ratified or not by public authority."[71] The Bubble Act of 1720, which, in a fit of understatement, one twentieth-century jurist called "wordy and obscure," coupled with the collapse of the South Sea Bubble later that year, somewhat retarded the development of formally incorporated enterprises in Britain.[72] Politicians were so appalled by the corruption and devastation caused by the Bubble that they interpreted the act very strictly until at least 1760, forcing entrepreneurs interested in larger-scale enterprises to form unincorporated joint-stock companies that operated in an uncertain and confused legal environment.[73]

Corporations became synonymous with odious monopoly, even though, strictly speaking, not all monopolies were corporations and not all corporations were monopolies. Until the passage of general incorporation reforms in the mid-nineteenth century, therefore, most large-scale British entrepreneurs had to form unincorporated joint-stock companies or trusts or to seek out royal letters patent.[74]

Due to Britain's limited and generally unsatisfactory experience with business corporations, "all that the American colonists took with them from England," legal scholar L. C. B. Gower noted in 1956, "was an embryonic law of corporations—municipal and governmental rather than business corporations."[75] If entrepreneurs in Britain proper had great difficulty obtaining a charter, it is not surprising that American colonists found it almost impossible to do so. Most therefore obtained charters, of questionable legality, from their colonial governments, or, more commonly, they formed unincorporated joint-stock associations in fields such as ironworking, mercantile trading, mining, and, most important, land companies. Many colonial "companies" were, in fact, general partnerships.[76]

The ability of colonies to charter companies was questionable because several colonies, including Massachusetts and Virginia, were themselves founded by corporations. They eventually went bankrupt, but the colonies they started lived on and, like all colonies, were considered sub-sovereign. Only the Crown—or, after 1688, the king in Parliament—had the authority to grant charters, a prerogative it exercised in America with the incorporation of the Hudson's Bay Company and the Ohio Company. Crown lawyers harassed nonprofit corporations like Harvard College and even partnerships that tried to engage in banking. (In the absence of banks, colonial scriveners, lawyers, and merchants acted as go-betweens between savers and entrepreneurs, lenders and borrowers.) In 1741, British policymakers eager to limit colonial economic independence explicitly extended the Bubble Act to the colonies.[77]

It is not surprising, therefore, to learn that historian Simeon Baldwin found that only six corporations "of strictly American origin or character" had been chartered before the Revolution: a fishing company in New York (chartered 1675), Pennsylvania's Free Society of Traders (chartered 1682), a trading company in New London (chartered 1732), a wharf in New Haven (chartered 1760), the Philadelphia Contributionship (chartered 1768), and a pier in Boston (chartered 1772). Little is known about the fishing company, the Free Society proved very costly to its shareholders, and the New London Society converted itself into a land bank and was eventually quashed. The wharves and the Contributionship, a mutual fire insurer that is still in existence, proved successful. In his survey, Baldwin excluded quasi-corporations created to drain swamps or supply towns with potable water. More controversially, he did not consider the "Corporation for the Relief of Poor and Distressed Presbyterian Ministers" (chartered 1759) to be a for-profit business, though it may well have been.[78] But even if we take an expansive view of colonial enterprise, corporations were extremely rare. In 1774, London policymaker Richard Jackson argued that both Crown and proprietary colonies had the power to incorporate businesses but that development was too late and too tentative to influence colonial economic development.[79]

With independence came freedom from the Bubble Act and other restrictions. American entrepreneurs began chartering corporations even before hostilities ended. The Continental Congress incorporated the Bank of North America (BNA) on December 31, 1781. Having opened subscription books months before and elected directors in November, the Philadelphia-based bank was able to begin operations in early January 1782. Due to doubts about the national government's authority to incorporate businesses, the BNA also obtained charters from the state governments of Pennsylvania, Massachusetts, and New York.[80]

After the Revolution, the pace of chartering quickened somewhat. Massachusetts birthed a bank, Connecticut incorporated a mine in Litchfield County, Pennsylvania created a competitor for its Contributionship, New York chartered an iron manufacturer, three bridge companies formed, and Virginia and Maryland both chartered the Potomac Company to assume the canalization project begun in 1762 by a voluntary association of the same name. Virginia also joined with North Carolina to charter the Dismal Swamp Company.[81]

That so few corporations formed between independence in 1776 and ratification of the Constitution was not due to a dearth of capital, an old and exploded canard. Throughout that period, America was home to numerous wealthy individuals and a thriving middling sort with the ability to save substantial sums in aggregate. By 1774, Americans owned an estimated £88 million (roughly $400 million) of nonhuman wealth. What prevented entrepreneurs from incorporating more businesses was fear. Businessmen were not interested in charters that did not afford them strong protections. They had to balance their new legal freedom to incorporate against the political realities of the era. Although independent, the new nation was far from stable, and significant domestic forces opposed the creation of large business units. As the next chapter shows, adoption of the Constitution allayed the first problem but not the second, which faded only slowly, with experience.[82]

Chapter 3

Corporate Iniquity

The powerful influence of good laws and their good administration on the
wealth and prosperity of nations, is in theory universally acknowledged. . . .
A wise and beneficent policy . . . may do more to advance the welfare
of a nation than the greatest natural advantages. . . . Who would carry
on business in a place in which wealth rendered the life of its possessor
insecure? Who would reside by choice in a country where the laws gave no
protection to life or property?

—Anonymous, 1829[1]

The U.S. Constitution does not mention business corporations because the
delegates to the constitutional convention that met in Philadelphia in 1787
decided not to give the federal government the explicit power to charter corporations of any sort. Ironically, ratification of the Constitution touched off a
chartering spree at the state level that has not abated to this day. The reason is
not difficult to discern. The rise of the American corporation nation was not
sui generis but rather rooted in what contemporaries called the genius of
American institutions. Most countries were poor because most suffered
under predatory governments. "There is no fact more evident," one writer
noted in 1818, "than that the bulk of mankind have been the hewers of wood
and drawers of water, for the use and pleasure of knaves and tyrants, from the
earliest ages to the present moment."[2] After ratification of the Constitution,
however, Americans eagerly sought to create wealth because they were assured that they could keep the fruits of their hard work and acumen. As an
anonymous author pointed out, the Constitution created a federal system
that allowed Americans to flee to another state much more easily than

oppressed Europeans could. Cognizant that "the smallest hope of profit" would "draw crowds of adventurers from Maine to Louisiana," American state governments typically quickly adopted the best policies and practices of their neighbors lest they suffer a debilitating net outward migration.[3] So the Constitution created a competent national government and also provided state governments with incentives to implement good policies.[4]

The American colonists had often evinced what was termed a "vigorous spirit of enterprise," but adoption of the Constitution unleashed a torrent of additional entrepreneurial energies.[5] In 1792, Philadelphia merchant and public policymaker Tench Coxe claimed that buildings and "public works . . . of every kind, and of species and values unknown among us till the present time, are undertaking every where" due to Treasury secretary Alexander Hamilton's monetary and fiscal reforms but also "our voluntarily imposing upon ourselves the wholesome restraints of just government." "Every good plan requiring capital, which is set on foot," he correctly claimed, found capital "quickly from the confidence of our monied citizens or from foreigners."[6]

Numerous other writers evinced similar sentiments, and not all were wealthy elites like Coxe. Justin Hitchcock, a hatter of modest means in Deerfield, Massachusetts, recalled the salubrious effect that "our National Government had upon all classes of people" in 1790. From widespread confidence in the new regime emanated "a new Spring to all kinds of business," including a strong desire among farmers to "cultivate their lands under a sure prospect of a ready market and good price."[7] Time and experience mostly strengthened the nation's institutional genius, so it is not surprising that in 1831, Swiss-born banker Albert Gallatin believed that "a general spirit of enterprise" suffused the nation, a claim echoed by other foreign observers such as Michel Chevalier and Alexis de Tocqueville.[8]

Good government created the conditions under which corporations could thrive. "It cannot be material to inquire whether these institutions can flourish at all, under the influence of a tyrannical government," argued a group of New York legislators in 1826, "but experience testifies to the truth of the position, that their principles will not submit to the control of arbitrary direction. . . . All history shows that they have flourished better and been the more safe and beneficial, in proportion as the government under which they have existed has approached the standard of rational liberty."[9]

Americans who felt that their lives, liberty, and property were secure under the new regime set out to improve their economic lives. As 80 to 90 percent of Americans were farmers, much of the action at first occurred on farms (and related industries such as mills), but much activity in infrastructure, both physical and financial, was palpable. Instead of a series of loosely connected marketplaces, Americans began to interact in regional, national, and international market economies where prices were both increasingly synchronous (moved up and down in tandem) and convergent (tending toward the same value), which increased competition and the efficiency of resource allocation, which, in turn, fueled further agricultural productivity gains and quickly changed the very structure of the economy. Freed from subsistence farming (with most goods consumed at home or traded locally, with enough surplus produced to purchase only a small quantity of manufactured goods and other imports), many Americans left the agricultural sector for services and manufacturing. That shift increased not only total output but the portion of it produced off the farms. A positive feedback cycle ensued as former or would-have-been farmers invented and disseminated goods, such as mechanical reapers, and services, such as transportation and finance, that made the remaining farmers even more productive, which, in turn, allowed yet more people to leave their farms for factories, wharves, and counting-houses. Corporations greatly facilitated that crucial metamorphosis.[10]

Corporate Critics

> [Corporations are] wormes in the entrayles of a
> naturall man.
> —*Thomas Hobbes, 1651*[11]

Although it clearly aided the development of the corporate form, ratification of the Constitution did not destroy the virulent anticorporate sentiments that many Americans inherited from the Old World. Fueled by partisan politics and fraudulent corporate activities, anticorporate angst slowed proliferation of the corporate form, until it was largely overcome during the period 1830–60 by pro-business Whigs and antimonopoly Jacksonians who concluded that corporate foibles were best mitigated by competition. Criticism of corporations, particularly specially chartered ones, therefore somewhat paradoxically sparked the chartering of yet more corporations and led eventually to liberal general incorporation laws.[12]

By 1790, Americans had experienced roughly three decades of economic stagnation brought on by British mercantilist policies, exacerbated by the

conflagrations of war, and succored by the imbecility of Confederation governance. Like most people inured to life in a zero-sum economy, they naturally
distrusted wealthy individuals and politically powerful institutions and found
it easy to give voice to their fears, especially of so-called moneyed institutions.
But even as the economy sprang to life in the 1790s and after, some Americans continued to fear large businesses and expressed very sophisticated critiques of the corporate form, many inspired by the pen of none other than
Adam Smith.[13]

It may strike some readers as strange that Adam Smith, the father of modern economic thought, disliked corporations, the seeming epitome of capitalist development. He was indeed a major critic of corporations—and for the
same reason that he sought to reform colleges and the church: because they
skewed incentives in ways that caused or perpetuated inefficiencies. Smith
believed that in "every profession, the exertion of the greater part of those
who exercise it, is always in proportion to the necessity they are under of
making that exertion."[14] Like churches and colleges, corporations were not
very good at eliciting effort; hence, at least whenever they attempted anything
other than routine tasks, they were doomed to succumb to competitors, to
leach off consumers as monopolies, or both.

Smith believed, and rightly so, that people tend to do precisely what they
are rewarded for doing. If incentives are not properly structured, agents (for
example, employees) will injure the interests of their principals (employers)
by stealing, shirking, or causing other so-called principal-agent problems, especially in larger corporations where the personal bonds of sympathy are
weakest. Salaried employees of corporations exerted enough effort to keep
their jobs—but no more, because the fruits of any additional labor accrued to
stockholders rather than themselves. Such minimal effort, Smith believed,
was sufficient in corporations such as canals, water utilities, insurers, and depository institutions, which required little thought beyond routine tasks.
Such weak incentives were almost certain to sink a trading company or other
business requiring flexibility, foresight, and so forth. Stockholders were unwilling or unable to improve incentive structures, Smith believed. One major
problem was that the more stockholders who owned shares in a corporation,
the bigger the free-rider problem and the bigger the temptation to wait for
other stockholders to handle any problems that might arise. "Negligence and
profusion, therefore, must always prevail, more or less, in the management of
the affairs of such a company," Smith concluded.[15]

In Smith's view, therefore, partnerships were far better organizational forms in most lines of business because each partner had all his wealth at stake in the venture and hence each worked diligently and intelligently to see the business thrive. Partners were also liable for one another's debts, so they monitored one another much more closely than stockholders watched over the activities of managers. Smith's views, however, did not jibe with the experiences of successful British corporations, of which early Americans knew little. Closer investigation of successful corporations would have revealed that the key to a corporation's success was not how much of its capital its managers owned but rather how much of each manager's personal net worth was invested in it. Managers who put their all into the company's stock, even if it was just a drop in a bucket of capital, worked as hard and smart as any partner and, of course, had the advantage of having more resources at their disposal. In short, corporations were not destined to be poorly governed, but not everyone had figured that out.[16]

Another problem that Smith identified was the tendency for corporations to acquire monopoly privileges. Because of the principal-agent problems at the heart of the corporate form just described, many early corporations found it difficult to remain profitable without becoming monopolies. Here, Smith followed Joseph Tucker, who in 1753 argued that chartered trading companies were much less efficient and enterprising than private merchants and hence had to have monopoly protections in order to survive. Smith, along with other eighteenth-century political economists such as Sir James Steuart, disdained monopolies, particularly permanent ones, and for many of the same reasons we do today: because they maximized producer surplus and profits at the expense of consumer surplus by selling fewer units at higher prices than would prevail in a more competitive market. Quality might suffer as well, partly because monopoly privileges rendered managers as well as stockholders complacent, stripping them of incentives to work more diligently or more intelligently. Many of the corporations that were granted monopolies failed, anyway, or, like the South Sea Company, morphed into government bond mutual funds, Smith pointed out.[17]

Because people were naturally rent seekers, Smith believed, they were apt to seek out monopoly privileges and other forms of government largesse. Corporations seemed especially adept at manipulating government officials. Governments therefore should be very careful about granting charters in the first place, Smith cautioned. Only businesses capable of routinization, ones that needed a larger capital than any individual or partnership could provide and that filled some great public goal should be incorporated, he argued. And he was not alone. Conservative British politician Edmund Burke called the statute incorporating the East India Company "a charter to establish monopoly, and to create power" and denounced that corporation's considerable influence in Parliament.[18] Another British wit defined the corporation as a "tyrannical, exclusive monopoly, generally consisting of gluttons, idiots, and oppressors."[19]

Critiques like those exerted much influence on early American corporate critics. In 1792, George Logan argued that salaried employees were "uninterested Agents" unlikely to do a very good job on behalf of their bosses or stockholders.[20] Corporate managers, many early Americans believed, possessed both the will and the means to defraud stockholders, creditors, and customers. In 1827, an anonymous critic argued that corporations were "made solely for the advantage of a few, and the probable injury of many."[21] In 1829, another anonymous critic argued that corporations had "great opportunities of making their apparent means greater than their real funds, and of defrauding in other modes, and are liable to great mismanagement."[22] "Human nature is the same every where," another critic explained in 1837; "a man's first and chief concern will be for *his own*." As a result, "a man's selfish interests will be *first* consulted, and will eat up the interests of his employers."[23] Others complained of two kinds of "evils ascribable to mismanagement . . . directing their operation to subjects not within the proper sphere of institutions of this kind" and assuming too much risk in their proper sphere, thus "encouraging a pernicious spirit of speculation."[24] Still others realized that managers could steal in a variety of ways, including self-dealing, empire building, and excessive borrowing.[25]

Even some businessmen doubted the ability of corporations to mitigate agency problems. "An Establishment comprehending a dozen different objects well chosen," an associate wrote Alexander Hamilton about the Society for the Establishment of Useful Manufactures (SEUM) in 1791, "conducted by an able direction, enlightened and honest managers and skillful Workmen might have the greatest success." But the correspondent wondered, could "the union of so many qualities, on which the success entirely depends be an absolute miracle? . . . [I]f one of them is Wanting," he explained, "you will find bad goods come out of the hands of unskillful workmen; dishonest managers make a fraudulent advantage at the expense of their employees, which in such a multitude of details will escape the eye of the directors." He claimed that even in Europe, large-scale manufacturers with several hundred employees well acquainted with the business and "employed for their own profit, and not as hirelings" were nevertheless "cheated in the details." Even if they were "all honest," employees "can never be stimulated by that interest which animates those who work for themselves. I repeat it, Sire, unless God should send us saints for Workmen and angels to conduct them, there is the greatest reason to fear for the success of the plan." The correspondent, likely Thomas Marshall, proved prescient; but the SEUM was not robbed by degrees but rather was boldly and directly pilfered by its president.[26]

Still other critics believed that limited liability induced stockholders to take excessive risks because "they share all the gains, but are responsible for none of the frauds or losses." For such critics, charters contained few protections because they were "for the most part drawn up by a cunning attorney . . . with so many invisible loop holes in it, that like a sieve, it lets out every thing they wish to get rid of, and affords ample space for the spirit of the instrument to evaporate entirely."[27]

The seemingly high frequency with which early corporations failed, especially during panic-induced recessions, further fueled anticorporate sentiments. In the view of many early Americans, failure in business, although inevitable from today's perspective, was a negative occurrence attributable more to character flaws and immoral conduct than to adverse market conditions and the effects of competition. "See the daily papers filled with Insolvencies, Bankruptcies and Forgeries, an eternal disgrace to the nation," as one writer put it in 1818.[28] Those associated with failed enterprises were often subjected to biting invective, feminization, and social ostracization. They were, in the parlance of the times, as "ruined" as an unchaste woman.[29] "No traces of the 'company' remain," one critic complained, "but the disgrace of the community and the ruin of thousands."[30] Corporate failures, critics reasoned, must be caused by placing big, complex businesses "into the hands of men having little knowledge of and no intimate connections with the commercial affairs of the country. Then it is that cupidity riots upon distress."[31] Such angst was largely pro-cyclical: in good times, little attention was paid to banks and other corporations; but following financial panics, people heaped abuse upon them.[32]

Many early Americans, like their English forebears, disliked securities trading for a variety of reasons but, most importantly, because it seemed to make a few unscrupulous or lucky individuals wealthy at the expense of the hardworking multitude. While trading in the public debt would have continued had there been no corporations, the proliferation of joint-stock companies greatly encouraged "stock" speculation. Early on, the term "stock" referred both to corporate equities and to registered bonds issued by national, state, or municipal governments. By 1850 or so, governments had begun to replace such "stock" with "the more convenient form of bonds payable to bearer," and the word "stock" began to refer only to corporate equities: shares in business corporations and joint-stock associations.[33]

If there was anything worse than commercial failure and securities speculation for early Americans, it was monopoly power. Monopolists were a powerful "class of men who live by taxes imposed upon the labour of others," one writer explained in the late 1840s, "and thus compel their neighbours to plough their way through mud or sand, and to live in half-built houses, that they may ride in coaches and live in palaces." The object of monopolists, he explained, was to extract economic rents from consumers "by selling bad commodities at higher prices."[34] Few shared Alexander Hamilton's narrow, modern conception of monopoly as "a legal impediment to the carrying on of the trade by others than those to whom it is granted."[35] For most, monopolies included any business believed to enjoy more than a modicum of market or political power. Monopoly, most believed,[36] "is a power exclusive in its nature. . . . [I]t bestows upon the few that which belongs to the many."[37] "A monopoly," as one observer put it in 1835, "consists in allowing one person, or class of persons, the exclusive enjoyment of certain privileges [sic] of a peculiar and personal character."[38] Banks were therefore considered monopolies even where they competed vigorously, even though anyone could buy shares in them, and even though they did not claim an "exclusive right of loaning money."[39]

Much anticorporate sentiment stemmed directly from fears that corporations would outcompete existing sole proprietorships and partnerships.[40] George Logan argued in 1792 that no one would want to apprentice in any line of work "in which he may be supplanted by a junto of monied men, under the immediate patronage and protection of Government."[41] In 1827, one corporate critic complained that successful manufacturing corporations "throw hundreds of useful mechanics out of employment."[42] Those opposed to the incorporation of a salt manufacturer in 1835 claimed that it would "complete the ruin of a large number of manufacturers, and to the creation of an unjust and odious monopoly."[43] And Peter D. Vroom, New Jersey's Democratic governor, advised that corporations "should be sparingly created . . . if they are to compete with private and individual enterprise" because "the contest between the two is an unequal contest, and the result is always in favor of the corporation."[44] The belief that corporations could not be as efficient as "individual shrewdness and diligence" was, ironically, used to try to convince critics that they had little to fear from corporate competition.[45]

On the political side, memories of the East India Company's attempt to monopolize tea in the colonies proved resilient.[46] "The East Indian Company," attorney Joseph Ingersoll wrote in 1834, "furnishes us an ever memorable example of the antirepublican character and of the evil tendency of such institutions."[47] "Corporations," many antebellum Americans believed, "are dangerous to the rights of the public, on the ground that they combine too much power and influence."[48] All those in business were suspected of rent seeking, of trying to gain government favors, but larger businesses were believed more likely to succeed. Indeed, corporations were thought capable of corrupting the political process in direct proportion to their size.[49]

Such sentiments were not without empirical merit. From the start, large railroad corporations engaged in heavy-duty rent-seeking behaviors. In April 1830, the South-Carolina Rail Road Company held a public meeting that voted "by an overwhelming majority" to memorialize Congress for aid. It also voted to request the South Carolina delegation in Congress to push the memorial. As local purists noted, it was ironic indeed that "some of the most respectable and influential citizens of South Carolina" would advocate a policy in direct contradiction of states' rights doctrine (a belief that in due time would lead to nullification and secession) and the "principle of opposition to all appropriations not authorised by the Constitution of the United States."[50] In the eyes of critics, such men were not economic entrepreneurs but political ones, "a knot of needy or greedy speculators."[51]

Corporations' political power stemmed from their ability to bribe legislators, either directly or indirectly through the payment of a so-called bonus to the state,[52] typically with the aid of "some dealer in political corruption, grown grey in the slimy vortex of shifts and expedients."[53] According to one particularly sarcastic critic, such lobbyists formed "holy" alliances with other "missionaries assembled from other quarters for similar purposes" in order to win "the general consummation of all their purposes."[54] Then, "guided by the sure instinct of rogues," the lobbyist "singles out his member" and "dogs him" around town assailing the legislator "with all the small, yet too often irresistible arts of long experience and hardened iniquity" until he relented and voted for the charter.[55] Financier and philosopher Alexander Bryan Johnson painted a similar portrait, calling lobbyists men who "disguised their venality by feigning to possess a reputable interest in the projects they undertook to support; or to be patriotic promoters of the measures for merely an alleged public benefit."[56] Other lobbyists were more direct, offering lavish parties, money, or (free or discounted) shares in exchange for legislators' consideration.[57] As a result of all that lobbying, corporations, especially banks, had, in the eyes of at least one contemporary, "polluted the streams of legislation [and] . . . transformed men of honour into legalized swindlers . . . more lustful in appetite, than the Juggernaut."[58]

Short of outright bribery or coercion, corporations could influence legislatures in more subtle ways that today would be taken for granted but in the nineteenth century were still considered backhanded or untoward. "With prompt management," a Kentucky bank promoter told Norvin Green in 1848, the bank's charter petition could "be gotten through the house," especially if Green would visit the state capital and "aid the friends" of the bank in their efforts.[59] "So potent" were the tools at the disposal of corporations, critics believed, "that a single night has been known to bring about the conversion of at least a dozen members. . . . It has not unfrequently happened, that a company or bank voted out of the house one day by a large majority, was voted in again the next, by a majority equally large, and that too without debate or discussion."[60]

Along with the carrots of nepotism, stock, and hard cash, corporations also had at their disposal the stick of the votes of their employees and other minions. After all, for all its vaunted democracy, antebellum America was still a land of viva voce and other types of open balloting that made vote monitoring possible.[61] By contrast, voting in many corporate elections was secret, explicitly so that stockholders could "avoid the odium and violence of party prejudice."[62]

Corporations with monopoly power were especially potent politically because they had ample profits with which to grease the political machine and equally ample incentive to maintain their market power. "The man who would be treasurer, or secretary, or governor," one critic of New Jersey's Camden and Amboy Railroad monopoly, one of the most notorious antebellum American monopolies, claimed in the late 1840s, "must conciliate their aid, or he cannot be elected. Senators and members of Congress, and Attorney-Generals must obey their orders, or they cannot be re-elected, or re-appointed." "No bill can become a law," he asserted, "however necessary to the convenience and advantage of its people, until it has received the Royal Assent, signified by viceroys acting on the part of the Railroad Kings of New Jersey."[63]

Corporations could also control public opinion to some extent. Railroads threw lavish parties including "plenty of Liquor of different descriptions and a most sumptuous dinner," dazzling guests like Richmond's Blair Bolling, who was "highly gratified with the entertainment" and amazed to have traveled "about eighty six miles" to and from the event "without accident."[64] By such devious manipulations of legislatures, electoral politics, and sentiment, many contemporaries believed, concentration of wealth would lead "to luxury, immorality, and final subjection to tyranny."[65]

Political corruption threatened to increase in intensity as corporations multiplied.[66] Many critics argued that banks, turnpikes, "or some other chartered companies" had "leagued against all honesty" and actually co-opted the government, especially judges and legislators.[67] Well-publicized instances of the apparent bribery of elected officials certainly did not help ease the public's apprehension on this point.[68] "Corporate powers have been extended too far in this Commonwealth," a Freeman of Massachusetts argued in 1834. He continued: "They have been gradually gaining ground, for a great number of years, until they have become dangerous to the rights of the people. Too much influence is accumulating in the hands of a few. The combined funds and influence of such bodies give them great advantage over individual rights; and they do not hesitate to use it."[69]

Some corporations further fanned the flames by behaving as their critics predicted. The Boston and Providence Railroad excited considerable derision by insisting on its right to build its line through a cemetery. It created quite a spectacle by exhuming the remains of some 150 people.[70] It did not help when cashiers publicly accused bank presidents of maintaining off-the-book slush funds in locked drawers for the purpose of making "contributions to various political parties." Rumors that banks reimbursed officers for their personal campaign contributions on the theory that "the bank was benefited" by the contributions did not bode well for the republic, either.[71]

"The history of banks," some argued, "is a history of monopoly."[72] According to one New York attorney, they were "at best, dangerous monopolies, & ere long will control the government."[73] He was far from alone. In 1803, New York Federalists warned that a proposed bank was "a grand political machine" that would bribe legislators with "douceurs of money." Big banks, they claimed, were a "prime mover in the management of all State Elections."[74] The Bank of the United States (1791–1811) was also routinely called a "powerful tool, which, under the impulse of an ambitious chief, could have smoothed and leveled the way to the reestablishment of tyranny."[75] The "odious charge" of monopoly was also used to destroy the second Bank of the United States

(1816–36) and its upstart sibling, the so-called American System of national banks, universities, and internal improvements.[76]

Bankers were considered "a very powerful body of men" who could foment wars, mandate the construction of enormously inefficient canal systems, and just about anything else that would raise interest rates and hence their profits. "The most dangerous and worst thing to be apprehended from the system of commercial banks," a Marylander wrote in 1817, "is, that it has a tendency to destroy the government of the United States, and to establish *a government of secret influence*."[77] "In a few years more," the author "Seventy-Six" claimed in 1818, "there may be men with bayonets in their hands to restrain or prevent our efforts" at reforming a system that gave "bankers a privilege to monopolize the very sinues [*sic*] of all commerce, to take all legitimate money out of circulation, and to substitute false promises, expressed on scraps of paper, in its place. . . . Any man who will take the trouble to examine critically, into the conduct of a majority of the legislature of [New York], in 1812," he continued, "will be satisfied what share of power and influence bankers have with our legislative authorities."[78] Banks in New York, New Jersey, and elsewhere often found themselves accused of bribing legislators for their charters or other favors. The problem abated only when legislatures began granting charters more liberally, typically in exchange for charter bonuses or other forms of taxation, a salubrious outcome not lost on reformers.[79]

Early Americans also generally opposed anything "perpetual," as it smacked of privilege and economic stagnation. While a few corporations would not lock up much wealth, ever growing numbers of them threatened to control all real estate, to the detriment of future generations and, of course, the political system. For that reason, most antebellum business charters were limited in duration, usually to a few decades. On September 13, 1785, Pennsylvania's state government annulled the charter of its first commercial bank, the Bank of North America. Critics of the bank voiced a variety of complaints, most of which displayed ignorance of corporations in general and commercial banking in particular. Some raised legitimate questions about the liberality of the bank's perpetual, unamendable charter. Despite having to buy back some of its shares from disgruntled stockholders, the Bank continued to operate in Philadelphia, perhaps under its congressional charter, perhaps under a Delaware charter obtained on February 2, 1786, or perhaps as an unincorporated joint-stock company (its status was never tested in court), until it received a new, much more restrictive charter from Pennsylvania on March

17, 1787. Despite the time limit imposed by its new charter, the BNA went on to have a long, illustrious career by obtaining the charter renewals granted to virtually all law-abiding corporations willing to accede to new charter terms. Charter sunset provisions, which soon became commonplace and remained so throughout much of the nineteenth century, also provided stockholders with a scheduled opportunity to close down marginally profitable companies.[80]

Municipal corporations and even nonprofits such as the University of Pennsylvania were suspected of being the vanguard of "aristocracy" and hence were also bitterly opposed at times. Their numbers quickly increased, however, because Americans were not against their towns, cities, and NGOs per se but against possible abuses of power. Once their powers were sufficiently checked by limiting charters to a specific number of years, expanding suffrage, and enhancing legislative oversight, chartering of municipalities as well as nonprofits occurred en masse.[81]

Strong anticorporate views slowed but did not stymie the proliferation of the corporate form because many anticorporate sentiments were merely rhetorical flourishes in political debates. In the words of one contemporary, "decrying corporations" was a good way to win some votes.[82] Then, as now, disliking corporations was easy for those Americans who disdained material prosperity. "Wealth is becoming the idol of the people of this country," one commentator lamented, "and the pursuit of it is absorbing all their best time and talents. There is already too much wealth in the country for the good of the people," he argued.[83] Another stated that "enriching the nation, as it is called, is by no means desirable."[84] Most early Americans, however, wanted more—if not for their country, then at least for themselves. So, as it turns out, many people who criticized one corporation were stockholders or directors in another: in early America, all corporations were bad, except one's own.[85] Early on, Jeffersonian Republicans were the most vocal critics of corporations; but soon, in the words of Pennsylvanian William Meredith, "by every party, and by every shade of party, that has ever been represented in the state legislature, have these institutions been founded."[86] Eventually, the sin became not direct public offerings of stock (DPOs) themselves but failing to open subscription books to as many investors as possible.[87]

Opposition to the corporate form per se was less pervasive than it might appear. Opponents of the Merchants Bank in New York in the early nineteenth century were said to be of two stripes: "some with weak minds" who thought the bank "a hideous monster who at a single gulp would swallow down

Republicanism from Maine to Georgia"; and others "stockholders in other Banks [who] thought they saw in it a diminution of the value of their stock."[88] Instead of being battles between pro- and antigrowth candidates, many elections pitted the proponents of one set of economic interests against the advocates of another. While candidates sometimes campaigned against specific corporations, especially big banks, few sought election on the grounds of being against all corporations. Hard times, like those following the Panics of 1819, 1837, and 1857, increased unemployment, hard feelings, ambivalence about extending the market economy, and, in some less commercial places, anticorporation feeling. Few people concluded that corporations themselves were to blame, though specific ones—most notably, the Bank of the United States (1816–36)—took their lumps. Indeed, many came to believe that by employing numerous people, manufacturers, utilities, transportation companies, and other corporations could alleviate economic distress.[89]

Some corporate critics believed that each new charter decreased the power and sovereignty of the government, essentially robbing citizens of control of their own government.[90] That argument held precious little water because everyone knew that the government would always maintain the upper hand in any contest with a mere business. Governments could tax corporations out of existence[91] or otherwise "annihilate them in a moment."[92] Rather than outright transferring power by creating corporations, therefore, the government merely delegated it to a subsidiary body beholden to it in every way. With that understanding, corruption, but not tyranny, remained the only possible untoward political outcome of corporate proliferation. Given that corporations helped to create wealth, the possibility of corruption was insufficient to subject them to the same fate that befell lotteries: near-extermination and then nationalization.[93]

Quieting Corporate Criticism

> The Good particular men may do separately . . . is
> small, compared with what they may do collectively,
> or by a joint Endeavor and Interest.
> —*Benjamin Franklin, 1751*[94]

Had most Americans believed that corporations were as pernicious as their critics claimed, the U.S. political system could and would have squelched them. If banks continued to oppress freeholders, a Marylander argued in 1817, "the people will in the fullness of their power, sweep all these cobweb Banks away with the broom of legislation."[95] "The only possible pretext and justification for increasing their numbers and influence," a New Yorker argued in 1827, was the likelihood that their benefits "do so counterbalance" their costs.[96] "It is not to be presumed," an anonymous observer argued in 1835, "that the national or state legislatures would build up institutions incompatible with the public safety."[97] In 1837, "A Citizen of Boston" argued, Locke-like, that corporations "were originally granted to promote the common good; and whenever they cease to accomplish the purposes of their creation, an end should be put to their existence."[98] "The public interests cannot fail to control the public administration," it was noted in 1845.[99] As "mere creatures of the Legislature," corporations could have their charters modified or outright revoked, as the Bank of North America's charter was. If such action would injure innocent stockholders too much to countenance, all governments would have to do is not renew charters as they expired.[100]

The argument that early U.S. governments maintained the upper hand against corporations was bolstered by the fact that those same governments successfully squelched private lotteries. Then, as now, more Americans bought lottery tickets than owned shares in corporations, but more people benefited from owning shares than from buying tickets. That is because lotteries are zero-sum activities. Like other forms of gambling, they redistribute resources from A to B, but, save perhaps for some marginal entertainment value, they do not create wealth. Corporations, by contrast, do add to humanity's stock of valuable things by increasing trade and technology. In fact, the American colonists tolerated the first lotteries not as a form of gambling or entertainment but as a way to fund public projects.[101]

Before the financial revolution inspired by Treasury secretary Alexander Hamilton in the early 1790s, American governments typically found it difficult to raise money by selling bonds, so they financed budget deficits by printing money called "bills of credit." The problem with that technique was that if the government printed more money than the economy demanded, inflation could ensue, which spelled political friction between debtors, who benefited from price increases, and creditors, who could suffer badly as the real value of sums owed to them deteriorated. Rather than print new bills every time it wanted to fund a project, therefore, colonial and confederation legislatures had to learn creative ways of raising the needful.[102]

And there is little more creative in public finance than a voluntary tax.

Rather than force everyone to pay for a church, school, road, or bridge that might directly benefit only a small portion of the population, legislators—who were, after all, elected—found it expedient to elicit contributions by promising a big payout to a lucky few adventurers. The human brain is rigged as such that it finds it difficult to turn down the opportunity to wager one for the prospect, however remote, of receiving 1,000 later. Since at least biblical times, lotteries have been run to exploit this weakness; by the eighteenth century, they were big business in Britain. Even conservative Quaker Pennsylvania eventually found the expedient too enticing to ignore. In 1735, for instance, just three years after Henry Fielding sang "A Lottery is a Taxation/ Upon all the fools of Creation," the Pennsylvania Assembly held a lottery for 100,000 acres of provincial land. By the mid-eighteenth century, colonial governments regularly held lotteries to establish, improve, or maintain bridges, churches, colleges, fortifications, lighthouses, public buildings, roads, and wharves.[103]

Private lotteries were also run, usually to dispose of real estate or other hard assets that, for whatever reason, could not be sold outright. In 1733, Bethiah Hughes of Rhode Island ran a lottery in which a two-story house with three fireplaces and a good well on a lot in Easton's Point, Newport, and several unimproved tracts and town lots were the main prizes.[104] Seven years later, a Philadelphian raffled off "A good New Pleasuring Boat Sixteen Foot Keel, with Mast, Sails &c."[105] In 1773, in the aftermath of the massive real-estate bubble associated with the French and Indian War, Lord Stirling resorted to the same expedient in an attempt to unload tens of thousands of acres of his holdings.[106] By the late colonial period, businesses began to look to lotteries as a source of finance. In 1771, the American China Manufactory of Newcastle, Delaware, attempted to raise £1,000 by means of lottery.[107] Shortly thereafter, the American Steel Manufactory held a lottery. In 1774, the American Flint Glass Manufactory resorted to the same expedient to unload its lands and inventory.[108] All told, such private ventures were few and typically limited to vending the property of insolvent debtors during periods of macroeconomic instability. Such distress lotteries were frequent enough to be occasionally mocked, as in "A Lottery for Old Maids," "wherein there shall be all Prizes and no Blanks," the former consisting solely of "superannuated Virgins."[109]

Some colonists clearly understood that lotteries, public and private, preyed upon people's weaknesses, including avarice and ignorance of statistics. The anonymous author of *The Lottery: A Dialogue Between Mr. Thomas*

Trueman and Mr. Humphrey Dupe, published in Germantown (Philadelphia) in 1758, tried to use humor and sarcasm to spread his anti-lottery message. When Humphrey asked "why should not the grand Prize fall to my Share as well as my Neighbour's," Thomas, the obvious protagonist, responded, "I own the Picture of ill Luck is not more visible in thy Face than in that of another Man's. For your Comfort, too the Odds against you is only five thousand to one." Intrigued by his neighbor's obvious agitation, old Humph asks why Thomas was "so bitter against Lotteries." "For this plain Reason only," Thomas immediately responded, "they are manifestly no better than public Frauds and Impositions, solely calculated to enrich the Proprietors at the Expence of those who are silly enough to adventure in them, viz. the *Credulous* and the *Covetous*." The laudable public purposes of most lotteries, however, kept them popular with the country's dupes. As Humphrey explained, "should every Ticket I purchase turn up a Blank, I have yet the honest Consolation of contributing towards the Support of so beneficial, so charitable, so pious, so excellent an Institution." This little pamphlet, along with a moving poem called "Christ's Example" ("Must we set up more lotteries/To maintain needless vanities/To turn Christ and Paul out of door,/With ragged cloaths, among the poor?") and other anti-lottery tracts, including one that made clear that lottery winners' inability to invest their winnings is not a recent phenomenon, helped lead to a partial ban on lotteries in Pennsylvania between 1762 and 1792. Continued demand for tickets, however, simply moved Pennsylvania lottery activities to Delaware, which became a sort of offshore lottery haven.[110]

Pressure from Britain to limit colonial lotteries intensified in the late 1760s and early 1770s but, of course, ended with Independence. During the Revolution, the new national government ran lotteries to try to fund the war. They raised some money but fell far short of what was needed. The new state governments also ran lotteries to support troops and succor the poor as well as build or repair the usual bridges and other public infrastructure, a practice that continued into the nineteenth century. Church lotteries were also resumed after the war but were palpably waning by about 1810, presumably because of religious scruples against gaming and the rise of other funding options.[111]

In the nation's first few decades, state legislatures granted a number of corporations (SEUM, canals, bridges) lottery privileges. For some corporations, lottery privileges meant little because they had such difficulty selling out their ticket allotments that drawings had to be postponed or outright canceled. Over the course of sixteen years, the Schuylkill and Susquehanna

Navigation Company and the Delaware and Schuylkill Canal Navigation Company sold only $60,000 of the $400,000 in lottery tickets that the government had authorized them to sell. That was a bonanza, however, compared with the lottery of the Potomac Company, which raised only $486.03 of the hoped-for $300,000.[112]

For others, lottery management became a major focus of their business despite legal prohibitions against using the proceeds to pay stockholder dividends; cash is fungible, after all. Through 1810, the Lehigh Navigation Company apparently raised far more than the $10,000 that the legislature authorized it to take in lottery profits in 1798. Between 1811 and 1833, the Union Canal, somewhat ironically formed by the merger of the aforementioned Schuylkill and Susquehanna and Delaware and Schuylkill canal companies, awarded prizes of about $33 million in some fifty different lottery schemes. Generally, corporations received lottery privileges only when they were considered of prime public importance or were stricken by a natural disaster. Pennsylvania granted the Bustleton and Smithfield Turnpike Company lottery privileges in 1806, for example, after it was wrecked by unprecedented flooding.[113]

By the first decade of the nineteenth century, lotteries—state and corporate, foreign (that is, out of state) and domestic—were so numerous in big cities like Philadelphia that many had difficulty filling. Corporations that had been granted lottery privileges complained that frequent lotteries "and the abuses which have been discovered in the management of some of them, have operated to render them so much the objects of suspicion and distrust, that the grant of a lottery has almost ceased to deserve the name of a privilege."[114] Adventurers, as ticket holders were called, complained that some lottery managers waited years before drawing prizes or never did so at all. For their part, lottery managers often found it difficult to collect from retailers trusted with tickets on credit. Nevertheless, lotteries remained so potentially lucrative that their number continued to grow, as did unscrupulous but lucrative side businesses such as "lottery insurance" and partial tickets. In some instances, retailers vended seven or eight "quarter" tickets.

By the 1830s, some 200 so-called lottery retailers had clustered in Philadelphia alone. "Their flaring and intrusive signs and advertisements," it was said, "meet the eye at every turn." Nary a town of 1,000 or more inhabitants lacked at least one lottery retailer, most of whom threw the term "lucky" into their shop's name. The retailers themselves were certainly lucky, as they generally received commissions of 20 to 25 percent. Most adventurers, however, were poor people who had become addicted to buying tickets even though they won back, on average, only about sixty-four cents of every dollar spent, facts that aroused the ire and indignation of the era's vociferous moral reformers who paraded before the public every heartbreaking story of lottery-induced bankruptcy, divorce, fraud, prostitution, suicide, or theft that they could uncover.[115]

For all those reasons, public opinion turned decisively against lotteries in the second decade of the nineteenth century. In 1814, a coal-mining corporation rejected lottery finance because "moralists" objected to them "as a sort of legalized gambling; while statesmen pronounce them to be an unequal, and expensive way of raising money."[116] "Seventy-Six" criticized lotteries in 1818 because they further impoverished the poor, spread morality and vice, and were unnecessary in a republic.[117] Beginning in about 1828, Pennsylvanians began to petition the legislature to take action. In 1831, Governor George Wolf argued that out-of-state lotteries could be suppressed only if domestic ones were suppressed as well. After several years of politicking, petitioning, and pamphleteering, Pennsylvania finally joined several other states and completely banned lotteries. Although nearby New Jersey was an early infamous holdout, more states followed, until by 1880, some thirty states had declared lotteries unconstitutional. Lotteries continued to operate underground as the "numbers racket" until state governments monopolized lottery privileges in the twentieth century and thus created the incentive to eradicate large infringers. (Small, nonprofit raffles are typically tolerated, though technically illegal in many jurisdictions, ostensibly because the cost of prosecution exceeds the benefits of suppression.)[118]

The type of corporation with the most lottery-like reputation was the commercial bank. "It cannot be denied," wrote Ferris Pell in 1819, that "the BANKING SYSTEM has . . . beggared thousands of our farmers . . . poisoned domestic enjoyment, and chilled the current of morality."[119] Unsurprisingly, banks were the most heavily regulated of all antebellum corporations and, in a few states, were banned outright or monopolized by state governments. Other lenders were also sometimes subject to opprobrium, typically during financial stringencies when many borrowers had difficulty staying current on their obligations.[120] And, of course, all monopolies were inherently evil. A railroad monopoly was thought to have rendered New Jersey "one of the poorest States in the Union, possessing the worst roads and the fewest of them, and the worst schools and the fewest of them, when she should be one of the richest."[121]

Banks and other types of corporations were usually seen as tools of economic development.[122] Like an ax, spade, or hoe, they could be used for wrongdoing but also for great good.[123] "The abuse of a thing," Americans realized, "is no argument against its proper use."[124] The proper policy, therefore, was not to stop their useful applications but only their deadly ones.[125] By the mid-1830s, "the nature of" corporate "influence, whether salutary or otherwise, upon the public welfare" was still characterized by "a great diversity of opinion."[126] Nevertheless, the claims of the most ardent corporate critics could be ridiculed as "the vague fancies of a distempered imagination, filled with chimaeras dire. . . . To these uncertain and intangible arguments it can only be necessary to reply," petitioners for a charter in Virginia argued, "that the uninterrupted experience of every State in the Union, including our own, has completely demonstrated their utter fallacy and groundlessness."[127] "The country that should attempt to throw any obstacles in the way of the combination of property," Americans realized, "would, if it were possible to enforce its laws, accomplish its own destruction."[128]

Though not without costs, corporations—unlike lotteries—palpably improved Americans' material lives in myriad ways. Perhaps most important, they contributed mightily to the coffers of state governments, partly through taxes and partly through government purchases of their securities, especially bank stocks. In Massachusetts and Pennsylvania, banks contributed 30 to 50 percent of total government revenues in the first three decades of the nineteenth century. In the 1830s, Alabama and Georgia were able to replace state property taxes with dividends from their state-owned banks.[129] Corporations also enriched state governments indirectly, by promoting economic growth and hence tax receipts. In 1829, an anonymous author admitted that, generally speaking, it could "scarcely be questioned that the readiness with which corporate powers have been granted have multiplied the resources and improvements of the country."[130] "The most beneficial results," a group of charter petitioners argued in 1835, "have arisen from them by the creation of a vast amount of productive capital, which has added to the wealth and augmented the resources of our common country."[131]

Even many candid bank critics agreed that in the districts where "country Banks have been established, animation has been infused [and] the faculties of the farmers have been brightened."[132] "If the banking system has been beneficial to the commerce and agriculture of the state of Maryland," one person wrote to the local newspaper in 1804, "which, I presume, the greatest sceptic will not deny, is it not necessary, to maintain the respectable standing we have hitherto held in the commercial world, that our bank capital should be increased in the same proportion that our neighboring cities increase theirs?"[133] Some observers even understood that banks *reduced* monopoly by preventing a few rich merchants from dominating credit markets; and, by lending to young adventurers, banks increased the competitiveness of various lines of business.[134]

Ultimately, corporations were able to counter most criticisms leveled against them as a business form. Some hired adroit rhetoricians who were quick to point out that injuring corporations ultimately hurt stockholders and hence that anticorporate attacks amounted to robbing "one class in the community for the benefit of another," an especially impolitic policy because many stockholders were widows, orphans, and others "dependant upon the dividends of companies for the means of support."[135] Many early critics believed that corporations were owned by a few wealthy folk, for a few wealthy folk.[136] That view was clearly incorrect by the early nineteenth century: in Pennsylvania alone, some 38,000 individuals bought shares in banks, turnpikes, and toll bridges between 1800 and 1821. A few of them were the rich "capitalists" of lore, but most were farmers, artisans, and retailers.[137] Angst receded as critics learned that most corporations were widely held (not compared with today, of course, but relative to the "close corporations" that most critics imagined) and that they helped "persons of small means and limited knowledge of business."[138]

Other corporations cried *homo homini lupus*: man is wolf to man. Yes, they admitted, some corporations had committed unconscionable acts, but individuals regularly defrauded one another and corporations. Some forged checks or counterfeited notes while others stole gas (used for lighting in many cities by mid-century) or water by tampering with meters.[139] Other corporate proponents wrote of the "presumed popular prejudices against corporations" as if they were entirely apocryphal. Others painted criticism as simple old-fogyism, a "common prejudice to all kinds of innovation," as some New Hampshire canal promoters put it.[140] Inventor Oliver Evans also criticized "the obstinate opposition that has been made by a great majority to every step toward improvement; from bad roads to turnpikes, from turnpikes to canal, from canal to railways."[141]

Americans increasingly came to believe that entrepreneurs who risked their own wealth in a potentially profitable endeavor deserved the public's praise, not its disdain. In 1860, a Texas editorialist called the "defeat of the charter" of the Raft Company "a gross outrage" because the proprietors sought no state money. "Was there ever a more preposterous refusal of justice—that people shall not be permitted, at their own expense, to clear out the obstructions of a great water course like Red River?"[142] The real danger, some perceived, was not investors but legislators. The former wanted to turn a profit and hence were less likely to back a losing proposition than the latter. They therefore complained when "Projectors" sought government aid instead of publicly offering "shares to the subscriptions of respectable men, of different parties."[143]

Critics of corporations were in earnest but were probably not as numerous or as strident as some historians seem to believe.[144] As part of their Revolutionary heritage, early Americans were very sensitive to any person or thing that could usurp their liberties and thereby re-enslave them to one or more tyrants. Properly checked, corporations proved incapable of reinstating tyranny—and, in fact, by strengthening the nation's economy, they helped ensure continued American independence. Ultimately, then, corporations needed to be monitored, not squelched. And the best way of monitoring them, Americans realized as early as the 1790s, was to allow them to proliferate and check one another through competition.[145] In an 1812 speech, Massachusetts governor Elbridge Gerry extolled the cleansing powers of competition. "Many institutions of this Commonwealth which have promised great benefit to the publick," he claimed, "would have met with much more success, had similar corporations been established. When one only of any kind is permitted," he explained, "it too frequently happens that a majority of the individuals composing it, indulge their private views and interest. . . . The multiplication of such institutions has a tendency, not only to prevent this evil . . . but to produce a competition, and to promote in the highest degree the utility of such establishments."[146] Subsequent experience in Massachusetts proved Gerry's views substantially correct. The perceived power of competition waxed over time, until it seemed essential to life itself. "Mr. Riggs has opened an Ice House, in addition to that of the Tallahassee Ice Company, which has usually been the means of supplying us with this refreshment," a newspaper editor chimed in 1840. "We are pleased to see that no monopoly will take place in an article so necessary to the comfort of our citizens, and so promotive of health" by reducing the incidence of heat stroke and improving the storage of food.[147]

It even became difficult to argue that competition did not have salubrious effects for bank borrowers. In 1807, the average length of discounts granted by the Philadelphia Bank was fifty-eight days, consistent with its policy of not granting any discounts for longer than sixty days. As the number of other banks in the city increased, however, the Philadelphia Bank felt pressure to increase its average loan length dramatically, to ninety-two days in 1824, 114 in 1828, and almost 150 in 1831. Similarly, the establishment of a branch of the Bank of the United States (1816–36) in Utica, New York, induced the local banks to cut their discount rate from 7 percent to 6 percent and to increase the average loan length from three months to five months. Competition also forced banks to update and innovate. In the 1830s, for example, the already hoary Bank of North America responded to competitive pressures by thoroughly modernizing its board and its business methods.[148]

By the 1830s, the concept of competition was pervasive enough to garner corporations support from an unlikely quarter: the followers of Andrew Jackson. Unwilling to abolish corporations due to public opinion or to curb their activities significantly through extensive regulation, many Jacksonians came to embrace competition as a solution to the corporation question. Jacksonians found special incorporation too restrictive, too apt to lead to "monopoly" conditions, too likely to aid a well-connected and well-heeled few at the expense of the many. So they pushed for general incorporation laws on the grounds that what "is open and free to all, can in no sense be denominated a monopoly." Jacksonians also sought somewhat more extensive regulation and the elimination of existing "monopolies" like the Bank of the United States (1816–36). In addition to being unconstitutional (or so they argued), that Bank was a monopoly in the sense of being the only federally chartered bank then in operation. Moreover, the Bank was so large that it had become, in the eyes of many Americans, a soulless monster capable of just about anything. Like lotteries, it had to be suppressed and was.[149]

More liberal incorporation promoted competition in the political sphere. As Samuel Tilden said, Jacksonians "do not assail property, we merely deny it political power."[150] Onetime Federalist Tench Coxe agreed, arguing that the existence of large numbers of corporations, especially banks, would ensure that they would not "deviate, in a dangerous degree, from their proper walk, into the ground of political combination and intrigue."[151] As rights rather than privileges, corporations would serve to check one another in the halls of power as well as the stalls of markets.[152] "The general laws sprinkled holy water on corporations," famed historian Arthur Schlesinger, Jr. claimed, "cleansing them of the legal status of monopoly and sending them forth as the benevolent agencies of free competition."[153]

Despite the support of some Whigs and Jacksonians, general

incorporation came slowly, over decades rather than in an avalanche. Politicking played a role, but so did a residue of skepticism about the efficacy of corporations and even the morality of the corporate form. "Corporations," one common aphorism stated, "have neither bodies to be kicked, nor souls to be damned."[154] Most attempts to pass laws, such as ten-hour-per-day laws, directed solely at corporations did not pass; but that they were proffered at all indicates the continued existence of anticorporate sentiments.[155] Other critics of general incorporation laws sought to restrict entry to qualified individuals, complaining that the "legislatures of most of the states" granted "corporate powers to great numbers of associations, in many cases no doubt injudiciously."[156] Criticism of the corporation continues to this day, largely along the same lines: they have too much market and political power and engage in socially irresponsible behaviors.[157] Nevertheless, by the 1830s, the most virulent criticism of the corporate form had been largely quieted, and legislators, north, south, east, and west, passed the petitions of entrepreneurs into law with regularity, if not alacrity. "Chartering corporate bodies," one contemporary explained, "furnishes one of the most ordinary occupations of the Legislatures of the different states."[158] The next chapter enumerates, for the first time, the rise of the United States as a corporation nation, the first nation to charter and put into operation large numbers of for-profit companies (mutual and joint-stock) endowed with perpetual succession, limited liability and entity shielding, transferable shares, and the right to sue and be sued as a single entity.

Chapter 4

Corporate Ubiquity

> The gathering and preparation of this work has been quite a task. . . . It has
> required a very close search and inspection—page after page—of . . . laws,
> both local and general. It is believed, however, that the importance of this
> undertaking will amply justify the labor expended and time employed.
> —J. S. Robinson, 1885[1]

Figure 1 plots, on a log scale, the number of special charters granted to businesses each year throughout the United States between 1790 and 1860. The sheer number of corporations was important to the rise of the corporation nation, but so was their size. Size is best measured by total assets; unfortunately, early corporations, especially nonbanks and especially before the 1830s, left few balance sheets to posterity. So Figure 2 plots—again, on a log scale—the next best measure: minimum authorized capitalization (MINAC), the lowest capitalization figure stated in corporate charters.[2]

Clearly, the old canard that the antebellum U.S. suffered from a dearth of "capital" needs to be jettisoned, just as it was in 1833 by author and internationalist Achille Murat, who noted that the speed "with which capitals augment in the United States, surpasses all belief. The demand for capital is such, and the enterprises, commercial, manufacturing, and agricultural, are so numerous, that whatever may be their amount, they are instantly absorbed."[3]

Figure 3 accounts for the growth in population, as measured by estimates of all Americans (slave and free). Figure 4 accounts for the overall economy, as measured by gross domestic product (GDP). Both figures show that corporations became more important over time, relative to both population and economic growth.

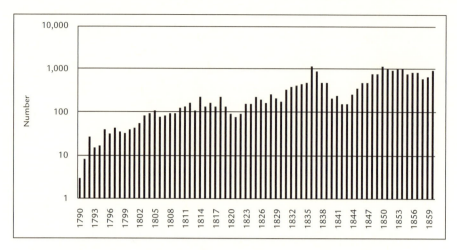

Figure 1. New special corporate charters, 1790–1860. Source: Richard Sylla and Robert E. Wright, "U.S. Corporate Development, 1801–1860," NSF SES Grant No. 0751577; complete database is available from the author.

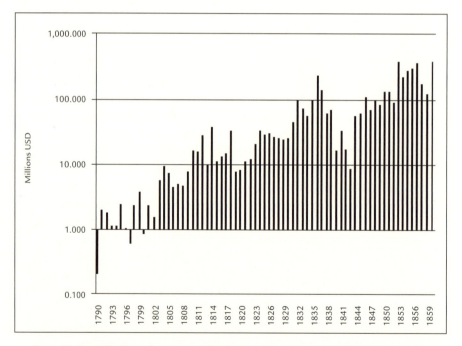

Figure 2. Capitalization of new, specially chartered corporations, 1790–1860. Source: Richard Sylla and Robert E. Wright, "U.S. Corporate Development, 1801–1860," NSF SES Grant No. 0751577; complete database is available from the author.

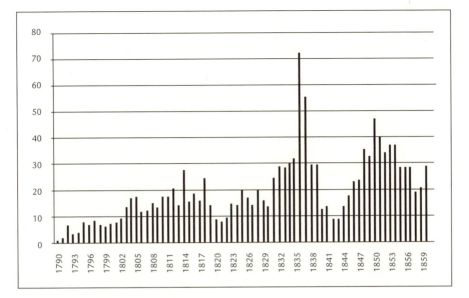

Figure 3. Number of new corporations per million Americans, 1790–1860. Source: Richard Sylla and Robert E. Wright, "U.S. Corporate Development, 1801–1860," NSF SES Grant No. 0751577; complete database is available from the author.

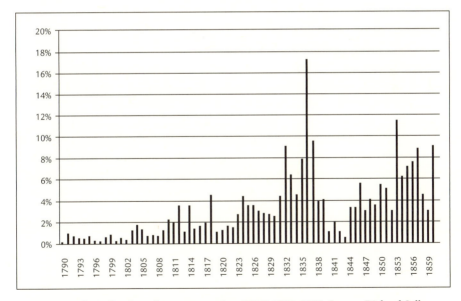

Figure 4. Capitalization of new corporations/GDP, 1790–1860. Source: Richard Sylla and Robert E. Wright, "U.S. Corporate Development, 1801–1860," NSF SES Grant No. 0751577; complete database is available from the author.

All four figures reveal that new corporate chartering was sensitive to the business cycle. During the steep recessions that followed the Panics of 1819, 1837–39, and 1857, the number and MINAC of new corporations dipped absolutely and also in per-capita and percentage of GDP terms. During the boom days of the early 1830s and the early 1850s, by contrast, corporation formation, corporation formation per capita, MINAC levels, and MINAC divided by GDP achieved new highs. Some lags in the data are to be expected, as legislatures generally met for only a few weeks, a few times a year. Revamping general statutes or other major legislative projects could also skew the data by delaying consideration of charter petitions. When legislators sought to pass sweeping reforms, as in New York in the 1820s and in Ohio in the mid-1830s to early 1840s, incorporation rates temporarily fell.[4]

Downturns probably did not greatly affect the total number of businesses that chose to incorporate or their MINAC over the long term, but they did influence their timing, inducing entrepreneurs to put off projects for one or more years or to implement less ambitious plans. Periods of economic or financial distress could negatively affect total authorized capital without diminishing the number of new corporations formed. In the early months of 1800, for example, numerous merchants in New York, Philadelphia, and Baltimore went bankrupt because of "Bankruptcies in Europe" and a "stagnation in commerce, & particularly in tobacco," which led to an "unfortunate State of Commercial Credit" and "great mercantile distress."[5] The number of corporations chartered in 1800 increased to thirty-nine from thirty-two the previous year, but MINAC slumped from almost $3.85 million to just $851,000.

The state of the overall economy affected new chartering activity because entrepreneurs were very sensitive to the costs and benefits of incorporation. During panics, interest rates soared to levels that rendered few projects profitable.[6] "Whilst the rate of interest in this country continued as it had been for many years past," an observer noted in 1840, "none but the most promising enterprises should have been undertaken by individual companies."[7] During the *"four panics"* that struck during the troubled 1837–39 period, interest rates soared "from 1 to 2 and even as high at times as 3 per cent. a month."[8] Such high rates created enough "pressure upon the money market" to render it difficult for the Troy Turnpike and Rail Road Company to raise money from its stockholders, some of whom were already peeved that the company was beginning with a turnpike rather than a railroad, or to borrow at affordable rates from "such persons, banks, or company, as would lend it for the benefit of the Company."[9]

During the Panic of 1857, interest rates increased to "a frightful extent" because of the failure of almost 1,000 businesses (most of which were not corporations) in Manhattan alone in the last quarter of the year. In such circumstances, corporations found it "impossible . . . to sell lands or bonds." Obtaining loans during panics was difficult, too, because crises wreaked havoc with some banks, such as the Bank of Pennsylvania, while sparing others, such as the Bank of Delaware County and most of the banks in Ohio.[10]

The recessions that followed financial panics eventually brought lower interest rates and prices that some corporations could not resist. The Lewis Wharf Company saved "at least $30,000" by building ten high-quality warehouses in 1838 after a panic.[11] For most businesses, however, recessions were an unpropitious time to attempt to raise capital or begin operations because investment funds were in short supply and expected revenues muted. The recession of 1839 "was immediately felt in the receipts of this company," reported one railroad, "by the large reduction which immediately commenced to take place in the number of travellers, and in the amount of merchandise transported."[12] Some railroads failed because of panics; others merely tightened their financial belts. The Pennsylvania Railroad missed a dividend payment in order to service its large "floating debt."[13]

Entrepreneurs were so sensitive to the economy that even relatively minor shocks could render them cautious. The number of new corporations chartered and MINAC dropped from 246 and almost $25.4 million in 1828 to just 198 and $24 million in 1829 because of a little-known "commercial revulsion" that "took place both in Europe and this country." The shock, industrialist Nathan Appleton explained, "was especially felt by the cotton manufacturers in England" but was severe enough that "several establishments in this country operating with insufficient capital, were prostrated."[14] Some banks had a tough time of it, too, because, in the words of one bank historian, "borrowers seemed to have been unable to meet their obligations."[15] Similarly, foreign shocks could have significant marginal effects. Some believe that the formation of new railroads in Massachusetts dropped off in the 1850s because of a recession in Britain.[16]

Expansionary periods, by contrast, may have increased new corporation formation by seducing entrepreneurs into launching corporations in order to take advantage of unrealistically ebullient capital markets. In other words, financial bubbles—periods of overinvestment, or rather, misdirected investment—may have caused some of the spikes in corporate activity shown above.[17] During such periods, not even bad news could derail large undertakings. In 1834, the DPOs of ten Ohio banks chartered within a few weeks of one another were quickly oversubscribed even though money market conditions were so tight that a newspaper editor claimed that the time for opening subscriptions "was the most unfavorable that could be."[18]

The 1830s look suspiciously bubbly, but the 1850s also witnessed a boom in business activity that may have been driven more by the California gold strikes than by fundamentals such as population growth and technological advances. According to that view, the Panic of 1857 brought asset prices, such as railroad and textile stocks, back to more realistic values. "The error was," W. P. Tatham told Baring Brothers in London, "in making [railroads] too fast."[19] Appleton agreed. "In consequence of the great profits in the year 1844, 5 and 6, both in England and this country," he argued, "the manufacture [of textiles] was extended beyond the wants of the country." Moreover, "disturbances in China have interfered materially with our increasing trade to that region."[20]

Court cases may have influenced incorporation rates as well. Supreme Court decisions favorable to corporations rendered by Chief Justice Roger B. Taney may have encouraged the formation of more corporations.[21] Several of his decisions, particularly *Bank of Augusta v. Earle* (13 Peters 519, 1839), opened new vistas by clarifying the legality of corporations that operated across state lines.[22]

Finally, some fluctuations in the incorporation data were due to political events. Maryland extracted taxes and investments from its banks in exchange for charter renewals and its promise not to charter new banks for a specified time. When that informal agreement ended in the early 1830s, the state quickly chartered seventeen new banks (five of which never opened).[23] Pennsylvania had gone even further in 1814, when it simultaneously chartered forty-one new banks, partly in response to the War of 1812 and the dissolution of the Bank of the United States (1791–1811).[24] For similar reasons, Kentucky chartered forty-six new banks in 1818, just in time for their balance sheets to be dashed on the rocks of the Panic of 1819. The demise of the second Bank in 1836 spurred an even more massive flood of new bank charters.[25]

Chartering activity was also sensitive to the ideology of those in power. The number of charters granted in Pennsylvania increased after the election of Governor Simon Snyder, who, as a member of the so-called New School faction, was a strong advocate of economic development.[26] Conversely, activity declined when a "champion of the people against the nabob interest," someone who believed that the "abuse practiced by corporate institutions" has "already been too seriously felt," was in power.[27] Government subsidies for railroads and pro-cartel policies increased the number of railroads chartered in Massachusetts, the former by increasing the pool of resources available to railroad builders, and the latter by decreasing cost and rate competition. Competition policies (antitrust), by contrast, tended to decrease new entry.[28]

The rivalry between Philadelphia and Baltimore pressured legislators in Pennsylvania and Maryland to keep chartering companies to supply their respective economies with enough banks, roads, and port facilities to allow their metropolises to compete against each other in trade. It was widely believed that experience had shown "that the city which can make herself the grand depository for such products [of the hinterland], is certain of arriving at great wealth and opulence."[29] With more corporations, Philadelphians claimed in 1804, they would be "enabled to extend their commerce to all parts of the globe" at the expense of Baltimoreans languishing in recession.[30] "Pennsylvania must have canals," one canal president asserted in 1811, because "she will not suffer her neighbours to outstrip her in internal improvements, and to draw from her those resources which will enrich them to her impoverishment."[31] "Corporations," Achille Murat reminded readers in 1833, "become an immense source of prosperity to the . . . town in which they establish offices."[32]

Such "rivalistic state mercantilism," as some scholars term it, was by no means limited to Philadelphia and Baltimore.[33] Philadelphia was also engaged in what contemporaries portrayed as a life-and-death battle with Manhattan that required the construction of a railroad from Philadelphia to the northeastern part of the Quaker State lest it be economically lost to New York, that "great toll-gate at the mouth of the Hudson River."[34] Pennsylvania also blocked a New Jersey canal's access to Delaware River waters to protect Philadelphia's trade with northeastern Pennsylvania.[35]

After Southern states began to build western railways to counteract the effects of the internal improvements of the North,[36] New York State countered by chartering several railroads that competed with its Erie Canal to protect Manhattan from encroachments by Maryland, Pennsylvania, Virginia, and South Carolina on its western trade.[37] Meanwhile, the widening of Canada's Welland Canal around the falls at Niagara spurred Boston railroad entrepreneurs to urge their city to connect to Ogdensburgh on Lake Ontario, on the theory that it would supplant Buffalo as the "foot" of Great Lakes navigation and free Boston merchants from the "tribute" it paid to Manhattan merchants.[38] Other instances of city rivalries and state competition increasing the number (and perhaps the size of) corporations abound.[39] Rival interstate interests sometimes interfered with the incorporation process. Pennsylvania legislators approved a railroad connecting the Susquehanna River to the Maryland state line, but because of fears that it would drain commerce to Baltimore, it larded the charter with illiberal provisions that some claimed almost destroyed the Maryland railroad that was formed to link to it.[40]

The tendency of corporations to fight the chartering of competitors, at times quite vigorously, undoubtedly dampened both the number and size of new corporations.[41] The New York and Boston Railroad faced "untiring opposition from the citizens of Hartford, and several existing Railroad Corporations."[42] That same railroad, ironically, sought to prevent the creation of a rival "Air Line" by the Charles River Railroad Company.[43] According to James H. Godman, president of the Bellefontaine and Indiana Rail Road Company, "a few persons in the Legislature connected with rival interests" saddled his corporation with an "illiberal" charter that made connecting to any other railroad "impracticable."[44] That was extremely damaging because of the prime importance of connections in the transportation business.[45] "A canal or railroad," one contemporary explained, "however insignificant in regard to length or other characteristic, assumes an importance far beyond its intrinsic value" when it became part of a transportation network.[46]

For decades, New Jersey's Camden and Amboy Railroad was a notoriously nasty defender of its presumed monopoly rights. For example, it blocked the attempt of a Pennsylvania railroad company to buy up and alter the charter of a New Jersey turnpike to allow it to compete more effectively with the Camden and Amboy on the important Philadelphia to New York route.[47] Rather than seeing the issue as a battle between competing states, many consumers correctly interpreted the situation as "an inordinate and favored appetite for exclusive privileges which has become too voracious to be restrained. In other words, . . . a MONOPOLY."[48]

As Table 1 shows, the special chartering of corporations varied significantly from state to state. As to be expected, the largest, oldest, and richest states chartered more corporations than the smallest, youngest, and poorest states did. What is somewhat surprising is the ranking of states in terms of corporations per million residents (free and slave) in 1860. Here, more marginal states, such as Rhode Island, Maine, New Hampshire, Vermont, New Jersey, and Nebraska, shine. Perhaps legislators and entrepreneurs in those states saw incorporation as a way to improve their state's ability to compete in

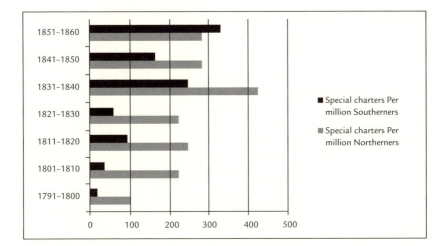

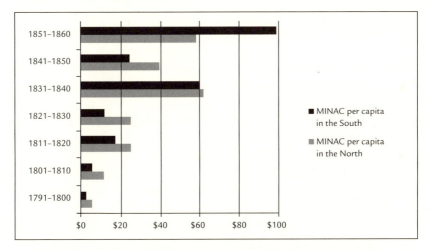

Figure 5. Number and capitalization of new corporations by decade and section, 1790–1860. Northern states: Connecticut, Delaware, Illinois, Indiana, Maine, Massachusetts, Michigan, New Hampshire, New Jersey, New York, Ohio, Pennsylvania, Rhode Island, Vermont, Wisconsin. Southern states: Alabama, Arkansas, District of Columbia, Florida, Georgia, Kentucky, Louisiana, Maryland, Mississippi, Missouri, North Carolina, South Carolina, Tennessee, Texas, Virginia. Excluded western states/territories: California, Colorado, Iowa, Kansas, Minnesota, New Mexico, Oregon, Utah, Washington. Source: Richard Sylla and Robert E. Wright, "U.S. Corporate Development, 1801–1860," NSF SES Grant No. 0751577; complete database is available from the author.

Table 1. Number and Capitalization of Specially Chartered Corporations by State, 1790–1860

State/Territory	Number	MINAC (mil. $)	Population in 1860	Number/Million pop.	Rank
Massachusetts	2,554	94.414	1,231,066	2,074.62	5
Pennsylvania	2,348	376.920	2,906,215	807.92	15
Virginia	1,862	270.708	1,596,318	1,166.43	11
New York	1,727	329.546	3,880,735	445.02	23
Maine	1,379	231.632	628,279	2,194.88	3
Ohio	1,302	236.012	2,339,511	556.53	19
Kentucky	1,151	264.449	1,155,684	995.95	13
New Jersey	975	82.380	672,035	1,450.82	8
Maryland	819	206.536	687,049	1,192.05	10
New Hampshire	818	86.601	326,073	2,508.64	2
Illinois	685	126.404	1,711,951	400.13	26
Vermont	663	41.747	315,098	2,104.11	4
Missouri	613	284.342	1,182,012	518.61	20
Indiana	602	23.116	1,350,428	445.78	22
North Carolina	560	80.858	992,622	564.16	18
Georgia	506	144.457	1,057,286	478.58	21
Rhode Island	441	57.027	174,620	2,525.48	1
Connecticut	398	57.731	460,147	864.94	14
Alabama	398	58.076	964,201	412.78	25
Michigan	324	54.553	749,113	432.51	24
Tennessee	322	47.309	1,109,801	290.14	31
Wisconsin	305	117.690	775,881	393.10	27
South Carolina	256	72.569	703,708	363.79	28
Mississippi	252	31.088	791,305	318.46	29
Texas	183	103.863	604,215	302.87	30
Louisiana	167	227.410	708,002	235.88	32
Kansas	164	254.203	107,206	1,529.77	7
Delaware	153	20.937	112,216	1,363.44	9
Minnesota	108	172.036	172,023	627.82	17
Florida	99	23.230	140,424	705.01	16

State/Territory	Number	MINAC (mil. $)	Population in 1860	Number/Million pop.	Rank
Arkansas	83	9.074	435,450	190.61	33
Nebraska	57	44.241	28,841	1,976.35	6
Oregon	55	13.879	52,456	1,048.50	12
Iowa	24	2.247	674,913	35.56	34
Utah	13	1.015	n/a	n/a	n/a
District of Columbia	12	2.177	n/a	n/a	n/a
Washington	11	16.660	n/a	n/a	n/a
California	11	0.000	379,994	28.95	35
Colorado	10	0.147	n/a	n/a	n/a
New Mexico	9	13.130	n/a	n/a	n/a
TOTAL	22,419	4,580.414	31,176,878	719.09	

Source: Richard Sylla and Robert E. Wright, "U.S. Corporate Development, 1801–1860," NSF SES Grant No. 0751577; complete database is available from the author.
Note: According to William Miller, Pennsylvania chartered 2,320 corporations between 1800 and 1860. The number here is larger because of the inclusion of the 1790s as well as differing opinions regarding the for-profit status of certain cemeteries and other borderline cases. See William Miller, "A Note on the History of Business Corporations in Pennsylvania, 1800–1860," *Quarterly Journal of Economics* 55, 1 (November 1940): 153.

an increasingly national marketplace. It should be noted that states that adopted successful general incorporation laws will be underrepresented in this and subsequent tables. Before the Civil War, only Iowa (1846), California (1849), Michigan (1850), Indiana (1851), Ohio (1851), Minnesota (1858), and Oregon (1859) prohibited all special charters, so the distortion is probably not great, except perhaps for Indiana and Ohio. Good data on general incorporations have proved difficult to obtain, for a variety of reasons.[49]

The strong growth of corporations in the South may surprise some readers, but it should not. Like their Northern brethren, most Southerners aspired to material comfort (if not outright opulence), reveled in economic independence, and condoned any institutions, including incorporated banks, canals, turnpikes, and—in some regions of Virginia, South Carolina, and elsewhere— even manufacturers, that were likely to further their goals. Figure 5 shows that in the 1850s, in per-capita terms, the Southern states specially chartered more corporations than the Northern states did and invested more in them. In the 1830s, Southerners invested almost as much in their corporations as Northerners did, in per-capita terms.[50]

Contemporaries also noticed that the formation of business corporations was a national, rather than a regional, phenomenon. "Multitudes of companies with corporate powers for banking, insurance, manufacturing, building bridges, roads, and canals," one author noted in 1829, "have been created *in all parts of our country*, and form one of the striking features of our social system."[51] "Now we see on every hand the most gratifying proofs of change," a Southern nationalist wrote in 1860, "and constantly we hear of some new enterprise [w]hich is to contribute to the general welfare of the community."[52]

Why the first big wave of incorporation came later to the South is a question that does not admit easy answers. Some have suggested cultural differences and wealth disparities. Northerners, particularly New Englanders, had a knack for association because of their Congregationalist religion and because they were so poor that they had to join together to get anything done.[53] Of course, measuring the effect of religious beliefs on economic activity is nearly impossible, and it is strange that Southerners joined to form corporations, as they grew even richer during the antebellum period. Ultimately, it was a development issue. Although profitable for slaveholders, slavery as an institution was a virulent form of pollution that kept the South several decades behind the free states of the North economically.[54]

All this suggests that earlier historians' infatuation with Massachusetts was largely, but not entirely, misplaced.[55] Massachusetts presumably led the way in incorporation because, as one historian claimed, "the Bay State mind . . . felt itself competent to improve upon any model."[56] General cultural explanations, however, are not amenable to empirical testing.[57] In addition, the available data provide us only with the equilibrium quantity, with the joint decisions of entrepreneurs and legislators. A state might have a middling incorporation rate, for example, because it was home to many eager entrepreneurs but reticent legislators or because its legislators chartered almost everything that the state's handful of entrepreneurs brought before it. While it is sometimes possible to use legislative records to track the percentage of charter petitions that were successful, it would be a gargantuan task to complete for every type of corporation in every state over the entire antebellum period.[58]

Table 2 shows that the most common and the most highly capitalized lines of business shifted after 1830, probably because of technological and structural economic change. As the top panel details, turnpikes were the most common form of enterprise in the earlier period, followed by manufacturers, banks, bridges, and insurers, while the most heavily capitalized corporations were banks, manufacturers, insurers, and canals. In the three decades before the Civil War, turnpikes and manufacturers remained the most common type of corporation, but railroads supplanted banks, bridges, and insurers to take the third spot. In terms of capitalization, railroads reigned supreme with over half of MINAC, followed by manufacturers, mining companies, and then banks and insurers. Readers should note that the data reflect only corporations formed under special charters and not those incorporated under general laws. So the total number of corporations chartered was larger than indicated in Table 2, and the numbers and percentages by business type may have been different, as most early general incorporation statutes covered only banking or manufacturing companies and tended to favor the chartering of smaller corporations.[59]

Policies such as the embargo of 1807 and the War of 1812 skewed the types of businesses formed, away from banking and marine insurance and toward manufacturing, mining, and quarrying, although not all at the scale requiring incorporation. The Philadelphia Manufacturing Society, for example, remained an unincorporated joint-stock company capitalized at only $50,000.[60] Many coal mines were run as proprietorships or partnerships, but others, especially those that built transportation links, incorporated. Later, gold and other metals would be mined almost exclusively by corporations because they were risky, expensive enterprises that served, in the words of a contemporary, "a grand industrial purpose."[61]

The end of the embargo and war adversely affected manufacturing interests, leading to decreased chartering activity in that sector.[62] "Under the influence of the war of 1812," Appleton recalled, "the manufacture of cotton had greatly increased, especially in Rhode Island, but in a very imperfect manner. The effect of the peace of 1815 was ruinous to these manufacturers." When Appleton visited Pawtucket in 1816, "all was silent, not a wheel in motion, not a man to be seen" except a few in "Slater's old mill, making yarns."[63] Appleton's recollections are corroborated by cotton manufacturers in upstate New York that did well during the War of 1812, only to falter after it. Whitesboro Cotton was worth $50 per share at one point on the basis of its "rich dividends," before falling when "the Factories [were] at a stand," in late 1816.[64] Manufacturers along the Brandywine in Delaware were also hurt by foreign imports after the war.[65]

Table 2. Number and Capitalization of Specially Chartered Corporations by Business Type, 1790–1860

1790–1829

Type of Business	Number	MINAC (mil. $)	Percent of Total Number	Percent of Total Capital
Turnpikes	1,175	29.776	28.40%	6.29%
Manufacturers	698	91.489	16.87%	19.34%
Banks	575	159.400	13.90%	33.69%
Bridges	476	8.177	11.51%	1.73%
Insurance cos.	314	64.134	7.59%	13.56%
Canals	223	50.294	5.39%	10.63%
Utilities	159	8.703	3.84%	1.84%
Navigation cos.	150	12.869	3.63%	2.72%
Waterway improvement cos.	137	12.731	3.31%	2.69%
Miscellaneous	80	6.060	1.93%	1.28%
Mining cos.	60	11.235	1.45%	2.37%
Railroads	44	17.380	1.06%	3.67%
Harbor cos.	34	0.674	0.82%	0.14%
Transportation cos.	12	0.215	0.29%	0.05%
Telegraph cos.	0	0.000	0.00%	0.00%
Total	4,137	473.137	100.00%	100.00%

1830–60

Turnpikes	3,648	142.540	19.95%	3.47%
Manufacturers	2,883	381.847	15.77%	9.30%
Railroads	2,559	2,281.238	14.00%	55.54%
Banks	1,855	312.316	10.15%	7.60%
Insurance cos.	1,806	148.763	9.88%	3.62%
Mining cos.	1,378	354.877	7.54%	8.64%
Miscellaneous	947	103.837	5.18%	2.53%
Bridges	892	27.418	4.88%	0.67%
Navigation cos.	741	135.535	4.05%	3.30%

1830–60				
Type of Business	Number	MINAC (mil. $)	Percent of Total Number	Percent of Total Capital
Utilities	736	70.523	4.03%	1.72%
Canals	223	73.245	1.22%	1.78%
Waterway improvement cos.	223	32.075	1.22%	0.78%
Harbor cos.	183	20.267	1.00%	0.49%
Telegraph cos.	136	7.375	0.74%	0.18%
Transportation cos.	72	15.421	0.39%	0.38%
Total	18,282	4,107.277	100.00%	100.00%

Source: Richard Sylla and Robert E. Wright, "U.S. Corporate Development, 1801–1860," NSF SES Grant No. 0751577; complete database is available from the author.

Manufacturing eventually rebounded, aided by a higher tariff passed in 1816 and the adoption of the power loom. By the mid-1820s, some New York manufacturers paid dividends of 10 or 15 percent. But the sector continued to suffer numerous ups and downs, some in sync with the overall economy, others due to the dynamics of tariffs and particular markets. In 1840, textile manufacturers in New England had a banner year while the rest of the economy slumped.[66] "Palmer Manufacturing Company, at Palmer, Mass., have lately made sale of the entire stock of manufactured goods they had on hand, at prices satisfactory to the manufacturers," a newspaper reported, "and have entered into a contract to supply all the goods they can manufacture at their establishment for six months to come, the Stark Mill and Amoskeag Manufacturing Companies have likewise lately made sale of all the goods they had on hand; the York Factory, at Saco, Me. has lately declared a dividend of twelve per cent. for the past twelve months."[67]

The tariff of 1846, by contrast, hurt incorporated cotton and woolen manufacturers despite a strong economic upswing, but simultaneously encouraged entry into leather manufacturing and related fields such as footwear.[68] In 1850, another period of general prosperity, "the high price of raw material . . . induced several of the Lowell Cotton Factories to suspend operations. One factory," a newspaper reported, "has discharged over 500 operatives and others are following their example. Probably over 3000 persons will be thrown out of employment in Lowell for this reason. The Boote Company, which turns out $60,000 worth of goods per month, have sold but $12,000 worth per month, during the last quarter."[69] The textile producer Granite Manufacturing Company planned to stop its factory for a month, then run it for a month, then shutter it again, as market conditions dictated.[70] At the same time, the Charleston Cotton Manufacturing Company announced plans to increase its capital from $100,000 to $500,000, "the additional capital . . . to be employed in the immediate erection and furnishing of a large cotton factory of 15,00[0] spindles, contiguous to the present factory at Hampstead." Half of the new stock was snapped up by "Gen. James, the celebrated machinist" while "the remainder has been taken by our citizens."[71] In late December 1850, Pepperell moved into a "large new mill," and the York announced that it would begin to run at double speed in January.[72]

Scholars such as William Roy and Mary Furner, who recently wrote that during the nation's first decades, "ingrained suspicions of concentrated economic power, along with the fearful legacy of the South Sea Bubble and other such schemes, had confined the corporate form to large-scale ventures in transportation and finance,"[73] clearly have underestimated the importance of early manufacturing corporations.[74] It is true that most manufacturing concerns were not corporations but rather sole proprietorships or partnerships that produced relatively modest quantities of arduous spirits, barrels, beer, bread, bricks, books, cabinets, candles, carpets, carriages, clocks, confections, coffins, draperies, furniture, glass, hats, iron, jewelry, leather, nails, paper, pottery, rope, sails, ships, shoes, shot, snuff, soap, starch, stones, sugar, textiles, vinegar, watches, or other goods. Increasingly, however, the biggest and most productive firms took the corporate form. By 1835, petitioners could claim that charters were "freely granted" to manufacturers "every where," largely because their positive effect on local employment and economic development was universally asserted by incorporators and widely accepted by legislators and their constituents.[75] The early ubiquity of manufacturing corporations has important implications for how scholars conceive of legislators' attitudes toward early corporations.[76]

Most earlier students of the corporate form have claimed that legislators would only charter corporations that provided clear "public" services such as currency, energy, transportation, or water. Only later, they argued, did lawmakers enlarge their view of what types of businesses could incorporate. The fact that early judges considered for-profit corporations as "private" institutions, along with the formation of a large number of manufacturing corporations before 1830, suggests a different interpretation. Rather than being quasi-public enterprises, as many scholars have assumed, early corporations, as a late nineteenth-century jurist put it, needed only to "provide some good that is useful to the public."[77] That is a huge difference, as explained by a jurist in 1851, who noted that a corporation "does not become a public Corporation, because public interests may be incidentally promoted by it."[78] Scholars have been confused because most incorporators claimed that their companies were "for the good of the public" in order to increase the odds of receiving legislative approval.[79] Supplying a *public good*, a good that is non-rival and non-excludable, and supplying a *good* for members of the public are distinct activities.[80]

Manufacturers certainly promoted public interests only incidentally, as did many of the nation's miscellaneous corporate businesses, which included hotels and spas, theaters, and cemeteries. They all incorporated because they needed a relatively large capital to thrive.[81] "Those citizens would be sensibly benefited," Tench Coxe noted in the mid-1790s, "were they able to relieve themselves of certain parts of their labour by the attainment of the auxiliary machinery, which is the purchase of larger capitals."[82] "One thing is certain," Appleton remarked. "[M]anufactures cannot be carried on to any great extent in this country in any other manner than by joint stock companies."[83] In other words, America would have spawned even more corporate manufacturers if scale economies had been more widespread.[84] Many miscellaneous corporations also needed the scale that only the joint-stock form or the occasional wealthy capitalist could muster.[85]

This is not to argue that legislators were yet entirely comfortable with granting charters for their own sake. In 1840, the Massachusetts legislature denied a charter to the American Friction Match Company by a large margin, "the yeas being almost inaudible." The reason given was that most legislators found "their object of a trivial nature." The "three or five persons" who owned the company held a patent and wanted to incorporate solely to make it easier and cheaper to sue infringers "providing any one of them should die or be taken sick, or become insolvent."[86]

Entry and Exit Caveats

> In the most material facts I have contented myself
> with round numbers; perfect accuracy would be as
> unnecessary as impossible. They are as correct as
> documents will admit.
>
> —*A Citizen, 1806*[87]

Despite their seeming certitude, the numbers in the figures and tables above should not be presented without important qualifications. Both the number of corporations and their capitals were built from legislative records. No early American government systematically recorded when a corporation did *not* begin business, but the smattering of information available on the subject shows that nontrivial numbers of chartered companies failed to begin operations.[88] In 1826, tax officials from Oneida County informed the New York state comptroller that thirteen companies chartered to conduct business in their county, including eight turnpikes, four manufacturers, and an aqueduct (water utility), "have never existed."[89] In Maine, twenty of seventy-one banks chartered between 1820 and 1838 did not begin operations.[90] Generally speaking, the less profitable types of corporations, such as turnpikes, were less likely to form than more profitable types, such as banks and railroads. In Pennsylvania, only eighty-four of 146 turnpike companies chartered before 1821 actually began operations, completing 1,807 of the 2,521 miles that they had been authorized to build. In New Jersey, only a little more than half of the fifty-four turnpikes chartered up to 1828 successfully constructed roads. One scholar concluded that in the Middle Atlantic states, "it is safe to say that at least one-third of the turnpike corporations chartered never built a mile of road."[91] The attrition rate among New England turnpikes was also about one-third.[92]

Those estimates of corporations that failed to form may be exaggerated because sometimes incorporators merely delayed beginning operations. One early railroad company refused to begin operations until a charter amendment could be passed because its original charter was "found to be so limited in its grants of power, so restricted in its policy, and so imperfect in its general provisions, that no efforts were made to carry it into effect, and it remained . . . a dead letter on the statute Book."[93] Adding to the confusion, some corporations changed their names. The Green Mountain Bank of Vermont changed its name to Stark Bank the year after it was chartered.[94] The Tonawanda

Railroad changed its name to reduce confusion as it connected Rochester to Batavia, New York, well east of Tonawanda, a northern suburb of Buffalo.[95]

Other data issues should also be noted. The charters of some companies were so short or ambiguous that their line of business or for-profit status could not be determined with certainty. A few corporations—typically, interstate bridges and canals—were chartered by more than one state. (We tried not to double-count them in the database even though the U.S. Supreme Court considered them separate corporations. Many other corporations were chartered in one state but maintained unincorporated offices in other states, a perfectly lawful behavior in most instances.) Some companies existed in other forms before incorporating. The Phoenix Iron Company of Chester County, Pennsylvania, operated as Reeves, Buck & Company, an integrated rail iron manufacturer, before receiving its charter. Sometimes corporations changed their line of business. In Maryland in the 1840s, seven savings banks converted into commercial banks. Many other companies were de facto banks masquerading as insurance companies, railroads, and so forth.[96]

"The nominal amount of capital in the acts of incorporation," New York legislator Jonas Platt astutely noted in 1811, "is very uncertain evidence of the real amount employed."[97] MINAC could deviate from actual capital for several reasons. Many charters also stipulated a maximum authorized capitalization (MAXAC), so those corporations lawfully could hold more than MINAC. The West Virginia Iron Mining Company had a minimum authorized capital of $100,000 and a maximum of $500,000. Other corporations ignored or circumvented the law and kept more capital or less capital than stipulated in their charters by outright lying or by loaning subscriptions right back to stockholders.[98] The South-Carolina Canal and Rail Road Company sold 6,000 shares in its DPO, but "several of the subscribers have failed to make their payments, and some from death and misfortune cannot now fulfil their engagements."[99] The company could resell those shares to other investors, but until it did so, it remained 192 shares short of its full MINAC. By the 1850s, some stock subscription agents expected that about 10 percent of subscribed capital would not be paid for, and they planned accordingly.[100]

Incorporators sometimes asked the legislature for a larger capital than they intended to raise, just to provide some cushion. The Boston Manufacturing Company, a textile manufacturer, was chartered in 1813 with a MINAC of $400,000. (It was actually located in Waltham and should not be confused with the Waltham Cotton and Wool Factory Company, which received a charter in 1812 authorizing a capital of $450,000.) "But it was only intended," according to one of the directors, "to raise one hundred thousand, until the experiment should be fairly tried."[101]

Another difficulty is that corporations sometimes bought their own shares in the market. Such purchases were probably roughly counterbalanced by the accumulation of contingency funds or undivided capital, profits that corporations retained for safety's sake rather than returning to stockholders in the form of dividends.[102] Some corporations actively managed their capital, which could fluctuate considerably from year to year. The capital of the Bank of the State of South Carolina was increased whenever the state treasury ran a surplus and decreased whenever anyone redeemed one of the state's 3 percent bonds, which took decades to accomplish.[103]

The charters of many early joint-stock corporations, especially in New England, did not authorize a specific amount of capital, though they all had some.[104] The Locks and Canals on Merrimack River (chartered 1792) had a capital of $60,000, not the zero recorded in the database used to create the estimates presented in the tables above. Furthermore, many corporations increased their capitals, some with and some without explicit legislative approval. The Merrimack Manufacturing Company was chartered in 1822 with an authorized capitalization of $600,000 but obtained amendments that authorized it to increase its capital by $300,000 in 1828, $500,000 in 1837, and another $500,000 in 1849.[105] Before the Civil War, 756 corporations received permission from their respective legislatures to increase their MINAC by a total of $281.4 million. Not all of that may have been actually raised, but it is unlikely that many corporations asked to increase their MINAC if their original MINAC had not been fully subscribed.[106] Some corporations asked to reduce their capitals, an indication that their MINAC had "been extended beyond the capital that can be employed."[107] All told, corporations asked for net increases of their MINAC amounting to almost $226 million.

Some states, including Maryland after 1854, allowed some or all of their corporations to increase their capital at will.[108] An unknowable number of other corporations simply increased their capitals without approval. The Boston Manufacturing Company, the corporation mentioned above that was not sure whether it could employ $100,000 to advantage, proved so successful that its capital was increased to $600,000, apparently without explicit legislative sanction.[109]

"In many of the banks, only a small part of the stock subscribed," Platt rightly pointed out, "has been actually paid or invested."[110] The shortfall was largely planned. The American Bank of Providence, Rhode Island, for example, had an authorized capital of $500,000 but issued only $193,000 when it formed in 1833. It later increased its capitalization to $300,000, then $400,000, and finally hit half a million in 1845. In 1851, it successfully petitioned the legislature for an increase to $1 million, and four years later, when it asked for an increase to $2 million, showed $983,750 on its balance sheet.[111]

Most antebellum U.S. corporations called in their capital slowly, over a period of months or years; so by design, full capitalization was not achieved until well after incorporation. In March 1835, the authorized capital of banks in Ohio was $12.2 million, but slightly less than $5.85 million was paid in at that time. By the end of that year, almost $6.4 million was paid in; and by December 1837, over $11.3 million had been called for and actually paid in by subscriber-stockholders.[112]

A comparison of a contemporary estimate of Philadelphia bank capitalization made by Samuel Breck with the MINAC from the database underpinning this chapter further illustrates this planned capital lag. Breck made his estimates in 1818 or perhaps 1817. Most of the corporations that he estimated to have capitals less than those authorized by law (those with positive numbers in Table 3's far-right column) had been chartered just a few years earlier. They were still calling in their capitals, a practice justified by its salubrious effects on both corporate governance (discussed in Chapter 6) and by the belief that corporations should begin operations as soon as possible so as not to render capital dormant for an extended period.[113]

The MINAC derived from the database is just $654,000 more than that reported by Breck. In 1845 and 1846, four of the biggest six banks in South Carolina had a database MINAC identical to that reported in their quarterly balance sheets those two years. Tax records from New York also bolster the view that MINAC and paid-in capital were often, though not always, quite close. Overall, such evidence suggests that, despite the sundry distortions discussed above and some claims to the contrary, the MINAC values reported in this chapter are good estimates of the capital eventually employed by early U.S. corporations.[114]

It must be noted that the data presented in the previous section refer to the *flow* of new corporations into the economy. Much less is known of the *stock* of corporations, the number in actual operation in any given year. Many early corporations survived the antebellum period and even the travails of the Civil War. Mutual Fire Insurance Company of Loudon County was still in existence in 1897, when its fifty-year charter expired. Others merged with other corporations or unchartered joint-stock companies. In 1784, the Bank

Table 3. Comparison of Corporate Capital Estimates by Breck and by Sylla and Wright

Corporation Name	Year Chartered	Breck's 1818 estimate ($)	Database ($)	Database— Breck ($)
Commercial Bank	1814	1,000,000	1,000,000	0
Germantown Bank	1814	152,000	300,000	148,000
Mechanics Bank	1814	534,000	1,000,000	466,000
Northern Liberties Bank	1814	250,000	500,000	250,000
Schuylkill Bank	1814	400,000	1,000,000	600,000
Bank of Pennsylvania	1793	2,500,000	400,000	-2,100,000
Farmers and Mechanics Bank	1809	1,250,000	1,250,000	0
Philadelphia Bank	1804	1,800,000	2,000,000	200,000
Bank of North America	1781	830,000	1,000,000	170,000
Insurance Company of North America	1794	600,000	600,000	0
Insurance Company of Pennsylvania	1794	500,000	500,000	0
Philadelphia Insurance	1804	400,000	400,000	0
Phoenix Insurance	1804	480,000	600,000	120,000
Union Insurance	1813	300,000	500,000	200,000
Delaware Insurance	1813	200,000	500,000	300,000
United States Insurance	1810	100,000	400,000	300,000
Marine Insurance	1809	300,000	300,000	0
TOTAL		11,596,000	12,250,000	654,000

Sources: Samuel Breck, *Sketch of the Internal Improvements Already Made by Pennsylvania* (Philadelphia: J. Maxwell, 1818), 46–47; Richard Sylla and Robert E. Wright, "U.S. Corporate Development, 1801–1860," NSF SES Grant No. 0751577; complete database is available from the author.

of North America was able to persuade investors in the Bank of Pennsylvania, a recently formed unincorporated joint-stock company, to give up their scrips in exchange for new BNA shares. In 1811, two Pennsylvania canal companies merged to form the Union Canal Company. About a decade later, the Merrimack Manufacturing Company acquired the Pawtucket Canal from the

Table 4. Comparison of Corporate Capital Estimates by New York Tax Officials and Wright

Name	MINAC ($)	Paid-in Capital per 1833 Tax Records ($)
Oneida Glass Factory	100,000	50,000
Oneida Manufacturing Society	200,000	124,000
Oriskany Manufacturing Company	100,000	61,000
Bank of Utica	1,000,000	600,000
Oneida Iron & Glass	100,000	92,500
Bank of Rome	100,000	100,000
Clinton Woollen Manufacturing Company	100,000	100,000

Source: Richard Sylla and Robert E. Wright, "U.S. Corporate Development, 1801–1860," NSF SES Grant No. 0751577; complete database is available from the author.

Proprietors of the Locks and Canals on Merrimack River by purchasing all its shares. Locks and Canals later sold excess waterpower to other manufacturers. It also built textile machinery until that part of its operation was "sold to a separate corporation" in 1845. A canal and a railroad in New Jersey also merged, ostensibly to protect the stockholders of the canal from the competition of the railroad.[115]

Yet other corporations successfully formed only to close down after a few years or decades of operation. Many went bankrupt; others deliberately folded, their unprofitability due to various business, economic, or regulatory pressures. The stockholders of the San Francisco and San Jose Railroad Company voted to dissolve their company in June 1860 "because they found themselves under an impracticable law, which the people could not safely endorse."[116]

Tracking the exit of all early corporations proved an arduous and impossible chore because of a lack of definitive records and sundry other difficulties.[117] Some corporations stopped operating for a time but later became active again. Ohio's Urbana Banking Company revivified in 1834 after failing some years earlier. That same state's Miami Exporting Company closed its doors in 1822, only to reopen them in 1834.[118] The following year, a Philadelphia newspaper reported that a silk manufacturing company in Northampton, Massachusetts, had been "resuscitated."[119] Moribund banks in New York also lay dormant for some years before beginning business anew.[120] In the words of a contemporary, the Society for the Establishment for Manufactures, "after struggling for many years through a series of difficulties, incident to the novelty of the undertaking— the infancy of the mechanic arts—a low impost, and foreign skill—... after heavy losses, has now at length, by good management and the accession of more active capital, become prosperous and valuable."[121]

If those corporations hibernated, others remained alive but comatose. In 1845–46, the stockholders of the Marine Insurance Company of Alexandria instructed the president and directors to stop writing new insurance and then to pay out their assets as dividends to them. The company at that time had about 30 percent of its assets invested in "Corporation Stock of Alexandria," valued at 95 percent of par, and most of the remainder in shares in the Bank of Potomac, valued at $72 per share. Interestingly, the stockholders instructed the managers to retain "a small portion of the Capital Stock, to keep the company alive, to enable the Stockholders to benefit by any compensation that the Congress of the United States may make for French spoliations previous to 1800."[122]

Extant records sometimes provide clues about early corporate exit rates. The Oneida County tax officials mentioned above also noted that five corporations chartered to operate in their county had failed by 1826.[123] Gallatin claimed that 165 banks, with more than $24 million in capital, failed between January 1, 1811, and July 1, 1830. "Of the actual loss incurred," Gallatin could "give no account" because sometimes stockholders suffered no loss, sometimes some, and sometimes all.[124] All told, 903 commercial banks failed before the end of 1860. Critics claimed that bank failures "frequently happen," but actually most failures occurred during the bank panics of 1819, 1837–39, and 1857, when up to 10 percent of all extant banks went under in a year or two.[125]

Some states fared better than others. Of the fifty-eight banks chartered (special or general) by Vermont before the Civil War, at least thirty-three remained in business long enough to become national banks under the National Banking Act of 1863.[126] In Maryland, nine of twenty-one banks had failed by the 1820s. The failed banks controlled $1.8 million, or 22 percent, of the state's total active bank capital. [127] New York chartered nineteen banks prior to 1812, three of which failed: the Columbia Bank and Middle District Bank in 1829;[128] and the Bank of Hudson in 1820. Between 1813 and 1829, New York chartered an additional twenty-four banks, five of which failed before 1831. Under the Safety Fund (1829–36), the state chartered or rechartered ninety-three banks, sixteen of which failed before their charters expired. In addition, fifty-seven New York free banks failed before the end of 1861.[129]

The record of savings banks also varied over time and place. New Jersey chartered twelve savings banks before 1860. The Newark Savings Institution, Trenton Savings Fund Society, Hoboken Bank for Savings, Burlington Savings Institution, Howard Savings Institution, and the Orange Savings Bank all thrived throughout the antebellum period, some into the twentieth century. Others, such as the New Jersey Protection and Lombard Bank, did not.[130] New York chartered nineteen savings banks before the Civil War. Before the end of the antebellum period, only three had failed: the Knickerbocker Savings (chartered 1851), Mechanics' and Traders' Savings (chartered 1852), and the Bloomingdale Savings Bank (chartered 1854).[131]

On December 1, 1837, the secretary of the Commonwealth of Massachusetts reported in operation forty-nine domestic marine and/or fire insurers with an aggregate capital of almost $9.5 million. The database on which this study is based, however, reveals that Massachusetts had chartered through that date 162 insurers with a total MINAC of almost $23 million. As those figures suggest, the percentage of corporations that failed might not be as important as the percentage of capital that was not remunerative. In 1827, for example, New York City had corporations with a capital stock estimated at $39 million, "about 35 of . . . [which] has been employed profitably for the holders," a decent record.[132] Stock information available on railroad capitalization in 1860 is only about half that of the flow presented above, suggesting that half of MINAC railroad capital was not paid in or had proven unremunerative.[133]

Corporate failures did not necessarily, or even usually, mean a loss of wealth to the community but only a change in the ownership of productive assets. In 1830, assets that the defunct Buxton Company had paid $40,000 for, "a valuable water privilege of 79 feet head, with about 200 acres of excellent land, several dwelling houses, stores, work shops, picker house, &c.," sold at public action "to Messrs. Wm. Wattemore & Co. of Boston for $6,000!"[134] Corporations often arose, phoenix-like, from the ashes of earlier failed corporations. The York Manufacturing Company in Maine "became the purchasers of property that was unsuccessfully placed there, and sold at a great sacrifice." The Cocheco was likewise "founded on the ruins of the Dover Company, in which fortunes were lost, or greatly impaired."[135]

Corporations apparently failed less frequently than individuals did, and, as an anonymous pundit wrote in 1837, "most persons, as a general rule, feel safer in trusting corporations than in trusting individuals."[136] "Sometimes, indeed, they do unprofitable business and fail," another contemporary noted of corporations. "[B]ut," he added, "that is very seldom."[137]

International Comparisons

> Americans of all ages, all conditions, all minds
> constantly unite . . . [in] commercial and industrial
> associations in which all take part. . . . I have since
> traveled through England . . . and it appeared to me
> that there they were very far from making as
> constant and as skilled a use of association.
> —*Alexis de Tocqueville, 1838*[138]

For the first six decades of the nineteenth century, America probably chartered more corporations than any other country on earth. Only Great Britain rivaled it for the top spot. While the full extent of the Mother Country's early corporate economy has only recently come to light, the best estimate is that about 1,500 corporations (ones with formal charters as well as unchartered companies with transferable shares and at least thirteen partners) formed in England, Wales, Ireland, and Scotland between 1720 and 1844.[139] While that figure does not include turnpikes, which numbered about 900 in England and Wales alone, the British likely chartered fewer corporations than the States did. British corporations, however, were likely more heavily capitalized on average than American ones.[140]

Nevertheless, many contemporaries, even some British ones, looked to the U.S. as the leading corporation nation. By 1850, *Fortune's Epitome of the Stocks*, the major international investment primer of the first half of the nineteenth century, began its section on the "securities of the United States" by saying that it was "utterly impossible within these narrow limits to go into a detailed account of the finances and resources of this great country."[141] Others observed that the practice of conducting business "by corporations has been much more prevalent in the United States than in England."[142]

British corporate governance and practices were similar to those in America, and British companies suffered from many of the same types of

fraud that U.S. companies did.[143] Many Americans harbored a grudging respect for the Bank of England, even though it grasped "a monopoly unfavour-
able to and inconsistent with the free spirit of our government."[144] In terms of
numbers, the early United States out-mothered the Mother Country, even
when accounting for Britain's many de facto corporations—its unchartered
joint-stock companies. As mentioned in Chapter 2, the Bubble Act of 1720
made formally chartered corporations exceedingly rare during Britain's industrial revolution. Unincorporated joint-stock companies were more common, especially in the types of businesses that Adam Smith believed were
best suited to the corporate form: turnpikes, canals, utilities, banks, and insurers. By 1794, British investors had sunk £5.3 million into canals, "a most
enormous sum!" according to one contemporary observer.[145] Some examples
of joint-stock bakeries, breweries, cemeteries, distillers, and sundry manufacturers have also been identified.[146]

Between 1740 and 1840, the capitalization of British joint-stock companies grew faster than the economy, from about £90 to £210 million (roughly
$350 million to $1 billion). Nevertheless, U.S. corporate case law by the 1820s
was already more advanced than in the Mother Country, and America held a
comfortable lead in the number of corporations, even after a bubble in corporation formation in Britain in 1824 and 1825. During that episode, 127 companies with £102.8 million in capital formed and remained in business until
at least 1827. They included forty-four mines, twenty gas companies, fourteen
insurers, and forty-nine miscellaneous companies. Another 118, including
sixteen mines, nine investment, twenty transportation, twenty steam, and
forty-three miscellaneous companies, with a total capital of £56.6 million,
were "abandoned" after they sold shares to investors. Another 236 companies, with a proposed capital of £143.6 million, published prospectuses but
never formed, or quickly failed, or did only a small amount of business. Another 143 companies were projected but were so ephemeral that the amount
of capital they attempted to raise was unknown but estimated to be about £70
million.[147]

The bubble chastened British entrepreneurs, investors, and legislators for
some years, but demand for full-blown corporate privileges mounted. An act
that was passed in 1826 allowing bankers and investors to form joint-stock
banks outside London was apparently intended to improve the stability of
English banking by allowing for the creation of larger institutions with larger
capital cushions and bigger hinterlands and branch networks for attracting
deposits and spreading out loan risks. Entrepreneurs formed only thirty-nine

such banks prior to 1833, when a new act allowed them to form in London as well. The ability to enter the metropolis spurred considerable activity, as by 1836 some ninety joint-stock banks, with an estimated total capital of £10 million ($40.87 million at mint parity of $4.8708),[148] had formed. By 1841, about 120 joint-stock banks remained in operation, some having already failed, with a total capitalization of about £17 million. But they were indeed safer and more profitable than the private banks, which shrank to about 300 in number by 1841, some by failure and some by conversion into, or merger with, joint-stock banks. The number of joint-stock banks peaked at 124 in 1896 and thereafter fell because of rapid consolidation, which left only two private banks and thirteen joint-stock banks, with more than 8,000 branches, in operation by 1924.[149]

In 1841, a list of the "principal joint-stock companies" in Scotland was six pages long and comprised only twenty-five banks; twenty-five life, fire, and marine insurers; seventeen railways; eighteen gas companies; and twenty-six miscellaneous companies. By the early 1840s, the number and capitalization (about £295 million—say, $1.4 billion) of British companies were impressive compared with any other country except the United States.[150]

In 1844, Parliament provided for incorporation by simple registration, but stockholders remained fully liable for their corporation's debts until 1855.[151] The law attracted few takers; railroads, for example, preferred to pay for special acts of incorporation from Parliament in order to acquire limited liability and eminent domain. But that did not stop the industry's growth. Between 1848 and 1857, total investment—bonds plus ordinary and preference shares (common and preferred shares, in U.S. lingo)—in British railroads increased from £200 million to just shy of £315 million.[152] By 1850, eighty life-insurance companies operated in London alone, and 155 throughout Britain.[153]

The effect of limited liability, finally granted to a wide range of companies in 1855, was palpable. In the words of British investment guru Robert Ward, acceptance of limited liability touched off a "mania" that "raged for speculation in the shares of joint-stock companies."[154] Between 1856 and 1862, almost 2,500 limited liability corporations formed in England and Wales, a third of which went bankrupt within five years. By that time, the U.S. economy had already overtaken that of Britain and, to this day, has yet to relinquish its economic and corporate leadership status.[155] In the mid-1920s, the U.S. was said by one expert to "turn out more of this particular transcendental product [the corporation] than all the rest of the universe put together."[156]

The French and other continental powers also got into the corporate game relatively late. The U.S. press took note of many innovative companies on the Continent, including a loan company set afoot in Hamburg in 1799, a coral fishery established in 1801, French transatlantic steamboat companies in 1840, and a joint-stock company formed in 1860 to conduct "farming operations on a larger scale." As in the British case, the number of corporations on the Continent lagged that of the United States. Prior to 1860, savings banks and credit cooperatives were fewer than two score in the area now known as Austria.[157]

Under Napoleon, France's business code spread across much of the continent; but, aside from railroads, continental corporations were few until after the enactment of general incorporation laws in the latter half of the nineteenth century. Between 1826 and 1837, French entrepreneurs formed 157 *sociétés anonymes*, "corporations in the United States sense, with limited liability for all owners," and about 1,100 *sociétés en commandites par actions*, limited partnerships with transferable shares. Between 1840 and 1848, French entrepreneurs created more than 1,400 *commandites* but only about 150 new *anonymes*. Only in 1863 did France embrace general incorporation. Other continental powers, such as Sweden and Germany, slowly but surely followed, first liberalizing business forms and then allowing general incorporation. By the end of the century, only the Russians and Ottomans still required special acts of incorporation. Russia's eastern neighbor, Japan, did not begin to stir economically until after the U.S. Civil War; and the rest of Asia was moribund until the twentieth century. China's relative dearth of corporations was a mystery to late nineteenth- and late twentieth-century observers alike. Asia was not devoid of corporations before the postwar period but, aside from Japan's *zaibatsu*, most business remained in the hands of small, noncorporate entities or large governmental or public-private enterprises.[158]

The non-U.S. New World was also slow to adopt the corporate form en masse. It is a mistake to think of early nineteenth-century Canada, as some scholars have, as an affluent country on a par economically with the United States. Some Americans had very close commercial ties to the "most fertile portion" of Canada, that part of Upper Canada (approximately present-day Ontario) near the northern and western shores of Lake Ontario. By the 1810s, many residents of that area were American by birth. Nevertheless, Canada's per-capita GDP and its overall level of development trailed those of the United States until after the Civil War and Canada's independence. Unsurprisingly, so did its corporate development.[159]

Quebec, or Lower Canada, remained especially backward, though observers considered it blessed with natural endowments "almost equally good"
to the "opposite portions" of the United States.[160] Prior to the Civil War, Quebec was home to just two Francophone banks—Banque du Peuple (chartered
in 1835 but called the DeWitt, Viger and Co. prior to 1844) and the Banque
Nationale, chartered in 1860—and a handful of Anglophone institutions such
as the Bank of Montreal and the Quebec Bank, which established branches
only in towns with significant English-speaking populations.[161] Before the
1870s, the French-speaking parts of the province were simply too poor to
establish many corporations of any type.

By 1840, there had been about fifty companies chartered in Upper Canada. There is little surprise in such paucity because as late as 1844, John Lang-
ton asserted that there were no profits to be made in Canada other than in the
law, storekeeping, tavern keeping, and horse dealing, none of which required
incorporation. Between 1841 and 1867, about 200 corporations, mostly public utilities and financial intermediaries, were chartered under special laws.
Only after 1855 did manufacturing or mining corporations appear in any
numbers.[162]

Canadian corporations followed the same general form as American and
British ones, undoubtedly because they were both rooted in the same
common-law tradition and often sought to attract investors in both places.[163]
The bylaws of the Montreal Mining Company, for example, held that the directors could "at any future time to appoint Agents in London, New York, or
elsewhere, and it shall be competent for them to issue Stock, either in Sterling
at the new par of Exchange, or in United States Currency, at the rate of five
shillings and one penny to the dollar, and such Stock shall be transferable at
the place of issue, where also any Dividend which may accrue thereon shall
be payable."[164] The first attempt to create a Canadian stock market apparently
took place in 1852, but there were no active exchanges in Canada until after
the outbreak of the U.S. Civil War. The Toronto Exchange, founded in 1854,
provided a physical venue for securities transactions that went unutilized, as
the existing over-the-counter markets were sufficient for the small trading
volumes then prevalent. The Toronto Stock Exchange, which began operations in October 1861 with just thirteen listings, was Canada's first true stock
exchange, but it, too, struggled with low trading volumes in its early years.[165]

The New World's other big country, Brazil, was not the economic or financial basket case that it would become in the twentieth century. Nevertheless, the number of corporations established there before 1900 lagged far

behind that created in antebellum America, even in per-capita terms. The Brazilian government granted special charters sparingly, and free incorporation was not enacted until 1882.[166] The story was much the same in neighboring Chile and undoubtedly throughout the rest of a Latin America plagued by tremendous disparities in wealth and political power.[167] But in the United States, H. S. Tanner argued in 1840, the situation was "essentially different; wealth and information being more generally diffused among the great body of the people, they possess and exercise a powerful influence in all affairs of a public nature, and of course, claim a large share of attention."[168]

Chapter 5

The Benefits of Big

> In most other countries, the great mass of the people, being destitute
> of wealth, have but little influence, and still less power to effect
> important objects; hence every work requiring large expenditure, must be
> accomplished by the wealthy few, whom it is well known, do not always
> consist of the most enterprising portion of a community.
>
> —H. S. Tanner, 1840[1]

Early American entrepreneurs, more than 131,000 of them, went through the trouble of obtaining a special act of incorporation for the 22,419 corporations documented in Table 1 in Chapter 4 because they expected that the total benefits of incorporation exceeded its total costs. They knew that investors were eager for the profits that promised to flow in the form of dividends or share or real-estate price appreciation. But why did entrepreneurs want to share their profits? To increase their financial success, they had to control more resources than they could personally command. "The convenience to a numerous body of men associated for any purpose, of having corporate powers and privileges, *is obvious*," wrote one analyst in 1829. "For many enterprises requiring the investment of large capital," he further explained, "a common partnership would be exceedingly inconvenient, not to say impossible."[2] Better to make $1 million and split it 1,000 ways than to earn only $100 as an individual. There were, in other words, big benefits in being big—economies of scale, optimal vertical integration, and market power foremost among them.

As New York chancellor James Kent put it, "the multiplication of corporations in the United States, and the avidity with which they are sought, have arisen in consequence of the power which a large and consolidated capital gives them over business, the facility which the incorporation gives to the management of that capital, and the security which it affords to the persons of the members and to their property not invested in the corporation."[3] Nineteenth-century investment guru Robert Ward, however, warned that corporations would be able to compete with individual proprietors only when "a very large capital" was an economic necessity. "A man, who has been brought up to conduct a particular business, and whose daily bread depends upon his constant attention to it and proper supervision of it," he said, echoing Adam Smith, "has an immense advantage over a company, whose affairs are conducted by a board of gentlemen, possessing knowledge of the business more or less incomplete, and devoting only a small portion of their time to the conduct of it."[4]

In the U.S. context, it meant that many endeavors would assume the corporate form and much more attention would be paid to reducing the agency costs noted by Smith, Ward, and others. According to French aristocrat and political scientist Alexis de Tocqueville, Americans relied on associations for almost every public undertaking because, unlike in Europe, few, if any, individuals, were rich enough or powerful enough to act on their own. No American had large numbers of citizen vassals whose loyalty he could command. Instead, Americans had to form voluntary coalitions to achieve goals or "fall into impotence" and eventually "barbarism."[5] In 1837, New Jersey legislators had not yet read de Tocqueville's book, but they chartered the Bergen Port Company explicitly because "large sums of money" would be needed to make the improvements it had in contemplation and because they "require the aid of capital to develope [sic] the same."[6]

Aside from the governance costs (discussed in detail in Chapter 6), entrepreneurs faced only two other costs of incorporation, both of them variable but typically light.[7] The first was lobbying and organization costs: the time, effort, and money expended on letters, pamphlets, petition drives, bribes, advertisements, and so forth necessary to obtain a charter and raise equity capital.[8] The second cost was bonuses or other forms of corporate-specific taxation.[9]

The costs of obtaining a special charter were certainly greater than forming an unincorporated joint-stock association or a corporation under a general statute.[10] Lobbying costs generally were not prohibitive. Costs associated with the general difficulty of obtaining charters later repaid themselves in the form of greater profits once incorporation was achieved because, as railroad man J. G. Hopkins understood, barriers to entry "effectually protect the stockholders in the privileges granted them."[11] Costs incurred due to resistance to specific charters, by contrast, could prove higher than expected, as when bank charter petitions in New York and elsewhere fell into labyrinths of partisan intrigue. In one instance, a bank backed by Alexander Hamilton and other Federalists struggled to pass a Republican-dominated legislature that was tricked into believing that the proposed bank was the creature of Republican vice president Aaron Burr.[12]

One tactic to minimize the threat of such outcomes was to submit charter petitions when the most favorable party or faction was in office, a tack taken by many early banks and some manufacturers. Another approach, which worked well for transportation infrastructure companies and water and gas utilities as well as some manufacturers, was to form a bipartisan coalition of incorporators, perhaps getting some key legislators or other political players involved as well, and pitch the charter as a general economic benefit to the state, region, or locale.[13] Similarly, attorney fees associated with drawing up a charter could be reduced by asking a lawyer or two to sign on as an incorporator. Of course, any work provided gratis had to be monitored closely. In 1850, the two lawyers who drew up the regulations for the West Boston Bridge Company wrote that the proprietors "shall meet annually on the first *Tuesday* in June, provided the same does not fall on *Sunday*."[14]

By the early nineteenth century, copying the provisions of earlier charters simplified the process and encouraged the adoption of best practices. The charter of the Phoenix Bank of Hartford, for example, "was almost a literal transcript of the Act incorporating the Eagle Bank" passed in 1811.[15] Charter standardization eventually took the form of templates, where all incorporators had to do was to fill in key variables left blank.[16] Even banks could form quickly—more quickly than today, in fact. The Phoenix Bank went from being the subject of casual conversation in late autumn 1813 to charter in May 1814 to stock sales on July 6 to the election of the first directors at the end of that month. Some states extended the template concept further by passing general regulatory statutes that special charters referred to. In 1805, Massachusetts passed a statute that specified the "general powers and duties" of turnpike companies[17]. Turnpikes still received special charters but all made reference to the 1805 law for the specifics. The technique saved legislators' time and reduced incorporators' bargaining power but still required application to the legislature and the concomitant political costs.[18]

Entrepreneurs had several options if their charter petition was denied. As discussed in Chapter 2, they could begin business as unincorporated joint-stock companies. In some instances, they could seek incorporation in another state.[19] The Jersey Bank, for example, was chartered by New Jersey and kept its vaults in Jersey City but the directors also "publicly and notoriously" maintained an office on Wall Street where loan applications were accepted and discount decisions made. To redeem the bank's notes for gold or silver, however, one had to cross the Hudson, which, in the early nineteenth century, was "always inconvenient, frequently difficult, and sometimes dangerous."[20] To avoid taxation by New Jersey, the bank later incorporated in New York as the Union Bank and fled the state of its birth altogether.[21] Similarly, William Gregg threatened to move to Georgia if South Carolina denied his textile firm a charter.[22] By the 1830s, such regulatory arbitrage was common, at least according to corporate critics like George Taylor.[23]

Corporations were also subject to taxation. Some taxes, like local real-estate levies, did not influence entrepreneurs' decision about organizational form because they applied to sole proprietorships, partnerships, and corporations alike. The Falmouth Manufacturing Company, the Potomac Silk and Agricultural Company, and the Fauquier White Sulphur Spring Company paid property taxes to their respective collectors, just as Virginia plantation owners did. Virginia corporations, however, also paid taxes on their dividends. Some companies, like the Eagle Gold Mining Company and the Virginia Hotel Company, paid no dividends and hence no taxes. Others, like the Virginia Central Railroad and the Bank of the Valley, annually paid thousands of dollars in dividend taxes by the Civil War era. New York corporations also paid taxes on their real and personal estate and, in some years, on their capital stock as well.[24]

In states such as Virginia and New York, total corporate tax bills ranged from just a few dollars to a few hundred dollars. While low by today's standards, specific taxes on corporations undoubtedly influenced entry decisions at the margin. The number of would-be corporations that remained unchartered joint-stock associations or never formed at all because of corporate taxation cannot be known with certainty but was probably small because the taxes were generally minor compared to the benefits of being big.[25]

Banks often had to pay bonuses, sometimes in stock and sometimes in cash, in exchange for their charters.[26] In 1813, Connecticut's general assembly made it known that it would charter a new bank in Hartford "if subscribers thereto would pay the State a bonus for a grant."[27] The Bank of North America had to credit Pennsylvania $120,000 for its 1814 charter renewal. In 1824, the

Farmers Bank of Virginia paid a $50,000 bonus to the state for its charter renewal. Pennsylvania exacted a $2 million bonus from the United States Bank in 1836. Pennsylvania also taxed bank dividends. By 1818, it was collecting almost $30,000 per year from the bank dividend tax, in addition to the $200,000 or so it earned in dividends on the $2 million or so worth of bank stock it owned. The state was in earnest about the levies; in 1822, the Columbia Bank of Pennsylvania and the Marietta & Susquehanna Trading Company lost their charters because they refused to pay the state's dividend tax. Massachusetts placed a 1 percent tax on bank capital, which, by the 1850s, brought in $400,000 in taxes annually. Nearby Rhode Island also taxed bank capital. Maryland imposed an annual tax of $20,000 on its banks, but later changed the levy to twenty cents on every $100 of capital. New Jersey taxed bank capital and also travel and freight on the Camden and Amboy Railroad. Governments also taxed banks indirectly by forcing commercial banks to lend to them at below-market rates or by mandating that savings banks invest in state bonds. Many Pennsylvania banks had to make sizable long-term loans to the government at the below-market interest rate of 5 percent.[28]

Pennsylvania, Massachusetts, Connecticut, New York, New Jersey, and other states laid taxes on nonbank corporations or their shareholders.[29] In Ohio, banks, insurance, and bridge companies annually paid tens of thousands of dollars in taxes on their declared dividends.[30] Taxes were, of course, politically controversial. In 1824, the New York legislature passed a new tax of 0.5 percent on the capital of banks and insurance companies. The mayor of New York called a meeting to remonstrate against the new system. "One of the largest ever known in this city" was held, at which Charles G. Haines and others spoke.[31] Haines later published a pamphlet expounding his views, which were that the state's previous tax system needed to be better enforced and executed, not replaced. Traditionally, banks and insurers paid taxes on their real estate on the same terms as individuals and other for-profit businesses did. To tax their capital stock, Haines argued, was actually to tax credit or to double-, triple-, or even quadruple-tax the tangible assets upon which credit was based, both iniquitous policies. Moreover, because of charter differences, location, size, and luck, some corporations were much more profitable than others; yet under the new law, all were subject to the same tax rate. Taxing the market value of stocks held by individuals, he concluded, would be much more equitable and accord more closely to the practices of many European nations.[32]

Investor Motivations

The sole object of the stockholders is, to make all the money they can.
—*A Citizen of Lowell, 1843*[33]

Early Americans countenanced and succored business corporations because they believed that corporations promoted economic growth and hence the common weal, that they were the best type of organizational form for entrepreneurs interested in pursuing large-scale projects, and, perhaps most important, that they provided financial securities that were good investments. A nationalistic desire to aid the development of the American economy may have motivated some investors. Others may have wished to stimulate regional development. Others mixed patriotism or regionalism with personal profit. In the words of investor Isaac Bronson, many Americans invested "in the hope of enriching ourselves, and benefiting the community."[34] Most demand for corporate securities, however, stemmed from more self-centered motives. As early corporation promoter Elkanah Watson exclaimed, corporations were "considered by us all a money making business."[35] "Patriots so disinterested, as to contribute their means to the public weal, without retribution," an observer noted in the early 1830s, is "an occurrence rare, in these, our days."[36]

Investment in corporations was not just the prerogative of the über-wealthy urban elite, as some scholars have assumed, though, as it is today, most members of the commercial elite were investors.[37] As two corporate scholars put it in the 1830s, "there is scarcely an individual or respectable character in our community who is not a member of, at least, one private company or society which is incorporated."[38] As another observer in the mid-1830s claimed, "a large proportion of the stock in banks and other incorporated companies, is owned by widows and children, and persons in moderate circumstances as to property."[39] Yet another noted that the bear market of 1834 injured "all classes of the community, the rich, the middling interest, and the poor" but that it hurt "women, minors, and public institutions" the most.[40] In 1838, the founders of a coal company called themselves "mechanics, tradesmen and farmers. . . . [I]n a word, we are not capitalists."[41] In 1856, the author of a stock market reference book set the price "at 25 cents, in hopes of insuring it a wide circulation among the very numerous class in the community who have occasion, from time to time, to invest in the various securities offering."[42]

In 1814 alone, some 20,000 Pennsylvanians purchased at least one bank share. The par value of the average holding was a fairly hefty $363, but the median was only $60.[43] "Every one is a man of business," Charles Ingersoll of Philadelphia explained, and "each individual feels himself rising in his fortunes."[44] Such widespread participation was no aberration, temporally or spatially. Between 1814 and 1860, more than 74,000 entities purchased shares in 764 direct public offerings of corporate stock in Pennsylvania.[45] In 1840, more than 12,500 investors owned shares in thirty-nine Pennsylvania banks. According to Elias Derby, "every artisan" in Boston aspired "to own his house. . . . Having secured his dwelling, he buys a single share in a bank, railway, or factory, and gradually becomes a capital. And large are the acquisitions of adventurous, frugal, and well-directed industry."[46] "A Citizen of Boston" argued in 1837 that corporate stock offered "peculiar advantages to persons of small means . . . and limited knowledge of business, who, by a concentration of their wealth, and a union of counsels, under the direction of competent agents, can come into fair and safe competition with the skilful and the wealthy."[47]

Such surprising numbers of less affluent or less powerful Americans owned corporate shares—directly or indirectly, via savings banks and insurers—because equities often offered the best mix of the holy trinity of investment factors: risk, return, and liquidity.[48] Like investment in land, equities offered investors relatively high levels of risk and return but were considerably more liquid than real estate. "The stocks of the monied institutions in a city like New-York," an observer noted in the mid-1820s, "are perpetually circulating—passing from one to another, and serving as commercial facilities, and commercial means to companies and to individuals. It is somewhat like money."[49] While securities trading volumes in antebellum markets were a far cry from what they would become in the late twentieth century, they were nevertheless impressive by the standards of the day.[50] In addition, stocks and bonds were not subject to entail or other archaic and arcane rights and rules that impoverished real-estate investors, enriched lawyers, and befuddled judges well into the nineteenth century.[51]

Putting money directly out to interest could be more remunerative than investing in corporations but was also far riskier. Moreover, corporations could legally pay dividends greater than state usury laws allowed for lending money at interest and often did so. Many investors reckoned that it was better to earn a legal, punctual, and almost certain 8 percent on bank or insurance stock than an illegal and tenuous 12 percent (or higher, depending on the time and place) by "shaving" notes (making loans by purchasing promissory notes at a steep discount) or lending on bond and mortgage.[52] Investments in corporations were so heavy in some areas, including Baltimore, Philadelphia, and Manhattan, that traditional person-to-person mortgage markets were said to have almost dried up in consequence.[53] Such claims were probably exaggerations—some estimated the person-to-person mortgage market in New York in the mid-1820s at $50 million—but the fact that such comments were made suggests the large sums of investment flowing away from person-to-person loans into corporate securities.[54]

Most early U.S. corporations (and unchartered joint-stock companies) sold shares via a direct public offering (DPO), which was similar to a modern initial public offering (IPO) but did not involve an investment bank or other intermediary. The incorporators, or special stock subscription agents named in the charter, advertised shares for sale and maintained the subscription books. The reputation of the incorporators was of prime importance to the success of the DPO. Often, they personally importuned prominent citizens and capitalists, such as Virginia's John Tayloe, or Massachusetts's Nathan Appleton or Israel Thorndike, to get the subscription moving quickly by assuring small investors that the scheme had powerful backers and was attracting the interest of what would later be called "smart money."[55] Obtaining the signatures of a few key men early in the DPO could ensure its success. As one observer noted in 1830: "The rapidity with which this large amount has been subscribed, when the known caution and circumspection, in money matters, of several of the principal stockholders, is considered, augurs well for the value of the stock."[56] Similarly, the incorporators of the Philipsburg and Juniata Rail Road cajoled subscriptions from iron masters who "subscribed to the extent of their ability, and . . . successfully exerted their influence amongst their working people, to obtain subscriptions from them; which produced the good effect of completing the amount of stock."[57]

Some DPOs never filled. Historians often portray failed DPOs as a failure of the system of private enterprise, symptomatic of a supposed dearth of capital, or in other negative terms. In fact, most failed DPOs represented the successful rejection of insufficiently remunerative projects. Consider the Aransas Road Company of Texas (chartered 1852; no capital specified in the charter, but a pamphlet says $4 million with shares of $100 par value each), which sought to deepen the channel between the Gulf of Mexico and Aransas Bay, to build a turnpike from the bay to Goliad, Texas, and to build a railroad from the bay to the Rio Grande. The ambitious company also foresaw "future connections, as they may be gradually developed by other companies, until the whole will constitute a system of incalculable importance."[58]

The development of a large "commercial city at Aransas Bay" predicted by the company never materialized. The president and chief engineer pitched the company as the owner of the easiest, best, and cheapest transcontinental route, the distance from the excellent port that the company planned to build at Aransas to Mazatlán, on Mexico's Pacific Coast, a mere 660 flat miles away. Moreover, once Texas was fully populated, at a surely not too distant time, Aransas would naturally become the point of departure of its beef, coal, and sea salt to world markets. Investors did not buy the story, or the stock. Some of the 1,250 shares (par value of $125,000) had been "issued to a few individuals, in payment for lands, services, and cash advanced for expenses. The remaining Shares," the president admitted, "belong to the Company, which has no debt, but a small sum for current expenses, and a few thousand dollars at interest."[59] Successful linkage of the east and west coasts of the United States to each other and to South America via a railroad in Panama by some New York capitalists in the mid-1850s effectively killed the Texas plan. Even before the railroad's completion, eight Atlantic and five Pacific steamship lines connected to it. The Panama railway later helped to facilitate the construction of the much more famous Panama canal, completion of which saved time and money for the ships that could avoid portage costs by traversing it.[60]

That some stalled DPOs filled after the legislature removed "objectionable features" from the original charter also suggests that the DPO process helped to squelch unprofitable projects before they expended valuable time and other resources.[61] Chartered in 1792 with a minimum authorized capital of $100,000, the New Haven Bank did not begin operations until 1796 because of the difficulties it faced raising capital during yellow-fever epidemics and the DPOs of banks in Hartford and New London. In late 1795, the government allowed it to amend its capital authorization to a range, from $50,000 to $400,000, and to change its unusual voting rule to one vote per share, whereupon $80,000 was quickly subscribed, directors elected, and business begun in February of the following year. The institution began paying dividends in 1807 and did so every year thereafter, until at least World War I.[62] Other DPOs filled only after the corporation received valuable extra powers, like banking.[63]

Some DPOs filled but only after a significant subscription period. The Lancaster Trading Company (later Lancaster Bank) of Pennsylvania had difficulty raising capital because it offered shares at the same time as four other banks in its county. One of its cohort, the Union Bank of Lancaster, failed to form for that very same reason. Another bank chartered as part of the same omnibus bill, the Farmers Bank of Bucks County, also found it difficult to raise capital in the wartime economy. Only eight shares were taken up on June 6, 1814, the first day of the offering, and a total of only thirty-eight by August 16. The Delaware County Bank, by contrast, appears to have had little problem attracting $100,000 of subscriptions.[64]

Some stalled DPOs just needed more time and effort. During its ten-day DPO in 1835, the Richmond, Fredericksburg, and Potomac Railroad raised only $305,200 of the $420,000 it needed by the terms of its charter. After unsuccessfully soliciting investments from various governments, it reopened the subscription books and managed to attract about $75,000 in additional private funds.[65] Other DPOs filled only because of the appearance of an angel investor. A canal in New Jersey was about to be abandoned "in despair, when a citizen of New Jersey, who had been absent from the state . . . came forward, subscribed a large part of the stock, embarked his whole fortune in the enterprise, and devoted his, time, talents and energy to its successful prosecution."[66]

Many other DPOs filled promptly.[67] According to a newspaper advertisement, the $110,000 capital of the Washington Insurance Company in Providence, Rhode Island, was "promptly subscribed" in 1800.[68] That same year, the DPO of the Mohawk Turnpike and Bridge Company also filled quickly because, according to a newspaper correspondent, the local inhabitants were "impressed with the great importance of improving their roads."[69] In August 1801, the Second Company of the Great Western Turnpike Road boasted that almost "300 shares are already subscribed."[70]

Some three decades later, the Camden and Amboy Rail Road subscription filled "at the opening of the books of subscription" and on the first installment call, there was not "a single defalcation."[71] In June 1830, the town of Petersburg, Virginia, launched the successful DPO of the Petersburg Rail Road Company by subscribing 2,000 shares. "On the following day, books were opened for the reception of stock subscriptions on the part of individuals," a newspaper reported, "when stock to the amount of one hundred and two thousand dollars was promptly subscribed."[72] About the same time, the Lexington and Ohio Rail Road Company of Kentucky raised $729,900 in just five days in Lexington before moving the DPO to Louisville.[73] In a single day in 1837, ninety-six individuals subscribed the full $500,000 offered by the Tonawanda Rail Road Company to "individuals residing in the section of country in which it was contemplated the road would be located."[74]

Some DPOs oversubscribed almost immediately. The books of the Germantown and Perkiomen Turnpike road "so rapidly filled," newspapers reported, "that more than a sufficient number of shares have been engaged."[75] Similarly, the Commercial Bank of Albany's $300,000 DPO was oversubscribed five times. In other words, it could have capitalized at $1.5 million. The Bank's DPO filled so quickly because of the reputation of one of its major backers, Joseph Alexander, the sixty-two-year-old Albany business leader who assumed its presidency.[76]

Some corporations emerged from their DPOs held by a surprisingly wide segment of the population, not just a handful of wealthy capitalists, as some historians later assumed. Confusion arose in part because many early corporations had strong minority controlling interests, usually largely coterminous with the directorate. The holdings of a dozen or so directors, however, usually left numerous shares to be taken up by small holders. Most early insurers were owned by hundreds of investors. Most turnpikes in the Middle Atlantic states were also not closely held, though partly because stock was sometimes given in partial payment to contractors. Shares in one early New York railroad were held in New York (542), Owego (411), and Albany, Utica, and Ithaca (1,807). The average number of stockholders in all extant New York corporations in 1826 was 74. In 101 bank DPOs held between 1814 and 1859 in Pennsylvania, the number of shareholders averaged about 400.[77]

A few early corporations were closely held, some by accident, others by design. The Locks and Canals on Merrimack River purposely had only nine stockholders as late as 1825. In antebellum Pennsylvania, the average number of shareholders in 144 mining companies was a mere ten. Shareholders in Pennsylvania manufacturing (thirty-six), transportation (forty-six), and utility (forty-six) companies were not much more numerous. The Ohio Life Insurance and Trust Company managed to fill its subscription books without going to the public trough at all and considered it a benefit because it meant that the original incorporators were more likely to maintain control, as the stock would be closely held for investment purposes and not become a "fancy" stock—to wit, the plaything of speculators.[78]

Some corporations that were initially closely held became less so over time because of sales in the secondary market, typically to "women, public institutions and thrifty mechanics."[79] The Cleveland Gas Light and Coke Company had just four shareholders when it formed in September 1849; but by December of that year, it had thirteen.[80] The Boston Manufacturing Company had only twelve shareholders when it formed in 1813. It remained closely held at first; but as its need for capital grew, it allowed additional investors in, a strategy followed by some other New England manufacturers.[81] By 1829, one informed observer claimed that manufacturing corporations were frequently owned by "a large number of shareholders, the stock of many of whom is comparatively small."[82] Similarly, shares in the Eagle Bank of Bristol, Rhode Island, were initially concentrated in the hands of a few prominent families; but within a few years, many of their shares had been sold to unrelated investors.[83]

Stockholders in smaller, more closely held corporations tended to be primarily local. Many stockholders in larger, more widely held corporations, by contrast, could live a considerable distance away. In 1824, stockholders in the Bank of Albany resided in fourteen counties, ranging from New York County in the south to Genesee in the west and Washington County in the north. The following year, Bank of Orange County stockholders hailed from seven New York counties, from Kings downstate to Onondaga upstate. In 1826, stockholders in the Farmers and Mechanics Manufacturing Company hailed from four counties. The average New York corporation in 1826 was owned by people in five counties; 10 percent of their shares were owned by investors who lived out of state.[84]

By the mid-1830s, railroads in Virginia had to set up bank accounts and stock-transfer agents in Philadelphia because so many of their stockholders resided there.[85] From the 1830s through the 1850s, stockholders in the largest Maine corporations were spread widely over the populated coastal regions of their home state as well as throughout the rest of eastern New England, Canada's maritime provinces, and even farther abroad. Not even stock speculators were limited to the big seaboard cities.[86] In little Oxford, New York, dwelled Thomas Butler, an attorney endowed with an "extraordinary spirit of enterprise." After losing a fortune as a merchant, he moved upstate, where he "entered upon a wide field of speculation in buying & selling wild lands, turnpike stocks &c. &c."[87]

The larger the corporation compared with the economy of the region in which it operated, the more likely it was to seek distant capital infusions. "The amount of spare capital in the west," noted two Indiana railway men in 1851, "as a general rule, is comparatively small, and most of the works look either directly or indirectly, to eastern capitalists for aid."[88] Investors in Boston and Manhattan[89] were said to be "large holders in manufactories" in countryside towns like Lowell as well as "in adjacent states" and were also known to invest heavily in railroads outside New England as well as in mines in Michigan and elsewhere.[90] Stockholders in the Bank of the United States (1816–36), capitalized to a then-mammoth $35 million, were said to be "dispersed and distant" from the headquarters in Philadelphia.[91]

The large amount of invective hurled at securities brokers and active traders ("speculators") strongly suggests that corporate securities were often actively traded among a fairly broad group of citizens. Otherwise, why bother to fulminate against them? Other anecdotal evidence bolsters the view that investors in corporations were numerous. After the defeat of Napoleon, one commentator complained that instead of perusing the paper for the details of battles, "now the price of cotton, flour, and tobacco, and the *prices of stocks* and the rates of exchange, are the principal, and almost the only object of enquiry or solicitude."[92]

Probate records listing the assets and liabilities of deceased individuals show that a fairly broad group of Americans purchased corporate securities. By the end of the eighteenth century, inventories of the assets of dead farmers in rural Massachusetts contained shares in banking, bridge, turnpike, canal, water, and insurance companies as well as government bonds and more traditional mortgages and personal bonds. Financial assets were found in the inventories of all four quartiles of decedents, suggesting that at least some of the members of all but the poorest strata of society, those too poor to need probate proceedings, invested in corporations. Some 13 percent of all estates sampled contained at least one financial security (stock or bond). Stockholders lived in both rural and urban areas but, of course, were more numerous in the latter, especially earlier in the period under study.[93]

Plantation owners in Louisiana, South Carolina, Virginia, and elsewhere stashed cash in financial securities, including corporate stocks. In addition to owning slaves, real estate, ironworks, mines, mills, sundry artisanal shops, hotels, taverns, and stagecoach lines outright, über-wealthy planter John Tayloe III of Virginia purchased shares in toll-bridge, canal, ferry, and steamboat companies as well as several banks, including the Bank of the United States (1816–36). Henry McCall of Evan Hall Plantation in Ascension Parish, Louisiana, listed four shares in the Bank of the United States among his assets when he completed a balance sheet on January 1, 1822. He was far from alone; other Louisianans then owned 302 shares in that bank, down from 891 in October 1820.[94]

The most compelling evidence of widespread stock ownership comes from stockholder lists and brokers' records. We know from such records that late in the 1780s, sixty-six entities owned 504 shares in the James River

Company. The average holding was 7.63, but the median was three and the mode only one. George Washington and the Commonwealth of Virginia were the biggest holders, each with 100 shares. David Ross held fifty shares, but no one else owned more than twenty-five.[95]

In 1815, 134 investors held an average of 2.5 shares in the Fauquier and Alexandria Turnpike in Virginia. No one owned more than twelve shares, and the median holding was just two shares. In 1819, forty-two investors owned between two and 125 of the 1,000 shares of the Union Bank of Elizabethtown, Kentucky. The average holding was 24.39 shares, but the median was only ten. The top six stockholders would have had to join forces to obtain a majority of the votes, but the bank's prudent mean voting rule (a concept described in Chapter 6) effectively prevented any small cabal from assuming control of the board.[96]

Over half of the investors in the Bank of Gettysburg in 1814 were farmers, and only a quarter were merchants or professionals. Most were among the county's wealthiest segment, but some had small estates. Similarly, when the Concord Bank of Massachusetts offered shares in 1832, 164 subscribers took up 1,084 shares. Those with less than $3,000 in taxable property constituted a little over 30 percent of all subscribers. Most were from Middlesex County, but a few hailed from Boston, Maine, and New Hampshire.[97]

In the mid-1830s, the Richmond, Fredericksburg, and Potomac Railroad Company attracted investments from 144 investors who held an average of 29.5 shares each. The median holding was only ten shares because two persons owned more than 400 shares each and two others owned 200 shares apiece. Due to the company's prudent mean voting rule, however, the top fourteen shareholders owned 57 percent of the company's 4,248 shares but controlled only 42 percent of its 1,282 votes.[98] Around the same time, the shares of "one of our principal banking establishments" was owned by the Connecticut state government "and Charitable, Ecclesiastical, and School societies. The remaining three fourths is distributed among 664 individuals. Of these, only 120 own above 20 shares each. Nearly two thirds of the remainder own not above 5 shares each, and the interest of a large proportion of the stockholders is but one or two shares each."[99]

Also in the mid-1830s, 3,923 shares of the 6,000 total shares in the Merchants Bank of Newburyport, Massachusetts, belonged, according to one of its directors, "to women and to public institutions, 1035 to working mechanics, and only 1042 to any description of capitalists." The 2,000 shares of the Mechanics Bank of the same town were owned by women and public institutions (946 shares), working mechanics (593), and reputed capitalists (461). "Not content with this," the director inquired and "found the general fact substantially the same . . . in different banks of the city of Boston."[100]

In the late 1830s, the 1,922 shares of the Troy Turnpike and Rail Road Company were owned by 171 economic entities, an average of 11.24 shares each. No shareholder owned more than forty shares, and most held five or fewer.[101] In the mid-1840s, the 390 stockholders of the Merrimack Company included sixty-eight females, eighty trustees of various sorts (administrators, executors, guardians), fifty-two retirees, fifteen farmers, and forty "secretaries, clerks, students, &c.," and even some employee operatives.[102]

In 1859, sixty entities owned one or more of the 1,327 shares in the Vicksburg Gas Light Company. The average holding was just 22.12 and the median only five. By contrast, that same year, only twenty-five entities owned the Covington Gas Company's 1,757 outstanding shares. The average holding was 70.28, the median fourteen, and five stockholders were related to the chief engineer.[103] Also in 1859, 320 entities owned the 10,000 shares of Virginia's Bank of Commonwealth. The average holding was thirty-one and the median a mere twelve. The same figures for the same bank for January 1, 1860, and January 1, 1861, are comparable.[104]

That early American women were cloistered from the marketplace, at best serving as consumers on behalf of their families, is a pernicious myth long since exploded. Women, especially widows but also spinsters and married women who managed to free themselves from the restrictions of coverture, worked as professional midwives, nurses, and teachers and sometimes even as lawyers, doctors, and printers. They also owned and operated a variety of businesses, including farms, taverns, retail and artisanal shops, and even wholesale commercial and real-estate enterprises.[105] Women were also active customers in banks, both as depositors and as borrowers. Ann McIlvain, for example, was the first woman to borrow from the Delaware County Bank of Pennsylvania, and she borrowed over $1,100, a princess-like sum for the time.[106]

Unsurprisingly, then, women also constituted an important class of investors in government and corporate bonds and equities.[107] Twenty women subscribed to the stock of the Germantown and Perkiomen Pike in Pennsylvania in 1801. About one-third of the stockholders in the Delaware County Bank on the eve of the Civil War were women. "Much stock is often owned by *widows and orphans*," asserted one expert on Maryland turnpikes.[108] "Manufacturing stocks," another expert observer noted, "are holden in large proportion by women, widows, orphan children, charitable institutions, and retired old men, who are dependent on them for their support."[109]

But not all women were passive investors. Some exhibited more skill than the median male speculator. Abigail Adams invested circles around her husband, president John Adams, and other male investors.[110] So did Elizabeth Powel, who, in January 1811, sold thirty shares in the Bank of the United States at 110 percent of par just before the price dropped when news arrived that Congress would not recharter the institution. Women could vote their shares and often did so, sometimes in person and sometimes via proxy. (A few women, however, were duped out of their proxies when they signed receipts for their dividends.[111]) Significant ownership of corporate stocks by women was not inevitable. In Britain, many companies actively discouraged female stockholders, calling them "unprofitable partners in business."[112] Where women are conspicuously absent are from the lists of incorporators and stock subscription agents. Of the quarter of a million or so such persons, only a few score had names like Anne, Elizabeth, Mary, Nancy, or Sally.

Governments were another major class of investors. Sometimes governments owned shares as business investments, as revenue-generating assets. The federal Navy Pension Fund, for example, purchased bank shares in the secondary market or subscribed during DPOs. The U.S. Treasury owned significant numbers of Bank of the United States (1791–1811) shares for a decade, 5,000 from 1792 until 1797 and 2,220 from then until 1802, and later owned millions of dollars of Bank of the United States (1816–36) stock.[113]

State governments were even bigger investors. Those favored with government money were typically pleased but those shut out were not. The problem with state ownership of shares was that it aligned the interests of the state with existing corporations and against new entrants. The New York State Bank in 1803 explicitly reminded the legislature that incorporating the Mercantile Company would "diminish and impair the funds of the State."[114] Indeed, by 1803, the state of New York owned $50,000 worth of Bank of New York stock, $20,000 in the Bank of Albany shares, and $150,000 in the New York State Bank. It took such a large equity position in its main depository partly at the urging of the bank's private stockholders, who shrewdly calculated that the state's patronage would shield it from political and economic shocks, much like Fannie Mae and the other ill-fated government-sponsored enterprises of recent infamy. (New York also owned $20,000 worth of shares [par value] in the Columbia Bank of Hudson, but it is not clear when it purchased the shares.) So it is not surprising that by 1812, New York had only about one-third as much banking capital as Massachusetts, Pennsylvania, or Maryland. Econometric evidence developed by financial historian Richard Sylla and his colleagues indicates that states indeed followed their own interests, chartering more banks where they laid taxes on their capital and fewer where, like New York, they owned significant amounts of stock in banks and hence relied on bank dividends as a major source of state revenue. Occasionally, however, a state became confused and levied taxes on a corporation in which it owned numerous shares.[115]

Somewhat less pernicious was the practice of governments purchasing shares for strategic purposes, in order to exert some control over key corporations. In 1798, Pennsylvania owned 2,500 shares in the Bank of Pennsylvania, its main depository. By 1818, Pennsylvania owned almost $2.8 million of stock in banks, turnpikes, bridges, and canals. Later, that sum swelled to some $6.2 million. Partly in an attempt to keep pace with Pennsylvania, Virginia also invested heavily in its transportation networks. It owned 70 of the 400 $250 par shares in the Dismal Swamp Company in the early nineteenth century, for example, and later established a special board charged with investing in almost all the state's transportation companies.[116]

Sometimes governments were, by law, the only stockholder in a corporation, usually a state bank. Such arrangements usually ended badly. The first bank chartered in Vermont, the Vermont State Bank (chartered 1806), was wholly owned by the state government. Its notes were so easily counterfeited that people complained that they were more numerous than the true bills. The bank also made numerous bad loans. It passed into the hands of receivers in 1813 and finally wound up its affairs sometime in the 1830s.[117]

By then, most forms of government investment in corporations had fallen into disrepute. The quantity of new purchases of corporate stock fell off, and existing investments began to be liquidated, a process sped up by the Panics of 1837 and 1839. Pennsylvania decided to divest in 1837[118] and, by 1843, had sold off many of its "depreciated stocks . . . for what they would bring in the market," some $4.2 million.[119] In 1842, Maryland still owned so much corporate stock that it hired agents to represent its interests at stockholder meetings and to collect information on its investments.[120] The following year, the state was under enough fiscal pressure to pass "an act to sell the state's interest in the internal improvement companies." The preamble noted that because of the "embarrassed condition of the finances of the State, and the great depression of business of all kinds, the public interest requires that the debt of the State should be paid off at the earliest possible day, that the people may be relieved from taxation." In addition, the state should be "separated from corporations, the connexion with which has involved it in the embarrassments under which it is now suffering."[121] Not all states joined the divestment bandwagon. In 1850, Kentucky owned $1.27 million of bank stock, 400 miles of turnpike roads, twenty-nine miles of railroads, and 290 miles of canalized rivers, dividends from which yielded it about $100,000 per year. That same year, Massachusetts received $87,000 in dividends from its shares in the Western Railroad.[122]

Banks and insurers often purchased shares in transportation and other corporations. In November 1829, banks owned over $1.5 million worth of road, canal, and bridge stocks. Nonprofit corporations such as churches and social associations also sometimes bought corporate securities, but they were not major stockholders in most corporations. Foreign investors, by contrast, were considerable players in some larger companies. Foreigners first became interested in U.S. government bonds and bought so many in the early 1790s that they were featured in the second edition of Thomas Fortune's *Epitome of the Stocks and Publick Funds*, published in 1796. That same source also described how interested investors could purchase shares in the Bank of the United States, which, like the U.S. government, offered to make payments in London or Amsterdam "without deduction."[123] Later, foreign investors became the "principle stockholders" in some state banks and invested "large sums in many of them."[124] During the height of the Napoleonic Wars, some Europeans even maintained deposits in American banks. Foreigners also sometimes ventured into turnpike shares. By the mid-1820s, New York had attracted "to her bosom" some $5 million of foreign capital, much of it in the shape of purchases of bank and insurance stock.[125] By 1809, foreigners owned some 18,000 shares in the Bank of the United States (1791–1811) and, by the early 1830s, some 80,000 shares in its successor. They also bought the bonds of banks, railroads, and some cities and states. (The bonds of Georgia were "very little known in Europe" in 1850, but investors were urged to look more carefully at the state because "latterly, there have been established several factories within the State, which have been found to be very profitable.")[126] Some railroads issued sterling-denominated debt to make their bonds more attractive to European investors. Most U.S. corporations denominated their securities in dollars and remained "wholly confined to the American Market," but British investors owned about £30 million ($150 million) of U.S. securities by the early 1840s.[127]

After initial skepticism, antebellum Americans for the most part welcomed foreign capital. "If a commercial state can induce foreign capitalists to invest five or ten millions of dollars in its funds, and while it pays five or seven per cent. interest, still realizes a profit of five or ten percent," explained an early political economist, "the most common understanding must perceive the profit and advantage which result to such state. It gives stability to her credit; it gives new means and facilities to her monied institutions; it gives business and profits to her merchants; employment to her ships and seamen; work to her mechanics and common labourers; opens a great market to her produce, and thus enhances the value of lands; raises rents and increases the value of houses and other tenements; lowers the rate of interest, and renders money more plenty, and, in fact, imparts life and animation to the whole productive industry of the community."[128]

"The common notion," wrote John Dix in 1827, "that the employment of foreign capital is prejudicial to the country in which it is invested, is nearly exploded. The most superficial examination will exhibit a gain, instead of a loss, in every such investment. The interest of this capital goes to the foreign capitalist, but the profits of the industry, which it puts in motion, comprehending the subsistence and compensation of the individuals employed is obviously a gain to the country, in which the investment is made."[129]

In the 1830s and 1840s, policies were implemented that reduced demand from overseas investors. Pennsylvania angered some foreign bondholders when it published their names without their expressed consent.[130] New Jersey made it illegal for anyone outside the state to own bank shares[131] because of the belief that dividends paid to foreigners drained the economy of specie and xenophobic complaints about foreigners' ability to "agitate our councils, divide our people, set law at defiance, and unnerve the arm of our general government."[132] New York state bonds were "very largely held in Europe" in the 1820s and 1830s; but in the 1840s, they were "steadily returning to America, not from any distrust . . . but from the action of the New York banking law, which requires all persons who may commence any new Bank to deposit with the comptroller of the State 100,000 dollars of New York State Stock for every 100,000 of Bank notes which they may issue."[133] Worst of all, in the wake of the Panics of 1837 and 1839, several states defaulted on their bonds; a few even repudiated their debts, much of which was owned by British investors.

In publicly traded corporations, ownership and control were never entirely the same, but the two increasingly separated over time. Rising incomes and lower share prices were two major culprits. The average par value of shares declined over time, from an average of over $250 in the 1790s to about

$75 by the 1840s and a median of just $50 in the first decade of the nineteenth century and thereafter. In Pennsylvania, the average number of subscribers in DPOs dropped by an order of magnitude, from about 500 to 50, from the 1810s to the 1850s, but lower par values allowed more investors into the secondary market by increasing market liquidity and by decreasing the cost of portfolio diversification (owning fewer shares in more companies). The result was more stockholders, and the cost was weaker governance.[134]

By 1811, Oneida County, New York, was home to ten manufacturing companies, including cotton and wool manufacturers Oneida, New Hartford, Oriskany, Oldenbarneveld, Whitesborough, Clinton; and Oneida Glass, Utica Glass, Mount Vernon Glass, and Rome Glass and Iron, all established by "men of substantial wealth" with significant control over the companies they established.[135] The same was true with early Lowell manufacturers, which, as noted above, were closely held at first, more like big partnerships than corporations. During that early phase, manufacturing corporations were "well managed and very prosperous" because the stockholders devoted "their personal attention, and . . . [brought their] shrewdness, energy and perseverance to bear for the welfare of their enterprises."[136] Later, after the incorporators and original stockholders died or became enfeebled, their shares passed into the market.[137] Average holdings dropped from $25,000 to $3,000, and the number of individual stockholders increased from 350 to 600 persons. At that point, the stockholders "rarely know each other at all" and were "scattered all over New England, and even other States."[138] In Worcester County, small, early mills were eventually bought up by Boston capitalists and run by former owners. Manufacturers that formed later in the antebellum period, such as the Pepperell, were owned at first by a few hundred people, and were so large relative to New England's old wealth that they had to attract a wide range of investors in order to begin operations. The new generation of stockholders were not proprietors but rather, in the words of a contemporary, "bought their shares as an investment, and with the delusive hope that somebody is interested in it who can and will take care of it."[139]

Much the same transformation took place in large urban banks to some extent but more so in railroads, the largest of which, in the postbellum period, would boast more than 10,000 stockholders apiece.[140] "It is painful to see," a railroad industry pundit noted in 1859, "how these interests [of stockholders] have been perverted in the management of nearly all the large railways for private gain. In the present loose manner in which elections are conducted and proxies given out," he complained, portending even greater governance difficulties in the future, "it seems almost impossible to secure an impartial, competent and honest board of directors."[141]

Scale, Integration, and Market Power

> Mr. Lowell adopted an entirely new arrangement, in
> order to save labor, in passing from one process to
> another; and he is unquestionably entitled to the
> credit of being the first person who arranged all the
> processes for the conversion of cotton into cloth,
> within the walls of the same building.
> —*Nathan Appleton, 1858*[142]

Some historians believe that horizontal integration (economies of scale), vertical integration, and market power are concepts too new or advanced to have influenced early entrepreneurs or corporate managers. They clearly underestimate their forebears. By the mid-eighteenth century, political economist Sir James Steuart could write about scale economies without controversy: "Several weavers, fishermen, or those of any other class of the industrious, unite their stocks, in order to overcome those difficulties to which single workmen are exposed, from a multiplication of expences, which can be saved by their association."[143] And, of course, Adam Smith's famous pin factory was as much an example of vertical integration optimization as of the division of labor. (That is why he had to discuss wool-coat production, too.) In some businesses, such as finance, scale economies are largely invisible, as they relate to the acquisition and analysis of market and applicant information rather than to tangible objects.[144]

In other businesses, especially manufacturing, scale economies were quite tangible. While antebellum U.S. industries were small by later standards, they were nonetheless significant in absolute terms. By 1827, the New England Manufacturing Company was milling four tons of flax a week. The Brattleboro Typographic Company ran eight power presses that were so large and efficient that rags that entered the factory in the morning came out as bound books shortly thereafter. The Hazard Powder Company's gunpowder was "well known throughout the country" because the company was able to make 750 barrels daily even though the seventy to eighty buildings on its mile-long campus were not working to capacity. In 1848, the scythe factory in

Dunnville, Maine, was "the most extensive work of the kind in the world, being capable of manufacturing 12,000 dozens a year."[145] By 1850, New England Glass Company needed a 230-foot-high chimney composed of almost 1 million bricks.[146] By 1860, the American Hoe Company could produce "one hoe per minute" on average, on a sustained basis. Few individual Americans or even partnerships could finance such extensive works.[147]

The importance of horizontal integration, or the scaling up of a business enterprise to make it more profitable by tapping economies of scale, can be discerned directly from productivity estimates and prices. In 1832, each worker in the mechanized, corporate textile mills of Worcester County, Massachusetts, produced an average of $974 worth of cloth. In the shoe industry, which remained organized as a largely unmechanized mass of individual workers through variants of the traditional "putting out" system, average output per worker was only $433.[148] Similarly, the American Watch Company could produce "a hundred watches . . . with the thought and labor expended on one" the manual way.[149] By exploiting scale, manufacturers drove costs relentlessly downward. Textile corporations could profitably sell cotton goods at six cents a yard in 1843 that had been sold at thirty cents not even thirty years earlier.[150]

The development of trademark law furthered economies of scale by helping to extend markets regionally and nationally. Well before the Civil War, corporations learned to mark their best goods to differentiate them from the inferior wares of free-riding local competitors. The Amoskeag Company, for example, developed in the mid-1830s a "ticket, or trade-mark, to distinguish the best of their tickings," and by the late 1840s, it had "acquired throughout the United States a very high reputation." The company sued (in the corporation's name, of course) when some New York merchants began to imitate the mark, a red oval with the letters ACA slightly below the center, on inferior tickings produced by the Dorchester Manufacturing Company.[151] Similarly, two brands offered by a gunpowder manufacturing company, Kentucky Rifle and American Sporting, were regarded by users as equal to any powder made in America or Britain.

Economies of scale were also a function of technological breakthroughs, particularly mechanization of production processes or information processing. The corporate form was, of course, most common where "a large capital is necessary to success."[152] Salt and many other types of manufacturers found that they had to scale up and adopt new technology or be outcompeted on price, quality, or both. The timing of the transition to the corporate form varied from industry to industry. As tanneries became larger and used more complex technology, a process that began in the 1810s and 1820s, they evolved from sole proprietorships to partnerships and finally, in the 1870s, to joint-stock corporations. Iron, by contrast, went corporate at least two decades earlier.[153]

Chartered in 1832, Richmond's Belle Isle Manufacturing Company was still a "work in progress" in 1837 but already, in the eyes of Blair Bolling, "an extensive Iron Manufacturing establishment."[154] The corporate revolution came to the bulk of the iron industry somewhat later than in Richmond, primarily because ironworks cloistered from British imports by cheap wood, high tariffs, and expensive transportation were able to persist, using older charcoal technologies. A few such furnaces managed to survive into the postbellum period, but by mid-century, most iron firms had to scale up, vertically integrate, and adopt new technologies or die, as many did. The newest, largest, most heterogeneous in terms of products, and most technologically advanced firms, such as the rolling mills and anthracite blast furnaces, were increasingly likely to be incorporated. During the 1850s, the industry shifted decisively toward incorporated producers and manufacturers in terms of output and capitalization, if not total numbers of firms. About half of all pig-iron products and more than 60 percent of all rolled-iron products came out of incorporated firms in that decade.[155]

Some services required significant scale to be profitable. In the antebellum era, American cities were home to some big hotels that were more spacious and lavish than those even in Britain. "They are vast concerns" one traveler noted, "and have a reputation of being ably conducted."[156] Many of the biggest and most luxurious were owned by corporations, such as the United States Hotel in Richmond, Virginia, which enjoyed a MINAC of $35,000 and a MAXAC of $200,000. In one year, repairs, including carpentry, plastering, locksmithing, and painting, amounted to over $2,500, insurance to over $75, taxes to almost $46, and advertising to some $37 per quarter. Its *old* furnishings sold for over $2,300 at auction in 1856.[157]

The more mountainous parts of New York, Delaware, Maryland, and Virginia were home to numerous incorporated health resorts, such as the Brandywine Chalybeate Spring Company of Delaware. The entrepreneurs who chartered the company clearly perceived a sort of arbitrage opportunity in the form of an underutilized asset called Brandywine Springs. It was well known that Native Americans had used the springs to cure the sick, but the property was under the control of a tavern keeper named Holton Yarnall, whose tavern, Conestoga Wagon, catered mostly to teamsters driving big Conestoga wagons laden with grain from the agricultural hinterlands to the Christiana River. Never well-off, Yarnall heavily mortgaged the property. When the lender, a single Wilmington woman named Jane Wilson, died, and the executor of her estate pressed for payment, Yarnall was not able to obtain refinancing or to sell the property. The sheriff obligingly auctioned it off. William Seal, president of the Bank of Wilmington, and others, undoubtedly on behalf of the Brandywine Chalybeate Spring Company, posted the winning bid of $2,805.[158]

On January 3, 1826, a distinguished group of Wilmington entrepreneurs, already well established in insurance, gas, railroad, and agricultural concerns, petitioned the Delaware legislature to charter the New Castle County Chalybeate Spring Company. They quickly replaced "New Castle County" with the much more appealing name "Brandywine," after the watershed in which the spring lay. In their petition, the incorporators argued that the springs were medicinally valuable but underutilized because of the dearth of proper facilities. They also claimed that only a corporation could erect "such Buildings as are essential for the proper accommodation of the public." The legislature agreed and chartered the company on January 24. The charter authorized the company to sell an unspecified number of $100 shares and provided each shareholder with one vote "and no more." The charter explicitly forbade the company from engaging in banking or owning real property worth over $25,000. The board comprised a president and twelve directors (called managers). Its twenty-year charter was never amended. The DPO apparently filled, stockholders elected a president and secretary, and the company borrowed $20,000 from the Delaware Fire Insurance Company.[159]

In July 1826, just half a year after receiving its corporate charter, the Brandywine Chalybeate Spring received some publicity—in faraway Maine, no less—where an editor noted that the spring teemed with "tonic and strengthening" waters, was located in a "high, healthy and pleasant location," treated visitors to "agreeable scenery," and was just a short five-mile stroll from the borough of Wilmington. Best of all, the editor reported, the spring was being "fitted up by an incorporated company," under a contractor whose workers erected on the site "a building seventy three by forty three feet."[160]

In March and April 1827, the company advertised for a tenant for the hotel that it had erected, which it described as "a large and convenient house . . . three stories high, and half basement story, finished in modern style, with spacious dining rooms, parlours, halls and extensive piazzas, front and back, and in other respects inferior to few buildings of the kind." The ad noted that the company planned to establish a "watering place of the first order" and mentioned the existence on the property of another house, "nearly new, which might be made a desirable lodging house for retired, or invalid persons," an icehouse, carriage house, and stabling. "The pleasure grounds," the ad continued, "are extensive and romantic." The spring was located near good roads that led to daily steamboat connections to Philadelphia and Baltimore. Perhaps most important, Professor Keating of the University of Pennsylvania attested that the waters of the spring were "pure Chalybeate," meaning that they were impregnated with salts of iron.[161]

An advertisement placed in June by the first tenant, Charles Stanley, explained that such waters were "particularly efficacious in bilious and other fevers" and were "celebrated as a fine tonic." Stanley described the company's grounds as "pleasant and shady" and "bounded by streams" and argued that it was the most conveniently located "watering place" in the nation. Stanley promised to rent gigs, carriages, and horses to his guests and to supply them with "dinners, collations, Ice creams &c." at a "short notice."[162]

Stanley apparently did not pan out because a year later, a Mr. and Mrs. Willson ran the house. But the company received some good press when a local newspaper noted that the springs were open and that "many have already availed themselves of the comforts of the house, the benefits of the water, and of the advantages of the bracing air consequent upon so high a situation." The article called the house "very capacious, elegantly furnished and kept in the best manner" by the Willsons, who refurnished the house, supplied it with the "choicest liquors," and arranged for grand summertime musical concerts and dances on the grounds, tickets for which it charged a full dollar.[163] The Willsons apparently put matters in good order because by 1829, the Brandywine Chalybeate Spring was called "justly celebrated," the hotel needed to be enlarged, and the springs had attracted competitors in nearby Newark.[164]

By 1830, residents of Baltimore could travel to the springs by steamboat and stagecoach in only six to eight hours for $2.75: $2.25 for the boat and fifty cents for the coach. Those transportation services continued for years at the same prices. Convenient steamboat service also connected the springs to Philadelphia. The hotel charged $1.50 per person per night, and dinner could be had for $0.625, sums that its "fashionable" clientele could no doubt pay with ease.[165]

The corporation nonetheless sank into dire financial difficulties. It had expended some $36,000 improving the property but could not generate enough cash to service the $10,000 that it still owed to Delaware Fire Insurance. On August 10, 1833, Matthew Newkirk, then one of Philadelphia's richest entrepreneurs, bought the company's physical assets for $15,500 and dissolved the corporation. A frequent visitor to the springs in the years preceding the purchase, Newkirk improved the property further by erecting warm and cold baths, clearing a nearby wood, and building and stocking a fishpond. He also remodeled the buildings and supplied the hotel with running water, a rarity in those days. He likely calculated that railroads would soon increase the resort's business by reducing travel times and costs.

Like the corporation he replaced, Newkirk had no intention of running the place himself. It was not unusual for early capitalists or corporations to acquire and improve physical assets, which they then rented to operating companies. Alexander Hamilton's brainchild, the Society for the Establishment of Useful Manufactures, for example, followed a similar strategy after it failed to manufacture successfully itself. Such arrangements were a means of financing extensive projects, like the improvement of Brandywine Springs, that individual entrepreneurs or small partnerships would have found difficult or impossible to fund themselves or to finance via bank loans or mortgages.

By 1837, a new tenant, George E. Shelley, had taken over the premises. By then, the attractions included a "highly popular Band," gardens tended by Europe's best gardeners, a wide selection of fine wines, billiard and bath rooms, "and various other amusements." Thanks to the new rail line, the springs, which Shelley called "one of the most fashionable and select in the union," would soon be only five hours from the nation's capital, and three from both Philadelphia and Baltimore.[166] By 1839, yet another tenant, this one an experienced Philadelphia hotelier named James Sanderson, ran the operation, but he, too, quickly vacated. Over the next decade or so, one tenant after another came and went.

In the 1850s, business had fallen off considerably, so Newkirk leased the property to Alden Partridge, who converted the hotel into a private military school. In December 1853, a fire destroyed the building—an irony, given that its construction had been financed by a fire insurer. Partridge died shortly thereafter. Fed up, Newkirk sold the property to a Philadelphia merchant for $15,000. Inexplicably, the merchant sold it to another Philadelphian for $5,000 just three months later. The springs themselves continued to attract attention, and a smaller hotel was erected from some of the outbuildings; but the locale never recovered its former glory. After the Civil War, entrepreneur Franklin Fell tried to start an Episcopal Girls School on the site but eventually abandoned the idea and operated a small hotel instead. The area later became a private amusement park and then, in the 1950s, a state park.[167]

That incorporation was necessary to run a successful first-rate resort was also suggested by Virginia's unincorporated Warm Springs, "the grounds and enclosures" of which were "very much neglected and the latter are in a state of dilapidation the spring used for drinking is small . . . it is covered by an old and decayed shelter."[168] The nearby White Sulphur Springs Company, which was chartered in 1834 with a MINAC of $500,000, survived at least into the 1880s.[169] When Blair Bolling visited there in 1839, his only complaint was that it took three days to arrive in crowded stages that departed in the wee hours of the morning. "So great was the croud [sic] at this popular resort of the seekers of pleasure as well as health that I coul [sic] not obtain admission and was compelled to seek refuge for the night elsewhere."[170] "The President of the United States, Mr. Van Buren, Mr. Poinset the Secretary of war and many other distinguished individuals grased [sic] the company with their presences," he noted, while describing the "usual" evening ball.[171] Bolling thought that the president attended merely to enhance his popularity, but he considered the balls "another link . . . to the chain that bind together this mighty union."[172]

"The White Sulpher spring" itself, Bolling observed, was "covered by a circular Dome or Temple supported by twelve columns . . . upon the centre of which Dome, is a statue surmounted upon a double pedestal also circular in form, the top most one the smallest, having the word HYGEA [goddess of health] inscribed on its edge in guilt letters." As in Delaware, the company provided guests the opportunity to play cards, to use a "most splendid Billiard table," and to listen to "a Band composed of six blacks who perform on wind instruments and a base [sic] drum, and entertain the company . . . with good music for an hour each day before dinner," which consisted of "mutton chiefly, good bread tollerable [sic] butter not much, and not very good milk and bad coffee."[173]

Another nearby resort, the Blue Sulphur Springs Company, was charted in 1835 with a MINAC of $32,000 and a MAXAC of $100,000. It offered visitors similar water and amenities but was situated in a place thought susceptible to "very high imbellishment." Sweet Springs, chartered in 1836 at $500,000, incorporated to keep up with the competition. Its "old" building was "in a very dilapidated condition and too small for the commodious accommodation of the number of persons that usually resort there during the summer and fall." Its waters were good for mineral baths as well as for drinking. Hot Springs, by contrast, was most famous for its "Gentleman's Spout," a five-foot-deep bath about ten-foot square "in which persons bathe, and apply those parts of the boddy [*sic*] or limbs most affected." It incorporated in 1840 with a MINAC of $100,000 and a MAXAC of $200,000.[174]

Even the nation's cemeteries needed to be big because early Americans had profound respect for the dead. "If we see a tree or a flower planted above [the deceased]," one noted, "we feel as if they must revive and rejoice in the pledge that their memory is still treasured by some who loved them."[175] To be successful, some cemeteries incorporated so that they could invest in large tracts of land, bridges, culverts, "direction boards" to help people to navigate the grounds, drainage ditches, fences, footpaths, gates, grading, landscaping, stables and sheds for visitors' wagons, an internal road system, and good roads leading to the front gates. They needed caretakers to keep it all up and astute business managers to ascertain competitive rates (less for children of different ages, including stillborns), to estimate the numbers of burials, and to plan the entire funeral experience. Roads had to be laid out so as to accentuate a "beautiful variety of hill and valley," to accommodate "the absolute necessity of the carriages getting near the Lot at a funeral," and to maximize the number of corner lots because they were especially "sought for . . . being desirable for the display of a monument or tomb." The larger cemeteries employed up to twenty-five hands during the busy season (spring, summer, and fall) but perhaps only three or four during the winter.[176]

Antebellum Americans attended plays in incorporated theaters. Philadelphia in the 1850s was home to four or five theaters, of which several were chartered and occasionally traded on the stock exchange. The Walnut Street Theatre was "prettily decorated," according to one customer, but "not so spacious as some in New York and Boston."[177] Baltimore also chartered a theater because its earlier, unincorporated theater was "rather thinly attended for so populous a place as Baltimore," according to one traveler, probably because "the entertainment was indifferent" because of the insufficient capital available to the stage managers.[178]

Scale diseconomies, where bigger corporations were less profitable than smaller ones, also existed and help to explain why early turnpikes were relatively short. The great trunk line from Philadelphia to Pittsburgh, for example, was controlled by eight turnpike and three bridge companies. Smaller corporations were easier to monitor, govern, and manage. At the same time, some turnpikes may have been too small to cover the fixed costs of collecting tolls, management, and so forth.[179]

Most early railroads were short as well because it was widely believed that they had to be to keep them "within a limit for the most economical work-ing."[180] Many were too small to cover the fixed costs of their rolling stock, so they slowly began to amalgamate. Some, especially interstate ones, joined forces by contract, not by charter.[181] "The companies owning" certain rail-roads, explained an observer, "are under contract to unite their whole lines in one common interest, to be under one general superintendence and manage-ment; and they are thus, for all practical purposes, one interest, though, as they pass in different states, separate corporations are necessary."[182] Others combined when one corporation leased other lines, as when the Housatonic Railroad leased the Berkshire Railroad and several other roads.[183] Others, though originally comprising multiple corporations, were able to "form a single interest under the management of a board of directors chosen by the stockholders of each in joint ballot."[184] The Northern Central was "the result of a union of four Companies." Laws passed by both Maryland and Pennsyl-vania were needed to complete the amalgamation, although previous to that time, one of the roads had been able to "virtually subject" two other roads "to its exclusive direction" while "preserving only the form of a separate corpora-tion."[185] In another instance, three railroads merged to form one continuous line (save for a steamboat ferry across the Susquehanna) from Philadelphia to Baltimore. After merging, "the expenses of the Corporation have been dimin-ished, the revenue increased, and the advantages, in energy, promptness and unity of action which had been anticipated from such a combination, have been thus far satisfactorily realized."[186]

Where scale diseconomies loomed large, businesses looked for ways to combine partially so as to gain some of the advantages of large size, such as market power. By the late 1820s, insurers in New York formed a cartel that sought to maintain premiums by imposing "a penalty for a breach," but the arrangement eventually crumbled.[187] As early as 1829, salt manufacturers in Virginia's (now West Virginia's) Kanawha River valley proposed what one his-torian called "an embryonic trust arrangement." The cartel fell through be-cause of coordination problems that were solved by forming unincorporated joint-stock companies that sold their products through stockholding agents in key marketing centers.[188]

Just as it was important for businesses to tap scale economies without growing too large and unwieldy, it was important to optimize their degree of vertical integration. In other words, corporations were most profitable when, as economist Ronald Coase explained in the twentieth century, they only performed functions within the business that they could not procure at lower cost in the market. A manufacturer of steel, for instance, should have purchased iron-ore deposits and fuel sources if, and only if, it acquired those crucial inputs more cheaply than by purchasing them from mining companies. And it should have sold its own steel to railroads and other consumers of steel if, and only if, it did so more profitably than selling via a wholesaler.[189]

Achieving such Coasean optimality was a moving target subject to frequent changes due to market fluctuations. If corporations were attempting to maintain the most profitable degree of vertical integration, therefore, we should observe them shedding and adding units with some regularity, bearing in mind that managerial discretion in the matter was often limited by charter restrictions. Manufacturing companies in New England were adroit at buying and selling off parts of themselves. The Boston Manufacturing Company sold off its machinery manufacturing operations to the Merrimack Company to further streamline operations, concentrate on its core competencies, and earn a quick return for stockholders. Similarly, the Brattleboro Typographic Company manufactured the paper that it used in the books it published. No similar business in the nation was so vertically integrated.[190]

Textile mills tended to sell their output to wholesale merchants. For example, B. C. Ward & Co. was the agent for the Waltham Company. The agency used its knowledge of market conditions and fashions to help Waltham decide which patterns to print on its fabrics and even hired a "regular designer" for the task.[191] Such arrangements, however, were not always as profitable as they could have been. In 1860, a committee reported to the stockholders of the Lowell Company that they could save "upwards of 11,000 a year" if the company "should establish a warehouse for the sale of their own goods in New York instead of selling them through commission houses." A stockholder committee concurred and canceled the company's contract with A. & A. Lawrence & Co., which apparently had been giving kickbacks to Lowell's upper management. Dividends almost doubled after the change.[192] A stockholder committee for the Taunton Company uncovered a similar inside deal in 1828 but was less successful at rectifying the problem; by 1832, the company was bankrupt.[193]

Metals firms also integrated vertically to various extents. The iron industry comprised various types of firms, such as furnaces that produced pig iron, forges that produced bar iron, mills that produced final goods made of iron, and ironworks that integrated all stages of the value chain.[194] The Lulworth Iron Company of Maryland (chartered 1847 with $500,000–$1 million in capital; renamed the Mount Savage Iron Company in 1848), for example, "consisted of smelting, puddling and casting furnaces, forges, rolling mills, steam engines and machinery for making and manufacture of crude, bar and cast iron, in the various usual processes." By 1846, it had "already invested . . . a capital of nearly a million of dollars." Situated in the northeastern part of the Cumberland coal field, just two miles shy of the Pennsylvania border, it connected itself to the B&O Railroad by a private railway constructed with "heavy rail-road iron" of its own manufacture. The corporation also built and rented "on the declivities of the adjoining hills . . . dwelling-houses for a population already exceeding 5000, all occupied in, or dependent on, the works."[195]

Railroads also waxed and waned vertically. Railroads that allowed common carriers to compete with them on their own lines on favorable terms, for example, found the other carriers to be a "formidable impediment" to profits and hence refused to renew their contracts.[196] Instead, railroads purchased and managed "their own passenger cars for the transportation of passengers, over their Railway."[197] Eventually, "the owners of all Rail Roads with a single track, in this country and England, . . . all excluded from their roads locomotives not owned by the proprietors of the roads."[198] Some railroads found it profitable to own and operate warehouses and wharves. Steamship lines, especially long-distance ones, often found that placing "the ownership of the entire route within one common interest and management, and under one responsible head" led to "increased energy, economy and security" and hence improved "pecuniary results."[199]

Sometimes, it was more optimal to set up a separate division with its own management than to shed a business unit entirely. The directors of the Illinois Central "thought it expedient to organize the Land Department as a separate and distinct branch of their business, and to commit its care and management to the special charge and supervision of one officer, subject of course to the advice and direction, from time to time, of the Board of Directors" because that part of the business, selling off the lands given to the railroad by the state, was so different from that of the rest of the corporation.[200]

At other times, management found it expedient to spin units off. In one instance, a coal field and its attendant transportation facilities were separated (into the Lehigh Coal and Lehigh Navigation companies, respectively) because some investors "were willing to join in the improvement of the navigation, but had no faith in the value of the coal, or that a market could ever be found for it among a population accustomed wholly to the use of wood. On the other hand, some were of the opinion that the navigation would never pay the interest of its cost, while the coal business would prove profitable. This gave rise to the separation of the two interests."[201]

The Schuylkill Navigation Company found that coal often "did not come through the canal, but sought some other route, simply because there were no boats in readiness to bring it."[202] At first, it tried to construct its own boats and wharves but soon found the expense too large because many of the boats remained "for months at Manayunk unemployed, lying there rotting." Thereafter, instead of manufacturing, owning, and operating their own boats, the corporation built boats for captains who paid fifty dollars a month to use them, until the corporation recouped its costs, at which point it gave them title to the boat.[203]

A canal near Sunbury, Pennsylvania, obtained the right of selling or leasing the 724 horsepower that its canal was capable of producing but decided "to make this more valuable to the stockholders, by using it in connection with a Lumber Manufacturing Company" since the stockholders also owned 50,000 acres of "good timber land in Potter County." So it incorporated another company, capitalized it at $800,000, but issued only half of its stock "until the wants of the trade shall demand an increase." It thought best to vertically integrate no further, however, and promised to sell the "right of stumpage" and any excess waterpower to other businesses.[204] Similarly, the Shamokin Coal and Iron Company formed in the 1840s through the amalgamation of a coal-mining and transportation company and an iron manufacturer. The combined company possessed "privileges which few corporate bodies in the State possess, and which, when used with prudence and skill, must make the stock of great value," at least according to the directors.[205]

Some corporations took integration too far and tried to combine only loosely connected businesses under a single management. Such conglomerates, especially if they included banks, were generally frowned upon. The New York State Bank's request to purchase the state's salt mines in exchange for an annuity caused a mighty uproar because it appeared to be just another lucrative privilege extended to a group with political pull. Some early conglomerates appear to have been a means of hedging bets. The Towsontown and Baltimore Road and Railway Company was both a turnpike and a railway that shared an eighty-foot-wide right of way in an era when rails were supplanting roads in many areas.[206]

The third major advantage of large size was market power, on both the buy (monopsony) and sell (monopoly) side. Corporations with monopsony power could cap wages and prevent workers from organizing through the use of blacklists and other strong-arm tactics.[207] In many manufacturing towns, such as Lowell, they often changed wages simultaneously.[208] In 1845, one editor claimed, "a great strife between capital and labor . . . is fast gaining the mastery. . . . [T]he combined, incorporated, and protected capital can starve out the workers."[209] Instead of being regulated "by the relation, one to the other, of supply and demand,"[210] wages were subject to "an organized combination of all the large manufacturing establishments"[211] that by "acting in concert, regulate the wages, the operatives may receive for their labor, and dictate to them by an irresistible fiat, the number of hours they shall toil."[212] The corporations combined to hire propagandists and agents who enticed surplus laborers to the factories, thereby further depressing wages. "Combinations of the operatives it is true are sometimes formed to counteract the oppression of corporation influences," one contemporary conceded, "but they are of no avail."[213]

The exercise of market power sounds exploitative, but the promise of the extra profits it afforded was often necessary to induce entry into newer and riskier endeavors.[214] Few early corporations actually monopolized markets. Unlike some early Dutch and British joint-stock banks and international trading companies, charters were more about large size and protection from direct assault by governments or competitors than dominating markets by fiat. Nevertheless, many corporations had a fair degree of market power—that is, some control over prices and quantities.[215] Due to their expansive definition of monopoly, however, early Americans claimed to see monopolies everywhere. They complained of the plural "monopolizers" of grain and even railed against "the monopoly of the Soil" in a nation endowed with enormous quantities of inexpensive land.[216] Many early Americans believed that although banks dotted their landscape, "the history of *banks* is a history of *monopoly*."[217] In one breath, New York attorney Henry Van Der Lyn complained that banks were multiplying too rapidly and then described them as "at best, dangerous *monopolies*."[218] That was because, like Albert Gallatin, he equated monopoly with barriers to entry rather than market structure. Clearly, no one bank, not even the Bank of the United States, controlled all banking capital. Equally clearly, banking was a local or regional business, so the number of banks readily accessible to any given American was usually small.[219] Manhattan and Philadelphia both suffered at times because the number of banks doing business in them did not keep up with their exploding populations. By the late antebellum period, however, banks were common enough in many markets to keep their profits down. "Competition," Gallatin argued in 1841, "rendered the privilege valueless. There is not a single city bank, chartered subsequent to the year 1833, the stock of which is not below par."[220]

Similarly, some bridges, ferries, turnpikes, canals, and railroads faced stiff competition from private or public competitors; but others enjoyed considerable local market power. The objectively worst cases of literal corporate monopoly involved interstate and international transportation. In 1787, John Fitch exhibited a steamboat that marveled spectators. As a reward, Pennsylvania, Delaware, Virginia, and New York granted him the exclusive privilege of navigating their state waters by means of steamboat; in 1791, Fitch took out a U.S. patent. In 1798, however, New York's legislature granted Robert R. Livingston, a wealthy landowner, politician, and jurist, a twenty-year monopoly on transporting freight by steamship on New York's waterways. In 1803, the extremely well-connected Livingston managed to get the grant extended until 1828. Not until 1807 did Livingston, working with Robert Fulton, finally produce a working boat, for which Fulton obtained a federal patent. In 1808, New York again rewarded the pair and their heirs with a new thirty-year monopoly, which also extinguished the remaining claims of Fitch's heirs. In 1811, the state passed yet another law, which evoked "incessant opposition . . . on all sides" because it authorized the impounding of unlicensed ships cruising in waters claimed by other states.[221]

Tensions increased after claims surfaced that Fulton's ship was in no way superior to Fitch's original. A New York court in 1811 revoked Livingston's monopoly privileges, but the decision was reversed on appeal. Meanwhile, an acrimonious pamphlet debate flared up, pitting antimonopolists William Alexander Duer and James Langdon Sullivan against Cadwalader Colden, attorney on behalf of the Livingston and Fulton interests. Duer and Sullivan noted that New York's monopoly impinged on U.S. patent law and the rights of the citizens of other states. Connecticut indeed complained loudly that the Constitution was supposed to provide "for the free and equal commercial rights of each and every one," and New Jersey, which felt very ill-used indeed, passed retaliatory legislation. Petitions against the monopolistic beast mounted, numbering almost 4,000 in 1823 alone. *Gibbons v. Ogden* (22 U.S., 9 Wheat. 1, 1824), one of the Marshall Court's most popular decisions, struck down the monopoly, noting that states could not grant patents or make other laws that restrained "a free intercourse among the States."[222] The decision spurred multiple firms to join the steamboat business, which drove down passenger rates from Manhattan to Albany from seven dollars to three dollars.[223] Out of the debates and trials emerged the consensus that patent monopolies should be confined to inventors and "not granted to those whose wealth, patronage or opportunities may have enabled them to seize on the inventions of others and bring them into public use."[224]

Gibbons may have fueled corporate growth by establishing free interstate commerce but also may have limited it by reducing expectations of market power. Interestingly, the decision did not bar states from establishing literal monopolies on purely inland waterways or within their own landmass, even if they interfered with interstate commerce, a loophole later effectively exploited by New Jersey's Camden and Amboy Railroad (hereafter the C&A R.R.). In 1832, the New Jersey legislature bestowed upon C&A R.R. a monopoly on merchandise and passenger traffic traveling through New Jersey between New York and Philadelphia. In exchange, the corporation gave New Jersey 1,000 shares and promised to pay it dividends and transit taxes totaling at least $30,000 per year. Under that arrangement, company stockholders shared their monopoly profits with New Jersey taxpayers at the expense of those who paid high fares to travel, in unprecedented discomfort and at timid speeds, between the Pennsylvania and New York metropolises. The company's market and political power caused considerable consternation, but its contribution to state coffers long protected it from critics' quills.[225]

The charter of the Boston and Worcester Railroad prevented any other railroads from coming within five miles of its line; other railroads received similar protections, but all fell far short of the sort of market power afforded the C&A R.R.[226] Some market protection may have been warranted. "Rivalry of this kind," the representatives of railroad companies claimed in 1854, "confers no real advantage upon the public; the losses incurred are often retrieved by higher charges afterwards."[227] Proponents of limiting competition also argued that allowing more than one railroad to service a route would prevent any projects from being completed. "Not the first spade would have been put into the earth," they claimed, "for all know that but one can be supported."[228] "When one Company can do and actually does all the business on the road vastly more advantageously and better than two Companies can do it," others queried, "why should another Company be admitted?"[229] Limiting competition between railroads was especially important because of the sunk costs involved, advocates of no "parallel lines" argued. "It is not like two stage lines or two lines of steamboats, which, in case the investment is not profitable, can be moved away and used in some other place."[230] Others demurred, arguing that canals, railroads, and other "appurtenances of vigorous improvement cannot be too much multiplied for the public good, where private expenditure will bear them," but the falling transportation costs for both passengers and freight made it difficult for reformers to gain much ground.[231] Because of railroads, it cost only twenty dollars and thirty-six hours to travel from Cincinnati to New York when "but a few years since," the same trip would have "required an expenditure for fare of $50.00, not including meals and incidentals" and would have "consumed more than a week of valuable time."[232] It was difficult to rail against railroad "monopolies" under such circumstances, especially when the railroads were well governed. Later in the nineteenth century, when railroad rates rose and many roads had clearly fallen into the grasp of cabals of directors or executives, matters would be different.

Chapter 6

Governance Principles

Principles, then, and not regard to men, should guide our conduct.

—Charles Sigourney, 1837[1]

Early corporate charters were somewhat experimental at first and hence marked by diversity. Convergence occurred with some rapidity as incorporators and legislators discovered what worked and what did not.[2] What worked was whatever prevented employees, managers, officers, directors, or large stockholders from stealing from a corporation's other stakeholders. As Chapter 7 will make clear, corporations were not always successful in their quest to prevent fraud and mismanagement. Were it more honest about itself, our species would call itself *Homo sapiens ereptor*, "man the wise thief." When corporations successfully protected themselves from the agency problems that their critics so feared, they almost invariably followed the principles of corporate governance described in this chapter.

Early corporate and political governance were deeply intertwined.[3] Many of the men who formed the nation's first constitutions were also those who formed its first corporations. George Washington, George Mason, and Thomas Jefferson were all founding stockholders in a 1774 joint-stock company thwarted by the Revolution.[4] "A nation itself," wrote nineteenth-century political philosopher Francis Lieber, "is the great corporation, comprehending all the others."[5] A corporation's charter (or an unincorporated joint-stock company's articles of association) was considered analogous to a nation's constitution. Its bylaws were akin to statutes, its board of directors to legislatures, and its officers to the executive branch. Corporations and governments were both essentially Lockean: if leadership/management did not benefit the citizens/stockholders, the government/management could be—indeed, should be—lawfully ousted.[6]

Also like a political entity, as the business grew larger, a bureaucracy arose from the skeletal constitutional framework to standardize routine tasks. As Charles Sigourney suggested in the epigraph to this chapter, what decided the fate of the business was the same as what decided the fate of nations: the degree of alignment between the organization's goals and the incentives it provided to its stakeholders, not the quality of men it attracted per se. If men were angels, to paraphrase James Madison, corporate governance would be as unnecessary as political governance. Because most people were decidedly unangelic, corporations, like governments, operated best when they were designed with rogues and knaves in mind, not the most virtuous.[7]

Legislators generally worked with incorporators and the interested public to create the most robust charter possible; but after that, governments closely monitored only a few corporations—mostly, banks in which they had deposits or owned shares. Individual investors, in other words, were more or less on their own. Perhaps their greatest protection from expropriation was the limit that charters most placed on managerial discretion.[8] "Acts of incorporation," explained an anonymous observer in 1835, "are generally granted for specific objects, and confer specific powers; and any deviation, on the part of the corporators, from the proper line of their duty, is attended with an exposure of their interest."[9]

Early corporations were only supposed to engage in activities explicitly laid out in their charters, a concept tied to the legal doctrine called "ultra vires."[10] "If the object or design of a charter is limited," William Wright argued in 1820, "the powers of the Body Corporate must be considered as limited by the object. No general capacity to act at discretion in pursuit of other objects, can be implied from the grant of corporate powers even in general terms."[11] Any corporation "created by Legislative grant, for a special purpose," lawyers Isaac Williams and Garret Wall explained in 1835, "is to be considered as having such powers only, as have been specifically granted to it, by the Legislature; or are necessary for the purpose of carrying into effect, the powers expressly granted." Thus a turnpike corporation chartered to build a wagon road from Trenton to New Brunswick could not lay rails without the approval of both the government and its stockholders.[12] The point of such restrictions, Williams and Wall explained, was "to prevent the usurpation and exercise of powers, not intended to be granted." An antebellum corporation could not even "hold any more real estate than is proper for the purposes for which it

was incorporated."[13] Section 4 of Louisiana's 1848 general incorporation statute explicitly stated that "it shall not be lawful for any corporation established
under and by authority of this act, to embrace or pursue more than one
branch of business or industry."[14] Ultra vires restrictions were necessary because early corporations with very liberal charters—such as the Canton
Company, which enjoyed "corporate powers more varied and extensive, than
were perhaps ever granted . . . in any other State in the Union"—naturally attracted the attention of directors and managers eager to bilk stockholders.[15]

Lone stockholders could, and did, successfully petition courts to issue an
injunction against corporations "to keep them within their legitimate limits."[16] If stockholders approved a measure that might be lawful, however, a
little wiggle room was created. Some corporations issued cash-like notes
without the explicit sanction of the legislature but with the consent of their
stockholders, on the theory that corporations could, in the words of a late
nineteenth-century jurist, "borrow money to carry on its business . . . but not
for speculating in outside matters."[17] To outlaw such borrowing, legislatures
had to pass explicit legislation stating that only banks could issue notes designed to circulate as cash.[18]

Incorporators/entrepreneurs also drew up bylaws to fill governance gaps
in the charter.[19] Bylaws were usually quite detailed because they were explicitly "adopted to secure a faithful administration of the affairs" of the corporation.[20] Some mandated very specific reporting requirements of income from
all sources, disbursements of all types, and lists of employees and their remuneration. Others mandated the deposit of corporate funds in a specific bank
or banks and the countersignature of checks drawn on those accounts. The
bylaws of the City of Sonora Tunnel Company stipulated that no money
could be disbursed until the board approved and the claim "shall first have
been audited."[21] Other bylaws created committees of stockholders charged
with examining the corporation's physical infrastructure and account books
on a regular basis. Yet others detailed when, where, and how stockholder
meetings would be announced, how many directors were needed for a quorum, and so forth.[22]

Bylaws could be changed with the assent of stockholders, but good ones
had a long shelf life. The thirty-two bylaws drawn up by the Farmers Bank of
Bucks County in 1815, for example, were not amended, according to the
bank's chronicler, "in any important particular" during the bank's first *century*.[23] Other banks cribbed them, and some of those operated for decades,
even a century or more, with nary a loss due to defalcation. Bylaws also often

specified stockholder voting rights, an important point discussed in more detail below. For example, the third bylaw of the Eastern Railroad of Massachusetts stipulated that each stockholder was "entitled to one vote for each share held by him," up to 10 percent "of the whole number of shares of stock."[24]

The board of directors sometimes drew up regulations to govern its meetings. Typically, notice of board rule or other interior management changes had to be given prior to voting on them to prevent shysters from changing rules on the fly. The number of directors on the board entailed a trade-off. More directors meant more information and more contacts and less likelihood of the formation of a dangerous clique. In 1804, for example, a newspaper editor argued that creating more banks was better than enlarging existing ones because "it would increase the number of directors, and give a greater scope of information as to who ought and ought not to be accommodated from the banks."[25] At the same time, larger boards suffered from free-rider problems: no one tried to solve difficult problems because he anticipated that others would bear the costs and risks of doing so. Individual accountability was also reduced as boards increased in size.[26]

Stockholder resolutions could also constrain management. In 1850, the stockholders of the Manassas Gap Railroad resolved that no part of the shares "subscribed after this date in the Counties west of the Blue Ridge to the Manassas Gap Railroad, shall be appropriated to building the Road east of the Blue Ridge."[27] Throughout the antebellum period, stockholders remained residual decision makers.[28] If in doubt, directors and officers were supposed to obtain stockholder approval as the "the President & Directors of the Dismal Swamp Canal Company" did because they did "not conceive that they" were empowered "to enter into any of the arrangements proposed" by a committee.[29] After stockholders approved a major policy, the directors did not possess discretion to change it "without their consent."[30] Stockholders were also the final arbiters of disputes within management. When the directors of a railroad failed to adopt the suggestions of a committee report, for example, the committee members threatened to appeal to the stockholders, "a great majority of whom" they thought would "instruct the Directors to adopt such report, and carry it into immediate execution."[31]

Today, at best, stockholders exercise control only in extremis. By contrast, antebellum stockholders reigned so completely at one mill that overseers had to ask them whether it was acceptable to change the time when workers took their breakfast. Stockholders also made decisions such as where an office would be located and whether it would be purchased outright or leased. The directors of the Farmers Bank of Virginia at Martinsburg "resolved, that the application [for establishment of a new branch] was one which the stockholders were alone competent to grant."[32] Stockholders in the Bank of the Northern Liberties voted 713 to two in favor of moving the location of the bank south of Pegg's Run in Philadelphia.[33] Generally, stockholders had to approve charter changes before they became effective and were not bound to continue paying any stock subscriptions that became due after a fundamental change in the original charter, even if the majority approved of the amendment. As one jurist put it: "[C]orporations can exercise no power over the [stockholders], beyond those conferred by the Charter to which they have subscribed."[34]

Charters, bylaws, directors' rules, and stockholder resolutions had to be lawful and constitutional in order to be binding, and bylaws and regulations could not run counter to the corporation's charter. As one nineteenth-century jurist put it: "The powers of the stockholders' meetings are defined by charter and Code. Those of the Board of Directors by the Code, charter and bylaws of the stockholders. Those of the subordinate agencies by the Code, charter, by-laws and regulations of Directors."[35] Such strictures were usually taken quite seriously, as extant directors' records are replete with references to "the act incorporating the company"[36] and often flatly stated that the company charter did "not allow them to agree to the proposition."[37] Directors and officers who wanted to engage in new lines of business, therefore, had to obtain a charter amendment from the legislature. America's first joint-stock life-insurance company obtained a charter supplement to allow it to conduct a trust business, to "act as trustees under last wills and testaments, as guardians of the estates of minors, or committee of lunatics, and as assignees for the benefit of creditors."[38]

Corporate capital structure was also under the direct control of stockholders and/or the state. Typically, management had to obtain shareholder approval to borrow from banks, to sell bonds, or to borrow in any other fashion other than regular trade credit. Charters sometimes constrained borrowing, too. To sell additional shares, corporations usually had to obtain legislative and/or stockholder approval and to offer new shares to existing stockholders first so that they could protect their pro-rata interest in the business.[39] The bylaws of the Boston and Barre Company (a manufacturer of woolen and cotton goods in Worcester County) flatly stated that the capital could not be increased "unless at a legal meeting of the Stockholders, they having been duly notified that the meeting is called for the purpose of taking into consideration the subject of such increase."[40] The Canton Company increased its capital stock in 1853 only "after considerable discussion among the *Stockholders*," legislative approval, and official approval by the shareholders.[41] Contemporaries considered such strict limitations on capital stock "that great rule of public policy" because it "effectually" guarded "against any such gigantic growth and power."[42]

Stockholders ultimately ruled most early American corporations just as voters ultimately ruled early American governments.[43] Like voters, stockholders found it necessary to delegate power to rulers and thereby opened the door to agency problems. Corporate presidents and directors were extremely powerful, enjoying, it was said, "great privileges and authority, very little inferiour to the petty despots of the earth."[44] But their powers were generally countered by various checks and balances, some structural, others interest-based.

Structural Balances

> The duties of the managers of an institution of this nature, are two-fold: towards the public and towards the stockholders, whose agents they are. Their interests are also divided: as stockholders, their interest is direct; as a part of the community, indirect and remote.
> —*Executive Communication to the General Assembly of Maryland . . . On the Subject of Turnpike Roads,* 1819[45]

In 1845, J. D. Bird tried to prove that his appointment as both president and superintendent of the Petersburg and Roanoke Railroad was a good idea by publishing a short pamphlet that claimed that his road outperformed another, similar road (the Richmond, Fredericksburg and Potomac), the president of which disdained the notion of "uniting the two offices." It may well have been more efficient to combine the offices; but doing so, many early Americans recognized, broke down important structural balances designed to limit corporate defalcation.[46]

Each corporation was the brainchild of one or more entrepreneurs called "incorporators," typically men of "standing and character" like Russell Freeman of Hanover, New Hampshire,[47] and Israel Thorndike, the "Federalist financier" from Massachusetts who was involved in the early stages of a number of companies beginning with the Essex Bridge between Beverly and Salem in 1787. Later, Thorndike and his eponymous son were involved in the formation of several turnpikes, canals, banks, insurers, railroads, and manufacturing concerns.[48] The men who formed banks in the Ohio River Valley in the eight years following the end of the War of 1812 were intensively studied by historian Harry Stevens, who found that they were older than the median age of men in the general population. Ranging from twenty-seven to sixty-seven years of age, they were rather numerous, accounting for over 5 percent of the population aged twenty-six or older. Most had been born elsewhere; all but one had moved to the area before the war. Many had been farmers at some point in their lives. A few were professionals—ministers, doctors, lawyers—but most were merchants or artisan/proto-manufacturers (nail makers, tanners, pork packers, millers, and a few textile manufacturers). Many more such studies are desperately needed to more fully understand this understudied and underappreciated group of adventurers, especially because the incorporators often became board members.[49]

After their business formed, the incorporators typically called a meeting where stockholders elected the first board of directors. In some corporations, the directors then elected a president from their number; in others, stockholders elected the president directly. One problem with the latter was that it was necessary to call a stockholder meeting should the president resign or die. The South-Carolina Canal and Rail Road Company suffered constant "inconvenience or injury" after its president died because by the terms of its charter, "without a President, the Board of Directors could do nothing," even though "urgent business required attention every hour of the day."[50]

Time and again, directors made clear that they believed "that they were elected by the stockholders to superintend their interests."[51] To achieve that goal, directors were supposed to provide strategic direction for the corporation, and, in fact, some people used the term "direction" as a collective noun to refer to the board of directors much as we use the term "management" today to refer collectively to a company's executives.[52] Rather than run the business day to day, directors provided leadership, vision, and monitoring of the president, and they hired managers. Directors made important decisions such as which applicants the banks or insurers should lend to or insure or which route a canal, railroad, or turnpike should take—for example, should the B&O Railroad terminate in Pittsburgh, Cleveland, or Cincinnati?[53] The board also typically appointed cashiers, treasurers, "and such other officers and agents.... And it may fix their compensation."[54] The directors them-selves received no direct pay, although sometimes they received a travel al-lowance or per diem for their attendance at board and stockholder meetings.[55] Occasionally, stockholders voted them gratuities or bonuses, as when stock-holders in the Taunton Copper Company voted $10,000 bonuses to two di-rectors for their "valuable services" to the company after the declaration of a 20 percent dividend.[56] In well-governed corporations, like the better textile mills of New England, "the Directors properly consist of stockholders most largely interested in the management of their own property. They receive nothing for their services" other than the fatter or more secure dividends on their shares, which could be substantial, derived from their efforts.[57] Simi-larly, in the mid-1820s, directors in New York corporations outright owned 28 percent of the companies they ran.[58]

Some charters specified that corporations were to be headed by "manag-ers" instead of "directors." The two terms were more or less synonymous, but the term "manager" connoted directors who were to have fairly substantial day-to-day operational authority. They should not be confused with salaried officers (executives, in today's parlance) or with upper-level supervisors (managers, in today's lingo). Because they interacted with the corporation and its customers more intensively than most directors did, managers had to be selected with "the greatest possible care." In the best-governed corpora-tions, managers received not "merely a salary" but instead were encouraged to "have a large personal interest in the affairs of the company"—to wit, to have most of their net worth in the company's shares so that they had a vested "pecuniary interest" in the company's profits.[59]

No one wanted to invest in a corporation run by rogues, so the quality and the reputation of directors (or managers) were crucial. The New York State Bank made an emergency loan to the Bank of Niagara during the Panic of 1819, for example, because "a favorable change had taken place in the Board of Direction, which was calculated to revive public confidence." The new president, in particular, was considered a man of "standing, respectabil-ity, and character."[60] The "Well known and prominent men" who formed the board of the Bank of the United States Buffalo branch were said to be respon-sible for that institution's success.[61] "The respectability of the members" of the Maine Fire and Marine Insurance Company, claimed a newspaper editor in 1800, "promises much public utility."[62] "Corporations, like individuals, will succeed or fail," industrialist Nathan Appleton opined, "as they are directed by skill and intelligence, or without them."[63]

Early Americans realized that even those with sterling reputations could create agency problems. To help ensure their fidelity, directors in many corporations, especially banks, had to resign if they took a directorship with a competitor. In almost all early corporations, a director had to resign if he was no longer a stockholder. Some charters also banned government officials from serving as directors. To help stockholders to monitor directors, the board had to maintain minutes and was often instructed to record even relatively routine matters.[64]

Directors (or managers) were usually elected for one-year terms and sometimes faced term limitations. Except for the president, directors in the United States Bank of Pennsylvania could not serve more than three years out of four.[65] Where term limitations were absent, good directors sometimes served for decades. Abraham Barker of the Merchants Bank of New Bedford served from the bank's inception in 1825 until his death, in 1871.[66] Bad directors, by contrast, were often ousted at the first opportunity. A steamship-company director named Josiah Dow was voted off the board because he "was a very troublesome kind of chap to do business with, there being no helm to his tongue, and that consequently it would at times yaw a good deal."[67] Many other directors self-selected out by resigning or declining reelection.[68] In aggregate, director turnover appears to have been low enough to minimize learning-curve costs but high enough to discourage entrenchment. Of the 157 directors of Virginia banks in 1827, forty were new; but in 1829 and 1832, only about half that number changed out.[69]

Some corporations staggered elections, as the U.S. Senate did. That rule made it impossible for an outsider to take over the board quickly but also delayed necessary board reformation—an important limitation, given that new boards sometimes saved troubled companies. After the Bank of Royalton suspended specie convertibility of its notes following the large losses it suffered during the Panic of 1857, stockholders elected a new board, and "without delay these men made great effort to collect money enough on the overdue notes to the bank to enable it to resume business."[70] When that proved insufficient, they borrowed money on their private credit. They had to officially write down the bank's capital to $50,000, but it later restored its capital to $100,000 and became a national bank.[71]

Presidents, by contrast, rarely faced term limitations. Bank presidents (and cashiers) tended to stay in power for at least several years and sometimes much longer. Charles Sigourney was elected director of the Phoenix Bank of Hartford twenty-two out of twenty-three years and was chosen president each year for the last sixteen of those terms before retiring. Shepherd Knapp's tenure at the Mechanics' Bank of New York extended from 1838 until at least 1855. Jesse Maris headed the Delaware County Bank during the nineteen years prior to his death, in November 1860. Chartered in 1814, that bank had just six presidents and five cashiers before the Civil War. James Cox was cashier of the Bank of Baltimore from 1796 until 1841. The first six presidents of the Bank of North America averaged about a dozen years in office. Two died at their posts. The first president of the Commercial Bank of Albany stayed in office for seven years, though he assumed the presidency when already aged sixty-two. That bank's second president remained in office from 1832 until 1854. The third lasted only until 1860. Moses Taylor was a director of City Bank of New York for forty-five years and headed the institution for twenty-six of those. After replacing the New Haven Bank's first president, who lasted only a few years, Isaac Beers ran the institution for fourteen years. His successor, Dr. Aeneas Monson, lasted nineteen years. The Merchants Bank of New Bedford had just two presidents between 1825 and 1876.[72]

Typically, presidents, like other directors, cast a single vote when a roll call was necessary to decide an issue. Their power relative to other directors stemmed from being chairman of the board and from possessing superior information about the corporation's operations. Unlike most other board members, presidents usually earned a salary, approved by the stockholders at the annual meeting. Stockholders often pared back presidents' salary aspirations. A motion to increase the salary of the president of the Ohio and Chesapeake Canal Company from $1,000 to $2,000, for example, was shot down unanimously. Presidents were often the highest-paid person in a corporation, but not always. The president of the Farmers Bank of Bucks County, for example, received $300 per year, the same as one of the clerks, while its cashier received $800.[73]

Presidents were usually subject to sundry checks on their power. The president of the Union Canal Company of Pennsylvania, for example, was forbidden to engage in "any kind of manufacturing, mercantile, or speculative concerns."[74] When necessary, presidents could be removed and replaced quickly. When one bank averted a run on its deposits only by conspicuously displaying a $25,000 specie loan from the Bank of the United States (1816–36), the president was ousted at the next board meeting in favor of a new president who addressed the bank's underlying problems by calling in outstanding loans, suing defaulters, cutting administrative expenditures, and improving the bank's loan portfolio.[75] Similarly, some board members managed to oust Azariah Cutting Flagg from the presidency of the Hudson Railroad Company in 1849 because they "deemed Mr. Flagg incompetent to the useful discharge of the duties of President."[76] He was simply too expensive, others argued. During his sixteen-month stint as president, Flagg received about $8,000 in salary payments and stock dividends.[77]

In addition to a president or board chairman, most early corporations employed one or more salaried officers, including a treasurer, secretary, or, in banks, a cashier. Such officers were typically selected and their salary set by the board, but they could appeal to stockholders if they could not come to terms with the directors. In 1810, Joseph Lawrence, the recently cashiered treasurer of the Providence Mutual Fire Insurance Company, called a meeting of the stockholders to hear his complaints regarding the niggardly compensation he received for obtaining over $1.6 million in insurance for the company over the previous six years. As part of his campaign, Lawrence spread handbills making "various accusations and imputations against the Directors."[78] Stockholders rejected Lawrence's claims and voted to publish the company's audited financial statement, presumably to assure policyholders that all was well at the company.[79]

Treasurers were entrusted to "receive all the monies of the Company, and carefully preserve the same, and disburse and pay over . . . and render a true and faithful account."[80] Because they handled the corporation's money, treasurers were in the best position to rob it blind. According to Appleton, the great New England textile corporations all assigned "a treasurer as the responsible agent, and a superintendent or manager of the mills. The principle on which these corporations have been established, has always been, the filling of these important offices with men of the higher character and talent which could be obtained. It has been thought, and has been found to be, the best economy, to pay such salaries as will command the entire services of such men."[81] Even the most honest of them, however, were allowed to withdraw cash from company accounts only by "a check . . . countersigned by the President."[82]

Cashiers also faced restrictions designed to limit their ability to fleece their banks. Generally, they were not allowed to have any significant outside business interests that could distract them or run them into debt. For those very reasons, Charles Sigourney, president of the Phoenix Bank of Hartford, sought in 1837 the dismissal of his longtime cashier, Mr. Beach. So long as the cashier "abstained from participating in the perplexities, hazards, and, at this time, the consequent embarrassments of trade, he did well," Sigourney noted.

"But, when in the cupidity of wealth, he engaged in extensive mercantile business, and largely in the purchase of western lands," the president continued, "he became a different man; and was drawn into a vortex, which may engulph him in ruin, and may endanger, at the same time, the funds and reputation of the Bank."[83] Some cashiers received merit pay. The New Haven Bank, for example, paid its cashier up to $1,600 if annual dividends exceeded 6 percent per year but only $1,000 otherwise.[84]

Secretaries (not to be confused with office assistants or receptionists) oversaw corporate clerks and often were made responsible for the corporate seal—an instrument used, typically in conjunction with signatures, to contractually bind the corporation.[85] Charters or bylaws often stipulated that the seal be kept by the secretary or some other bonded officer. Early corporations usually forced officers to secure a performance bond to limit their incentive to commit fraud, to put outside sets of eyes on their activities (the sureties', which could number up to a dozen), and to secure some compensation for theft or other breaches.[86] The bylaws of the Washington Mutual Assurance Company of New York stipulated that the "Treasurer shall give bond, with two sureties to be approved of by the Directors, in the sum of ten thousand dollars, for the faithful performance of the trust reposed in him." The secretary had to do likewise, though only for $5,000.[87]

Cashiers and other bank employees typically had to acquire performance bonds of relatively high value because of the large sums they came into contact with daily. In January 1846, the cashier of the Farmers Bank of Virginia was required to obtain a bond of $50,000, the first teller and first accountant one for $10,000 each, the second teller and second accountant for $6,000 each, and the runner for $3,000.[88] In the bigger banks, cashiers employed assistant cashiers who were also heavily bonded. Smaller banks sometimes employed a "first teller" or "first discount clerk" who oversaw the activities of one or more subordinates. To limit pilfering and other forms of peculation, banks rewarded employees for monitoring other employees up and down the chain of command. It often worked: in 1855, the assistant cashier of the Mechanics' Bank of New York accused the cashier of embezzlement and brought the matter before the board of directors, which agreed. The cashier resigned before he was fired. The assistant cashier's diligence was fortunate because the president and directors had been lulled to sleep by the cashier's "high standing . . . in this community, for integrity and ability."[89]

Below directors and officers came the supervisor, "one well-paid and efficient manager" who provided detailed instructions to underlings that was much better than "the very inefficient management usually obtained by a board of directors" because the supervisor devoted "his whole time to the business of his company, and thoroughly underst[ood] it."[90] Meritorious supervisors received raises and even pensions. In 1855, for example, the Merrimack Manufacturing Company started paying a life annuity of $2,000 to John D. Prince for his service of almost thirty years. Like officers, supervisors did not have to own stock in the corporations for which they worked; but occasionally, they were paid shares in addition to their salaries as another way of tying their interests to those of their employers.[91]

Early in the nineteenth century, communities and industries were small enough that potential supervisors were often personally known. One of the early New England textile mills, immediately upon incorporation, secured the services of Paul Moody of Amesbury, "whose skill as a mechanic was well known, and whose success fully justified the choice." When local talent could not be acquired, directors or other bigwigs might search for talent as far away as Britain. One of the Boott brothers, for example, voyaged "to England solely for the purpose of engaging engravers" to make calico printing cylinders.[92]

Supervisors used several techniques to induce their subordinates to work hard and smart on behalf of the corporation. One was to bond them.[93] Another was to pay relatively good wages. "The new rates of wages were assimilated to those paid by various Railroad and Canal Companies in the neighboring region of country," one supervisor explained in 1840, adding that "it is believed, that, they are entirely adequate to the procurement, of the most sober, steady, honest and industrious persons."[94] A third technique was to promise advancement. Clerks, foremen, and tellers were told that they could move up to supervisor or cashier, and enough did so to make the promise credible. Peleg Howland, for example, began working at the Merchants Bank of New Bedford in 1846, at age sixteen. At twenty-one, he became a teller. In 1854, he became assistant cashier and, in 1858, cashier. He remained with the bank until his death, in 1885.[95] Some corporations—most notoriously, the Lowell textile mills—acted paternalistically toward employees, regulating everything from the time they awoke to the food they consumed. In addition to garnering favorable publicity because they were ostensibly preserving the "morals" of the "young of both sexes" who worked in their factories, paternalism mitigated agency problems.[96]

Antebellum Americans took the balances built in to their corporate structures very seriously indeed and used their strong governance provisions to lure foreign investment. "A peculiar value is attached to these provisions in the United States," a group of life-insurance incorporators informed potential British investors in 1836. "It is believed," they explained, "they render it morally certain that the Company will never pass into the management of improper persons. . . . They place it out of the power of speculators and adventurers."[97]

Gaslight engineer John Jeffrey developed a detailed system of governance that allowed him to work for, and invest heavily in, more than a dozen gas companies throughout the South and the Caribbean basin without being physically present most of the year. The rules may have been particularly rigorous in the gas business because any deviation from safety procedures caused "great *danger of explosion.*"[98]

Regulations for Gas Co.

1st. It shall be the duty of the President to make all contracts & authorize all payments; nor shall any payments be made without the special sanction of the President. He shall give all orders for materials required for the carrying on, or extension of the Gasworks. He shall take the general control & supervision of all the Books, accounts & concerns of the Gas Co. & do & perform such other duties as may from time to time be required of him by the Board of Directors.

2nd It shall be the duty of the Board of Directors to carefully examine & check all the cash accounts, statements & exhibits of the other Officers & be held personally responsible for the correctness of the same.

3d It shall be the duty of the Secretary Treasurer & his Clerks, under the directions & control of the President, to keep all the requisite Books, & make out all the accounts of the Company, to receive, collect, & pay out, the cash as authorized by the President retaining proper vouchers therefore. And generally do & perform such other duties as may from time to time be required of him & his clerks by the Board of Directors. The Secretary Treasurer to give bond with approved security to make good any possible deficiency in the cash or other accounts.

4th It shall be the duty of the Engineer-director to visit & superintend all the practical operations of the Gas Works; to instruct & control all the officers & mechanics engaged in the Engineering & Mechanical departments of the Gas Works, & to furnish all plans, reports, estimates & specifications as required by the Board of directors;

& make all requisite maps, surveys &c &c connected with the Gas Works.

5th It shall be the duty of the manager of the Fitting shop, under the instructions of the Engineer, personally to superintend all the affairs of the Fitting shop both in the shop & in the consumers houses; and <u>make returns monthly to the Secretary</u>, showing an account of the time & wages of men employed, & of the pipes chandeliers & other materials used by the Fitting Shop. He shall prove all the new fittings put up, in consumers houses, & see that the same are in proper order, & in size, according to the printed Rules & Regulations adopted by the Company & make returns monthly to the Secretary, showing the numbers & sizes of all Meters & burners put up or discontinued in the city. He shall see that the consumers meters are in proper adjustment & that their indices are correctly taken <u>monthly, & make returns of the same to the Secretary</u>.

6th It shall be the duty of the Inspector, under the instructions of the Engineer, personally to superintend & direct the laying down of Street Main pipes, service pipes, meters & public Lamp pikes <u>& make returns monthly to the Secretary</u> of the time & wages of men employed, & of the piper, & other material, used in said work. He shall also inspect the Public Lamps, & see that the same are kept in proper order & repair, and are lighted & extinguished at the proper hours; and do & perform such other duties in the Street department as the Engineer may from time to time require.

7th It shall be the duty of the superintendent of the Gas Station, under the instructions of the Engineer, to personally superintend & direct the operations of Gas making & extensions at the Gas Station, <u>& make monthly returns to the secretary</u>, showing the time & wages of men employed, & also all material used at the Gas Station. Also to make monthly returns of the Carbonizing account, & of the sales, & receipts, of materials & of the stock on hand at the Gas Station. And do & perform such other duties appertaining to the Gas Station, as may from time to time be required by the Engineer.[99]

The structural balances laid out in Jeffrey's bylaws prevented individual officers from expropriating value from other stakeholders but could not prevent management from acting in concert to steal from stockholders. To keep his interests aligned with those of the stockholders, therefore, Jeffrey took shares in exchange for his services. To mitigate self-dealing by Jeffrey, stockholders exercised effective checks against managerial malfeasance built into the bylaws of the companies in Jeffrey's orbit, such as those of the Covington Gas Light Company:

Bye Laws Covington Gas Light Co.

Every stockholder to have a vote for each share of stock bona fide held by said stockholder which stock shall have been paid in full. . . . Each director to own at least two shares of stock and should any Director cease to be a stockholder his seat at the Board shall in consequence become vacant. . . . Special meetings of the Board may be called by the President or any three Directors or by a majority of the votes of Stockholders, at such other times as may be deemed expedient, written notices being served on the Directors at least one day previous to the Meeting. Special meetings of the stockholders may be called by the same parties, by advertisement in the public newspapers of Covington, written notices being also served on each stockholder at least thirty days before such meeting. [Four directors are needed for a quorum.] Shares of Stock transferable only on the books of the Company. Should it be deemed advisable by a majority of votes of stockholders at any future period to increase the amount of the Capital stock of the Company, then it shall be the privilege of the then Stockholders first to have the option of subscribing for and taking the new stock pro rata to the amount of stock then bona fide held by said stockholders. [The president to] exercise a general control over all the concerns of the Company. All checks and drafts to be signed by the President and countersigned by the Secretary. [The secretary shall on the second Monday in January and July make a] balance sheet statement of the affairs of the Company showing all the business transactions and finances. [Secretary to give bond. Superintendent of works to make monthly returns to the Secretary showing all time worked, wages, carbonizing account, all materials, meter readings, etc.] The Foreman of the Gas Works shall personally assist in the operations of Gas making. All officers and agents of the Company to be appointed by the Board of Directors and removable at their pleasure. [Directors shall also fix salaries.] No alteration or addition to be made to these Bye Laws without the same being submitted and approved at the annual meeting of Stockholders.[100]

Jeffrey's system articulated most of the governance principles common in successful antebellum corporate enterprises, and it appears to have worked everywhere that it was implemented. Where it was not, as in Havana, Cuba, profits were low for a monopoly business, and the relations among managers, workers, stockholders, and customers often turned contentious.

Stockholder Checks

> Frequent stockholders' meetings are necessary in
> order to secure an interchange of opinions and views
> respecting past and future managements, and if
> unsuccessful the opportunity will then be afforded
> to hold the officers to a strict accountability.
> —F. H. Stow, 1859[101]

As noted above, everyone conceded that stockholders were the true owners of the corporations in which they owned stock. That meant that stockholders retained the power to terminate the employment of anyone, from the daily laborer to the president, who did not work to further their goals, typically increasing, if not outright maximizing, profits. "The stockholders have the undoubted right to make" changes in management, admitted the directors and executives of the Canton Company in 1851, "whenever the views of a majority of them are not coincident with those of the Board."[102] When the structural checks mitigating agency costs just discussed proved insufficient, stockholders retained the ability to retake control of their property and place it under new, or even their own, direction, management, and supervision. Brandishing meetings and votes, investigatory committees, and other powerful weapons could induce all but the worst men to toe the stockholders' line.

Today, most corporate elections are decided before they are even held because of the control that management has over proxies. In antebellum America, by contrast, corporate elections could be, and sometimes were, hotly contested affairs because so much was at stake for so many. Joshua Lippincott, for example, questioned the new toll structure of the Schuylkill Navigation Company because it severely hurt the company's receipts and hence Lippincott's income because he had "with my family, a large stake in the institution." With a significant portion of his wealth on the line, Lippincott had "no other wish, motive or desire, by any of my acts, than to promote its permanent interest, and thus to endeavour, by a reformation in its management, to enable it to make dividends to its Stockholders."[103] Even during quiet periods, many local stockholders showed up at meetings. In 1859, twenty-two of the Vicksburg Gas Light's sixty stockholders, representing 1,071 of the company's 1,327 outstanding shares, appeared at the company's annual meeting. Eight of the rest of the company's stockholders were dead, and their shares had not yet legally transferred; so essentially, only thirty shareholders, representing a mere 213 shares, did not appear. Most of those apparently sent in proxies.[104] Distant stockholders were, of course, much more likely to vote by proxy than in person. In 1846, a period when the Canton Company of Baltimore's stock was held mostly in New York and Boston, owners of only 119 shares "personally appeared" while the owners of 4,922 shares "appeared by their proxies."[105]

The election of directors was often noted in newspapers, but ballot totals were rarely reported, even in meeting minutes. Sometimes newspapers indicated that the directors had been elected "unanimously"; usually, no specifics were provided. The few that were recorded often show evidence of pitched battles for control, undoubtedly because controversy brought with it the desire for proper documentation. The bylaws of the Manassas Gap Railroad stipulated that a ballot vote "upon any questions, shall be taken, whenever required by any seven stockholders present" but otherwise could be done by acclamation. To prevent disputes or cheating, that company's bylaws required that an alphabetical list of stockholders and the "number of votes, which each is entitled to, set opposite his or her name, shall be made by the clerk, and laid before the stockholders at each meeting."[106]

Most stockholders today are complacent. If they dislike management, they sell their shares and buy those of another, presumably better-managed, company in the same industry. With fewer investment options to choose from and somewhat higher transaction costs, early Americans, like early Scottish investors, often stood their ground rather than sell out.[107] In 1850, "an opposition ticket was started under an erroneous misrepresentation, that the present directors were in favor of investing the receipts from the sale of the steamer Republic in other packets; but it having been ascertained that they entertained no such views, and, on the contrary, were in favor of a division of the capital among the stockholders, the opposition ceased."[108] Freemen accustomed to getting their way in political elections, one steamboat captain and stockholder explained, were not about to give control of companies to "certain individuals 'in perpetuity.'"[109] Stockholders could proffer their own slates of "proper persons for directors,"[110] which were often heavily laden with merchants even in manufacturing corporations because of their overall wealth and business acumen. In 1796, stockholders in a bank in Baltimore published ten different directors' tickets, some with overlapping candidates, others not.[111] Due to space considerations, newspapers seldom reported the lists, and few stockholders would pay to advertise them but circulated them privately instead.[112]

Even when stockholders merely decided on candidates picked by management, they generally knew much about them. Newspapers sometimes described directorial candidates in detail. In November 1839, the *New York Herald* described one candidate for bank director as "a good farmer; a man of most excellent sense . . . as a practical man, very few superior." Another, Quaker silk merchant Caleb Cope, it called "too venturous in business . . . [and] apt to trade beyond his means."[113]

The voting rights of stockholders were taken very seriously in antebellum America. The initial board of the Hollywood Cemetery in Richmond, Virginia, for example, disbanded because "of the small number of the subscribers present" at the meeting. Board members had to be reelected at a later meeting where subscribers representing fifteen shares appeared and another twenty-eight shares, making "a majority of the whole number that could be given," were represented by proxy.[114] Proxies were votes cast on behalf of an absent stockholder and, at first, were a convenience that increased stockholder participation in corporate elections. In 1816, almost 500 residents of Norfolk, Virginia, gave their proxies to Littleton Tazewell to vote on their behalf in the corporate elections of the Bank of the United States (1816–36). (Proxies were later used by executives to perpetuate their reigns, a point discussed further in Chapter 9.) Early on, stockholders could remove directors at will (they can no longer do so), and proxy fights for control of companies occurred with some regularity. In 1858, Hiram Sibley of Rochester, New York, wrote to Louisville to obtain the proxy of several large stockholders there because a "move" had "lately been made . . . to take the control" of a railroad from "the Board & transfer it to certain parties" in Manhattan. "As the battle now stands," Sibley confided, "the 400 shares might be important."[115]

None of this is to say that shareholders enjoyed anything remotely like "democracy," where the rule almost invariably is one vote per person. As law professor Usha Rodrigues rightly argued, the democracy analogy does not hold because "shareholders are not citizens; their investments are voluntary and relatively liquid, and their proxy ballots lack the meaning and power of citizens' votes."[116] The correct analogy is that of a republic. The members/citizens of corporations and nations need to protect their interests through the use of various institutional checks and balances. The right to vote, in other words, is but one of numerous checks against tyranny and expropriation.

One vote per share (or policy or dollar of insurance in some mutuals) was the most common voting rule in corporations and unincorporated joint-stock companies. Early on, however, a substantial percentage of corporations opted for "prudent mean" voting rules like those championed by Alexander Hamilton. Or, more simply, they followed one vote per share but capped the number of votes that any one shareholder could cast. (The percentages are not reported here because the voting rules for most companies were embedded in their bylaws rather than in their charters and hence are unavailable. That fact, combined with a misreading of common and case law, has led some scholars to argue, erroneously, that most antebellum corporations had one-vote-per-shareholder rules.) Prudent mean and capped rules increased voting power at less than a one-to-one ratio to balance the power of small shareholders with larger ones without going to the other extreme of granting each shareholder one vote.[117]

Economic historian Eric Hilt found that in New York corporations chartered before 1825, prudent mean voting rules were most commonly found where stock ownership was relatively concentrated.[118] If the goal was to increase demand for shares by preventing small holders from selling out (or not investing in the first place), the rules worked because the stock prices of corporations with them were higher than those that allowed one vote per share. Because prudent mean rules could be lawfully circumvented by dividing "stock between transferees, to increase their [voting] power,"[119] prudent mean and capped rules eventually lost their ability to shield minority stockholders. By 1835, corporate critics could claim without cavil that large blockholders (stockholders with many shares) "would override the small stockholders" regardless of the voting rule in place.[120] For that and perhaps other reasons, prudent mean rules petered out within half a century or so, albeit in the uneven fashion typical of American state-level governance, leaving one vote per share alone in the field until twentieth-century innovators created shares with super voting rights (a point discussed further in Chapter 9).[121]

In states such as Maine and Massachusetts, corporations were supposed to keep lists of stockholders so that they could contact one another to discuss corporate affairs. Although such policies may have reduced the stockholders' coordination costs, they created problems of their own. Sometimes stockholders did not want their names published because of privacy and tax concerns. Also, incidents were reported where some banks took revenge on rival banks by declining to make loans to rival stockholders.[122]

As in political governance, voting alone was insufficient to avoid tyranny—specifically, the tyranny of the majority described by de Tocqueville and the joke about the two wolves and one sheep voting on the dinner menu. In 1842, for example, Maryland cast 10,279 votes in favor of accepting an 1841 charter amendment (passed by the same state of Maryland) for the Chesapeake and Ohio Canal. All other stockholders present, representing 5,675 votes, voted no and protested, but to no avail.[123] Voting, however, was sometimes an effective check against potential malfeasance. Individual stockholders held veto power in two instances: when a proposed policy change affected "the right of a stockholder or changes the fundamental and organic purposes"[124] of the corporation; and when a company attempted to do something outside its charter or to borrow more than necessary to conduct its business. "Courts of equity," one judge explained in 1851, "treat such proceedings by a majority, as a fraud upon the other members, which they will neither sanction or permit."[125] Voting rights were strongest when coupled with other rights, including the right to call meetings, to receive timely and accurate information about the corporation's affairs, to pay for shares in installments, and to form investigatory committees.

In addition to annual meetings, which were standard in all but corporations already controlled by rogues, stockholders could call special meetings. For example, sixty or more shareholders in the United States Bank of Pennsylvania who owned a total of 1,000 or more shares could summon the other stockholders to a special meeting if they provided at least six weeks' notice thereof in at least two Philadelphia newspapers.[126] Similarly, the owner or owners of 100 shares in the City of Sonora Tunnel Company in California could call "a general meeting of their body, whenever they may deem such a meeting necessary for the protection of their interests, or for the consideration of important business connected with the Company."[127]

Stockholders actually exercised their special meeting rights with some frequency, though, of course, disgruntled stockholders did not always get their way. In 1804, stockholders who disliked the planned route of the Fourth New Hampshire Turnpike called a special stockholder meeting to discuss the matter, which had already been voted on and approved overwhelmingly by the stockholders. Their concerns were heard, and "several motions were made" to reconsider the route, but "no vote passed concerning them." The meeting adjourned. A month later, another meeting was called to discuss a different part of the planned route.[128] Similarly, "A Stockholder" in 1820 threatened to exert himself "for a total change in the direction as soon as possible" unless the current directors of the Congaree and Santee Steam Boat Company stopped plying routes on Sundays. "This may be lucrative," the stockholder argued, but it was not "conformable to the spirit of our civil laws, or our religious institutions."[129] Sabbatarians who opposed all travel on the Sabbath, except to and from church, rarely defeated Mammon. In 1849, Charles William Ashby complained to government official Joseph Holt that most of the stockholders in the Orange and Alexandria Railroad Company had wanted to stop Sunday train mail routes, but the motion was defeated "by connecting it with other matters entirely irrelevant."[130]

According to Nobel economist Joseph Stiglitz, "market forces do not necessarily lead to full (or efficient) disclosure of information, so there is a good rationale for disclosure requirements."[131] Stiglitz's claim does not jibe with financial history. Early corporations were not legally bound to share information with shareholders but did so, anyway; otherwise, they would not have been able to attract or retain much equity investment. As Albert Gallatin argued and as most contemporaries conceded, "publicity is, in most cases, one of the best checks which can be devised: it inspires confidence, and strengthens credit; whilst concealment begets distrust, and often engenders unjust suspicions."[132] Instead of full public disclosure, as the government attempts to mandate today, early corporations shared information with investors selectively. Selective disclosure allowed them to supply more and better information to those investors that needed it without providing crucial data to competitors.[133]

Instances of selective disclosure abound. In 1828, Littleton Tazewell informed prospective investor Christopher Tompkins that an agent of the James River Steam Boat Company would "shew you their books, and can give you any information you may desire to have in relation to its value and situation."[134] In 1835, the Richmond, Fredericksburg, and Petersburg Railroad opened its journal "to the inspection of the stockholders if they should desire further information as to more minute details."[135] The following year, Blair Bolling was able to visit and view the "different shafts that have been commensed preparatory to raising coal" by the Midlothian Coal Company, "of which," he noted in his diary, "I am a stock holder to a small amount."[136] The 1849 bylaws of the Cleveland Gas Light & Coke Company stipulated that the company's account books be "kept at the Office of said Company subject to the inspection at all reasonable business hours of the Stockholders."[137] When the Mechanics' Bank of New York ran into difficulties with its cashier in 1855, "many stockholders and others called, in apparent alarm, at the bank, to inquire the cause" of the president.[138] Stockbrokers such as Abbott Lawrence also kept regular tabs on corporations for their clients.[139]

Selective information disclosure was a vital right throughout the period. In 1839, twenty-six stockholders asked the directors of the Mohawk and Hudson Railroad Company for a "statement of the income, condition, resources, &c. of the Company . . . at as early a day as may be convenient." They then requested nine specific pieces of information, including annual receipts for passengers and freight, disbursements, cash on hand, assets, liabilities, measures taken "to reduce the expenses of the road," and the condition of the tracks and rolling stock along with "any other information, that you may deem important or useful to Stockholders."[140] In 1846, Thomas W. Ward, an agent for Baring Brothers, commissioned a report on the progress of the Chesapeake and Ohio Canal by William H. Swift and Nathan Hale. According to Swift and Hale, the president and engineer of the canal provided "every assistance in obtaining the necessary information" to write the report and even traveled with the authors "over a great part of the Canal, from Georgetown to Cumberland, including the finished and unfinished parts of it, and also through a part of the mining region near Cumberland" so crucial to the canal's success.[141] Similarly, the annual report of Illinois Central noted that the directors had endeavored "by several publications in the public papers and otherwise, to keep the Stockholders informed, from time to time, during the year past, of the condition and progress of the works of construction."[142] Scholars have subsequently called that railroad's reports "thorough" and a "model" that even current corporations could learn from.[143]

Selective disclosure was not a governance panacea because without other checks and balances in place, directors could simply lie to stockholders or prospective investors for personal gain. When combined with other governance principles—including significant directorial equity ownership (which acted to reduce incentives to talk the company down), ultra vires restraints (which acted to reduce incentives to talk the company up), and legal and social penalties for fraud and lying (which acted to reduce incentives to lie in either direction)—selective disclosure generally provided investors with sufficient, quality information.

To limit the time spent satiating the information needs of individual or small groups of stockholders, corporations soon learned to communicate them quasi-publicly, through circular letters or annual reports. By 1846, the board of directors of the Buck Mountain Coal Company could casually refer to their "customary Annual Communication."[144] That same year, the directors and managers of the Canton Company published an annual report because its stockholders expected them to do so.[145] Around the same time, a tariff advocate noted that "purchasers [of manufacturing shares] know how to discriminate. They have, in truth, all the information that they could desire for doing so. The accounts of the companies cannot be concealed from stockholders, to whom a full annual exhibit is always made. Still less can be concealed from directors."[146] Some reports were largely propaganda pieces but contained valuable information nonetheless. Others walked a fine line between massaging complacency and striking fear in stockholders. Somerville Pinkney walked that line when, as president of the Annapolis and Elk-Ridge Rail Road Company, he informed stockholders that the company had $20,000 in the bank but still had much work to do to complete the line.[147]

Annual reports were often "extensively circulated" and available to "any one who feels an interest in the subject."[148] Even if their circulation was more limited, the mere act of publication opened the information to non-stockholders via word of mouth and newspaper summaries. Most companies lost their early instinct to remain as secretive as possible, coming to believe that protecting future plans was much more important than maintaining secrecy of past performance. "The leading operations of the Company," argued one railroad stockholder in 1849, "can require no veil of mystery—no secrecy—*except the ordinary business caution in respect to prospective movements*. Anything which is done and concluded, may be, and ought to be, freely communicated to all Stockholders, who are the real parties interested in anything adverse or advantageous which occurs."[149] But the secrecy of plans had to be maintained "for reasons too obvious to need comment."[150] "Spreading before the public all the proceedings of a private corporation" another observer noted, was an "obvious impropriety." Publication of "the books of a mere business concern—thus exposing to every eye what should be seen and known only by those interested" should only be done, contemporaries believed, when it benefited the corporation in some way.[151]

Corporations therefore sometimes shared information publicly, especially when they sought to raise capital at home or abroad or when they wished to cultivate positive public sentiment.[152] The directors of the Northern Railroad Company beseeched "the capitalists of our own State [New Hampshire], and of Massachusetts, to come, and survey, and calculate for themselves. We invite inquiry; we solicit comparison," they wailed, trying to prevent "hasty action" that would lead to the creation of one or more competing lines.[153] Similarly, the Manassas Gap Railroad published 500 copies of its charter and bylaws to excite subscriptions.[154] Investors needed to see "a reasonably fair prospect of reliable results" or their "aid will not be granted,"[155] so before offering stock directly to the public, most corporations (and joint-stock associations, whether they planned to obtain a charter or not) published or otherwise promulgated a prospectus laying out their general business plans, their charters and bylaws (when applicable), market conditions, and other information pertinent to prospective investors.[156] The stock commissioners of the Hudson River Rail Road Company delayed their company's DPO "in order to present to the public such statements, based upon good data, in reference to the prospects of the undertaking, and the profits be derived from it, when in operation." They believed that their arguments and their assurance that they held "perfect confidence in the entire success of this highly important work" would "induce a very general subscription to the stock of the company."[157]

Some prospectuses were relatively brief. The Spot Pond Aqueduct Company sent out a one-page circular letter inviting subscriptions and providing basic information about its plan for supplying the water needs of Boston by laying pipes from the 283-acre pond whose name it bore.[158] Most prospectuses were much more detailed. In 1837, the West Virginia Iron Mining Company described its 105,000 acres "situated on the Elk River, in the countries of Nicholas, Kanawha and Braxton" in an area of Virginia that was allegedly "one of the healthiest in the world." The Elk, it claimed, was "a smooth flowing stream, navigable from its mouth almost to its source, thus furnishing through its own and the streams of the Kanawha and Ohio, a natural and uninterrupted channel for the productions of the country to the markets of the west and the world." Furthermore, the tract was "covered with timber of the finest quality and of every variety suited to the purposes of commerce and economy." But, of course, the main attraction was the tract's abundant "deposits of iron, coal, salt and other minerals."[159]

For turnpikes, railroads, and navigation companies, "the population and property of a country" were considered "perhaps the best measure of its transportation" unless actual tonnage traffic was available, as it sometimes was. Hills and mountains raised construction costs for railroads but not necessarily operating costs (at least when the weather was good), as extra energy expended on the ascent was, to a large degree, saved on the descent. In bad weather, however, "the danger of the wheels sliding upon the ice is in proportion to the grade."[160] Prospectuses of turnpikes and railroads also often tried to appeal to local landowners as well as potential capitalists. The New York and Boston Railroad reminded landowners along its route that "experience shows that upon all great lines of communication, the increased value of real estate alone, situated within a short distance of the improvement, on either side, is sufficient, exclusive of other advantages to cover the entire cost of the improvement."[161]

Corporations were also eager to assuage the concerns of stockholders who still owed them money on their stock, as an 1833 episode involving the Ithaca and Owego Railroad amply demonstrated. "Some embarrassments occurred last summer in the financial concerns of the company," the president and directors explained in a pamphlet, "arising from misrepresentations and misconceptions, upon which a few stockholders in New York were induced to refuse payment upon the calls of the company. The President, Treasurer, Secretary and Engineer repaired to New York with the books, maps and vouchers, and made a full and ample exposition of the concerns and affairs of the company, with which those stockholders were satisfied."[162] Beholden to subscribers for additional funds, corporations eagerly supplied them with information, especially with good news. The directors of the Washington Manufacturing Company of North Carolina informed stockholders that the water loom that they had purchased "answers their most sanguine expectations" and that the only thing stopping the company from progressing further was "the negligence of subscribers in paying up their instalments."[163]

Stockholders could owe their corporations money because of the ingenious and almost universal practice of selling scripts, or call (buy) options on shares, instead of full shares during the DPO. The option could also be characterized as a put (sell) because subscribers could essentially return the share to the issuing corporation by refusing to pay additional installments. The process can be traced in detail for some corporations, such as the Louisville Hotel Company, through account books showing the name of the subscribers, the number of shares they subscribed, and the installments they paid.[164]

Scholars traditionally considered the buying of shares on installment to be a form of credit purchase, a common practice in America since the early colonial period. The sale of shares on installment did serve a credit function; but more important was its governance feature. Purchasing shares in a start-up venture was intrinsically risky, as the company could fail to form, perform poorly, or even turn out to be an outright sham. Few could be induced to pay a full twenty-five, fifty, or hundred dollars or more for a share, given such high risks. So corporations instead sought only a small earnest payment on each share and the right to ask for subsequent installments up to each share's par value. In many companies, only when shares were fully paid in did stockholders receive actual stock certificates. Before that, investors held so-called script. Holders could make installments when called for, sell their script in the open market if they needed cash, or, if the company met with difficulties, withhold further payments. By the mid-1850s, incorporators estimated that about 10 percent of subscribers would fail to pay for one reason or another.[165]

The alternatives facing corporations that sought to recover from delinquent stockholders varied over time and place but were rarely strong. In Massachusetts and Connecticut before 1820, corporations could sell the shares of delinquent stockholders only at auction.[166] In Virginia in the mid-1830s, a corporate board directed Edmund F. Wickham to pay the total sum due on his twenty-five shares or else "the board will consider that he does not desire to be a stockholder and will allow the number of shares for which he subscribed to be subscribed by some one else."[167] Later, that same corporation threatened thirteen other shareholders, who had subscribed to a total of sixty-five shares, to pay up or "their shares will be sold." Three shareholders paid, but the others had their shares sold at public auction. The Yadkin Navigation Company went a step further by threatening to sell shares at auction and then to "sue for and recover the balance," though the legal grounds for the latter were shaky at best.[168] A few companies strengthened their leverage by inducing subscribers' to collateralize their installments with their personal bonds.[169]

With the legal deck usually stacked against them, directors were often lenient with delinquents. In 1809, the directors of the Onondaga Gypsum Company "procrastinated the time for the payment" of a fifty-cent-per-share installment for a full year.[170] Despite the Panics of 1837 and 1838, the directors of the Lewis Wharf did not sell the shares of its "delinquent Stockholders" but rather let them pay when they could. All eventually did, except for four shares "held by the executor of an estate."[171] Corporations such as the Concord Bank offered a carrot: interest at 5 or 6 percent to anyone who paid his installments before they fell due; others offered the stick of punitive late charges.[172] The North Branch Canal charged delinquent stockholders 2 percent interest per month and denied them the right to vote in corporate elections.[173] To "restrain projectors from subscribing more shares" in the Bank of Baltimore "than they were able to pay for," the bank's charter stipulated that failure to pay any part of the first installment would lead to "forfeiture of all Rights and title to the share or shares subscribed by" the defaulting party.[174]

In some instances, the corporation or its creditors could legally enforce subscriptions, late charges, and so forth, but subscribers could obtain a release if a substantial change from the original plan, including "an unreasonable delay in carrying on the work," occurred.[175] Such a rule sought to punish delinquents while allowing stockholders with a bona-fide beef to avoid legal liability. Although most corporations managed to enter business with relatively little difficulty, others encountered such difficulties that stockholders felt it best to cease making installments on their shares. In 1850, subscribers only paid enough into the Jersey City and Bergen Point Plank Road Company to build three miles of road, spurring a local newspaper to editorialize, sarcastically, that the road was "destined to be a regular and favorite route of residents of Staten Island to the city of New York."[176] Other corporations suffered early governance breakdowns severe enough to send subscribers scurrying. "Payments are not made on the stock," explained a shareholder in one such concern, and "these resolutions afford reasons why payments are not made. Wise men will not pay, who are not permitted to have a voice in the selection of their agents."[177]

Sometimes calling in subscriptions was slowed when expected aid from the state failed to materialize. The directors of the Columbia Bridge complained that calls on stock subscriptions were difficult to collect "owing to the death and removal of many, the insolvency of others, and the backwardness and reluctance of the rest, as soon as they found that the application to the Legislature [for a capital infusion] had failed. The result was, that of the $123,000, which had been subscribed, only $78,000 was collected." So the directors decided to engage in banking to increase the company's expected profitability. The ploy, though arguably illegal, worked. "The people applauded the design; subscribed nearly the whole capital remaining [$400,000 total]; paid it in."[178] Not all such instances ended so happily. Capitalists "refused to invest" in a railroad through mountainous New England when governments refused to subsidize the route and an attempt to tunnel through an imposing mountain failed. "Some of the original subscribers" decided not to exercise their call option and "have been unwilling, and have refused, to pay the assessments made upon them."[179]

Corporations that were formed to tackle especially risky projects sometimes made the option-like nature of their scripts explicit in order to remove all doubts from investors' minds. In a speculative enterprise to supply a parched Manhattan with New Jersey water via an aqueduct to be constructed under the Hudson River, one company opened "a subscription to the stock so far as to leave the subscribers the choice of taking their shares or not, on the report and estimate being made." By putting up a small sum, the projectors explained, subscribers received "the option of a considerable amount" if the aqueduct proved feasible.[180] Similarly, "A Friend to the Charleston Water Company" claimed that adventurers would be at "liberty . . . to withdraw" if early surveys of available water supplies, elevations, distances, and costs were not to their satisfaction.[181] Similarly, a Boston salt manufacturer promised to call for only one-quarter of the stock price until it proved "that the undertaking . . . yields more than 30 per cent."[182]

The major cost of the installment system was that new corporations were often starved for cash. Known to be slow in making payments to their creditors, corporations suffered from higher costs as contractors learned to include expected payment delays in their bids and overall "procrastination, dissatisfaction, and increased cost" when working on corporate projects. Projects could peter out from a lack of funds, driving directors to beg stockholders for funds. "The time of its completion depends, gentlemen, upon yourselves," directors in a struggling concern told stockholders who were debating whether to sink more funds into a project still months from completion.[183]

Corporations also sometimes made voluntary public disclosures to drum up business. In 1800, the directors of the Massachusetts Mutual Fire Insurance Company "thought proper to lay before the public, its principles, and general state of its funds, to induce all persons owning houses or other buildings within the Commonwealth, to become Members of the same."[184] In 1837, the Pennsylvania Company for Insurance on Lives published a pamphlet announcing new, lower premiums based on "rates of mortality observed among actual insurers and annuitants in Europe and America."[185] A decade later, in an apparent attempt to show the reasonableness of its expenses, the directors of the Brooklyn Female Academy, a for-profit school, published a pamphlet that listed all the school's purchases, down to five-dollar fees for recording deeds and an eight-dollar blackboard.[186] In 1850, the Manassas Gap Railroad printed and distributed 5,000 copies of a leaflet showing the projected prices of shipping goods to Baltimore from Warren, Shenandoah, and Rockingham Counties on their road.[187]

The problem was not, then, the proclivity of corporations to share information but rather the quality of the information that they set forth. Claims could be exaggerated, important details left out, and so forth in order to make the company appear more valuable than it actually was. The Adirondack Iron and Steel Company claimed that it owned "inexhaustible and unrivalled mines of iron ore," claims that were later doubted by "intelligent men . . . induced to examine the subject of these ores for themselves."[188] The Potomac and Alleghany Coal and Iron Manufacturing Company boasted of "extraordinary coal seams, and . . . altogether inexhaustible beds of iron ore."[189] A mining company in California admitted that the value of its shares was "impossible to estimate" but, in the very next sentence, suggested that "at least" $1,000 per share, for shares with a $100 par value, would soon be the going market rate.[190]

Public disclosure improved over time as financial accounting procedures became more sophisticated and audited or sworn statements became more common.[191] So by 1851, the Housatonic Railroad could inform the public with precision that "the balance $19,354.27 is the amount which in consequence of the extraordinary expenses, the net earnings fell short of paying rents, interest and dividend."[192] By that time, corporations could also make cost and revenue estimates based on comparisons with similar businesses. Statements that were not properly audited, however, were so easily gamed as to be less than worthless.[193] One Pennsylvania life insurer advertised a capital of $250,000 when it had only $15,800 actually paid in. Legislators discovered that banks tried to "place themselves in such an attitude as to present the best possible appearance in their annual report." In New York, "it was found that the security which the Legislature supposed would result from compelling an annual report was entirely deceptive" when a bank failed "involving an almost total loss, within a very few weeks after having exhibited a report verified upon oath, showing it to be perfectly solvent."[194]

The value of genuine information was clear to all, so there were incentives to both provide and seek it. By the Civil War, potential or actual stockholders who could not fully understand relatively sophisticated financial statements could look to the press for aid. "How does he get data for this assertion?" asked one newspaper editorialist of claims made by the president of the Pennsylvania Railroad in 1860. The president, he claimed, "seems to have but a low estimate of the mental powers of those who are publicly criticizing his present policy."[195] Investors also sometimes published detailed analyses of why they did or did not subscribe to a particular DPO.[196] "It is calculated," wrote one such analyst in 1830, "that the stock [in the railroad] will yield a dividend of more than 8 per cent (when the work is completed) even though the price of transportation were 50 per cent below the rate allowed by the charter, provided the cost of the work should not exceed one million dollars."[197]

Finally, early corporations provided information about their condition, generally twice a year, in the form of dividends. When directors were honest, dividends broadly represented real corporate earnings.[198] (As discussed in Chapter 5, taxes were not yet a major factor.) Paying dividends out of capital or borrowings was verboten because contemporaries realized that when directors paid "large dividends of more than the actual profits," it had the effect of redistributing the capital to the stockholders and giving "a fictitious value to the stock in market."[199] Not that matters were always clear-cut. Although many charters stipulated that directors were to "cause dividends of the nett [sic] profits of the company,"[200] they did not rigorously define net profits or similar terms such as clear profits, actual profits, or income.[201] Inevitably, tricky questions such as whether the appreciation of securities owned but not sold should be used in dividend calculations cropped up. Some charters made it clear that the company's capital "shall never thereby be impaired" by dividend payments but offered little guidance on gray areas such as dividend smoothing or adequate surpluses.[202] For the most part, contemporaries believed that corporations were "kept in good, sound condition; and, then, dividends are made as far as prudence will admit."[203] Nineteenth-century corporate accounting, however, was biased a bit toward the "sanguine"[204] because it did not handle capital depreciation well.[205]

Corporations sometimes created large surpluses for strategic reasons. The Bank of New York did so in the 1780s to hide its profitability from hostile legislators and cautious stockholders, who might have been exposed to unlimited liability before the bank's incorporation in 1791. The surplus was later used to smooth dividend payments by boosting them when they fell short of the norm, a practice at some other corporations as well.[206] Smoothing somewhat distorted the information contained in the dividend stream, but some stockholders preferred it to "feast" or "famine" and, of course, it could be implemented only so long as the company was profitable on average.[207] After the Panic of 1819, the Farmers Bank of Bucks County continued to pay the large dividends that its stockholders had come to expect, but soon found it necessary to pare back, as it faced a sustained rash of defaults and lawsuit expenses.[208] To reduce the gaming of dividends, some states instituted dividend clawbacks whereby creditors could sue stockholders for any dividends they received that were in excess of actual profits. Nevertheless, malevolent directors who were not closely monitored by stockholders could expropriate wealth from investors by raising dividends (and hence share prices) when business conditions were unfavorable and they wanted to sell, and by lowering dividends (and hence prices) when conditions were propitious and they wanted to buy.[209]

With those caveats, shareholders could rely on dividends and share prices to provide accurate information about their corporations' actual financial standing with less of the noise created by accounting conventions and income taxes today. Dividend reductions or decreases in share price therefore usually spurred a quick response. It was not unusual for disgruntled stockholders to offer the management concrete suggestions, which were sometimes heeded. When the Farmers Bank of Virginia slashed its dividends in response to losses caused by bad loans and employee fraud, the stockholders adopted a resolution at their January 1823 meeting recommending that the bank slash its expenditures by 20 percent. The board decided to cut everyone's salary by that amount rather than to lay off some workers. The total payroll was thereby cut from $10,000 to $8,000 for the cashier, two tellers, two bookkeepers, discount clerk, runner, and porter.[210] In 1842, the Citizens' Bank of Louisiana failed and that October went into state-controlled receivership, at which time "the stockholders . . . ceased to have any share or participation in the management of its affairs." The state intervened on the grounds that it stood as surety on the bank's $7.2 million of foreign bonds. According to a group of shareholders who owned over $4 million in stock, the government's receiver had misapplied "the funds of the institution, to the detriment both of the State and of the bondholders . . . to the extent of nearly half a million of dollars." Among other faults, the receiver was too lenient with delinquent mortgage holders. "The consequences for the Institution and for the State are ruinous," the stockholders noted, "when a mortgage debt is suffered to accumulate beyond the value of the property securing it."[211]

Antebellum Americans did not invent stockholder activism (that honor goes to the Dutch[212]) but often exercised their rights with alacrity. Dividend reductions or rumors of misdeeds could spur stockholders to create formal investigatory committees with broad powers. In one instance, stockholders obtained a charter amendment that allowed them to vote seven wayward directors off the board several months ahead of time and to enlarge the board and its quorum from seven to thirteen and from four to seven, respectively.[213] Other times, investigatory committees were written directly into the bylaws: in 1847, stockholders of the Upper Appomattox Company in Virginia resolved "that a committee of three be appointed at each biennial meeting of the stockholders, whose duty it shall be to ascertain the condition of the improvement and enquire into the management of the same and the manner in which the books and financial affairs of the company are kept" and report to the stockholders on the same.[214]

When stockholders, for whatever reason, found themselves powerless to change corporate policy, they retained the right to sell. "It behoves those, who have already become shareholders," suggested British investment adviser Robert Ward, "to watch with interest the proceedings of the companies in which they are interested, and to take an early opportunity of relieving themselves of their responsibilities, if they find the success of their company is doubtful, and they have no means of arresting its downward course."[215] "No matter how outrageous abuse of the properties," an American commentator chimed in, stockholders could let their displeasure be known in the stock market.[216] Directors, another contemporary noted, could not "control two or three hundred stockholders, so far as to prevent them from putting their shares into the market."[217]

Early investors usually priced shares as they would bonds, treating expected dividends like coupons and discounting accordingly. Share prices were more volatile than bond prices, however, because dividend expectations were malleable. "The gradual rise in its price from par to seven dollars and ten cents per share above par," noted the directors of one railroad, "furnishes strong evidence that in the judgment of the community," the corporation would thrive in the future.[218] Sales, however, would have a negative effect: a decreased stock price or pressure on other stockholders to buy shares. Constant sales had the effect of concentrating the corporation's shares in the hands of fewer stockholders, which often frightened casual investors away, putting further downward pressure on prices. It also created regulatory problems for the few companies whose charters stipulated that the enterprise would lose its corporate privileges if ownership became too concentrated. The West Virginia Iron Mining Company's charter said that whenever 80 percent of the capital stock became concentrated "in the hands of less than five persons, or more than one half of the same shall be and remain in the hands of one person for more than six months, all the corporate powers and privileges granted by the act . . . shall cease."[219] The justice of the market here was complete: those in control had to buy more and more of the corporation or suffer a collapse in its value that would injure their personal net worth and make raising additional corporate capital prohibitively expensive. If the insiders' business policies were profitable, they reaped the rewards; if not, they suffered the loss. When the Sutton Bank failed in 1829, 90 percent of its assets were loans to businesses owned by a single family, the Wilkinsons. But that family also owned 90 percent of the bank's stock.[220]

The net effect of limited liability on governance was ambiguous. On the one hand, it undoubtedly increased the number of investors, the amount invested, and the liquidity of shares, thus improving market-monitoring mechanisms. By shifting much of the risk of bankruptcy onto creditors, it also limited management's ability to borrow in order to engage in risky projects. Unlimited liability allowed managers to expropriate the credit of wealthy stockholders by allowing them to borrow large sums to undertake risky projects or to underwrite profligate practices. The losses could accrue before such activity "is known to the stockholders in general, or perhaps even to the managers themselves." Under limited liability, managers were constrained because the "credit of every corporation" was a function "as it ought to be, [of] the amount of capital paid in, the business it is doing . . . in short, by the character of the corporation." So the ability of limited liability corporations to borrow was limited compared with that of full liability ones, but that provided a salutary check, a point undoubtedly understood by the shareholders who lost their homes because of the failure of the unincorporated Pacific Knitting Company of Manchester, Connecticut, which had $80,000 in liabilities but only $50,000 in capital when it succumbed. If directors wanted to borrow, they could still do so by becoming "personally responsible for loans or purchases; but the advantage would be that they would know precisely what their obligations were, and could not have their estates put in peril without being aware of it."[221]

On the other hand, as Adam Smith noted, limited liability tended to render stockholders torpid, unwilling to monitor management closely enough to mitigate even significant agency problems. And portfolio diversification meant that stockholder losses would be relatively small compared with their net worth, thus decreasing their incentive to monitor the executives of the many corporations in which they invested.[222]

Stockholders were not the only stakeholders with incentive to monitor corporations. Customers and creditors, including bondholders, depositors, and debt guarantors, also had incentive and were, in the words of political scientist Gerald Berk, "hardly as 'passive' as the conventional wisdom suggests."[223] When they encountered activities or products that ran counter to their interests, customers could complain to corporate stockholders, directors, supervisors, or employees directly, either privately or publicly, or they could vote with their feet and purchase elsewhere. "We call the attention of the Canal Company to the great inconvenience, and real danger of the bridge at Roebling's Mill," wrote some concerned citizens of Trenton, New Jersey, to a local newspaper in 1860. The bridge was old and provided "no accommodations for foot-passengers whatever, though hundreds have to cross it every day," including "scores" of children who ran "the risk of being jammed by the wagons or thrown into the canal. . . . We trust," they closed, "the Company will heed their complaints."[224] The ability to complain publicly could be gamed to some extent, however, as when published complaints were authored by competitors and not bona-fide stakeholders.[225]

In a period when deposit insurance was rare, depositors, especially larger and more sophisticated ones, kept close watch on their banks and withdrew their funds at signs of trouble. The Merchants Bank of New Bedford, for example, pulled its deposits out of the Chemical Bank and put them into another New York bank after the Chemical could not satisfactorily answer questions about the condition of its balance sheet.[226]

Bondholders and the holders of preferred shares, a hybrid debt-equity instrument that promised a guaranteed dividend senior to (paid before) that of common shareholders, were typically more passive than stockholders but sprang into action if an interest or guaranteed dividend payment was missed. Common stockholders were sometimes preferred shareholders or bondholders, too, which only increased their incentive to monitor management. In at least one instance, an investigatory committee was composed of stockholders who were also bondholders because instead of calling in more of the subscribed capital stock, directors of the Troy Turnpike and Rail Road asked stockholders for a loan and they complied.[227]

When they were not the same group of people, stockholders and bondholders often found their interests at odds: the latter wanted interest paid punctually and nothing more; the former typically desired profit growth. To limit conflicts of interest between stock- and bondholders, railroad industry pundit F. H. Stow recommended converting bonds into equity whenever possible.[228] Conversion also reduced the risk of insolvency by decreasing the corporation's debt burden. In 1835, the Philadelphia and Reading Railroad Company commenced building a double track from the company's specially designed wharves on the Delaware River to Mount Carbon, ninety-four miles up the Schuylkill valley, primarily to bring coal to market. The high interest rates and depressed economic conditions of the late 1830s and early 1840s, however, hurt the company's financial position. Its progress "greatly retarded by pecuniary embarrassments" and "discouraging sacrifices," the company took on debt "to a great amount" while making only slow progress constructing the line. By the mid-1840s, stock- and bondholders in New York and Boston had had enough and commissioned a committee of consultants "having no interest whatever in the property" to make "an accurate and detailed statement" of the company's "financial condition and of its resources." Before the committee could report formally, the managers, who "showed at all times, a disposition to promote a free and full inquiry," greatly improved the company's condition by converting $1.1 million of the company's bonds into equity. With the help of higher rail rates and increased traffic, they also purchased needed equipment and paid down additional debt. The securities holders must have been pleased to learn that signs of managerial malfeasance were few and that "the track both in line and surface is superior to the roads generally in the Middle States, and compares favorably with those in the Eastern States." Given increased demand for coal, the company's prospects, while not bright, were not dire, provided that management could keep costs down and refinance its debts on more propitious terms.[229]

Chapter 7

Governance Failures

> Persons disposed to use [corporations] as mere engines of speculation,
> are generally without pecuniary means of obtaining the control of healthy
> and well-conducted establishments. They have sometimes seized upon
> the scattered remains of some ruined project, and after raising it to a
> temporary consequence by a legerdemain peculiar to themselves, gathered
> the fruit of a short-lived imposition upon public credulity.
> —Report of the Committee on Banks and Insurance Companies, 1826[1]

Chapter 6 explored how and why most early corporations were able to mitigate the principal-agent problem that their critics believed would overwhelm
them—or, in the words of a contemporary board of directors, how corporations were able "to promote the permanence, value and usefulness of the
work, a reduction of excessive charges and prohibition of all unnecessary expenses, and an economical, systematic and efficient organization of the su-
perintendance of and management of the same."[2] When the principles of
governance were properly applied, the interests of employees, supervisors,
officers, and directors (or managers or trustees) were closely aligned with
those of stockholders and other securities holders. Various structural checks,
including stockholder voting rights and investigatory committees, as well as
structural balances, from carefully designed charters to bylaws to board regulations, kept them aligned.[3]

This chapter, by contrast, explores how and why governance principles
sometimes broke down and what happened when they did. The first section
explores breakdowns in management (directors and/or officers) that led to
inefficiency or waste sufficient to palpably injure corporate profitability or

sustainability.[4] The second section examines governance breakdowns severe enough to allow management to bilk stockholders or other stakeholders directly.[5] The first section is basically about incompetence and the second about fraud, but one often led to the other.[6] As a contemporary noted, manufacturers failed because of excessive leverage brought about by "a fall in the price of manufactured articles; an improvident expenditure which renders the cost of the manufactured article higher than it can be sold for; losses by the failure of agents and factors, or other persons indebted to them; a fraudulent division of the property among the stockholders."[7]

What will not be considered here are outright scams and flimflams. Although most often associated with the late nineteenth and early twentieth centuries because of books such as *Grafters of America*, sundry swindlers also inhabited antebellum America. It was easy to set up in business as, say, a liveryman, work hard and honestly for a few weeks, gain credit, and then abscond westward with as many horses, banknotes, and other property as one could handle. Such scams were common but relatively small. Corporate frauds, although relatively rare in America (as in Britain), were typically for large sums and hence somewhat economically and politically destabilizing even when perpetrated by outright criminals such as Frederick Hoffman, who was apprehended in upstate New York in July 1860 for forging two checks and overissuing at least $150,000 worth of stock in the Pacific Steamboat Company.[8]

Mismanagement

> Much, very much, of the success of joint-stock
> undertakings depends upon their management.
> —Robert Ward, 1865[9]

Investment guru Robert Ward pointed out that many corporations "fail simply from mismanagement, or rather from want of management at all."[10] Management was still an emerging amalgam of art and science in the nineteenth century, but many modern practices were known, at least by some. Proliferation of best practices was glacial at times because of the lack of management-specific education and relatively slow and expensive information-diffusion technologies. Books were expensive in real terms. Some primers on accounting were available, but few books were devoted to general management issues, leaving many business leaders reliant on classical learning and gut instincts—at times, an ugly combination, especially in more technical endeavors such as insurance and accounting. Many early life-insurance officers were "totally ignorant of the whole science of Life Insurance," at least from the perspective of trained actuaries.[11] "Accountants are bewildered in their endeavours to find in what consisted, and what has become of the capital" of failed companies, another contemporary noted.[12]

Given that context, we should perhaps be surprised at how good early management could be rather than how bad it sometimes was. As Mohandas Gandhi once pointed out, history tends to skew toward catastrophes and wars because they leave more evidence in the historical record and are more interesting than quotidian activities. Similarly, more books tend to get written about business failures and frauds than about successes such as the Boston Manufacturing Company during its well-managed heyday. Or the Baltimore and Susquehanna Rail Road Company, which reported to stockholders in 1835 that "notwithstanding the limited extent of our rail road, and the consequent small amount of transportation furnished at the points at which it has arrived, yet by the skilful and prudent management of its general operations, and the strictest economy in the application of its resources, it has yielded enough, not only to meet all its expenses, but to defray the cost of some valuable improvements lately made, and to liquidate a considerable portion of the debt which had been contracted in its construction."[13]

Similarly, the Manchester Cotton and Wool Company (chartered March 1832) received authorization from the Virginia legislature to raise up to $100,000 in equity capital by selling shares with a par value of $100 each. Its five directors were selected under a one-vote-per-share rule, with no cap. By June 1835, the company was already selling cotton yarns that it produced at its new factory, which was filled with "machinery of the most approved construction" and staffed by "superintendents and assistants every way qualified for the business" enticed away from cotton factories in the North. In 1836, the legislature authorized an increase in the company's capital to $250,000. In March 1838, the company offered an additional $100,000 of its stock for sale, apparently to help it expand its line of offerings, and gave its current stockholders first dibs. In 1846, the legislature extended the company's charter and reiterated that it could raise its capital to $250,000, which it successfully did at some point.[14]

No company thrives all the time, however. The Manchester Cotton and Wool Company survived the Civil War but almost succumbed during the decade leading up to it. In November 1855, a quorum did not appear for the annual stockholder meeting. The rump stockholders nevertheless created a committee to examine the company's condition and report "whether the Factory had best be sold, the administration changed, or what had best be done under all the circumstances." The committee reported a month later that the early 1850s had been "perhaps the worst ever known to the Cotton Spinners of the United States" and the losses "were shared in full measure by your Company." From the beginning of 1852 until the middle of 1855, the company had regained profitability. In the second half of 1855, trouble struck again because raw cotton prices soared while prices of items manufactured from cotton held firm, rendering losses almost certain.[15]

Despite those market setbacks, the company was ahead almost $11,000 since the start of the decade. Moreover, it had successfully repaired and improved its mill. "The improvements, which are particularly striking in the carding and spinning departments, (being of all the most important,) are very judicious," the committee reported. "The character of the work is now better, more of it can be turned off even at less cost than heretofore," it continued, and "the new machinery being so constructed as to turn off better work and more of it with fewer operatives." Finally, the committee reported that the company was only about $19,000 in debt and had a skilled agent in Richmond ready to work full-time on behalf of its interests. The stockholders voted to stick it out, in part because the $206,527.89 spent on cotton machinery could not be recouped easily, as there was no known market for second-hand machinery at that time.[16]

The Canton Company of Baltimore was another management success story, a real-estate improvement company at first run by "wily and designing stock-jobbers" who paid exaggerated dividends to run up share prices. After the stock fell far below par, locals bought up the shares and installed a president and directors who resisted "any measures, the object, design or effect of which would be to inflate, or depress the price of the stock in the market, to the prejudice and injury of its permanent and *bona fide* holders." The company's revenues steadily increased, as did its stock price, which, by 1855, had bounced off an all-time low of $47 to hit $104. The company made it through the Civil War, a tumultuous time indeed in Baltimore's history, in a "wholesome and satisfactory" condition.[17]

The managers of the Buck Mountain Coal Company also managed to reverse misfortune. With $40,000 of debt pressing upon them, they placed the company's "Mines and Machinery in such a condition as would allow them to be worked with true economy, and to deliver the wealth of the Company at a point where it could be rendered available as the means of removing incumbrance and eventually of remunerating for outlay made."[18]

Numerous other examples of good management could be adduced as well. The work of Alfred Chandler to the contrary notwithstanding, good management practices did not arise sui generis from large railroads but rather evolved over centuries of creeping industrialization. Some supervisors were astute enough to understand that what mattered most was worker productivity, or output divided by the wage, not just the wage level. Amasa Morton put it this way when discussing a particularly good steamship captain: "His judgment and services are something like a Lawyer who has studied and toiled a long time to inform himself; and although the charge for advice sounds high, still if you see how much time he has spent to get the information, the charges are moderate." Because of his high competence, the good captain's boat always had "on an average nearly double the number of passengers to the other boats."[19] Many of the better manufacturers, like the Pepperell, paid bonuses to supervisors who kept costs down while meeting production quotas.[20] Some corporate leaders tried to reduce agency problems with contractors and other nonemployee agents by offering rewards for good work. The Chesapeake and Ohio Canal offered prizes worth between $10 and $50 to the contractors who built the best constructed locks, culverts, and other canal works.[21]

Although imbued with the racist attitudes of the era, the management of the Panama Railroad well understood the advantages and disadvantages of laborers from different countries. Irish laborers, they believed, "perform a fair amount of work" before their six-month tours ended. Chinese laborers (coolies) were "at first feeble and inefficient, but being steady workmen, temperate, and but little affected by the climate, as they become accustomed to the use of the tools, and acquire strength from regular and wholesome food, they make useful workmen." The natives were generally "elastic" and "hardy" and "the most efficient common laborers" because they were, "excepting the Coolies, the most economical."[22] Other corporate managers carefully weighed the costs and benefits of free versus slave labor. "Slave labour is usually cheaper than free," one group concluded, but only if adequate financing for their upfront costs could be secured.[23]

Some managers were equally adroit at analyzing the strengths and weaknesses of individual employees. In 1855, W. D. Reid wrote Norvin Green that in their company's New Orleans telegraph office, "the operators are all constantly at their posts & seem to be industrious & capable." One of the managers, one Baker, was "just the man" whom Reid and Green "took him to be. He is constantly at his post, has our interests at heart, and will always account for the last dollar he receives." Baker, however, lacked "decision and an enlarged business capacity . . . a not minor" objection in Reid's estimation, given the importance of the New Orleans office. The manager of that office, Reid argued, should have the ability and power to identify and discharge any weak operators anywhere along the line to Vicksburg, but Baker was "not the man to exercise this sort of function." Another important employee was an Anglo-French man who spoke "both languages fluently" and was "favorably . . . known," though more for his humor and drinking than his skill. Yet he was far superior to Tanner, a "worthless . . . fellow" who was "worn out," and his sidekick Dorris.[24]

Antebellum America suffered from a dearth of good engineers, but some were remarkably astute. Gaslight engineer John Jeffrey, for example, understood his business from raw material through delivery so thoroughly that he was able to establish and maintain the profitability of numerous gasworks throughout the U.S. South, Mexico, and Cuba. (There was quite a surprising amount of U.S. business interest in the Caribbean basin in the 1840s and 1850s.) He preferred gasifying coal, at prices up to $30 per ton, over rosin or oil because the former produced salable by-products, including coke and coal tar, while the latter produced only pollution.[25]

Many corporate managers also showed that they could learn from mistakes, including steamboat, powder-mill, and iron-mill explosions, as well as train crashes.[26] According to Thomas G. Cary, most mill managers were men in the last twenty years of their careers, with "long experience in commerce on an extensive scale, and to whom the management of important affairs is nothing new."[27] According to another contemporary, life-insurance officers also showed that they could "correct themselves in any error they may have made; they are not blind to their own experience, but they profit by it."[28]

Most early managers were capable of doing cost-benefit analyses[29] but were sometimes too sanguine, overestimating revenues and underestimating costs. Some implemented more sophisticated concepts such as net present value, although, of course, they did not use modern terminology. In 1847, the president of the Baltimore and Ohio Railroad argued in favor of a southern route because "the northern route leaves us with little prospect of return before the final completion of the road" while the southern would "insure us a large amount of trade and travel" sooner and an "immediate return upon our capital" because it would wend through coal country.[30]

Some early corporations even used derivatives, especially forward contracts. The Illinois Central saved a substantial sum when it contracted for cars and locomotives "of superior quality" before a "large advance in prices of labor and materials used in their construction" considerably raised their spot prices. (The manufacturer suffered somewhat from the deal as matters worked out; but by agreeing to the long-term contract, it had successfully hedged against a price decline.) At the same time, the Illinois Central constructed fewer miles of track than planned because its management had not foreseen "the great demand for labor on other public works and its consequent scarcity."[31] Similarly, the too-numerous managers of a rich vein of lead wasted $73,100 on smelting works that they subsequently abandoned and on imprudently long-term contracts for materials and hauling. They "could not have done things worse," a contemporary critic argued. "They seemed to try to sink all the money they could, and blamed the mine for what they themselves were to blame."[32]

Some mismanagement was rooted in the principal-agent problem at the heart of the corporate form. "I have lost my confidence in Factory Stocks as I have become more familiar with them & have seen how some of the best of them are managed," Patrick Jackson wrote Francis Cabot Lowell in 1856. "There must someday be a terrible reckoning. I do not believe the business can be permanently prosperous 'till it is managed as a man would manage his private business."[33] Many episodes of mismanagement were simply failures to do the basics—to "block and tackle," in more recent jargon. Supervisors for Pennsylvania Central Railroad Company, for example, failed to sufficiently monitor the company's conductors, who began pilfering cash fares and reselling tickets that they had neglected to punch "cancel." The wayward conductors were caught when one of them paid $12,000 in cash for a new house while another, with a salary of $750 per year and no other visible sources of income, rented fancy digs at $800 per year. Before their capture, a ticket seller and seventeen conductors managed to scam $170,000.[34]

Other instances of mismanagement were due to the intrinsic difficulty of managing large, complex organizations in a competitive environment. Consider the travails of a steamboat company, as reported in the press: "The Troubles of the Great Eastern seem to have no end. The directors are scarcely out of one danger before they are plunged into another. A fatality awaits the company at every stage of their proceedings. But some of the difficulties are to be traced to indecision at the Board, springing from difference of opinion as to the equipment of the ship and her destination. . . . In the management of such an expensive ship, well matured plans are indispensable. . . . Want of capital may very probably upset all the calculations of the managers; but . . . change of views, and not monetary tightness, has led to the prospect of litigation."[35]

Banks were especially prone to mismanagement. Albert Gallatin concluded that the Bank of the United States (1791–1811) had been "wisely and skilfully managed"[36] and that despite some early difficulties at its Baltimore branch, "the character of the president and directors of the Bank of the United States [1816–36] was as irreproachable, as that of the directors and officers of any of the banking institutions of New York."[37] Other early banks were run so recklessly that they were borderline fraudulent. According to Gallatin, many country banks were "improperly administered" and failed "for want of experience."[38] A bookkeeper in one badly managed bank claimed that he had not informed the president about the cashier's questionable practices because he had not wanted to make "difficulty."[39]

The use of stock notes was particularly dangerous. A stock note was created when a stockholder borrowed back the par amount of his stock, which was usually pledged as collateral for the loan. Such an arrangement could be legitimate but could also be used to make an institution look better-capitalized than it actually was. The practice was so widespread in Ohio by the 1820s that its governor was prompted to remind everyone that to "insure the solvency of a bank, its stockholders should be lenders and not borrowers of its money."[40] Although a solid principle, the governor's admonition was a foreign concept to many early bankers, including William Wright, president of the Columbia Bridge Company of Pennsylvania, which was both a bridge and an illegal bank. With the knowledge of the bridge's board, Wright borrowed from its bank as treasurer of the Wrightsville Canal Company, a partnership that included a second director on the Columbia Bridge's board. Several partners in the canal partnership defaulted, but Wright posted collateral for the whole and "only asked for indulgence," to wit, more time to pay.[41] Similarly, the Manual Labor Bank of Philadelphia failed before it incorporated. Headed by T. W. Dyott, the institution was ostensibly a savings bank but issued notes curiously similar to those of commercial banks before it failed after a short and volatile existence, apparently predicated on bad banking practices.[42]

When the Bank of Columbia failed in 1829, the state of New York initially attributed it to "fraud, neglect or mismanagement of some or all of its officers and agents."[43] A court case and legislative investigation eventually revealed that the bank's failure was due "not to any recent mismanagement of its concerns" but rather to the impairment of its capital in 1813. The bank stayed in business because it was able to borrow $150,000 for fifteen years on the personal responsibility of the directors. Unable to service the loan and rebuild its capital, it finally succumbed.[44] The Citizens' Bank of Louisiana was said to be "one of the strongest in the Union," until its government-appointed directors placed it "in such a position as to forfeit its charter" and put it into liquidation. "Great as the mismanagement of the Bank has been," however, many stockholders believed that if properly liquidated, the bank's assets should have covered its debts entirely.[45]

Many troubled banks simply lent too much money to too few people. It seemed that the directors of the Bank of Middlebury (chartered in 1831 at $60,000) "judiciously and safely managed" their little Vermont Bank, until it became known that they had lent large sums, relative to their capital, to the Rutland and Burlington Railroad Company and two other corporations. When those big borrowers defaulted, the bank teetered on the edge but ultimately regained its footing by calling on stockholders for another installment of capital. It clung to life long enough to become a national bank in 1865.[46] In 1822, a bookkeeper in the Bank of the Northern Liberties allowed three companies, including one he owned with his brother, to overdraw their accounts by over $284,000. The run that ensued was stopped only because of the timely aid afforded by other Philadelphia banks. The following year, the bank stopped paying dividends, wrote down its capital by $100,000, and replaced its cashier. It rebounded quickly, paying a small dividend in November 1823. After the episode, it received the nickname "Old Plug Top" because the harder the knocks it received, the firmer it stood. The bank was still in operation at its centenary.[47]

Other banks were not so plucky. In 1825, the Eagle Bank of New Haven failed after the Hinsdales of Middletown defaulted on a loan thought to be in excess of $600,000. Although the bank's president was also mayor of the city, the bank's notes immediately sank to thirty to forty cents on the dollar.[48] In some cases, mere mismanagement gave way to governance failure. In 1847, the Lancaster Bank fell under the sway of its new president, David Longenecker, and new cashier, Benjamin C. Bachman. The pair immediately began discounting their own promissory notes. They listed the notes in the minutes but never mentioned them out loud, thus giving the appearance that they had been approved by the board. By the time the bank failed in 1856, the dastardly duo had borrowed $565,833. In this instance, the bank's stockholders and directors had clearly fallen asleep at the switch.[49]

They were not the only ones. In the 1850s, the president and stockholders of the Ontario Bank in New York were imposed upon by their cashier, who overdrew accounts, falsified records, intercepted letters, and apparently paid his subordinates to look the other way. Once a tight-knit band consisting largely of the incorporators and their associates, over time the stockholder base evolved and widened to include numerous widows and the denizens of distant states, including California, and even Europe. In the end, the receiver was able to pay stockholders only 5 percent of the par value of their shares.[50]

As noted above, Gallatin believed that the Bank of the United States (1816–36) was governed by honorable men and that, for the most part, its structural checks and balances mitigated fraud. The major exception, a scandal at the Baltimore branch, proved the rule. Philadelphia merchant Stephen Girard was the second Bank's largest shareholder; but because of the institution's prudent mean voting rule, he did not have as much influence as Baltimore merchant George Williams, who gamed the system brilliantly by purchasing 1,172 shares in 1,172 different names and then assigning himself power of attorney over them all. As a direct result, the second Bank was led at first by a bankrupt drunkard named William Jones instead of a prudent and experienced banker. Jones believed in lending early and often, and most loans ended up in the hands of cronies and stock speculators bent on puffing up the stock price through "dashing intrepidity and unblushing confidence." Jones was ousted in January 1819 but not before he allowed directors to circumvent various charter restrictions and not before the cashier of the Baltimore branch managed to pilfer a couple hundred thousand dollars by making bad loans to his friends without the consent of the board.[51]

After Andrew Jackson vetoed the federal bill that would have rechartered the second Bank, the situation changed dramatically. Within a few years, its successor, the Pennsylvania-chartered United States Bank, proved a titanic failure. Many foreign stockholders thought the new institution a renewal of the second Bank, "and almost all of them gave their power of acting" to Nicholas Biddle, "a circumstance that proved particularly unfortunate in the end." (Those who preferred their capital back after the dissolution of the federal bank "obtained it readily, and more, by selling their shares to others.") "Intoxicated with a supposed omnipotence in banking," Biddle tried to informally re-create the second Bank by buying small banks in other states to serve as quasi-branches of the Philadelphia-based institution. "He found competitors every where," however, so "his intentions were defeated" and he "began to feel the want of those exclusive privileges, throughout the Union" that the second Bank "had previously enjoyed." In response, he employed "a

great deal of money in a kind of loans, for which banks were never designed—
long loans to states, and to incorporated companies," including Southern railroads, a direct violation of the bank's charter. Unfortunately, Biddle "overrated
his own sagacity and ability" and, "clothed with power from the distant stockholders," shut down "any of the directors" who "were disposed to interfere."
Matters worsened after some "independent" directors "resigned, or were displaced."[52] "If the stockholders in Europe," one contemporary argued, "had occasionally sent sensible men to look after their affairs, and to see how things
were managed," the bank would not have failed. Just as important as stockholder apathy, however, was the breakdown in the United States Bank's governance structure. Unlike the second Bank, which distributed its capital
among numerous branches, each with its own president and directors, the
United States Bank put its entire capital under Biddle's control alone. In the
words of a contemporary, "those wholesome checks were removed which had
previously existed in the various boards of directors attached to the several
branches, who watched *him* as he did them."[53]

Unprincipled Governance

> Every instance, without exception, which has yet
> occurred, of a bankrupt Bank, has grown out of the
> overweening confidence of stockholders in some
> one individual, who had the address to insinuate
> himself into their favor, and by obtaining an
> ascendancy in its councils, and control over its
> funds, then use the Bank, to its deep injury, or
> destruction.
>
> —*Charles Sigourney, 1837*[54]

As the United States Bank episode and the epigraph to this section suggest,
governance failures can always ultimately be blamed upon gullible or lazy
stockholders who failed to monitor directors, presidents, or corporate officers. Contemporary observers often complained that stockholders in large
corporations, such as railroads, did not "meet often enough to inform themselves of the acts of their directors." A more constructive approach is to analyze the circumstances in which stockholders were more likely to take an
active interest in the (mis)use of their property.[55]

Stockholders did not want management to destroy the value of their shares, but none could afford to monitor a corporation's affairs intensively. That was one reason that investors purchased shares instead of directly engaging in finance, manufacturing, or transportation themselves. Basically, they relied on governance principles (described in Chapter 6) to safeguard their property. What they needed to watch out for, then, were not specific instances of peculation or other agency problems but for gaps in, or erosion of, governance principles. Some did not understand that, however, and others were not sufficiently incentivized to search out and mend the holes that inevitably appeared in the numerous checks and balances devised to prevent peculation.

Stockholder monitoring was at its best when directors as well as major shareholders were locals, as they were in many community banks, such as the Concord Bank and the Merchants Bank of New Bedford. Locals were most likely to show up at stockholder meetings and could keep an eye on corporate affairs inexpensively by simply observing its condition and actions. Small, local, or related groups of stockholders found it relatively easy to communicate and coordinate with one another. Many believed, however, that share ownership should be spread as widely as possible. Offerings of stock, therefore, should be public and not private placements among a few cronies. Secret lists of "particular friends" smacked of political corruption and favoritism and did nothing to quiet fears of "monopoly" and special privilege, especially if scripts (the options to buy full shares, discussed in Chapter 6) began trading above par. Many early Americans believed that a closed subscription would lead to the election and perpetuation of a small coterie of directors in office, a bad omen for quality governance.[56]

In at least one case, the Mohawk Bank of Schenectady, New York (chartered in 1807 at $200,000), a flawed DPO was said to have caused later governance problems. In 1814, a group seeking to establish a second bank in Schenectady convinced a legislative committee "that in the apportionment of the said capital stock among the subscribers thereto, difficulties arose from the vague and indefinite powers with which the commissioners named in the act of incorporation were vested, and the unsatisfactory manner in which those powers were exercised." Those unspecified difficulties "produced others in relation to [the Mohawk Bank's] management and control, seriously affecting the peace and harmony of the great body of the people in the county of Schenectady and its vicinity."[57]

Early insurance expert Harvey Tuckett agreed that relatively widespread stockholder ownership was best. "For the security of the insured," he argued in his 1850 treatise, "the capital stock of a Life Insurance company should consist of a large number of shares of small amount . . . and the extreme number of shares in any person's hands should be limited." A capital of $2 million divided into 40,000 shares of twenty-five dollars each and capped at 100 shares per investor, he suggested, would ensure rapid compliance to capital calls and "effectually prevent . . . a body of fourteen or fifteen persons, in whose hands a majority of a small stock—already eaten up by expenses—may be vested, from having an entire control over the affairs, and in operation rendering it a private institution with corporate powers and limited liability."[58] Virginia believed so strongly in widening the base of stockholders that its corporation code stipulated that when a DPO was oversubscribed, the stock commissioners "shall reduce the subscriptions . . . deducting the excess from the largest subscriptions in such manner, that no subscription shall be reduced while any one remains larger."[59] In many states, including New York and New Jersey, some corporate charters mandated that shares be sold in certain geographical areas or to certain occupational groups. Massachusetts allowed manufacturing corporations to issue shares with a par value of $1,000 each to small, close-knit groups such as the so-called Boston Associates but sometimes limited the number of shares that any one person could own, as was the case with the Essex Mill in 1822.[60]

Widespread stock ownership also bolstered the corporation's political base. By widely disseminating its shares throughout western New York, the proponents of the Western District Bank argued, "all would have a common interest in supporting the credit of the bank and its benefits and accommodations would be extended to all."[61] The directors of a New York to California steamship line purposely sought "to obtain as many shareholders as possible" in California "to identify this enterprise more fully with the vital interests" of the new state.[62] Interstate projects also required widespread subscription, if only to reassure investors in one state that, if necessary, they could garner political support in the other state(s). The New York and Boston Railroad, for example, tried hard to induce citizens of Connecticut to buy shares "as a guarantee for the proper management of the work, and security against unjust and partial legislation in regard to it."[63]

"Whatever precaution may be exercised in placing charters in safe hands," some contemporaries realized, "the stock being transferable, may pass into the possession of persons irresponsible in character or property."[64] More damning yet, as shareholders became more numerous and more widely dispersed, their monitoring, communication, and collaboration costs soared, as did the urge to free ride on the diligence of other stockholders. Maryland legislators, for example, feared that a corporation "under the direction of so many persons, each having a slight interest, would be very badly managed" because most stockholders could not be bothered to attend meetings.[65] "The Meeting of the Stockholders of the CITIZENS BANK," in March 1847, for example, "was very thinly attended."[66]

The legislators' concerns were not misplaced, as collaboration costs could quickly become prohibitively high. In October 1859, for example, stockholders in Virginia's Richmond and Danville Railroad scrambled to prevent management from building yet more lines instead of concentrating on improving the profitability of the existing ones. In a letter to William Dickinson, Asa Dickinson noted that another stockholder, L. E. Harris, had written to urge him to ask "the country stockholders" in the railroad to either attend the next stockholder meeting in person or to give their proxies to Harris. Dickinson agreed because he believed that if "the company is to be a Dividend paying concern, it is a matter of some importance to private stockholders to have their interest taken care of. I as one of its stockholders want all the Dividends that I am entitled to, and am unwilling to expend mine, to build roads elsewhere." If the directors wanted more roads, he exclaimed, let them invest "*their own* money in them." Tellingly, Asa wrote William, apparently his kinsman, because he did not "know what stockholders are in your neighborhood except yourself."[67]

Good governance could still be observed in widely held corporations but only if a few large stockholders had much of their net worth on the line or if the corporation's shares were frequently traded in the stock market. In the former case, the large stockholders had ample incentives to monitor their investments carefully. In the latter, the decisions of many investors could discipline management by decreasing the stock price, as described in Chapter 6. Having more shareholders typically increased liquidity and thereby made securities markets more efficient and less susceptible to market operators like those who had infected British securities markets in the 1690s.[68]

Although technologically less sophisticated than today, early securities markets were fairly efficient, in part because they allowed insider trading.[69] Those with quality information drove prices toward their fundamental values by buying when prospects were good and selling when they were not.[70] Under that system, securities prices were certainly subject to manipulation attempts; successful ones perpetrated by the likes of Daniel Drew and Jay Gould are legendary. Rumors of such attempts, however, undoubtedly outnumbered actual, successful machinations. Directors in the Manhattan Bank, for example, were accused of inducing policymakers to allow petitions for new banks to gain ground so that they could speculate on price fluctuations.[71] Few such schemes appear to have succeeded, at least for very long. Before the Civil War, most directors were "unwilling to incur the imputation of puffing" up the value of their shares by spreading false rumors, but some were not above bashing rivals. Rather than "suffering their property to be unjustly depreciated in public estimation," the rivals responded, often touching off pamphlet wars to "expose . . . fallacies . . . [and] jealousy . . . [and] biased . . . judgment."[72] The net effect of such battles on stock prices, it appears, was negligible. As in seventeenth-century Amsterdam's stock market, the bulls and the bears generally canceled each other out. As Thomas G. Cary noted in 1845, "the market price . . . is the true indication of the value of the share. Fifty men, at least, stand ready to buy or sell as any advantage is to be gained either way. Their calculations are founded upon an exact knowledge of fundamentals like 'the stock of goods unsold' and 'the latest report of prices from Canton or New York.' "[73]

Unsurprisingly, shysters were attracted to the types of corporations where stockholder incentives to monitor the health of the governance structure were lowest because it was there that they could most easily make the changes necessary to cloak their intentions and actions. That generally meant midsize companies with numerous, well-dispersed stockholders and stock that traded too infrequently to be regularly quoted in newspapers, much less traded on the nation's many regional stock exchanges. Whenever stockholders were inactive, any of the major governance principles (discussed in Chapter 6) were susceptible to manipulation or even outright eradication. When cronies controlled companies, for example, bylaws relating to performance bonds could go unenforced.[74] In the worst cases, managers behaved, in the words of one aggrieved insurance stockholder, "as if they were the proprietors & not the servants of the Company!"[75] Foreshadowing future developments, the worst antebellum managers attempted various ruses designed to "perpetuate their own continuance in office," as stated in the records of one court case.[76]

Dividends were supposed to provide investors with nearly ironclad signals about corporate financial health because honest directors did not pay dividends when the company's earnings did not clearly merit doing so.[77] After suffering numerous setbacks, the directors of one bridge company "resolved, unanimously, that it is inexpedient and highly improper to declare a dividend at this time."[78] Dividends could be gamed to some extent, as the directors of one railroad did when they came up with the cash to pay a 4 percent dividend by factoring the road's passenger receivables at 1 percent interest per month.[79] According to its new directors and managers, the previous leaders of Baltimore's Canton Company had declared dividends that were "practically fraudulent" in order to "puff and inflate" the share price, making the stock one of the "fancies of Wall Street."[80]

Then, as now, accounting issues were important but ranged from confusing to intractable. To what account should stolen product be posted? When should liabilities be recognized—when a verbal contract for services is made, or when the service is actually performed, or when it is invoiced or due? Answers to such questions could make the difference between a 4 percent dividend and a decline in the stock price or the usual 5 percent payment.[81]

A related problem was that new corporations did not have a solid history of dividends that investors could go by. They therefore had to rely upon financial statements but, as insurance actuary Harvey Tuckett explained, those could be even more easily manipulated than dividends. He advocated the use of auditors to examine corporate accounts and to make officers "explain the receipts, the compound interest, the expenses, the valuation of policies, and the basis upon which he proposes to grant a bonus or dividend." Only if all is satisfactory should the auditors, "men of high commercial standing, . . . paid for the examination of the accounts, but in all other respects, unconnected with the company," recommend that the dividend be voted on at the next stockholder meeting.[82]

Directors were supposed to have much of their net worth invested in the corporations they governed so that if the company went down, so would they. They were not supposed to receive any other remuneration but often did, indirectly, in the form of contracts with the corporations they ran. Such contracts, of course, put their interests (highest contract price possible) at odds with those of stockholders (lowest contract price possible, level of quality constant). "Men cannot be found to devote themselves to an enterprise of this kind for the public benefit," one contemporary complained, "but from selfish, interested motives."[83] "The direction," Albert Gallatin complained in 1841, "must necessarily be placed in the hands of a few men, who have comparatively but little interest in . . . all public bodies . . . and as they are not paid,[84] it is impossible to expect that they should attend without deriving some compensation for the sacrifice of a portion of their precious time," in the form of favors.[85] Bank presidents and directors often received large loans from their institutions. If the loans were made on commercial principles, carried the same interest charged to other customers, required the same collateral and endorsements, and were kept to a small percentage of total loans and total capital, they were innocuous, or so most contemporaries argued. [86] When made at no or reduced interest to borrowers who would not normally gain the bank's favor, or when they consumed a large portion of a bank's capital, loans to directors could be quite pernicious.

Sometimes, directors or officers simply ignored charter provisions or by-laws. The treasurer of one railroad placed the company's funds in a bank in his own name despite a bylaw prohibiting him from doing so because of the "insecurity attending this mode of taking care of the company's funds."[87] In another instance, stockholders resolved that they were opposed to the passage of their railroad through a cemetery and that they believed the corporation had no right to dig up the dead. As described in grisly detail in Chapter 3, the directors proceeded nevertheless.[88] In another case, the officers and directors of the Middlesex mill in Lowell took $89,000 by claiming that they used the money, "without any consent or even knowledge of the stockholders," to bribe members of Congress.[89]

Even stockholder voting rights could be corrupted, as when directors enjoyed the right to select election inspectors, men who were supposed to ensure that elections were fair. That was like allowing the fox to guard the henhouse. In 1810, for example, Cornelius Low and John Jackson served as inspectors in an election of directors in the Wallabout and Brooklyn Toll Bridge Company. Jackson was elected president and Low a director in that election.[90] Another technique for limiting stockholder influence was to keep meeting agendas secret so as to discourage attendance. In 1797, one stockholder of the Baltimore Insurance Company went into the country for a few days instead of attending the annual meeting. A measure passed, increasing the president's salary to $2,500, instead of the $800 or $1,000 that the stockholder believed sufficient. "When a salary is to be established," the stockholder rightly complained, "all those who have a vote, ought to be notified to attend."[91]

Sometimes, crooked officers conveniently forgot to inform stockholders of meetings or advertised them in unusual places. Sometimes, they held meetings in rooms that were too small to hold more than a few handpicked shareholders or held them so early in the morning that those coming in from the country on trains were put to the extra expense of a hotel room. Others deliberately scheduled their meetings at the same time as other widely held corporations, which had the effect of dividing the in-person but not the officer-controlled proxy vote.[92]

Perhaps the most infamous way of subverting stockholder voting rights was the use of proxy votes. By common law and often by charter or bylaws, stockholders had a clearly defined right to cast a vote at a stockholder meeting by authorizing someone else to vote on his or her behalf.[93] The practice was allowed because many stockholders found it too costly or inconvenient to attend in person. In many corporations, voting by proxy afforded more stockholders an opportunity to participate in governance. At least three stockholders in Virginia's Berryville and Charlestown Turnpike Company appointed John W. Leake as their "Proxy to vote for a President Two Directors & a Treasurer . . . at an election to be held in Charlestown on the 1st day of October 1850" as well as "to transact all other business that may come before the respective meeting." Two stockholders stipulated that the proxy was to be good "at all future Elections" until countermanded, but the third exercised his right to grant it for one election only, unless explicitly renewed.[94]

Abusive tactics turned proxies into a potent tool of management interests. A proxy holder was supposed to vote as the stockholder wished and could be called to account if he did not, but many proxies were given without restriction. Letters and pamphlets seeking proxies usually claimed that some competing faction sought to gain control in order to engage in unwarranted insider lending or other types of fraud. In most instances, it is impossible to evaluate such claims. Even today, politicians rarely claim that their opponents, if elected, will steal from or otherwise defraud the public. Rather, they claim that their foes will enact unpopular policies such as higher taxes, abortion, gun control, or whatever. Proxy fights rarely revolved around business issues per se.[95]

By the Civil War, the cognoscenti knew numerous techniques that could be used to subvert shareholder rights. "A volume could be filled with similar cases," one contemporary claimed, "since these tricks, subterfuges, and expedients, are in constant use from year to year."[96] The biggest schemers creatively employed numerous tactics simultaneously. In the mid-1850s, the Atlantic and Pacific Railroad claimed to have raised $100 million in capital, over $74 million of it subscribed by twelve men not worth $1 million altogether and the rest no richer. "In the above subscriptions," one critic wryly noted, "there is more humbug and less money than can be found on any subscription paper on the face of the earth." All sorts of shenanigans then commenced. Robert J. Walker, one of the company's trustees, obtained a payment of $10,000 from the company (which he used to pay a call on his stock) in return for a contract of dubious authenticity or merit allowing the company's road to cross northern Mexico. Walker and two fellow Southern slaveholders, Jeptha Fowlkes and T. Butler King, then took over the company's accounting mechanisms and, soon after, gave away millions of stock to cronies. Those men later blamed the actions of the governor of Texas aimed at suppressing the road for the fact that subscribers had stopped making payments. To induce shareholders to pay up, the trio claimed that the Texas lands that the company would obtain from the state were the most fertile in the nation and laden with coal, too. They also unveiled a scheme to accept in payment for these paradise-like lands only bonds issued by the railroad. That alone would ensure huge profits, but the railroad itself would also be lucrative, they claimed, because it would be the cheapest way of getting mail and passengers to California and of returning its gold and the riches of the Orient to the east coast. Dividends of 28 percent per year were a foregone conclusion and huge additional surplus payments very likely. To top it off, they claimed that the railroad would be certain "to render our Union indissoluble, under the guaranties and limitations of the Constitution."[97]

Most early Americans believed that if anyone suffered from a corporation's failure, "it ought to be the Stockholders," and, in nonfinancial corporations, that was generally the case.[98] But with financial institutions, especially banks, the matter was different. Institutions that issued bearer liabilities were particularly susceptible to governance breakdowns because stockholders and managers could ally to defraud note holders and depositors. Issuance of banknotes, claimed the cashier of the Merchants Bank of New Bedford, was "the only circumstance that justifies that constant and minute interference with the concerns of the banks that the legislature has always exercised."[99]

The promissory notes that infamous bank shyster Andrew Dexter gave in exchange for the loans he received from the banks he controlled show the matter most clearly: "I Andrew Dexter Jun. do promise to pay to the President and directors of the Farmer's Exchange Bank, or their order ____ in ____ years from the date with interest, at two per cent per annum. It being understood, however, that the said Andrew Dexter Jun. shall not be called on to make payment, until he thinks proper, he being the principal stockholder, and best knowing when it will be proper to pay the same."[100] The bank failed in late February 1809, with $86.50 in its "vault" to cover hundreds of thousands of dollars of demand liabilities. Dexter was simply a failed businessmen who tried to salvage his dreams through increasingly shady means. Early in the Civil War, many Missouri bankers deliberately made huge loans of dubious quality to Confederates. In addition to defrauding note holders, their actions helped to fund guerrilla violence in the frontier border region.[101]

Defrauding note holders was also the motive of Isaac Mack of Rochester, New York, and E. S. Townsend of Palmyra, a small town near Rochester. In April 1833, the Essex Bank of Guildhall, Vermont (chartered in 1832 with capital of $40,000), began its short, ugly life with a nominal capital of $20,000, over $18,000 of which consisted of stock notes (the promissory notes of stockholders). The bank labored to convert its notes into specie until March 1839, when all but fifty-five of its shares were purchased by Mack and Townsend, who knew that the bank's capital "was mostly fictitious and false" but intended "to raise the credit of the bank, which was then at a low ebb, by redeeming its bills promptly in New York City." After lulling the market into complacency, they planned to "then flood the country with them and let the bank fail." The only thing that stopped them from consummating their fraud was "their own failure, which took place soon after" they came into control of the little country bank.[102]

Antebellum New York's worst governance scandal, the so-called conspiracy of Jacob Barker and other upstart financiers in the mid-1820s, was also perpetrated at the expense of creditors, the holders of so-called bonds (really post notes) issued by quasi-banks such as the Life and Fire Insurance, Western Insurance, and Mercantile Insurance companies. To stay afloat, that small flotilla of allied companies engaged in a complicated series of accounting and securities frauds that ultimately cost its creditors and minority stockholders hundreds of thousands of dollars. Further frauds and losses were stopped, thanks to the actions of activist stockholders in a bank taken over by the conspirators. The state ultimately proved incapable of successfully prosecuting any of the conspirators but at least evinced a desire to see justice done.[103]

Even before the problems at the Baltimore branch of the second Bank discussed above, Baltimore never had much of a reputation for probity in banking. Accusations of favoritism and, worse, illegally large loans to directors, were rampant at many banks but not the venerable Bank of Maryland—not until, that is, it fell under the control of Evan Poultney in the summer of 1831. Poultney dismantled the bank's governance mechanisms by seeing to the election of cronies and men, like Reverdy Johnson, who were too engrossed with their own affairs to pay much attention to the bank. One director was never informed that he had been elected and hence had never attended a board meeting. Poultney and his cronies then made large loans to themselves, which they used to speculate in the bank's stock and to form an insurance company, among other activities. Poultney and the directors lost a little when the grossly overleveraged bank crashed and burned in March 1834 but far less than the $200,000 loss that Baltimoreans who held the bank's notes and deposits suffered. In 1835, they rioted in retaliation and stoned Johnson's house, although he had been cleared of any wrongdoing.[104]

After Poultney's gang took over, the bank's stock price jumped to $500 per share and stayed there until the end without wavering. But clearly, in the words of a contemporary, the price "presented an appearance of things which had no substantiality in it."[105] Most likely, the newspaper reporting the price could not bring itself to stop coverage on the old stalwart until it went bankrupt, which, by all accounts, was "totally unexpected."[106] A group of Baltimore merchants and tradesmen concluded in retrospect that the failure was the result of "a few individuals . . . all of whom have been actuated by a spirit of wild and licentious speculation," but did not enter into details of the fraudulent transactions.[107] A newspaper editor professed that there were aspects of the failure that could not be "readily understood by anyone; and they are ugly enough to look upon."[108] Whatever the specific problem, it was largely limited to the old bank, the resources of which proved to be several hundred thousand dollars short of its liabilities. After a brief panic and run on the banks, most of which held firm, money market conditions in Baltimore and its extensive hinterland returned to normal.[109]

Unprincipled governance brought down other antebellum banks, too. Although personally bankrupt, Thomas Allibone in 1857 became president of the Bank of Pennsylvania and, in the words of one stunned contemporary, "immediately abstracted large sums for his own purposes," some $1.2 million, or about three-quarters of the bank's capital. To cover his tracks, Allibone ran the bank in a wild and reckless fashion, wiping out the remaining capital. Unsurprisingly, the bank failed in the opening stages of the Panic of 1857. Allibone fled to Europe, only to stand trial years later and earn acquittal.[110]

Governments responded to episodes of corporate mismanagement and defalcation like those described in this chapter in a variety of ways. Chapter 8 assesses their efforts, some of which were salubrious and some of which were not.

Chapter 8

Regulation Rising

Too much legislation has often been found to be a great evil.
—Substance of Argument of Respondents' Counsel, 1838[1]

Entrepreneurs and legislators first responded to lapses in corporate governance like those described in Chapter 7 by tightening charters and bylaws.
After William Duer simply walked off with corporate securities owned by the
SEUM, for example, corporations began to hire treasurers and buy chests that
could be opened only by two different keys turned simultaneously. When
later fraudsters drew on corporate bank accounts, corporations responded by
mandating the use of countersignatures on all checks of significant size. After
mutual life insurers failed in droves in the 1830s and 1840s, the surviving
companies tightened up by making medical examinations more rigorous, by
using improved mortality tables, and, most important, by cutting back on
premium notes and dividends. Given a big enough prize, however, crooks
eventually could crack any safeguard. Over time, the inability of stockholders
to eliminate fraud and other forms of governance failure opened the way for
increased state-centered regulation. The door opened wider when contemporaries began to believe that states with stricter state-centered regulations,
such as New Hampshire, suffered fewer defalcations. The best that state regulators achieved, however, was the same level of success that stockholders had
achieved: temporary victories in the many skirmishes in a never-ending war
to exterminate that hardy species, *Homo sapiens ereptor*. And in the long
term, state-centered regulation proved itself to be more costly and less responsive than stockholder governance.[2]

Governments and corporations were always deeply intertwined because the former granted the latter legal powers that other types of business organizations could not fully enjoy (though some businesses, as we have seen, tried to obtain them, anyway). Corporations provided quasi-public goods such as transportation facilities, currency, industrial might, employment, and taxes in exchange for the state's legal protection. Disgruntled corporate stakeholders therefore naturally turned to the government for aid when other avenues of redress appeared blocked. It was also natural for legislators to look into episodes of possible malfeasance when the governance principles mentioned in Chapter 6 appeared inadequate to the task. The main question, one with no easy answer, was how far the government should regulate corporations' interactions with society and among corporate stakeholders themselves.[3]

From the corporation nation's inception, some charters mandated periodic information disclosure to one or more government officials. Early on, many corporations simply failed to comply with charter provisions that mandated information disclosure to the government, and officials generally allowed the mandates to lapse. The Fourth Turnpike of New Hampshire did not send any financial information to the government until 1830, twenty years after it was supposed to have begun doing so. Perhaps legislators realized that unaudited financial reports were too easily gamed to bother collecting. Though the United States Bank of Pennsylvania made regular monthly returns to Pennsylvania's auditor general, the bank still failed—and spectacularly, at that. Many other charter provisions, including minimum subscription mandates, were also ignored or sidestepped with simple lies.[4]

There was no doubt, however, that governments could force companies to disclose information to them or impose just about any other regulation up to and including charter revocation (typically via a common-law writ called "quo warranto"). Before the *Dartmouth* decision, governments could and, as we have seen occasionally, did unilaterally amend charters. Corporations, of course, argued that their charters were inviolable, but that did not make it so. After *Dartmouth*, a government could still unilaterally amend a charter if it explicitly retained that right in the original act of incorporation or a general statute, a stratagem that many states followed, if only to quiet criticism that the Supreme Court had given corporations too much power. Section 25 of Louisiana's 1848 general incorporation act explicitly stated that "nothing in this act contained shall in any wise be construed or interpreted as a contract between the State and the stockholders of any corporation formed under it, or with such corporation when formed, but the Legislature shall have at all times the right to alter or amend this law." As most charters contained sunset clauses, governments also could (and did) insist on any desired reforms as a condition of recharter. Pennsylvania, for example, trimmed the Bank of North America's authorized capital, required more legislative scrutiny of its affairs, and put restrictions on foreign stock ownership when it rechartered the already hoary bank in 1814. It added more restrictions when the bank's charter expired again in 1825.[5]

Legislators were attentive to governance failures, even in other states, and some were eager to learn from them. "I know sir, the banking system has been carried to great excess in some parts of new-England," New York legislator Jonas Platt noted in 1811, soon after Andrew Dexter's downfall, "and I hope we shall profit by their example."[6] A New York senate committee noted fifteen years later that "abuses arising from the frauds of officers and agents, are such as every branch of mercantile business is exposed to, and are fit and proper subjects for legislative interference." The big question, then, was the form that "interference" would take. Would legislators attempt to support the private governance mechanisms discussed in Chapter 6, or would they attempt to bolster or even supplant it with state power?

Tightening Corporate Checks and Balances

> It is not to be expected that any legislative provisions
> can entirely protect the creditors of corporations
> from all risk of loss by their failure.
> —*Anonymous, 1829*[7]

Early on, legislators' first instinct was to bolster existing governance principles, not supplant them with government oversight. Depictions of early U.S. governments as laissez faire are clearly overdrawn, as governments from Washington to county seats and town boroughs were involved in many aspects of the economy, from setting the weight of bread to investing money in corporate stocks and bonds. But early governments were laissez faire in the sense that they were relatively small parts of the economy and, as such, did not—indeed, could not—engage in extensive regulation of private businesses, even in areas, such as transportation infrastructure, over which they would later take almost complete control. When tears in the fabric of corporate governance began to appear, therefore, they initially worked with entrepreneurs and stockholders to try to mend weaknesses in charters and bylaws. Simply enforcing common charter provisions, such as ensuring that corporate capital was bona-fide paid in, would help governance tremendously, many believed.[8]

So, too, would sensible new rules. When several scandals revealed that rogues were able to secure their election to boards of directors by buying shares just prior to stockholder meetings, charters (and bylaws) began to withhold voting rights from shareholders who had recently purchased their shares. In the case of the United States Bank of Pennsylvania, only those who owned their shares for "three calendar months before the day of election" were qualified to vote and only on the shares that they had owned over that entire period.[9] The Delaware County Bank and numerous other corporations eventually implemented similar rules, which delayed (without preventing) control contests, ostensibly to give stockholders more time to analyze and organize.[10]

Increasingly, legislators began to meddle with market mechanisms that appeared not to protect stakeholders sufficiently. In the late 1840s, "A Citizen of Burlington" accused the directors of the Camden & Amboy Railroad of fraud in the pages of a pamphlet and in the *Burlington Gazette*.[11] The New Jersey state legislature responded not by referring the matter to the corporation's stockholders but by forming a commission to investigate. It showed that the accusations went far beyond the truth but did conclude that "culpable misconduct" had taken place in the railroad's canal subsidiary. Such actions were rare before the Civil War, and the case in question was ostensibly justified by New Jersey's reliance on taxes paid to it by the railroad. But clearly, legislators were beginning to believe that stockholder governance did not always ensure optimal outcomes.[12]

The shift toward state-centered regulation was clearest in banking. For decades, banks in urban areas generally held sufficient reserves of gold and silver because liability (note and deposit) holders could force payment of the banks' liabilities into hard money on demand. Reserve ratios were not mandated, but the state was supposed to encourage banks to keep sufficient reserves by punishing banks that ran out of reserves by revoking their charters, forcing them to pay interest to holders of inconvertible liabilities, and by fining directors. Banks in rural areas faced looser constraints because their notes circulated over a much larger area. The farther they strayed from the bank of issue, the less valuable notes became because the cost of returning them for payment in hard money increased. A risk premium subtracted from the face value of the notes of the riskiest banks complicated the situation. In most of the nation, the Bank of the United States and brokers handled the note valuation problem by dealing in (regularly buying and selling) country notes at posted prices. The system incentivized people to keep country notes close to the bank of issue and to return ones that strayed via the lowest-cost method.[13]

In New England, a different system arose that managed to keep the notes of all the region's banknotes at par, at the cost of some coercion. One Boston bank, the Suffolk, managed the system by collecting country banknotes and returning them en masse until the bank of issue agreed to keep (zero-interest) deposits at the Suffolk sufficient to redeem their notes. Country banks in New England were thus less leveraged and hence less profitable than they otherwise would have been, but they were also much less likely to fail. They survived the Panic of 1837, according to one country banker, without causing any "inconvenience" or "loss," proof positive, he argued, of the system's "soundness" in the face of "such a deep and wide-spread commercial convulsion."[14] Later, private regional clearinghouses fulfilled much the same regulatory niche.[15]

For the nation's first twenty years, market regulation and private governance were clearly sufficient because nary a bank failed. After banks began failing at a significant rate because of the Panic of 1819 and subsequent recession, legislators and incorporators reformed charters to increase bank capital actually paid in, to reduce leverage to two or three times capital, and to force the dissolution of banks that failed to pay specie on demand for their notes and deposits. According to Albert Gallatin, all but the leverage requirements had salutary effects, at least at first.[16] To enforce such strictures, some states imposed double or higher liability on stockholders; others concentrated on directors who willfully violated the restrictions. "Public policy," one jurist argued in 1829, "requires that the directors shall understand distinctly that if they so manage the concerns of the institution as to produce insolvency, the property and effects of the institution will be taken from them entirely and be placed in the hands of those who will investigate their conduct fearlessly and impartially."[17]

As Figure 6 shows, the market regulation of banknotes and the improved governance of banks in the 1820s did not prevent all bank failures, but they did return the system to a fair degree of stability. From a modern economic perspective, with its high tolerance for what Joseph Schumpeter called "creative destruction," the private system worked quite well, the failures being symptomatic of nothing more than competition, learning, and rational risk-taking.

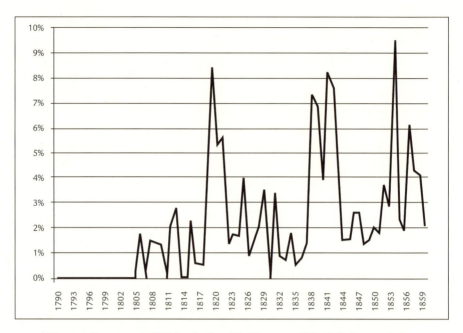

Figure 6. Percentage of U.S. banks that failed by year, 1790–1860. Source: Robert E. Wright, "Governance and the Success of U.S. Community Banks, 1790–2010: Mutual Savings Banks, Local Commercial Banks, and the Merchants (National) Bank of New Bedford, Massachusetts," *Business and Economic History Online* 9 (2011); complete data file is available from the author.

Many legislators had a different view, arguing that bank failures mandated more state-centered bank regulation. They justified that stance on the grounds that "the public have an interest in these institutions, connected as they are with the currency, and influencing as they do, all the business operations of the community, paramount to any interest which the individual stockholders can have; the conclusion would seem to follow, that it can neither be regarded as an invasion of private right, nor in the slightest degree justly offensive to the most fastidious, that the government should send its agent to overlook its interests."[18] New York's lawmakers were the most keen to involve the state, adopting in 1829 the nation's first banknote-insurance scheme, the controversial Safety Fund.[19]

Some contemporaries saw the Safety Fund as a public interest measure. Lawmakers were "alarmed by the failure of several banking institutions, anterior to the passage of this law, the affairs of which upon investigations, turned out to be desperate in the extreme." They therefore sought "a more secure system of banking, than the one which they had before relied upon." Others saw more sinister motives, "a deep designed political scheme, to preserve the ascendancy of that political party to which Mr. [Martin] Van Buren is attached," the Albany Regency. Still others saw an attempt to ensure that Manhattan would be the headquarters of an anticipated third Bank of the United States.[20]

Whatever the driving motivation behind its passage, the Safety Fund tried to fix problems with the bank charters then in force, which were thought to leave too much discretion to the directors, including the sums to be paid in on the MINAC, the percentage of capital lent back out as stock notes, and the ratio of notes and deposits to specie. Prior to beginning operations, each Safety Fund bank had to prove that its entire capital was "actually paid in . . . and that no loan has been made to any stockholder to enable him to pay for his stock." Banks were also forbidden to take their own shares to collateralize loans, to issue banknotes beyond twice their capitals, or to pay dividends or buy their own stock "except from actual surplus profits." If the bank's capital was impaired, it had to be fully restored before dividends could be paid. Banks were also prohibited from lending more than one-third of their capital to their directors and from purchasing their own liabilities for less than their face value. Finally, to help improve stockholder monitoring, all Safety Fund banks had to allow stockholders to inspect "transfer books and lists of stockholders, . . . for thirty days previous to every election of directors."[21]

Some of those provisions worked well because they ensured that the incentives of stockholders and the corporations in which they held stock were closely aligned. Limiting stock notes was salubrious, for example, because stock notes "afforded the means to designing persons of acquiring the control of other institutions where capital had actually been paid in, and of course the power of dissipating that capital and the other means of the institution." Designing persons "possessed of a given amount of stock in one institution, an individual by hypothecating it, could raise the means of purchasing other stocks, and thus get the control of another institution, and despoil it of its effects." By such means, individuals of little property were able to control several New York corporations and even "grasped at the control of some of the largest of the others, and even the Bank of the United States." "It was fortunate for the community," one contemporary opined, "that the bubble [associated with Jacob Barker, discussed in Chapter 7] burst, and exposed losses, which amounted to no more than one or two millions." Moreover, borrowing the value of one's stock from the corporation was not actual stockholdership but rather a debtor relationship. Stockholders wanted their respective corporations to succeed but corporate debtors did not.[22]

Prohibition of post notes, on the other hand, was much lauded but probably unnecessary. Post notes (banknotes that were payable at some future date rather than on demand) had been issued as early as 1792, when the Bank of the United States had hundreds of thousands of dollars' worth in circulation. The Bank of New York, which exists to this day, had some $15,000 in post notes outstanding in 1799. Numerous other banks used them as well. Indubitably, the ban stemmed from the fact that in the mid-1820s, several New York insurance companies acting illegally as banks had used post notes fraudulently. At first, the insurers were merely seeking entry into Manhattan's lucrative but highly restricted banking market. After suffering large losses on loans, they abused post notes to stay afloat.[23]

The Safety Fund's injunction against insider lending was probably also unnecessary and could easily be circumvented by shysters simply by having the bank lend to shills who then relent the sums to the directors. Its limitation on banknotes was downright specious. When Albert Gallatin examined the financial statements of more than 300 banks, including some that had subsequently failed, he found "not a single one" in which "the loans . . . amounted, so long as specie payments were in force, to three times, or the issues to twice the amount of their capital. It is clear, that provisions applicable to such improbable contingencies are purely nominal."[24]

The Safety Fund legislation forced banks chartered or rechartered under the Safety Fund to pay 0.5 percent of their total capital annually, up to 3 percent of their respective capitals, to the state treasury, which held it to indemnify the creditors of insolvent member banks. The insurance component of the legislation necessitated much more careful supervision by the state because it reduced the incentives for private monitoring by note holders and increased moral hazard (risk-taking) on the part of bankers. So the law also subjected member banks to visits by government examiners "three times in each year, and oftener if required by any three banks; to examine the books, papers, and funds of the institution, and to ascertain the true condition of each institution, and its ability to meet its engagements." The examiners were empowered to question the bank's officers upon oath and to inflict heavy punishments for "false swearing" and "false books, or entries." The examiners could ask the chancellor for an injunction to suspend the operations of any bank if half its capital was lost or if it refused to submit to examination. The examination system was later extended to the state's free banks (of which more anon) but was jettisoned in 1843, when lawmakers and the examiners themselves admitted what early critics had suspected: that they could not discern the "true condition" of the banks they inspected. There was simply too much to know and too little incentive to know it.[25]

Overall, the Safety Fund was probably an improvement over what came before except for the fact that New Yorkers thought it unjust because it made properly governed institutions responsible for improperly governed ones and because its costs fell most heavily on the large, relatively safe urban banks.[26] The system also exacerbated moral hazard by eliminating the risk premium on country notes, leaving the discount solely a function of "the expense and time, requisite to send the paper home for redemption" regardless of how reckless the country bankers behaved. Essentially, then, the Safety Fund allowed roguish country banks to increase their note issue on the credit of conservative city banks. The new system also favored country banks by guaranteeing only notes, not deposits, even though they were functional equivalents. "They perform the same office, and there is no substantial difference between them," explained one contemporary. "Both are alike payable on demand, and are used and intended to answer the purposes of money"; but as bearer obligations, notes were much more popular in thinly inhabited areas while deposits predominated in urban ones.[27]

As critics predicted, the Safety Fund proved "a very great fallacy"[28] because it attracted the interest of rogues who took the opportunity to establish "rag institutions" that were quickly rubber-stamped by legislators who believed that their "boasted law will cure every disorder & Bankruptcy." A lawyer familiar with the situation accurately predicted, "Soon a crush among those ephemeral plants will dissipate the boasted safety fund into air & open the eyes of the government to the gross delusion." One of those rag institutions was the Chenango Bank, which failed on February 15, 1830, with about $130,000 of notes in circulation after it had fallen under the control of James Birdsall and Thomas Millner, who conspired to conduct "secret depredations upon the property of the Bank, until they have run ashore amidst rocks & breakers."[29] During the macroeconomically troubled late 1830s and early 1840s, Safety Fund banks proved more likely to fail than the banks that remained outside the system. Other early banknote-insurance systems, in Michigan and Vermont, also failed to stop bankruptcies or to fully protect creditors.[30]

The Safety Fund remained in place, but no new banks were chartered under it. For new banks, New York embraced free banking under bond security. Free banking allowed anyone who could meet the minimum entrance requirements to charter a bank under a general statute. It regulated banks by mandating that each cover its note issue by depositing bonds to a like amount with the government.[31] According to one contemporary, the law "entirely restored confidence in the New York Banks" because, although banks still failed, note holders were usually fully reimbursed.[32] It worked well enough to serve as a model for free banking laws in other states and the National Banking acts implemented during the Civil War.[33]

A more state-centered attempt by Louisiana to regulate banks by strictly enforcing reserve requirements, the Forestall Act, appears to have increased bank stability, although at the cost of slower capital accumulation.[34] Good free banking laws, by contrast, increased both banking capital and competition. Some free bankers, such as Loveland Paddock, son of a Patriot mariner turned Utica farmer, lent widely to the younger, smaller, poorer, riskier entrepreneurs, including farmers and manufacturers, typically eschewed by old-line banks. According to contemporary reports bolstered by careful scrutiny of his bank's records, Paddock "was very liberal with his customers, and . . . some of them speak feelingly of the assistance he gave them at trying periods in their business career."[35] Borrowers at other banks also spoke or wrote feelingly for the bankers who helped to make their careers. One even offered to repay a debt long since extinguished by law and almost forgotten to memory, but the bank refused, saying, in effect, that the borrower's default had been fair and square.[36]

Not all free banking laws worked. Contemporaries considered the free banking legislation passed in Michigan "a complete failure, and . . . the source of innumerable frauds."[37] Michigan legislators rather dully allowed bankers to collateralize their note issues with the par value of bonds instead of their market value. That incentivized shady bankers to deposit risky bonds with the state and thus encouraged so-called wildcat banks that were no easier to find than the elusive feline predators that they were named after. And although Michigan's bank examiners realized that they were encountering the same coins in the vaults of different banks as they moved across the state, they had no incentive to do anything about it. Vermont in 1851 passed a free banking act, but only one institution was formed under it, allegedly because the public thought banks chartered under general laws inferior to, and less well regulated than, those created by special charter because they seemed to lack the imprimatur of the state.[38]

Other general incorporation laws also attempted to improve corporate performance with a combination of state-centered regulations and market mechanisms, especially competition. At least as far back as Sir James Steuart, political economists realized that the easiest way to minimize corporate market power was to encourage the creation of competing corporations. General incorporation fit that bill perfectly. "We believe in general legislation," a New York newspaper editor argued in 1860, because it allowed for the "advantages of corporate action . . . without the risks of unlimited liability" while simultaneously encouraging "competition" that led to "cheapening to consumers."[39]

Ironically, the increased levels of competition fostered by general incorporation laws imposed hidden costs that helped open the door to more intrusive government regulation later in the century. Most important, corporate competition was highly disruptive of older, more paternalistic relationships between employers and employees, turning the latter into mere "hired hands." Nowhere was the transformation clearer than in the mills of Lowell, Massachusetts, which, in its early days, was a relatively comfortable place for farm girls to work a few years, gain some independence, and save money for marriage. When recession struck in the late 1830s and early 1840s, however, competition forced the corporations to cut wages, spurring a nasty war of words, during which corporate critics such as "A Citizen of Lowell" called the town's largest employers "hard hearted money changers, and a gold-worshipping and poverty-oppressing aristocracy." Such critics already saw a class struggle between laborers on the one side and "an interested aristocracy . . . a pensioned press, and a bought priesthood," on the other. To them, factory operatives suffered more severely than any "class of persons in the U. States . . . even the slaves of the South" (many of whom also labored for corporations, especially railroads but also some manufacturers).[40] Workers would be pushed past their limit "until arrested by extending to them legislative protection." "Here then," a contemporary concluded, "we see the necessity for legislative protection to the operatives in the factories."[41]

General incorporation laws, at least those accompanied by the elimination of any special chartering options, provided governments with an opportunity to restrict entry to only those entrepreneurs willing to follow stringent governance guidelines and, increasingly, public disclosure clauses. By eliminating the ability to lobby for weak charters, governments ostensibly ensured the adoption of best practices by all its corporations. General incorporation laws opened up the corporate form to all while simultaneously narrowing the range of acceptable alternatives, sometimes to one.[42]

When general incorporation laws proved overly restrictive, new entry was minimal, signaling legislators the need for reform. In 1851, Massachusetts passed a general incorporation act for manufactures that was not used much until after 1855, when the maximum allowable capitalization was raised from $200,000 to $500,000 and issuance of preferred stock was allowed.[43] Not all states were as responsive to market signals. Ohio's general banking law of 1842, for instance, was considered too severe. The legislature amended it in early 1843, but even the revision proved unpopular because the law continued to mandate unlimited liability and taxed both capital and dividends. As one newspaper pundit put it, "no man would trust himself or his property in such a scheme, and not a cent of the stock was subscribed."[44] As Ohio banks closed when their charters expired, the notes of banks from nearby states flooded into the Buckeye State, fueling agitation to amend the defunct general law. A new general banking law, which incorporated aspects of New York's Safety Fund and bond security banking systems as well as an entirely private state bank with branches, was passed in February 1845. Despite continued political agitation over banking, the legislation proved liberal enough to entice minimal reentry and new entry. A new free banking law was passed in March 1851 and quickly attracted thirteen new entrants but none thereafter, ostensibly because of high taxes on capital and dividends. Unsurprisingly, as the number of chartered banks declined and interest rates rose, so did the number of (technically illegal) unincorporated banks in operation in Ohio.[45]

The first general incorporation acts applied only to companies in specific industries and generally did not prohibit special chartering, even in those. Massachusetts, Pennsylvania, New York, and other states passed general incorporation laws for churches and municipalities in the eighteenth century. Pennsylvania passed the first general law for the organization of municipal corporations in 1834. North Carolina passed the first business general incorporation statute, for canals, in 1795. It is not clear if any companies formed under it, however, likely because it stipulated that the canal would escheat to the state once the proprietors earned back their principal with interest at 6 percent. More could be made, more safely, by investing in mortgages.[46]

Massachusetts enacted a general law, for aqueducts (water utilities), in 1799 because "there is perhaps no subject of public interest on which there is more unanimity of opinion," according to civil engineer J. L. Sullivan, "than the importance of a liberal supply of pure water to large cities from some external source."[47] The law appears to have been largely a nonstarter, perhaps because it did not accord limited liability to investors. A March 1809 law that allowed for the formation of unlimited liability manufacturing companies in the Bay State, however, attracted 130 corporations by the end of the War of 1812.[48]

In 1811, New York passed a general incorporation act for manufacturers of woolen, cotton, and linen goods, glass, bar iron, steel, hoop iron and iron mongery, sheet copper, sheet lead, shot, and white and red lead. Extensions in 1815 and 1817 added clay and earthenware articles and leather, respectively. The act capped capitalization at $100,000, corporate life at twenty years, and the number of directors at nine. Voting was one vote per share, without limit. The act was renewed in 1821 and remained in force until passage of a new general incorporation act in 1848. Under the terms of the 1811 law, the state issued 362 charters. Over the same period (1811–48), 138 manufacturing companies received special charters in New York. The generals were capitalized at about $23 million and the specials at about $14.16 million. That works out to an average MINAC of just over $100,000, suggesting that the general act's capitalization cap was not a major limitation. Unlike the Massachusetts act, the New York act tried to limit liability, perhaps to twice the par value, but was so poorly worded that stockholder liability remained uncertain for some years.[49]

In 1837, Connecticut passed a general statute for manufacturing, mining, and quarrying companies. Called the Hinsdale Act, it was long considered "the first modern corporation law." It added telegraph companies in 1848, banks in 1852, and plank roads in 1854. As Table 5 shows, it was certainly the most important general incorporation act for which data are available, in terms of the number of businesses incorporated.[50]

Unfortunately, complete general incorporation data for New York were not available at the time of this writing. Between 1847 and 1854, the Empire State enacted twenty-eight general incorporation statutes, most for business corporations ranging from bridges to railroads and manufacturers to insurers. The laws were usually liberal, with fifty-year charters, limited liability (though sometimes only after the capital was fully paid in), very low minimum capitalizations, no capitalization caps, and one-vote-per-share rules. Directors were subject to personal liability if they failed to follow the regulations specified in the applicable statutes. Passage of special charters by New York continued, but only until 1856. Antebellum Pennsylvania passed two general incorporation acts: one for silk manufacturers, in 1836; and one for woolen, cotton, flax, iron, paper, lumber, and salt manufacturers, in 1849.

Table 5. Number and Capitalization of Businesses Chartered by Virtue of General Incorporation Statutes by State through 1860

State	Number	MINAC (mil. $)
Connecticut	1,473	23.796
Illinois	385	154.704
Indiana	95	0.000
Iowa	103	0.350
Massachusetts	197	15.310
Michigan	185	0.000
Minnesota	13	9.886
New Jersey	164	0.000
New York	685	0.000
Ohio	544	89.967
Virginia	69	0.000
Wisconsin	42	2.295
TOTAL	3,955	296.308

Sources: John Cadman, *The Corporation in New Jersey: Business and Politics, 1791–1875* (Cambridge, Mass.: Harvard University Press, 1949), 208; L. Ray Gunn, *The Decline of Authority: Public Economic Policy and Political Development in New York, 1800–1860* (Ithaca, N.Y.: Cornell University Press, 1988), 235; various state archives and departments of state.
Notes: Zeros are listed when extant records do not indicate capitalization. Records for some states with general incorporation laws, including Louisiana, have not been found and may no longer exist.

Records of companies formed under them are spotty. Massachusetts passed a general incorporation act for insurers in 1856.[51]

In 1850, New Jersey passed a general banking act on the New York plan— easy entry and notes backed by government bonds and (up to one-third) by mortgages on improved, unencumbered lands within the state and with a value of three times the mortgage (that is, a maximum loan to value ratio of 33.33 percent). Under normal circumstances, interest payments on the bonds and mortgages flowed through to the issuing bank; but in periods of distress, the state treasurer could keep them to bolster the note redemption fund. In 1851, eighteen banks formed under the general law. One merged and survived into the twentieth century. Another merged and converted into a national bank in 1865. All the others failed by the end of 1855, but that did not stop another fifty-nine banks from forming before the Civil War. The state responded to the failures by beefing up supervision by customers and state officials and empowering the chancellor to shutter any bank that flaunted the state's regulations. Basically, the policy sought to crack down on wildcat banks hiding in the state's inhospitable regions, such as its pine barrens. It was partially successful, as twenty-two New Jersey banks chartered in the 1850s survived long enough to convert to national status in the mid-1860s.[52]

By 1850, most states had enacted at least one general incorporation law, but most of them still allowed entrepreneurs to seek special charters if they wished. One early exception was Iowa, which, in 1846 and again in 1857, forbade special charters in its constitution. Investors in Iowa's general corporations were afforded limited liability unless their companies failed to comply with some basic regulations such as publishing their articles of association. While general incorporation grew more popular with each passing decade, it was not until well into the postbellum period that special incorporation shrank into insignificance. According to the faculty of Yale Law School, "almost every State in the Union" by 1900 had implemented "constitutional provisions" that prohibited the creation of "private corporations by special laws."[53] Between 1904 and 1996, only 3,932 corporations, a tiny percentage of the total created over that span, received special charters.[54]

The Growth of State-Centered Regulation

> The authority of public inspection is no curb upon
> the trade; the individuals who serve the company are
> cut off from the possibility of defrauding; no
> mysteries, no secrets, from which abuses arise, will
> be encouraged; trade will become honourable and
> secure, not fraudulent and precarious; because it will
> grow only under the inspection of its protector, who
> protects it for the public good only.
> —*Sir James Steuart, 1767*[55]

As shown in the previous section, state legislatures by the 1830s were taking steps to ensure that corporations, especially banks, were following the rules laid out in their charters and in consolidated statutes. The best reforms were those that sought to provide stockholders with the powers and incentives they needed to monitor their own property for themselves. When some banks in Massachusetts fell under the control of cliques of directors "who used them for their own purposes, squandered their funds, or diverted them . . . into the hands of their friends," "the Legislature cured all these evils at once by enacting a law requiring full and abundant notice of stockholders' meetings to be given to each owner, and prohibiting every officer of a Bank from soliciting, taking, or carrying a proxy vote. Our Banks," a contemporary boasted, "are now among the most conservative, popular, and well-managed institutions in the State. Not one has failed since that law went into operation, nor can it be justly charged that they are unfairly administered for the private advantage of anybody. . . . Their officers are responsible to their owners once a year, and this responsibility holds them to their integrity and the faithful execution of their trust."[56]

Most antebellum Americans believed that government is best that regulates least: the government should intervene in as few markets as possible and do so as narrowly as possible because it was not likely to improve the status quo much but could cause significant damage if it erred.[57] "The principles upon which real and substantial credit is founded, or the means by which that credit is to be sustained," a committee of New York legislators argued in 1826, "can no more be prescribed by legislative enactment, than it can change or detract from the force of mathematical truth."[58] "The highest legislative wisdom, can never equal the sagacity of private individuals in devising plans and methods of conducting business," another group argued. It quickly added that its criticism was "no reproach on Legislatures" because "they were not constituted for such purposes."[59] Unsurprisingly, antebellum securities and banking regulations were typically either market-oriented or rarely enforced. Stock exchanges like those in Boston, New York, and Philadelphia regulated their own members, for example, while laws against futures contracts and usury primarily dwelled in state statute books rather than quotidian reality.[60]

Nevertheless, some observers began to follow Sir James Steuart's thinking in the epigraph to this section and argue for a bigger role for the state. "As the ingenuity of man contrives new modes of effecting fraudulent purposes, and as these develope [sic] themselves," a committee of New York state senators argued in 1826, "the wisdom of the legislature ought to be vigilantly exerted in devising salutary restrictions to prevent and punishments to deter."[61] In 1841, Albert Gallatin argued that only "limited confidence" could be placed in corporations that were "not laid under efficient restrictions, and subject to strict inspection and examination."[62] In the 1840s and 1850s, labor activists began to agitate for government regulation of wages that corporations paid to their workers. Others, in the name of safety, urged the government to mandate how corporations ran their businesses. In 1860, the New York Board of Aldermen ordered the Hoboken Land Improvement Company to replace the "very old and rickety" thirty-four-year-old boats it used to shuttle people between Hoboken and New York.[63]

Around the same time, calls for stricter regulation of railroads were growing louder and more frequent. "In several of the States they are subjected to annual examinations from railway commissioners, and to sworn forms of returns," noted one pundit, "but in a large portion there is no law to compel an annual exhibit of their internal affairs." Without more oversight, he intimated, it "would be impossible . . . to remedy all the evils consequent upon improper management."[64] Safety was also a concern in railroading, but some remained willing to consider incentive-based solutions. An 1858 cartoon argued that the best way to "insure against railway accidents" was to strap a couple of directors to each engine. Although clearly in jest, the cartoon suggested that making directors more accountable for accidents would have beneficial effects.[65]

By the 1850s, several states had established regulatory agencies for banks, insurers, and/or railroads, albeit with limited powers and discretion.[66] Insurance regulation sprang, in part, from the failure of some companies to honor life-insurance policies with minor errors in applications. "I have heard of an office," wrote one disgusted actuary, the officers "of which boasted of their power to litigate a claim for three years."[67] Some states concluded that direct regulation was a better solution to such problems than market mechanisms such as publicizing claim disapproval rates or making it easier for policyholders to sue insurers and their directors. But direct tactics remained controversial. In 1852, critics railed at New York's new life-insurance regulations because they made insurers "subject to the perpetual inquisition of State Actuaries."[68] Most state-directed regulations stuck, however, because they benefited governments, legislators, and, all too often, the regulated companies themselves, with much of the cost falling on their respective constituents and customers.[69]

In 1834, a resolution asking the banks of Pennsylvania to make weekly reports to the legislature of basic balance-sheet and cash-flow information met with staunch resistance. Party politics were clearly at play; it was hoped that the reports would embarrass many state banks and thereby help the Bank of the United States, then locked in a life-and-death struggle with Andrew Jackson, make its case for recharter. Opponents of the so-called monster bank argued that requiring and publishing bank reports was outright "unconstitutional." Others believed that the regulation, although authorized by statute, was illegal, inexpedient, and "calculated to do mischief" by impairing confidence in the state's banks. Proponents of the policy countered that publishing the reports could not frighten any cashier who knew "his bank to be sound."[70]

Information transparency, policymakers began to see, could create confidence as well as destroy it, particularly in troubled times. "Another result from these disclosures," the legislator who called for the bank reports argued, "is, that the public confidence is increased, because the public are now made acquainted with the extent of their resources—with the extent and soundness of the basis upon which their credit rests." And if the banks were "unsound, it is time they should be exposed; better now than after the evil shall have become uncurable." He argued that only by knowing the detailed condition of each bank could the state decide where to deposit its money, which banks to borrow from in time of fiscal distress, and which banks to tax, but he never made clear why such information had to be published. As "guardians of the public welfare," legislators would make better monitors than stockholders and large depositors, he suggested.[71]

American governments, however, dared not travel very far inside the firm. The corporation's internal affairs remained sacrosanct throughout the nineteenth and twentieth centuries. "So strong," wrote economist John Kenneth Galbraith in the late 1960s, "is the protective convention that even radicals respect it."[72] Although they could revise or even revoke charters and thus dissect or reconstitute corporations virtually at will, governments usually did not interfere with corporate management. Protected from the threat of catastrophic interference, corporations often supported the development of state-centered regulations that favored their interests. They encouraged regulators, for example, who sought to protect "domestic" (in-state) companies from "foreign" (out-of-state) ones. "Far from even toleration," complained insurance actuary Harvey Tuckett, "every annoyance has been thrust upon the foreign offices . . . heavy taxation, amounting almost to prohibition, fines and penalties, and 'PARTY' declarations of future special legislation."[73] When regulation could not be stopped, it could often be diverted into harmless channels. Pennsylvania insurance companies, for example, were able to convince legislators that they should be required to publish only their assets, not their liabilities! That, combined with gullible policyholders, allowed shady insurers to pay outrageously large dividends, attract additional suckers, and walk off with more loot.[74]

Instead of trying to fight all state-centered regulation, corporations increasingly tried to influence its development, first on the legislative floor and then in the halls of the bureaucrats themselves. Rutherford B. Hayes called the government over which he presided (1877–81) a "government of corporations, by corporations and for corporations."[75] By the late nineteenth century, many U.S. senators were widely considered to be bought men, agents of emerging megacorporations (trusts) and other economic interests.[76] The effect of any legislation potentially damaging to corporations could be mitigated by co-opting the bureaucrats assigned to enforce it (such as those Michigan bank examiners who saw the same coins in every bank vault that they visited). Whether exaggerated or not, the widespread belief that many regulations were proffered by big business, in the interest of big business, slowed the growth of state-centered regulation. It was better, many concluded, to keep the state out of the economy altogether than to allow it to become the tool of powerful corporate interests.[77]

Progressives believed that they could reform governments sufficiently to render them effective corporate regulators. By the late nineteenth century, experts were advising corporations that they "should not look forward to any general reduction in the amount of state regulation" because government had an interest in determining whether "the profits arising from . . . huge corporations have been equitably divided between the three parties in interest: the company itself, the consuming public, and the employees."[78] The last two relationships remain important,[79] but, as Chapters 9 and 10 show, the biggest threat posed by corporations today lies in the first: the expropriation of shareholder value. That is because most of the antebellum governance checks and balances have eroded to the point of incompetence and the state-centered regulations and third-party gatekeepers designed to fill the lacunae have largely proven ineffectual.

Chapter 9

Corporate Governance and Regulation since the Civil War

> No legislation can wholly prevent the evils and dangers so often
> complained of. Foolish people cannot be legislated into common sense,
> nor can reckless speculation be entirely prevented by the wisest laws. . . .
> No penalties can be imposed by law which will compare in efficiency with
> the common instinct of self-protection.
>
> —Henry Hitchcock, 1887[1]

Traditional criticisms of the corporation survived the Civil War and apparently intensified over time.[2] In 1873, James A. Garfield told the student body of Hudson College that business corporations were a threat to the republic because "the vast powers of the railroad and the telegraph, the great instruments by which modern communities live, move and have their being" were "owned and managed as private property, by a comparatively small number of private citizens." The future president also reminded his listeners of the agency problems confronting large corporations. "The great managers," he noted, "have in many cases grasped the private property of the corporations themselves; and the stocks which represent the investment have become mere counters in the great gambling houses of Wall street."[3] Fifteen years later, a jurist noted that a "general prejudice against corporations" was apparent. "It is almost a proverb," he claimed, "that juries find against them whenever opportunity offers."[4] That was certainly untrue in the antebellum period, when juries often found in favor of banks, insurers, and utilities.[5]

Stockholder monitoring of their investments did not end with the Civil

War. In 1870, stockholders ousted almost the entire board of directors of the Pepperell Manufacturing Company because of a scandal involving the company's sales agent. In 1881, some British investors published a pamphlet lambasting Franklin Gowen, former head of the Philadelphia and Reading Railroad. The pamphlet purported to show Gowen's "unspeakably bad finance, his incapacity to deal safely with figures, the desperate expedients to which he will resort, his utter want of accuracy, his habit of quarrelling with and abusing his opponents, and his proneness to rely on wild and fantastic estimates."[6] In 1907, the *New York Times* noted that Dutch investors were able to "upset the old and somewhat inefficient management of a railroad in the Southwest."[7] Nevertheless, during and after the Civil War, state-centered regulation of corporations began to play an ever larger role, until by the late nineteenth century, Americans, in the words of James Bryce, had "grown no less accustomed than the English to ... the action of government."[8] While most Americans remained skeptical, some began to believe that government regulation sounded "well" in some economic areas, such as railroads and other public utilities, labor relations, and food and drug quality. One important issue was discerning in which types of business competition was a sufficient regulator and in which types companies enjoyed enough natural market power to require regulation.[9]

After 1900, governments increasingly regulated information disclosure and other topics traditionally in the purview of corporations. First came state-level securities statutes called Blue Sky Laws, which regulated the sale of corporate securities; then came several New Deal acts that closely regulated securities issuance and information disclosure and that radically transformed the banking system. Many such regulations were justified by the erosion of the governance checks and balances common in the postbellum period, especially the decline in stockholder rights, in the words of corporate scholars Adolph Berle and Gardiner Means, "from extreme strength to practical impotence."[10] Ironically, many of the new regulations furthered the ascendance of corporate executives over stockholders and other stakeholders without adequately controlling corporate behavior.[11] "It would be easy," wrote one postbellum jurist, "to point out ... patent defects in the general incorporation laws of the various States. Some consist in the ill digested and patch-work character of the law itself, the result of piecemeal and frequently inconsistent legislations; others in the lack of uniform requirements ... others in wholly insufficient and defective provisions for enforcing or supervising the fulfillment of the statutory requirements; others in the unrestrained permission to create mortgage and floating debts . . . others in the lack of precaution against the issue of stocks or bonds without real and adequate consideration."[12]

Separation of Ownership and Control and the Erosion of Traditional Governance Checks and Balances

> No such check or guard exists or can exist in a . . . company made up of persons . . . from Canada to California, incapable of knowing each other or acting in concert, even should wrong and mismanagement be known to exist. . . . From the nature of the case there could be no concerted action to reform or correct admitted errors.
>
> —*Anonymous, 1852*[13]

The separation of ownership and control that began in the late antebellum period deepened after it, when the nation was beset upon by "plundering rings of railway managers, who organize, at the expense of the road . . . parasites which prevent railway investments . . . from returning anything like the profit which railway enterprises actually yield."[14] In 1878, the *New York Times* warned that a few men ran the railroads and telegraph companies "mainly in their own interest," pointing to a rash of "embezzlements and irregularities" as proof.[15] Ten years later, a pamphlet titled *The Long-Suffering Shareholder: Railroad Directorial Mismanagement and Governmental Oppression* called railway governance "an aggregation of abuses, unscrupulousness, and dishonesty that is startling."[16]

Initially, checks such as the concept of ultra vires and caps on capitalization prevented railroad directors from furthering their managerial empires by straying into other lines of business. By 1900, the potency of ultra vires was rapidly disappearing;[17] by 1930, it was, in the words of legal historian Morton Horwitz, "if not dead, substantially eroded in practice."[18] Moreover, railroads and other corporations chartered or rechartered in the late nineteenth century and thereafter could engage in any lawful activity with whatever amount of capital that they could acquire without legislative or stockholder approval. In the words of Massachusetts legislators in 1902, the presumption had become "that, in the absence of fraud in its organization or government [governance], an ordinary business corporation should be allowed to do anything that an individual may do."[19] A fundamental governance balance thus disappeared, greatly increasing stockholders' monitoring burden, which had already been substantially raised by the large scale and scope of railroads and giant, multistate manufacturers. Gone were the days when most stockholders could casually and cheaply monitor their investments as they went about their daily activities.[20]

As executives came to control corporations and stockholders came to be seen as annoyances rather than owners, selective disclosure of corporate information slowly died. Executives began to tell stockholders that to divulge information at any time other than annual meetings would do an injustice to the other stockholders. By the early twentieth century, the only way that many stockholders could be assured of receiving a copy of a corporation's annual report was to appear at its annual meeting.[21] By that time, many annual reports were of dubious quality, ranging from the almost-useful type to the worse-than-useless "dance-card, bald balance-sheet, or picture-book variety."[22] The reports of the Royal Baking Powder Company failed "to register any fiscal information at all . . . for more than a quarter of a century."[23] Moreover, executives discouraged attendance in sundry ways, some not very subtle.[24] By 1950, aside from a handful of "corporate gadflies," small shareholders at annual meetings were as "rare as a polar bear in the tropics."[25]

Market pressures forced some corporations, such as U.S. Steel and GM, to minimize errors of omission as well as commission in their reports. "It evidently pays," noted one 1920s investment guru, "with bona fide investors to be frank." "Enigmatic accounting" that obscured "the distinction between capital and income" rendered even well-meaning reports of dubious value.[26] "The methods employed for the purpose of giving a wrong impression to the stockholders or the public as to the company's condition," wrote an accountant in 1909, "are almost innumerable."[27] "The means of corporation officials for misleading creditors and then diverting assets to defraud them," another critic noted, "are so varied and inscrutable that creditors are likewise helpless."[28]

"Though not technically fraudulent," many companies used "complicated systems of book-keeping" that contemporaries found "misleading and deceptive."[29] "Directors and their accountants may frame their figures, within limits," two experts complained, "much as they choose."[30] As a result, shysters found it relatively easy to induce investors to overpay for securities, especially high-yielding (risky) ones issued by railroads, oil and mining prospecting companies, land developers, and patent-development schemes of dubious quality. Apologists for the status quo even argued that stockholders ought to be beguiled.[31]

State governments responded to the demise of effective selective disclosure and the resultant increase in securities fraud by passing public disclosure and so-called Blue Sky Laws. Both, however, proved of dubious merit. Between 1911 and 1933, all but two states regulated securities through such laws. The laws were popular, partly because securities salesmen were always depicted as vultures, grafters, swindlers, and confidence men, and the buyers were always innocent widows, orphans, farmers, workingmen, or the feeble-minded. The regulations also proved popular because they protected the profits of small, local banks by raising the costs of securities issuers and investors. The federal government joined the fray during the New Deal by passing the Securities Act of 1933 and the Securities Exchange Act of 1934, which established the Securities and Exchange Commission (SEC), the Investment Company Act of 1940, and subsequent securities regulations. The regulations were necessary, though far from optimal, because returning to a regime of selective disclosure would have been meaningless because of stockholders' loss of control over their property.[32]

By the early postbellum period, many corporations were dominated by directors no longer beholden to stockholders or other stakeholders. In 1868, one critic complained that New York's railroad law was predicated on the assumption "that the directors are not agents at will, and subject to consultation and instruction from their principals the stockholders, but that, for the period of their office, they are, with but slight qualification, absolute masters of affairs."[33] "The Stockholder," another complained later that year, "is fast becoming only an embarrassing recollection to ambitious, scheming and self-willed Boards of Directors."[34] Because the "great majority of shareholders" had "no practical way of making their influence felt" and because directors were no longer easily removed from office during their tenure,[35] another observer complained, board members could run amok.[36] The Erie Railroad was particularly notorious because, in the words of another contemporary, "a large part of the owners have been for many years, not only entirely excluded from the management, but kept in ignorance of the company operations; and that irresponsible power and secrecy of management has been taken advantage of to commit a series of frauds and robberies upon the stockholders and public."[37]

The reign of the director was relatively short, as salaried executives soon seized more control from directors because of their superior access to important information about increasingly large and complex businesses and their control of the proxy voting system.[38] Increasingly, entrenched executives ran the show "in defiance of the stockholders, or any combination of them that can be made," as well as of the directors, who, even if they met weekly, could not exert effective control over behemoths like the Pennsylvania Railroad or U.S. Steel.[39] Many directors became mere shills—"dummy directors" hired by executives to serve as window dressing.[40] By 1875, Anthony Trollope could write a novel (*The Way We Live Now*) in which the promoters of a great railway between the United States and Mexico exploited the names of famous but clueless directors who met only once, for a few minutes, before the entire concern burned in a speculative crash.[41] Fiction was fact half a century later, when George Gould consented to be elected a director in Commonwealth Trust Company of New York only because the company's executives promised that he did not need to appear at any meetings. Gould later testified that he "never went near the Trust Company, knew nothing of its affairs, gave no attention to its business, took no action."[42] And shills were cheap because by 1900 or so, directors needed to own only a single share to remain eligible.[43] By 1915, contemporary observers knew that the "typical director" of a large corporation was "totally ignorant of the actual operations" of the business and "feels and exercises no responsibility for anything beyond the financial condition and the selection of executive officials." By then, executives were "practically supreme."[44]

"The interest of the managers of a modern corporation," economist Thorstein Veblen understood, "need not coincide with the permanent interest of the corporation as a going concern."[45] The takeover by management did not happen at all corporations or all at once but rather evolved over several decades, pushed forward by the erosion of stakeholder voting rights and other governance checks and balances and changes in legal conceptions of the corporation. The demise of prudent mean voting rules and the rise of uncapped one-vote-per-share voting rules reduced the power of minority shareholders. The minority stockholder associations that sprang up in the postbellum period, such as the Minnesota Electoral Reform Association and the New York Cheap Transportation Association, had salubrious effects in some cases.[46] But by the late 1880s, critics spoke of "the farce of voting by self or proxy,"[47] and, by 1910, Woodrow Wilson could write that the "position of the minority stockholder is . . . extremely unsatisfactory. I do no wonder that he sometimes doubts whether corporate stocks are property at all."[48] The *New York Times'* 1878 cry for a one-vote-per-shareholder rule was a nonstarter.[49]

Cumulative voting rights, "the corporate analogue of proportional representation,"[50] were also eventually beaten back in most states.[51] After an initial push for cumulative voting rights in Illinois, Pennsylvania, and Missouri in the early postbellum period,[52] minority stockholders slowly lost the power to cast all their votes for a single director beholden to their interests, even though many believed that just by being present, "the minority director, watching the interests of the minority stock" was often sufficient to "prevent a wrong."[53] Instead, stockholders were forced to dissipate their votes among the entire directorial slate. Voting rules were also transformed. Originally, a majority meant half of all stock, but by the end of the nineteenth century, it often meant just half actually "present and voting." Minority stockholders thereby lost the power to block board actions merely by abstaining, and important acts became, for the first time in U.S. corporate history, "legalized through assent of a small fraction of the electorate."[54]

In the first decades of the twentieth century, owners of preferred shares lost their right to vote except in the case of default. Then common shareholders lost voting power through the creation of different classes of stock with different voting rights.[55] Class B shares, for instance, often held super voting rights and were not regularly traded in the market but rather were used by family members or executives to control corporate elections. Artificial silk manufacturer Industrial Rayon, for example, issued 598,000 shares of nonvoting class A stock and 2,000 shares of (voting) class B stock. Executives so often owned the class B shares that they were also known as "management stock" and were clearly created to ensconce executives in office.[56] Shares with restricted voting rights were one of the tools in the chest of J. P. Morgan reorganizations. By the 1920s, it was "possible to incorporate a company in which practically all the shareholders are deprived of the right to vote."[57] The disfranchisement movement was rolled back, thanks to an uproar initiated by Harvard professor and corporate governance expert William Z. Ripley. Despite Ripley's claim that nonvoting stock was "dead beyond recall" and stock exchange resistance to it, various forms of voting restrictions appeared again in the 1950s and gained considerable strength thereafter, as a result of a variety of loopholes that effectively disfranchised most smallholders. By the 1960s, John Kenneth Galbraith could state without contradiction that most stockholders technically could vote but that their votes were "valueless."[58] Today, U.S. corporations rarely issue shares with super voting rights, probably because stockholders have long since stopped voting.[59]

During the late nineteenth and early twentieth centuries, it also became increasingly futile for stockholders to successfully sue self-dealing directors, even after corporate bankruptcy. Postbellum policymakers repeatedly displayed indifference to the plight of stockholders because jurists came to see them as passive investors rather than as active members with an important role in governance.[60] Courts increasingly gave executives broad discretion with the promulgation of the "business judgment rule,"[61] which held that executives were responsible, as the Pennsylvania Supreme Court stated in 1872, for "any losses resulting from fraud, embezzlement or willful misconduct" but not for "mistakes of judgment."[62] The business judgment rule is sensible if applied intelligently; but in the 1880s, directors and officers pressed for even more discretion, including exemption from all personal liability.[63] By 1890 or so, in the words of law professor Herbert Hovenkamp, "those in control of the corporation were legally answerable for virtually nothing."[64] By the 1920s, numerous charters explicitly allowed directors to have a personal interest in their corporation's contracts and absolved them "from any liability that might otherwise exist." In many cases, directors could even vote on contracts in which they stood to profit. In other words, directors could self-deal with complete impunity. Many apparently did, in a stunning variety of ways. Limited liability became sacrosanct at this time because deteriorating governance meant that most corporations could not raise capital without it.[65]

Increasingly, salaried executives supplanted large stockholders on boards of directors, even though most executives owned relatively little stock themselves. In one corporation, the president owned only a single share, and the rest of the directors and officers owned only 17,760 of the 2.426 million shares outstanding. Laws that required directors to own stock were emasculated until stock ownership became a mere formality. By the early 1930s, "those in control h[e]ld only a negligible proportion of the total ownership," according to early governance gurus Berle and Means.[66] As executives moved into directorships, the independence of most boards waned—in some cases, to virtually nil. By the turn of the century, regulators complained about "one-man banking" because directors had ceased monitoring their institutions' loan portfolios or even their overall business strategies. Instead of meeting weekly, as was traditional, many bank boards had to be forced to meet monthly.[67]

Eager to build empires that would enrich and aggrandize themselves, some executives in the 1880s began to form large, interstate trusts.[68] After courts broke up the sugar and oil trusts in the early 1890s, corporations began to charter themselves in the states with the most pro-management rules: first, New Jersey and, later, Delaware.[69] (Confusingly, large interstate corporations continued to be called "trusts" long after they jettisoned the form in favor of the New Jersey holding company, a process largely completed by 1904.[70]) A sort of race toward the bottom ensued[71] as states with the most pro-management laws soon became the nominal headquarters of the nation's largest and most important corporations.[72] States with more stringent laws could not retaliate by taxing the corporations of "chartermongering states"[73] such as New Jersey, Delaware, Maine, South Dakota, and West Virginia out of their states because interstate coordination was difficult and the threat of counterattacks too grave. Within a few years, more than half of the nation's corporations were chartered in lenient New Jersey, where, according to a leading legal historian, a corporation chartered after 1889 "could do virtually anything it wanted"[74] and was no longer subject to the relatively staid corporate laws of Massachusetts, New York, Pennsylvania, or even Colorado.[75]

Rather than try to buck the trend, other states soon liberalized their corporate laws in an attempt to win market share from New Jersey, the treasury of which had quickly grown fat on incorporation fees and taxes.[76] The corporation servicing company for South Dakota advertised in a Boston newspaper that South Dakota's charters beat those of New Jersey because they cost only "a few dollars" and the state's secretary boasted that 95 percent of the time applications were approved "within ten hours after the application is received here."[77] The corporate laws of Maine allowed management "without approval of the shareholders, to dispose of the assets at any price; to purchase whatever property it might see fit, at any figure; to contract loans without . . . hindrances; and to issue new securities also *ad lib*."[78] By the 1930s, critics complained that state corporation laws were riddled with "loopholes through which astute and skillful lawyers can drive an automobile and still have room for a passing truck."[79] Delaware eventually won the race with laws and court precedents that favored executives over shareholders—for example, by allowing executives to pay dividends out of capital.[80] Today, 90 percent of large U.S. corporations are chartered in Delaware.[81] Active competition now focuses on the charters of shell corporations—legally valid corporations with no shareholders, assets, or paid-in capital that, "if . . . not found in the law books," as one corporate critic put it in the 1930s, "might be thought a reflection of one of Alice's more extreme adventures on her sojourn in Wonderland."[82] In the process, shareholders typically lost access to the names of other shareholders. They could still inspect company account books but only with a court order.[83]

The liberal, pro-management states empowered directors (now either executives or beholden to them) to acquire services, assets, and even corporations with stock at valuations that the directors themselves decided. "Valuation of anything other than cash," Berle and Means wryly noted, "always raises some questions."[84] Executives were also empowered to form holding companies with no business of their own. With that, ultra vires, already mutilated by the government's reluctance to enforce the seemingly decrepit ancient concept, was completely emasculated and directors could acquire other corporations without clear limit. Although invoking ultra vires and easing entry barriers worked in the Texas oil industry and a few other places, most corporations responded to increased state-centered regulation by rechartering in states with weaker restrictions. Competition (antitrust) policy therefore shifted to the federal level. After passage of the Sherman Act in 1890, the federal government did a good job of stopping "loose" combinations such as cartels but proved relatively powerless to stop firms from integrating, vertically or horizontally, because most nonfinancial firms held state charters. Corporations responded by jettisoning cartels in favor of "tight" combinations such as holding companies and outright amalgamation. Formally combining with competitors satiated the desire for market power traditionally fulfilled by cartels imperiled by the Sherman Act. The process culminated in the so-called Great Merger Movement, the period between 1897 and 1904 when 4,227 companies combined into just 257 giant corporations. The agglomerations were justified economically by the economies of scale opened up by new technologies and large national and international markets. Mergers could also lower the cost of capital because larger companies found it easier and cheaper to tap emerging national capital markets.[85]

The merger movement, however, accelerated the separation of ownership and control, or in other words, it accelerated the trend toward ownership by markedly more numerous and more widely dispersed small stockholders.[86] As the number of smallholders increased, the effectiveness of their monitoring of management decreased because of free-rider problems and the large fixed costs associated with attending meetings and analyzing financial statements, an always onerous chore rendered more so by the increased gaming of dividends after 1900. When asked if dividends should be paid "if they are not earned," the president of a major corporation answered in 1916: "That's an open question."[87] Dividend smoothing also became more pronounced as executives found it easy to hide assets until needed during a downturn to keep dividends at the expected level. Large surplus accounts also made dividend smoothing easier.[88] The rise of the income tax further reduced the signals that dividends once provided. To reduce their taxes, stockholders urged executives to stop paying dividends and retain earnings or buy back stock instead. Soon, stockholders came to desire rising stock prices rather than a dividend stream.[89] That change allowed executives to more easily expropriate stakeholders through the use of what one contemporary called "accounting monstrosity—or shall we call it acrobatics?"[90]

Bondholders and creditors were not very effective monitors any more, either, because in the 1880s they lost much of their power to help govern corporations that went into default or bankruptcy.[91] By the late nineteenth century, courts allowed executives of failed corporations to stay in power and turned railroads over to receivers rather than to bondholders and other creditors. Henry Wollman complained in 1894 that the courts "appoint receivers for corporations on the flimsiest of grounds . . . but prevent the creditors doing anything, except to sit by and see the executives operate them as they deem proper."[92] By 1910, the management of all corporations operating across state lines had like power over creditors.

Many foreign bondholders, owners of about a quarter of all foreign-held U.S. corporate bonds, responded to those developments by selling off their bonds to American investors. More investors did not flee the markets because they believed, usually correctly, that powerful financial intermediaries protected their interests. Between the Civil War and World War I, a period sometimes dubbed "the age of financial capitalism," investment banks played important roles in the governance of U.S. nonfinancial corporations. Relatively unimportant financial intermediaries prior to the Civil War, investment banks grew rapidly in number and prominence during the Gilded Age. By 1900, investment banks such as J. P. Morgan and Kuhn, Loeb & Co. were thought to dominate the industrial and transportation sectors for their own benefit. Such claims were exaggerated; but by controlling access to capital markets, the banks did exert considerable influence on the boards of most major corporations.[93]

Before the Civil War, general securities laws were rare and of little practical effect because most regulation was handled privately on regional exchanges and the New York Stock Exchange. Financial disclosure requirements on the latter, however, were rarely enforced, so public financial information was rare and, especially when unaudited, of low or even negative value. Instead of specific information, therefore, investors in the late nineteenth century relied on the reputation of institutional investors such as J. P. Morgan to help them discern safe investments from risky ones. Investment banks served as a sort of insurer for investors, stepping up their monitoring whenever one of their issuers ran into financial difficulties. Monitoring ranged from costly to impossible: the bankers readily told stories of being outmanned and out-gunned by corporate executives who controlled the flow of information to the board. Nevertheless, the bankers were often able to obtain the information and policies they needed because they controlled access to the capital market.[94]

The ability of investment banks to act as governance intermediaries for retail investors waned with the passage of the Clayton Act of 1914. Financial capitalism did not sit well with many Americans, who believed that it gave too much power to the likes of J. P. Morgan. The system came under espe-cially heavy attack after the Panic of 1907. Congressman Arsene Pujo's 1912 investigation of investment banking and the 1914 publication of Louis Brandeis's anti–investment bank diatribe *Other People's Money* made policy-makers ill-disposed toward Wall Street titans.[95] Pujo's report correctly noted that no one—no one living, anyway—had ever heard of small stockholders "overthrowing an existing management in any large corporation" or even se-curing "the investigation of an existing management of a corporation to as-certain whether it has been well or honestly managed" because in all "great corporations with numerous and widely scattered stockholders . . . the man-agement is virtually self-perpetuating and is able through the power of pa-tronage, the indifference of stockholders and other influences to control a majority of stock."[96] Instead of acknowledging the major governance role played by investment bankers, Pujo, Brandeis, and other critics conflated them with executives. Some, such as Walter Lippman, argued that the aston-ishing fact was that businesses were "managed by men who are not profiteers. The managers are on salary, divorced from ownership."[97] Many correctly per-ceived that Morgan and his men were all that stood in the way of managerial dominance of the nation's biggest companies.

Nevertheless, regulatory attacks on financial capitalism continued until the system was all but dead by the end of the New Deal, as a result of the pas-sage of Glass-Steagall and the creation of the SEC. Glass-Steagall forced the complete separation of commercial (take deposits and make loans) and in-vestment (securities issuance) banking. The restriction solved no economic problems but helped legislators get reelected by purportedly fixing a pre-sumed cause of the Great Depression. Glass-Steagall also aided the big invest-ment banks by limiting competition from the large commercial banks with securities affiliates that had been winning market share from them for dec-ades. That same legislation also protected small unit banks by providing them with deposit insurance instead of encouraging the formation of the large, well-diversified branch banks that weathered the Depression so successfully in California and Canada. Other reforms limited entry into banking and created a quasi-cartel by limiting the interest rates that banks could pay on different types of deposits. Those and other reforms, when combined with the unexpected inflation of the 1970s, led directly to the Savings and Loan Crisis of the 1980s.[98]

With the financiers scotched, executives extended their powers and prerogatives further than ever before. By the 1920s, stockholders could not even discover how much salaried executives paid themselves.[99] Governance guru William Z. Ripley complained of "the steady encroachment of management upon the traditional rights of shareholders" but pointed to contrary sentiments and court decisions that promised to catalyze a revival of stockholder control.[100] By the 1930s, however, other observers lamented that the "old vested rights" of the stockholder were "gone or going."[101] A dark malaise had settled over corporate governance. "Too often," lamented one depressed, Depression-era observer, "we find stockholders who do not vote, directors who do not direct, and officers who do not obey."[102] This meant, as Berle and Means famously put it in *The Modern Corporation and Private Property*, "the divorce of ownership from control."[103]

Some stockholder activism still occurred, especially in egregious cases of managerial expropriation; but under normal circumstances, widespread stock ownership and proxy control provided executives with overwhelming power. "When corporations have stockholders numbering in the many thousands," wrote corporate critic I. Maurice Wormser in 1931, "it becomes impossible to hold corporate meetings which amount to anything. Proxies are signed blindly at the request of the management, which in this manner is enabled usually to continue its control at the shareholders' expense." "Stockholders, especially small ones," Wormser lamented, "are surprisingly indifferent to all corporate ills and abuses, especially while dividends are being paid."[104]

Cognizant that high levels of expropriation could lead to their ouster or their company's failure, executives shared profits with stockholders, especially when there were plenty to go around.[105] Between the Civil War and World War II, executives became more specialized, educated, and professional as they learned to coordinate the activities of corporate enterprises unprecedented in size, scope, and complexity. According to renowned business historian Alfred Chandler, the "visible hand" of management and strategic planning improved upon Adam Smith's "invisible hand" of the market.[106] By the early twentieth century, it was possible to argue with a straight face, as corporate finance scholar William Lough did, that "the active managers of a corporation are more prudent or more farsighted than the majority of their stockholders and for the good of the corporation" desire a different set of policies.[107] But advocates of strong, able technocratic executives, such as Lough and Chandler, forgot about Adam Smith's critique of the principal-agent problem inherent in the corporate form. Executives might be better equipped to make business decisions than stockholders are, but that does not mean that they will do so. If not properly checked, they might use their superior expertise, acumen, and knowledge to self-deal in any number of ways.

As argued in Chapter 5, from the founding of the republic, significant numbers of investors owned most large U.S. corporations. Before the Civil War, however, even the largest corporations could be effectively governed by smallholders in the absence of large blockholders because of the checks and balances described in Chapter 6. Those checks eroded just as the size of the largest corporations and the number of small shareholders ballooned. By the interwar period, most of the 200 largest U.S. corporations had tens or hundreds of thousands of dispersed shareholders, most completely unable to exert any meaningful control. Although many substantial companies, such as Pepperell in Biddeford, Maine, were still owned by 1,600 or so stockholders, including important local financial intermediaries, the most widely held companies were per force owned by large numbers of laborers, housewives, and clerks. Most of those large, widely held corporations were controlled by entrenched executives, but some effectively remained in the hands of majority stockholders or minority groups that cobbled their votes together, along with whatever proxies they could obtain, to create what was called "working control" of the company.[108]

In the first decade of the twentieth century, "railway stocks," in the words of a contemporary investment analyst, "tended . . . to pass more into the hands of the smaller investors," who numbered in the tens of thousands.[109] By 1909, Pennsylvania Railroad had more than 60,000 stockholders and United States Steel almost 110,000. In 1910, the average holding of the American Sugar Refining Company's 19,359 stockholders was fewer than fifty shares. Almost half of all shareholders held ten or fewer shares. By 1924, the number of shareholders in Standard Oil had jumped to 300,000 from just 6,000 in 1911; the American Telephone and Telegraph stockholder list increased from 7,500 in 1900 to 343,000 in 1924 to 642,000 in 1931. By 1930, about 438,000 people owned shares in Cities Services, 269,000 in General Motors, 232,000 in Pennsylvania Railroad, and 141,000 in United States Steel, a number matched by corporations "too numerous to enumerate."[110] Many of those smallholders were corporate employees awarded stock for what one contemporary called "length of service or for meritorious service."[111] By the 1920s, employee stock plans were widespread. They were thought to reduce support for unions and socialism and further enhanced managerial power with pro-management proxies.[112]

According to one flawed but widely cited study, the total number of stockholders in all U.S. companies increased from about 4.4 million in 1900 to about 14.4 million in 1923 to 18 million in 1928. By the end of 1967, more than 22 million Americans directly owned shares, with AT&T alone claiming more than 3.2 million of them, and untold millions more indirectly owned shares through intermediaries such as insurers and pension funds. By then, none of the largest corporations had fewer than 10,000 shareholders each.[113]

Increased stock market liquidity also meant that shareholders had little incentive to look out for the corporation's long-term interests. Even for those who sought long-term investments, selling was easier than fighting if they became disgruntled or uneasy. As the Commission on Industrial Relations put it in 1915, "stockholders as a class . . . have no guiding interest in the permanent efficiency of the corporation [because] in a busy week on Wall street, the number of shares bought and sold in one of the great corporations will greatly exceed the total number of shares that are in existence." The same source claimed that "the ordinary stockholder in a large corporation actually . . . has less knowledge of its actual operations, and less control over its management, than the ordinary citizen has over local, state and national governments."[114]

Such a large increase in the number of shareholders was made possible by large increases in the number of extant shares.[115] Before the Civil War, capital stock could be defined fairly concretely: as stockholder contributions to the corporation. Although sometimes in the form of land or services, those contributions were typically in cash that was used to purchase productive assets such as machines, mines, or portfolios of financial assets and were legally held in trust for the benefit of the corporation's creditors first, and then for its stockholders as residual claimants.[116] By the early twentieth century, however, stock was heavily "watered." "Watered or fictitious stock," wrote one late nineteenth-century jurist, "is that issued when the full amount has not been paid up. If none be paid—or less than par—this is watered. Generally fraudulent, though it may be authorized."[117] Watered stock, wrote economist Alfred Marshall, "is issued without any actual payment of a corresponding sum of money."[118] "Watered stock, of course, has no real value back of it," wrote one corporate critic early in the Depression.[119] "By watered stock," he further explained, "is meant stock issued as being paid up in full though the consideration for it was grossly inadequate or non-existent."[120] For example, the Whisky Trust issued promoters over $24 million of stock in return for $3.5 million in cash. The Tin Plate Trust promoters received only $10 million but supplied nothing but vaguely defined services in return.[121]

According to one expert in the 1930s, "even if full allowance is made for intangible assets, patents, good will and dividend-earning power, a majority of our corporations have a vast amount of nominal capitalization for which there is no real equivalent in present or prospective value."[122] Today, all stock is watered in the sense that the market capitalization (share price times number of shares) far exceeds the value of tangible corporate assets. The market capitalization of many corporations also exceeds the value of the intangible assets such as goodwill. ("Goodwill," wrote one wag, "is the outward expression of inward unsubstantiality.")[123] That is possible because investors value corporations as an expected stream of earnings discounted to the present. Then and now, market prices reflect stock watering in that the price per share will decline as the nominal number of shares increases and earnings expectations remain constant.[124]

Manipulation of earnings expectations is much more difficult for markets to detect. "Watering" expected profits is relatively easy, at least in the short and intermediate terms, by manipulating quarterly earnings expectations. By 1900, it was widely believed that corporate insiders manipulated stock prices for their own benefit, to the detriment of "little holders of stock who stand shivering on the outside the management." In the first decades of the twentieth century, earnings became largely an accounting concept only loosely tied to economic reality, a number that could be gamed in seemingly endless ways. Concepts such as capital depreciation were inherently fuzzy. Accountants were urged to be "conservative" in their estimates, but there were few guidelines about what that meant. Sometimes executives ran factories or other physical inventory into the ground to appear more profitable than they actually were. "Few investors," economist Alfred Marshall lamented, "allow for such influences." Even seemingly straightforward tasks such as valuing corporate assets were also inherently ambiguous. As Marshall explained in 1919, valuing assets at their historical cost, as was traditionally done, was not necessarily accurate. "A railway in a deserted mining district is almost value-less," he explained, even if acquired at a high cost. Conversely, cheaply pur-chased land may subsequently rise in value "five-fold."[125] One corporate accountant justified rosy accounting by noting that "unwilling forbearance on the part of creditors" could save corporations from failure until they brought "everything around right."[126] Of course, "unwilling forbearance" could also be used to expropriate wealth from creditors and stockholders.[127]

Managerial Power after World War II

> We can learn from a largely jettisoned corporate
> governance configuration, in which well-informed,
> active, committed, and responsible corporate
> monitors added a dimension of control that is often
> sadly lacking at the beginning of the twenty-first
> century.
> —*Jeffrey Fear and Christopher Kobrak, 2010*[128]

World War II indirectly weakened stakeholders by creating a strong economy that easily hid defects in the governance system. America and its so-called cen-ter firms were on top of the world in the 1950s and 1960s, and their dominance allowed them to achieve high levels of profitability and low levels of corporate indebtedness. That fact, coupled with the New Deal's eradication of financial capitalism, allowed executives to maintain and even expand their control of corporations at the expense of stockholders and other stakeholders.[129]

Not all large corporations were controlled by executives, but a study con-ducted during World War II showed that at least half of the stock of the 176 largest corporations was held in blocks of less than 1 percent of the total is-sued. In less than a third was the interest of a blockholder large enough to allow potential control. The gap between ownership and control continued to widen in the postwar period as stock ownership in the largest corporations continued to broaden. In 1963, some 85 percent of the largest 200 nonfinan-cial corporations were effectively controlled by management. Adolph Berle, the granddaddy of governance gurus, noted in 1967 that the nation was still "digesting" the fact that owners did not manage and managers did not own, so "the corporate collective holds legal title to the tangible productive wealth of the country—for the benefit of others."[130] Berle's coauthor, economist

Gardiner Means, noted that the "corporate revolution" marched on. "The separation of ownership and control," he argued, "has released management from the overriding requirement that it serve stockholders."[131]

By the postwar period, the executive officers of most big companies no longer conceived of themselves as the stockholders' agents because a "managerialist" theory of executives as trustees, stewards, or professionals had taken hold.[132] "By mid-century," Alfred Chandler noted, "even the legal fiction of outside control was beginning to disappear."[133] The illusion of stockholder ownership persisted, however, because management found it a useful myth. "Corporate liturgy," as Galbraith called it, was attended with much solemnity to give the appearance that directors made decisions rather than merely rubber-stamped the "recommendations" of management. But in most instances, the incentives of the "old men" who serve on boards would make "rejection . . . unthinkable."[134] Stockholders were also allowed to believe that they had information and power as "products and even plants are inspected" and "handsomely printed reports" doled out. Even cranks were listened to "with every evidence of attention" and assurances that their cockamamie ideas would be "considered with the greatest care." Instead of the raucous affairs of the past, annual stockholder meetings became "perhaps, our most elaborate exercise in popular illusion."[135] But real "stockholder power," Galbraith lamented, had been the victim of a program of "euthanasia."[136]

Galbraith argued that the most important power "in modern industrial society is exercised not by capital but by organization, not by the capitalist but by the industrial bureaucrat." Gone were the great men of business history, the Carnegies, Rockefellers, and Fords, replaced by men unknown outside their industries. Owning "no appreciable share of the enterprise[s]" they run, they were "selected not by stockholders but . . . by a Board of Directors which narcissistically they selected themselves."[137] Despite Galbraith's critique, the separation of ownership and management was heralded in most academic circles. The Capital Asset Pricing Model (CAPM) that was developed in the 1960s allowed investors to buy securities with limited information about the issuer or its business, let alone its governance, rendering Galbraith and other critics' views seemingly obsolete. Major retirement fund legislation passed in 1974 (ERISA) stressed portfolio diversification in its version of the "prudent man rule," relieving pension funds from the duty of trying to discern good corporations from bad ones and further reducing the perceived importance of monitoring. By the postwar period, capital was plentiful and limited liability completely sacrosanct, so the incentive for stockholders to monitor management was low.

Bankruptcy law continued to allow executives to reorganize broken businesses while retaining control of the organization. In the words of a contemporary, executives enjoyed "power without property."[138]

With the nation's economy reaping the rich rewards of postwar economic dominance, executives could do little wrong. "The economic system of the United States" was by the 1960s "accepted by all but the malcontent as a largely perfect structure."[139] Through the 1960s, U.S. corporate success was undoubted. The problem facing policymakers was how to curb corporate excesses, not how to prevent executives from pilfering stockholders, many of whom had been co-opted by investor-relations departments and free lunches. Agency costs, however, remained sky-high and needed only the macroeconomic upheavals of the 1970s to expose them.[140]

By the 1960s, many executives were entrenched enough to augment their salaries not by making their companies more efficient but by making them larger. To do that without running afoul of the Justice Department and the Sherman Act, they formed conglomerates: huge organizations comprising disparate parts. By the 1970s, inflation and foreign competition had eroded both profits and the leeway that executives relied upon. Most conglomerates turned out to be colossal wastes of stockholders' money that improved executives' salaries, offices, and the like. Stock prices for the parent company dipped below the value of its parts until the unwieldy conglomerates were broken up, sometimes by management but more often by outsiders seizing an obvious profit opportunity. Once-mighty corporations such as U.S. Steel, Sears, Chrysler, and RCA began to teeter but were too administratively fat and managerially brain-dead to regain their balance easily. As the prospect of profits dwindled, so, at long last, did the patience of stakeholders. Increased product market competition due to globalization winnowed out incompetent executives, but, according to two leading experts, the effect of the new market realities was "hard to measure."[141] The effect of renewed stockholder activism, however, was not in doubt: it was large and salubrious. As Galbraith noted, "it is in times of such failure of earnings, and then only, that the stockholders of the large corporation can be aroused."[142]

In the first half of the twentieth century, stockholders were occasionally active enough to engage in proxy fights to defend their interests against entrenched executives despite the fact that the "loser of a proxy battle, if he is an outsider, must pay the cost." "If the company has been seriously mismanaged," Berle and Means noted in the early 1930s, "a protective committee of stockholders may combine a number of individual owners into a group which can successfully contend with the existing management and replace it."[143] That old-school option could be bolstered with other forms of "offensive shareholder activism," particularly the act of buying up large stakes in under-performing companies and then forcing management to make reforms likely to increase stock prices. That tactic was introduced by the "white sharks" of the 1950s, honed by the corporate "raiders" of the 1970s and 1980s such as T. Boone Pickens, Carl Icahn, Sir James Goldsmith, KKR, and more recently developed further by hedge and private equity funds. The massively ineffi-cient conglomerates that executives cobbled together in the 1960s were among the first targets.[144]

Some activist shareholders returned companies to profitability by induc-ing executives to make them more efficient via restructurings, downsizing, outsourcing, offshoring, and the implementation of leaner production meth-ods, just-in-time inventory control, and so forth. Other activists were accused of looting and scooting; but overall, they appear to have had a salubrious ef-fect on corporations as well as the overall economy. The existence of a vigor-ous "market for corporate control"—the mere threat of a takeover, in other words—became enough to send executives scrambling to make their busi-nesses more efficient, or at least to give that appearance, though perhaps at the cost of focusing managerial attention on short-term gains rather than on long-term strategic projects.[145]

Offensive stockholder activism is, unfortunately, now subject to a range of takeover antidotes, such as poison pills and other tactics and laws that protect entrenched executives. According to corporate guru Jonathan Macey, the market for corporate control "has been crippled by statutes and regulations, rendering the hostile takeover virtually obsolete."[146] As noted above, hedge and private equity funds have filled some of the lacunae, but they, too, are under attack.[147]

More fundamentally, the market for corporate control functions best when a corporation's share price is lower than its value under better manage-ment. Knowing that, executives game the accounting system to get stock prices up (or the apparent value of the company down, but that is less likely because of the compensation system discussed below). Accounting shenani-gans today can be much more extensive than gaming dividends in the nine-teenth century were. Due to the tax structure and the theory that all but the most mature corporations should reinvest most of their profits in their busi-ness, dividends are now minute. Ascertaining a corporation's earnings is now an exercise in judgment with very little connection to hard reality, at least in the short and intermediate terms. That is how businesses valued at billions one day can be worthless the next. Accounting ambiguity is the heart of what law professor Lawrence Mitchell has termed the "speculation economy," a system built more on financial and accounting conventions than bona-fide productivity improvements.[148]

The speculation economy has thrived since at least the 1920s, when Harvard professor William Z. Ripley and accountant Arthur Andersen (the person, not the recently disgraced firm) railed against financial statements that ranged from deceptive to downright abusive.[149] "Apart from intricate corporate methods of bookkeeping which an archangel would find difficult to unravel," complained one observer during the Great Depression, "it is a truism that knowledge of the true facts is confined to a very small group of insiders."[150] Accounting practice slowly moved away from its traditional, pro-creditor emphasis on balance sheets, the so-called proprietary theory of accounting, toward a more stockholder-friendly entity theory of accounting that emphasized income statements. Nevertheless, accounting remains the corporate governance system's weakest link, the easiest way of inducing investors to pay more than they ought to for corporate securities. Stockholders can sue, but only if financial statements are "grossly negligent." The Securities Acts of 1933 and 1934 mandated disclosure whenever a corporation issued securities and as long as its securities remained publicly traded, but its impact was muted by a big jump in exempted private placements and in the continued evolution of accounting ambiguities.[151]

The systematic overvaluation of corporate securities is a major problem. As a British judge accurately reasoned, "if it became known to the world that the balance sheets of English companies could not be relied upon, it would be a very serious thing for this country."[152] Thankfully, equity markets have a mechanism for chastening corporations that game the accounting system too much. It is called "shorting." An investor who thinks that a corporation is overvalued can borrow some of its shares from a broker, sell them at the inflated price, and then, after the stock price declines, buy the shares back, return the shares to the broker, and pocket the difference (minus transaction costs, of course). When it is allowed, shorting helps to keep asset bubbles from puffing up too much. Short sellers do not generally exert any influence on governance; in other words, corporations with inflated share prices are not subject to the same governance pressures as those with deflated ones because few want to buy something that is overpriced that they cannot control. The even more disturbing flip side is that stockholders of overpriced corporations tend to remain content because they believe that they are getting rich. Instead of scrutinizing the business carefully, they sit back and watch the ticker with glee.[153]

Another reason that publicly traded corporations game their accounts to look more valuable than they actually are is that executive compensation is now closely tied to stock prices. As Thorstein Veblen once noted, managers have incentives to create a discrepancy "between the actual and the putative earning-capacity of the corporation's capital."[154] Modern executives, in the sense of top-level managers compensated primarily by salary rather than an ownership stake, began to proliferate in the wake of the great merger movement at the end of the nineteenth century. According to one prewar survey, executives in U.S. corporations owned about 25 percent of the capital of the corporations they ran, *on average*. But while some companies were almost completely owned by their executives, many were less than 2 percent owned by their top managers; and in some, executives owned no shares whatsoever. By World War I, salaried executives dominated the ranks of many of the largest industrial firms, though some old-school proprietary managers compensated largely with profits remained. Executives' salaries stayed the same or increased but never went down—and they have been increasing ever since the 1940s. "While earnings show the ebb and flow of changing business conditions," two contemporary economists noted, "the salaries of managers remain unchanged" in the short term, adjusting only after short-term gains proved "in the end to be pure gain."[155]

When corporate performance was found lacking, many companies adopted cash bonus plans that paid executives a percentage of annual profits on top of their base salaries. During the Great Depression, some stakeholders complained that unwarranted bonuses were being paid surreptitiously. World War II brought with it higher marginal tax rates and a shift in compensation toward tax-favored fringe benefits such as insurance, pension, and stock-option plans. Although popular, the stock-option plans remained a relatively small part of overall compensation at most corporations from the 1950s through the 1980s, partly because of an initially cold reception by the courts, less favorable tax treatment after 1964, and complaints by stockholders who saw potential for abuse. Because directors were de facto selected by proxy-wielding executives, not by stockholders, some critics predicted that boards would regularly lower the options' strike price if the company's stock price slipped, effectively rewarding executives for decreasing shareholder value. Option repricing indeed became a major problem in the 2000s.[156]

Since the 1970s, executive compensation has been growing much faster than worker income, even in declining industries such as auto manufacturing, as executives learned to pack "golden parachutes" for themselves that ensured their financial safety, even if they flew their companies into the ground. Much of that additional compensation has taken the form of stock options because they appeared to work wonders in the 1980s, partly because of changes in the tax code that favored them and partly because academics such as Michael Jensen and William Meckling pushed the idea that options would induce executives to work more diligently and more intelligently.[157] Workers continued to own shares as well; but to have the intended incentive effect, nonexecutive employees had to invest most of their retirement savings in their employer's stock, with disastrous results in the case of Enron and other failed corporations. As we have seen, the notion that owners work harder and smarter than mere employees was an old one rooted in the thought of Adam Smith and other corporate critics. As classical economist John Stuart Mill put it: "Management . . . by hired servants, who have no interest in the result but that of preserving their salaries, is proverbially inefficient, unless they act under the inspecting eye, if not the controlling hand, of the person chiefly interested: and prudence almost always recommends giving to a manager not thus controlled a remuneration partly dependent on the profits."[158]

Stock options essentially turned executives into owners, or so the academics argued. But they were wrong, for four fundamental reasons. First, stock options gave executives only the upside benefit of ownership, not the downside risk, and hence essentially rewarded them for taking risks with other people's money. Second, options increased executive income even when stock prices increased as a result of macroeconomic fluctuations, such as lower interest rates, rather than managerial acumen. Third, options provided executives with short-term incentives, not the long-term incentives of true owners; short-term incentives encouraged risk-taking and also stock-puffing. Fourth, option backdating removed any remaining incentive alignment capacity of this type of compensation; claims to the contrary notwithstanding, option repricing does not improve company performance or even improve retention of key employees.[159]

Governance matters do look bleak at present; but in Chapter 10, I will suggest ways of improving corporate governance today by harking back to the checks and balances that were slowly eroded away between the Civil War and World War II.

Chapter 10

Reforming Corporate Governance

> A wise legislator will look to the experience of the past for lessons of
> prudence to direct him in the disposition of the various subjects of public
> interest that come under deliberation. . . . This review of the past is often
> beneficial, though the analogy of cases may not be perfect, whenever the
> similarity is sufficient to trace the general effect of the principles that govern
> any political system.
>
> —Report of the Committee on Banks and Insurance Companies, 1826[1]

Despite their weakening governance systems, U.S. corporations have continued to grow larger, more numerous, and more complex, and have become an
ever larger component of the national economy. In the late nineteenth century, one corporate jurist noted that few entities other than corporations promoted "wealth, or science or charity, . . . and the statute books are filled with
acts of incorporation."[2] By 1916, more than 300,000 corporations were active
throughout the nation, and the largest ones alone had an aggregate market
value of some $8 billion. By the mid-1980s, more than half a million new
corporations formed each year. In 2001, some 5.5 million corporations were
operating in the United States.[3]

By the late twentieth century, most corporations, new or seasoned, were
vanishingly small, but the 3,000 or so largest corporations were enormous,
controlling about 75 percent of all corporate assets and sales. Those are the
ones that stand in serious need of reform. In the last dozen years or so, an
alarming number—Enron, WorldCom, Bear Stearns, Lehman Brothers, and
AIG, to name a few—have failed because of factors ranging from gross mismanagement to egregious fraud. Corporate apologists consider them rotten

apples, but closer inspection makes clear that they are symptomatic of a much deeper problem: failed systems of governance and regulation.[4]

In Chapter 1, I raised the specter of the U.S. economy being devastated by a combination of wrongheaded regulation and a loss of confidence in corporate governance. A crisis of confidence in the broad nonfinancial sector could occur if investors learn that they cannot accurately value corporate shares because of the poor state of corporate governance and accounting. Erastus Bigelow, a prominent inventor and textile manufacturer, once remarked that when investors "decide to invest capital" in corporations, they usually do so "on the grounds of general confidence. They invest because others are investing; they believe, without knowing exactly why, that such investments are safe, and will be profitable."[5] They follow the herd, sometimes toward risky equities, as during the dotcom bubble of the late 1990s; but sometimes away from them, as during the long bear market that began at the outset of the Great Depression and lasted until the Korean War.

While the probability of a repetition of such a large and angry bear market may seem low, that is what most people thought about the possibility of a subprime-mortgage-related crisis in the mid-2000s. And even more is at stake now because a broad crisis of confidence could not be reversed by bailouts, as the sums involved would be too vast. Instead of the systemic crisis of 2008, the U.S. would face an existential crisis on the order of the Revolution or the Civil War. As its critics predicted, the corporation, like a Frankenstein, may turn out to be an impressive piece of technology that destroys its creators. Directors, executives, shareholders, and policymakers need to learn again how to mitigate the agency problem inherent in the corporate form before it is too late.[6]

The key will be to restore the principles of governance common in the antebellum period, not additional state-centered regulation. As Professor Johann Neem pointed out to me in private correspondence, reviving the nation's political culture—increasing voter turnout, raising the level of political discourse, and revivifying democracy—would be a great aid here.[7] Government regulators play a perverse game of cat and mouse or Whac-A-Mole because "the ingenuity of concealment," as one early nineteenth-century banker put it, was "naturally as great as the ingenuity of detection."[8] The evil ascribable to mismanagement rears its ugly head in one hole. As regulators prepare to give it a light whack, the mole disappears, only to reappear shortly thereafter in another hole. The only people with incentive to strangle the evil mismanagement mole and fill its hiding holes are corporate stakeholders, especially stockholders. New holes will always be dug, but stockholders are more likely than regulators to predict where they will appear and to react to them with appropriate speed and vigor.[9]

Much of the recent debate about corporations centers on whether they should maximize profits (shareholder value) or act in presumably more socially conscious ways by considering their impact upon other stakeholders, including employees, communities, and the environment. That very ideologically based debate largely misses a more important point: most corporations today are run in the best interests of executives, not stockholders, let alone God's critters. Executives jumped on the corporate social responsibility bandwagon whenever it personally benefited them to do so because it assuaged their consciences or made their lives easier. They encourage the debate because it helps deflect attention from the real problem: their complete control of most large, publicly traded corporations.[10]

In the late 1920s, corporate governance expert William Z. Ripley claimed: "The house is not falling down—no fear of that! But there are queer little noises about, as of rats in the wall, or of borers in the timbers."[11] In the intervening period (nearing a century), creepy critters have had enough time to endanger the house and, indeed, the economy's entire foundation. As recently as the late 1990s, it was possible for well-informed observers to consider Anglo-American corporate governance successful. "Complementary monitoring patterns—one professional and the other governmental—provide assurances in the Anglo-American markets of the reliability and currency of corporate information," Jonathan Baskin and Paul Miranti wrote in 1997, with little guff from reviewers (including myself).[12] At that time, boards of directors and so-called gatekeepers—accountants, attorneys, investment bankers, consultants, credit-rating agencies, securities analysts, stock exchanges, and other professional monitors—seemed to be doing a good job, and the government "provided a second level of monitoring."[13] Moreover, the mere threat of additional federal regulation appeared to keep management in line.[14]

After the bursting of the dotcom bubble in 2000, the corporate accounting scandals of Enron, WorldCom, and others, and the financial crisis of 2007–9, such sanguine views appear almost naive. Instead of providing a second level of monitoring, government regulators lulled investors into a false sense of security.[15] Far from being afraid of federal regulation, executives adroitly maneuvered reform efforts into legislation that hurt their small competitors and channeled hundreds of billions of taxpayer dollars into their corporate coffers.[16] Finally, professional monitors were compromised by deep conflicts of interest.[17] Credit-rating agencies inflated the grades that they assigned to new issues. So, too, did securities analysts: during the dotcom bubble, a "buy" recommendation really meant "hold"; and "hold" meant "run like hell."[18]

In short, the gatekeepers turned out to be mere agents with incentives that were not entirely, or even especially closely, aligned with those of investors. That became painfully clear in the aftermath of the accounting scandals at WorldCom, where executives played a variety of accounting games to make the company look profitable when, in fact, it was deep in the red.[19] When what the press termed "three unlikely sleuths" uncovered the fraud, the company immediately fell into bankruptcy.[20] Put simply, WorldCom executives classified operating expenses, which have to be accounted for quarterly, as capital expenses, which can be depreciated over many years. That and other niceties allowed the company, now dubbed by wags as World-Con, to overstate profits by $3.8 billion over five quarters. WorldCom's external auditor, Arthur Andersen (the company, not the person), aided and abetted the scheme because of a massive conflict of interest: it received big consulting fees from WorldCom. Andersen has since been shuttered, and consulting by auditors has been outlawed. But executives at financial institutions have since pulled similar accounting shenanigans. The frightening thing is that the cons could have gone on much longer, suggesting that other WorldComs and AIGs still lurk. "And what has been done" at WorldCom, to steal the words of a late nineteenth-century corporate governance reformer, "has, to a lesser extent been done in thousands of other corporations, and is *possible* in all."[21] The cause of the whole mess was allowing executives to choose the auditors, rather than allowing stockholders to do so, as was prevalent in the earlier history of Britain and the United States.[22]

Almost as insidious and far more common are corporations in cloistered markets that are not as efficient as they could or should be because executive pay is not closely tied to company performance. Some labor economists have tried to explain high executive pay by creating mathematical models that assume that even minor differences in executive ability can lead to huge differences in corporate performance. It is important, they contend, that corporations be allowed to pay as much as necessary to acquire executives presumed to possess top talent. Others think that high executive salaries are a means of inducing effort on the part of middle managers all eager eventually to win a prize in the form of a high CEO pay package.[23] Both views may have some validity without vitiating the notion that executives can and do earn high pay without improving corporate economic performance. "Flawed compensation arrangements," governance gurus Lucian Bebchuk and Jesse Fried wrote in 2004, "have been widespread, persistent, and systemic and they have stemmed from defects in the underlying governance structure that enable executives to exert considerable influence over their boards."[24]

CEO turnover is quite high—about 15 percent per year—but that may simply be because it does not take long for a CEO to grow wealthy at the expense of stockholders. Even as executives extol shareholder value, they continue to exert their absolute "right to manage" as if they were early modern divine-right monarchs.[25] Stockholders eventually become dissatisfied with the old CEO, and takeover rumors begin to circulate, leading to his (or, today, sometimes her) ouster, but the replacement CEO will probably demand an even higher compensation package for no better leadership. Meanwhile, the directors responsible for the fiasco "face very little risk of being ousted."[26] Although many corporations have blockholders that own 5 percent or more of the total outstanding stock, U.S. corporations continue to be dominated by management, not stockholders or even so-called independent directors, many of whom are not truly independent, despite media hype to the contrary. Executives and their boards are therefore free to agree upon the "Heads, I win big; tails, I win even bigger" contracts that cause financial and economic catastrophes such as the Panic of 2008. The agency problems that worried Adam Smith and other early corporate critics have returned with such vengeance that old assumptions about the efficiency of private property no longer hold. Executives virtually unchecked by law can get rich by meeting the needs of customers at a good price or by bilking corporate stockholders and other stakeholders. Too often, the latter proves faster and easier. "The prevalent philosophy," Ripley wrote in 1929, "is still that of a body in which a substantial identity of interest between all parties concerned necessarily exists. This, it is evident, is becoming each day more out of accord with the facts."[27] Eighty years ago, executives were not investors' friends; and they still are not, as their interests, if not diametrically opposed to those of other stakeholders, are far from closely aligned.[28]

U.S. corporate governance is broken, and corporations are too economically important not to try to fix it. Most business enterprises are not joint-stock corporations, but joint-stock corporations are much larger than their brethren, accounting for some 90 percent of sales reported by all businesses. Corporations account for more than 70 percent of sales in finance, manufacturing, transportation, and utilities. Corporations are too important to continued economic growth to allow them to be manipulated into the ground by management the way that Enron, WorldCom, Bear Stearns, Lehman Brothers, and so forth were. In each case, stakeholders complacently muddled on while executives and other inside directors stuffed their pockets with stockholders' money (and employees' jobs) in the form of unwarranted bonuses, golden parachutes, and excessive risk-taking; the last technique is the most ironic because defenders of the status quo theorize that well-diversified stockholders want to take on more risk than executives, employees, and creditors do.[29]

Although the need for reform is widely acknowledged, little consensus exists about the direction of future reform efforts. Some believe that vigorous competition (antitrust) policy forces corporations to adopt governance best practices.[30] Others argue that what should be sought are "novel directions in corporate governance."[31] In that vein, three scholars from the University of Zurich (Switzerland) believe that the compensation of star athletes in major North American sports leagues (NBA, NFL, MLB) provides a model on which a new system of executive compensation, one with salary caps or "luxury taxes" on high salaries, could be built.[32]

I believe, as the epigraph to this chapter suggests, that any reforms should be rooted in systems that worked well in the past. Regardless of the exact path taken, the best time to reform U.S. corporate governance is now. "If you want to change the world," wrote two corporate reformers in the mid-1980s, "there is no time like the present."[33] Solid reforms could stave off a nasty bear market and perhaps reinvigorate[34] the savings rate, something that America desperately needs, according to Ronald Wilcox.[35] "If the public felt assured that the interests of all the stockholders would be protected," corporate governance reformers argued in the 1870s, "it would be far easier than now to enlist the capital of the eastern States in manufacturing enterprises."[36] Ripley argued much the same thing in the 1920s. "Nothing will more surely conduce to popular thrift," he wrote, "than to throw all possible safeguards about the investments of the common people."[37]

Many believe that more state-centered regulation is called for, but anyone who has studied the sordid history of government regulation has to be skeptical of the government's ability to improve the situation. In addition to being slow, inflexible, and incapable of foreseeing future trouble spots, government-centered regulations actually crowd out stockholder monitoring and sound management by directors and executives. Most regulations cause more

problems than they solve, a situation that is a leading contributor to a phenomenon that I have termed "Fubarnomics." Sarbanes-Oxley (aka SOX or
SARBOX), the government's response to the accounting scandals of the early
third millennium, tried to restore the integrity of the governance and disclosure systems and thereby bolster investor confidence. It achieved the latter to
some extent but not the former, as the subprime mortgage debacle and Panic
of 2008 made clear.[38]

One of SARBOX's main innovations, the Public Company Accounting
Oversight Board (PCAOB), sought to improve auditing standards for publicly traded companies and to impose harsh penalties on CEOs and CFOs
who lied about their companies' finances. It also forced corporations to disclose their corporate governance procedures on the (largely flawed) theory
that investors would chasten those with loose controls. Like most reforms
before them, the new regulations appeared entirely sensible; but they did not
work because the mole of fraud had already scampered away to a new hole.
SARBOX was not too little, but it was way too late. In the words of Rutgers
economist Eugene White, "central problems of governance have not been addressed" by that legislation.[39]

At heart, SARBOX was an attempt to root out rotten apples but did nothing to stop subtler expropriation techniques or to change the fact that executives have significant influence over their own pay.[40] It relies upon the hoary
concept of the "independent audit"[41] but does not solve the dilemma of how
a truly independent auditor can ever have enough information to discern
chicanery and fraud. Generally Accepted Accounting Principles (GAAP) is
probably better than no rules at all but was easily gamed by Enron and others.[42] Mark-to-market accounting can help bring some transparency back
into the system, but the technique does not work as well for nonfinancial
companies with firm-specific assets that do not trade regularly and hence
have no current market price. Despite all the rules, regulations, and reforms,
many corporations remain grossly overvalued, though some more than others. According to hedge fund manager David Einhorn, Allied Capital, a business development company that receives substantial government funding,
has actually paid dividends out of new capital contributions, basically rendering it a government-sanctioned Ponzi scheme.[43]

Dodd-Frank, the regulatory reform that emerged out of the financial crisis of 2007–9, is still too new to fully assess but has garnered low marks so far
because it did not address the key causes of the world's largest financial debacle since the Depression. Most important for the discussion here,

executives are again raking in huge bonuses on purely accounting profits and will continue to do so under the new regime. Frequent claims to the contrary notwithstanding, more inputs into state-centered regulation will not improve matters sufficiently.[44]

What, then, can be done? Over two centuries ago, Lord Chancellor Edward Thurlow noted that corporations possessed "neither bodies to be punished, nor souls to be condemned, they therefore do as they like."[45] That remains true, but executives do have bodies. The best role for government today, as in the antebellum period,[46] is to impose fines and other penalties on executives' and directors' bodies and personal estates, not on the corporations themselves.[47] "You cannot punish corporations," future president Woodrow Wilson argued in 1910, because "fines fall upon the wrong persons . . . upon the stockholders and the customers rather than upon the men who direct the policy of the business."[48] (Wilson probably knew about late nineteenth-century railroad legislation that hurt small stockholders while enriching directors and other insiders.)[49]

A century ago, it was well understood that "there are two methods of preventing the mismanagement of corporations, . . . requiring security of the directors and officers for their faithful discharge of their duties and subjecting them to greater liability for the corporate debts; and the other in supervision by strangers to the management."[50] The *Wall Street Journal* noted over a century ago that "suing is too much like locking the stable door after the horse is stolen."[51] But if lawsuits induce future directors and executives to lock up the horses before theft occurs, the harsh personal penalties will have served their purpose.

It's an old canard that if executives and directors are made personally responsible for their actions, they will decline to serve. That simply is not true, as the history of Anglo-American corporations shows. Many antebellum U.S. and British corporations were led by able individuals, despite considerable director liability under the common law, charters, and, in Britain, the Companies Act of 1867 and the Directors' Liability Act of 1890. Honest companies will form, and they will find honest people to run them, no matter how stringent the laws against wrongdoing become, so long as directors and officers are not unfairly convicted of offenses that they did not commit.[52]

At the very least, courts have to stop coddling the executives and directors of bankrupt companies. "If the officers knew in advance that when their companies failed they would lose control," noted Henry Wollman over a century ago, "they would be much more conservative."[53] Courts should also step in more vigorously on behalf of aggrieved stockholders, especially in heinous cases such as the sweetheart deal that Disney gave Michael Ovitz.[54] Stockholders need judges who will restore losses inflicted upon them by majority stockholders, venal executives, or shill directors.[55] As Wilson argued a century ago, "society cannot afford to have individuals wield the power of thousands without personal responsibility. It cannot afford to let its strongest men be the only men who are inaccessible to the law."[56]

Investors need to be disabused of the notion that some benevolent, omniscient bureaucrat, even one lawfully and ideologically constrained from meddling in corporations' internal affairs, can and will look after their property for them. America's public educational system does precious little to teach financial literacy but does a superb job of imbuing students with visions of the power and benevolence of government. The message from on high is clearly that individual stockholders cannot monitor their investments for themselves, so few even try.[57]

What investors and policymakers do not realize is that the emasculation of U.S. stockholders was not inevitable and was not the product of a Darwinian struggle for existence among competing forms of organization or governance. Stockholders once ruled directly. Later, after corporations grew too large to be directly monitored, stockholders ruled with the aid of intermediaries. By the early twentieth century, directors controlled by executives assumed control; but as legal scholar Mark Roe pointed out, "American politics deliberately weakened and shattered financial intermediaries thereby making managers more powerful than they otherwise had to be."[58] Jonathan Macey argues that the best mechanisms for governing corporations and for ensuring that managerial promises to investors are kept "are either heavily regulated or banned outright." The least effective, by contrast, "are facilitated, encouraged, and even directly or indirectly required by regulation."[59]

Once the history of corporate governance has been laid bare, discerning the path to take is relatively easy: policies should be implemented that will allow stockholders to protect their investments, both directly and through institutional investors. I do not mean giving them day-to-day control but simply providing them with sufficient governance checks and balances to prevent tyranny and expropriation. The goal of shareholder voting rights should not be to create "a general active participation by the whole body of shareholders" because that would be "bound to go wrong from the crossing of the wire."[60] The average stockholder, most observers acknowledge, "is entirely unqualified to engage actively in management," and "town-meeting government" is inefficient.[61] The general belief that stockholders are entitled to corporate information, not a voice in its affairs, is almost correct.[62] What investors need are corporate republics, not incorporated democracies; stockholders again need "the power, even if rarely exercised, and then only under extreme provocation," as Ripley explained in 1929, to "check and balance" executive venality.[63] Berle and Means likened the right of stockholders to vote to "that of a populace supporting a revolution."[64] Liberal voting rights for minority stockholders should, like a policeman's club, be "only occasionally used, but it serves a very useful purpose and while idle does no harm."[65]

Actually implementing governance changes will be difficult because reforms with real bite will face vigorous opposition. It is in the interest of bureaucrats to seek more government regulation, not a return to self-governance. As Macey reminds us, executives "will staunchly resist corporate governance reforms that put their jobs in jeopardy or threaten their ability to remain independent from outside entities such as activist hedge funds and corporate raiders or that otherwise make their lives more difficult."[66] Managers, Roe adds, have fought tooth and nail to maintain their preeminence and will continue to do so. And they have backers in academe who are willing to make outrageous claims such as "shareholders are not principals and managers are not their agents" and "shareholder claims to corporate surplus [are] dubious."[67]

To date, executives have successfully maintained the status quo. In 2007, the SEC supported the continuation of rules that make it easier for executives to control proxy votes and directorship candidate slates. No change is in sight, as many Republicans conflate corporate governance reform with "intrusive regulation" and managerial dominance with "the market." They wonder why stockholders need more rights when they rarely exercise the ones they already have, missing the point that the rights that stockholders currently enjoy are nearly valueless; their criticism is akin to giving someone an engine-less automobile and then complaining that he doesn't drive it.[68]

Reformers have not helped their cause by proffering simple but inadequate suggestions such as forcing a high degree of leverage upon executives (borrowing to the hilt). By limiting "free cash flow," the argument goes, a large debt service keeps managers on the straight and narrow the way that dividends once did. Interest payments and dividends, however, are contractually quite distinct. Bad macroeconomic conditions, not just bad management, can cause a debt default because interest, unlike dividends, must be paid regardless of the state of the economy. Other simple fixes, including giving stockholders more "say on pay," making increased use of so-called independent directors (basically, nonemployee directors), and implementing stricter accounting standards, have all fallen short, primarily because they leave executives in absolute power, which corrupts as absolutely today as in Lord Acton's era.[69]

Bebchuk and Fried call for more transparency in compensation arrangements and more controls to ensure that pay is tightly tied to actual managerial performance and not to stock market or macroeconomic performance.[70] That would include limiting or even eliminating golden parachutes and the ability of executives to "pump and dump" their shares. To ensure arm's-length contracting between executives and boards, the latter need to be composed of directors who are not just independent of managers but dependent upon stockholders. Although a hoary concept,[71] independent directors are the latest flawed fad in corporate governance best practices.[72] Executives acquiesced to nonemployee directors because they knew that the outsiders could be easily duped or co-opted. "It is the rare board that . . . can say 'no,'" noted two governance gurus in the early 1990s, because "the CEO-chairman simply dominates the board's decision making, even though independent outside directors constitute a clear majority."[73] More recently, Michael Bednar has exposed many independent directors and the media hype that often accompanies their appointment.[74] "Even so-called independent directors," explained corporate governance expert Jonathan Macey, "are highly susceptible to being captured by the very management teams that they are supposed to be monitoring." What are needed, Macey insists, are "dissident" directors beholden to institutional investors, not executives.[75]

Roe suggests that instead of mandating rigid governance procedures, policymakers should encourage experimentation, and Macey concurs, suggesting that shareholders should have the right to expand or contract the range of issues over which they can vote. "Any time shareholders feel they need special voting rights to constrain agency costs," he argues, "courts should rush to their defense." He recognizes, however, that shareholder voting is not a panacea because "shareholders do not have the time, expertise, incentives, or inclination" to vote intelligently on most issues.[76] Critics of reform also often note that stockholders "have neither time, impulse, nor capacity" to monitor corporations closely.[77] As individuals, that is certainly true. An early twentieth-century investment adviser cautioned individual investors to "make your own investigation in investments," but such advice was exposed as impractical.[78] Investigating the numerous companies needed to compose a relatively diverse portfolio was cost-prohibitive, "an aggregate burden of bother," in the words of one investment guru, "which would be backbreaking" unless it could be spread out via shareholder associations or other intermediaries.[79]

But then, as now, investors often aggregated their holdings. "If suitably developed under proper safeguards," opined William Z. Ripley in the mid-1920s, "these concentrated investments, handled by competent persons . . . might well participate in corporate government in an intelligent and entirely helpful way." He then described an early mutual fund at Columbia University. He acknowledged that agency problems between intermediaries and investors could arise.[80] Such problems, however, can be minimized because of the relative transparency of mutual funds' business models and daily mark-to-market accounting. Mutual funds per se are not typically overvalued because net asset value (NAV) is quite straightforward. Investors can therefore relatively easily distinguish good funds from bad funds and invest accordingly. (Hedge and private equity funds are another matter. The key, as always, is to ensure incentive alignment between the investor and the fund manager.) Moreover, mutual fund investors can chasten fund managers much more easily than stockholders can chasten executives because they can redeem their shares for cash, not just pawn them off onto other investors, as stockholders must. "Redemption," Roe wrote, "is a serious risk for sub-par mutual fund managers."[81]

Institutional investors—banks, insurers, and pension, mutual, hedge, and private equity funds—could play a much bigger role in corporate governance. Clearly, they have the economic power to exert considerable pressure on management: by 2000, they owned over 60 percent of all corporate shares, up from 33 percent in 1980. Since the demise of financial capitalism, they have rarely done so because, as noted previously, the government has constrained most of them from engaging in governance in a major way. Unlike in Germany and Japan, powerful intermediaries were stymied because, as Roe has argued, "federalism, populism, and interest group pressures pulverized American financial institutions."[82] Exceptions, which include Peter Lynch of Fidelity's Magellan Fund, John Bogle of Vanguard, CalPERS (California Public Employees Retirement System), and TIAA-CREF (the leading investment vehicle of university professors), suggest that financial intermediaries *could* play a positive role in governance.[83] To date, they have not done so. Institutional investors did not stop the crises of 2007–8, and their inability to force large, complex financial institutions to be more transparent and accountable exacerbated the situation.[84] Most fund managers preferred the "Wall Street shuffle": the dumping of stocks at the first sign of trouble.[85] "We vote with the management. If we don't like the management, we sell the stock" is the hoary mantra of many institutional investors.[86] Of course, such stock "churning" might become less prevalent if the barriers to intermediary-led governance were reduced.[87]

Advances in telecommunications have made it easier and cheaper for investors small and large to monitor corporations and institutional investors. "If there are big governance gains," Roe argued, "they will come not from unleashing mutual funds alone, but from *networking* several intermediaries."[88] Such networks have improved greatly since he penned those words in the early 1990s. Laws that prevent intermediaries from coordinating their governance efforts should be repealed and changes in their culture and human capital made, as appropriate.[89]

*   *   *

In summary, I recommend implementation of the following corporate governance reforms. These reforms, which stem from the history of U.S. corporations developed in this book and the ruminations of corporate governance experts, can be implemented by individual corporations with the urging of activist investors, institutional or otherwise. Once they have proved their value (again), they can be incorporated into law by state and national governments. The overall gist is to make corporations more like republics by giving their citizens (stockholders) the ability to prevent their legislatures (directors) and their managers (executives) from acting like tyrants by engaging in excessive self-dealing:

1. All directors, except the chairman of the board (the president in the old parlance), should be independent, outside (nonemployee) directors. This is much stronger than the current Dodd-Frank rule, which merely mandates that compensation committees be composed of independent directors.[90] They should not receive any direct compensation other than reasonable expenses for attending meetings. All directors should be stockholders and nominated by themselves or other stockholders only, not by the chairman or corporate officers.

2. Directors should negotiate executive compensation packages subject to affirmative approval by a majority of the stock eligible to vote. This is much stronger than the current Dodd-Frank "say on pay" rule, which is not binding on directors and may simply legitimize suboptimal compensation packages.[91] Directors who cannot commit significant time and effort to monitoring executives should not serve. Institutional investors that hire individuals to serve as directors on their behalf should carefully structure the compensation of those individuals and disclose the same to their own investors (for example, mutual fund owners or policyholders) as well as to other stockholders in the governed corporation.

3. An industry-appropriate percentage of executive pay (the riskier the industry, the higher the percentage) should take the form of long-term deferred cash compensation tied as closely as possible to appropriate empirical measures of corporate efficiency rather than to stock prices per se. The system should include negative bonuses (deductions from their retirement account) proportioned to the same degree as bonuses. This is stronger than the current Dodd-Frank rule, which encourages the clawback or recovery of incentive compensation awarded erroneously.[92] Contracts that limit downside risk for executives, including golden parachutes, should never be agreed to. Corporations should not pay for directors and officers liability insurance and should forbid directors and officers from purchasing such insurance.

4. To minimize incentives to raise stock prices artificially, executives should not own shares or options in their employers. Ex post renegotiation of performance metrics should not be allowed, of course.[93] Conversely, executives should be required to place almost all their familial assets in their company's stock and not be allowed to sell their stakes for a year or more after their retirement or departure.

5. To ensure proper screening, executives should be hired from within the corporation's managerial ranks whenever possible.

6. One vote per share should be preferred to super voting rights in most cases. And one vote per share per year of ownership rights should be experimented with and adopted if they improve long-term corporate performance. Prudent mean voting rules can be worked around fairly cheaply, so they need not be resurrected. Voting by proxy, on the other hand, should be banned because its original purpose, to allow

stockholders to vote at meetings that they could not physically attend, has been subverted and is now obsolete. Corporate meetings, including votes, should be conducted electronically over several days so that all stockholders can "attend" and vote. All yes or no votes—for example, on compensation—should require an absolute majority so that no measure can pass because of stockholder apathy. Stockholders should be allowed to cast all their votes for a single director if they see fit. It should always be cheaper and easier to vote in a corporate election than to sell shares.

Implementation of these rules will not solve all the world's problems, but it should increase investor confidence in the equities markets, thus preventing their possible implosion. These rules should also improve corporate efficiency and hence economic performance, if not in competitive industries or during booms, at least in uncompetitive ones and during downturns. If nothing else, after all, good governance is insurance against bad times.[94]

Chapter 1

1. V. H. Lockwood, "How to Reform Business Corporations," *North American Review* 164 (March 1897): 294.

2. Kenneth Lipartito and David B. Sicilia, "Afterword: Toward New Renderings," in Kenneth Lipartito and David Sicilia, eds., *Constructing Corporate America: History, Politics, Culture* (New York: Oxford University Press, 2004), 343. Others have also likened corporations to battleships, including John Micklethwait and Adrian Wooldridge, *The Company: A Short History of a Revolutionary Idea* (New York: Modern Library, 2003), xix, who noted that "the rise and fall of the juggernauts of corporate America forms a large part of our story."

3. Laws and judges have categorized corporations in a large variety of ways over the years. Use of the term "business corporation" is not anachronistic; the term was in use in America during the period under study. "Corporations, in America, may be divided into three classes: Municipal, eleemosynary, and business corporations." "Eleemosynary" referred to "hospitals, colleges, &c.," or what we would today call nonprofits. A Citizen of Boston, *Remarks upon the Rights and Powers of Corporations, and of the Rights, Powers, and Duties of the Legislature toward Them* (Boston: Beals and Greene, 1837), 5. See also Charles C. Abbott, *The Rise of the Business Corporation* (Ann Arbor, Mich.: Edwards Brothers, 1936), 10–11, 49; William Miller, "A Note on the History of Business Corporations in Pennsylvania, 1800–1860," *Quarterly Journal of Economics* 55, 1 (November 1940): 150–60; Arthur Selwyn Miller, *The Supreme Court and American Capitalism* (New York: Free Press, 1968), 6–7; Carl Kaysen, "Introduction and Overview," in Carl Kaysen, ed., *The American Corporation Today* (New York: Oxford University Press, 1996), 3. Louis Hacker wrongly claimed that "it was not until the 1840s that the doors were thrown open to the creation of corporations." Louis Hacker, *Alexander Hamilton in the American Tradition* (New York: McGraw-Hill, 1957), 4. Esteemed business historians George David Smith and Davis Dyer also got it wrong when they wrote that "in its early American setting, the corporation was rarely employed for undertaking even small-scale enterprise." George David Smith and Davis Dyer, "The Rise and Transformation of the American Corporation," in Kaysen, ed., *The American Corporation Today*, 29. So did Tony Freyer when he claimed: "From Ratification to 1860 . . . [p]eople . . .

were self-employed in small, generally unincorporated enterprises or who were principally agrarians [*sic*]." Tony A. Freyer, "Business Law and American Economic History," in Stanley Engerman and Robert Gallman, eds., *The Cambridge Economic History of the United States*, vol. 2: *The Long Nineteenth Century* (New York: Cambridge University Press, 2000), 436. See also Stuart Bruchey, *The Roots of American Economic Growth* (New York: Harper & Row, 1965), 139 and Abbott, *Rise of the Business Corporation*, 46–47. E. James Ferguson, one of the best historians of the early American economy, believed that "by 1815, several hundred companies had been chartered for the construction of turnpikes, bridges, aqueducts, canals, for insuring property, for banking, and for operating factories." In fact, the total number was almost 1,900. The error may have originated with Curtis Nettels, *The Emergence of a National Economy, 1775–1815* (New York: Harper, 1962), 289, who inexplicably provided much more accurate numbers on 291. See E. James Ferguson, "The American Public Debt and the Rise of the National Economy, 1750–1815" (working paper, May 9, 1976), 17. Sadly, Prof. Ferguson was unable to publish the paper because of a tragic automobile accident. Other venerable economic historians also underestimated early corporations. Naomi Lamoreaux notes that the "general consensus" is that "corporations were critical to the task of mobilizing capital for large-scale industry . . . by the end of the nineteenth century." Naomi Lamoreaux, "Partnerships, Corporations, and the Limits on Contractual Freedom in U.S. History: An Essay in Economics, Law, and Culture," in Lipartito and Sicilia, eds., *Constructing Corporate America*, 29. Scholars such as William Roy, Lawrence Mitchell, and David Skeel largely assume away the antebellum corporation: William G. Roy, *Socializing Capital: The Rise of the Large Industrial Corporation in America* (Princeton, N.J.: Princeton University Press, 1997), xiii, 3; Lawrence Mitchell, *The Speculation Economy: How Finance Triumphed over Industry* (San Francisco: Berrett-Koehler, 2007), ix; David Skeel, *Icarus in the Boardroom: The Fundamental Flaws in Corporate America and Where They Came From* (New York: Oxford University Press, 2005), 10, 18–19, 24.

4. Micklethwait and Wooldridge, *The Company*, xiv, 47.

5. Andrew Allison, *The Rise and Probable Decline of Private Corporations in America* (1884), 243.

6. A. S. Miller, *Supreme Court*, 43.

7. Edwin Merrick Dodd, *American Business Corporations Until 1860: With Special Reference to Massachusetts* (Cambridge, Mass.: Harvard University Press, 1954), 7; Adolf Berle, "Property, Production and Revolution: A Preface to the Revised Edition," in Adolf Berle and Gardiner Means, *The Modern Corporation and Private Property* (New Brunswick, N.J.: Transaction, 1991), xxxiii; Micklethwait and Wooldridge, *The Company*, 142; John Taft, *Stewardship: Lessons Learned from the Lost Culture of Wall Street* (Hoboken, N.J.: John Wiley, 2012), 80–82.

8. Henry Wood, *The Long-Suffering Shareholder: Railroad Directorial Mismanagement and Governmental Oppression* (Boston: W. B. Clarke, 1889), in Robert E. Wright, Wray Barber, Matthew Crafton, and Anand Jain, eds., *History of Corporate Governance: The Importance of Stakeholder Activism* (London: Pickering & Chatto, 2004), 5:283.

9. Minnesota Electoral Reform Association, *Minority Representation in Stock Companies* (Minneapolis: Minnesota Electoral Reform Association, 1874), in Wright et al., eds., *History of Corporate Governance*, 4:354–55

10. Mitchell, *Speculation Economy*, 93.

11. Jonathan R. Macey, *Corporate Governance: Promises Kept, Promises Broken* (Princeton, N.J.: Princeton University Press, 2008), vii.

12. I. Maurice Wormser, *Frankenstein, Incorporated* (New York: McGraw-Hill, 1931), 135.

13. Charles Calomiris and Carlos Ramirez, "Financing the American Corporation: The Changing Menu of Financial Relationships," in Kaysen, ed., *The American Corporation Today*, 129.

14. Cary Coglianese and Robert Kagan, *Regulation and Regulatory Processes* (London: Ashgate, 2007); Skeel, *Icarus in the Boardroom*, 210–12.

15. Wormser, *Frankenstein*, 87.

16. Micklethwait and Wooldridge, *The Company*, 154.

17. Joshua Gilpin, "Journal of a Tour from Philadelphia Thro the Western Counties of Pennsylvania in the Months of September and October, 1809," *Pennsylvania Magazine of History and Biography* 50, 1 (1926): 64–78. See also "Since the Opening," *Milwaukee Sentinel and Gazette* (June 5, 1850), 2.

18. A Citizen of New York, *What Is a Monopoly? Or Some Considerations upon the Subject of Corporations and Currency* (New York: George P. Scott, 1835), 9.

19. *An Inquiry into the Nature and Utility of Corporations, Addressed to the Farmers, Mechanics, and Laboring Men of Connecticut* (1835), 4.

20. Citizen of Boston, *Remarks upon the Rights and Powers*, 6.

21. Sir James Steuart, *An Inquiry into the Principles of Political Oeconomy* (Chicago: University of Chicago Press, 1966), 389. See also John W. Eilert, "Illinois Business Incorporations, 1816–1869," *Business History Review* 37, 3 (1963): 169–81; Robert E. Wright, "Corporate Entrepreneurship in the Antebellum South," in Susanna Delfino, Michele Gillespie, and Louis Kyriakoudes, eds., *Southern Society and Its Transformation, 1790–1860* (Columbia: University of Missouri Press, 2011), 195–214; Robert E. Wright, "Rise of the Corporation Nation," in Douglas A. Irwin and Richard Sylla, eds., *Founding Choices: American Economic Policy in the 1790s* (Chicago: University of Chicago Press, 2011), 240–41; *An Inquiry into the Nature and Utility of Corporations*, 3–4; John Randolph Tucker, *Notes of Lectures on Corporations* (Lexington, Va.: Washington and Lee University, n.d.), 9; A Citizen of New York, *What Is a Monopoly?*, 11–12; Entity shielding: The corporation "is so distinct an entity from the corporators, that neither is it liable for or bound by their acts, nor are they liable for its acts. And therein it differs from a partnership. The latter is not *one made of many*. The personality of the partners is never lost—never merged in the firm [emphasis in original]." Tucker, *Notes of Lectures on Corporations*, 6, 10. Howard Bodenhorn and other scholars believe that entity shielding was as important as limited liability to the rise of the corporation. Howard Bodenhorn, "Partnership, Entity Shielding and Credit Availability" (working paper, December

2006). See also Henry Hansmann, Reinier Kraakman, and Richard Squire, "Law and the Rise of the Firm," *Harvard Law Review* 119, 5 (March 2006): 1333–1403; Abbott, *Rise of the Business Corporation*, 3; Henry G. Manne, "Out Two Corporation Systems: Law and Economics," *Virginia Law Review* 53, 2 (March 1967): 260–65; William Lough, *Corporation Finance: An Exposition of the Principles and Methods Governing the Promotion, Organization and Management of Modern Corporations* (New York: Alexander Hamilton Institute, 1909), 13–15.

22. Henry Hitchcock, *Annual Address before the A.B.A.* (1887), 236.

23. Cadwallader Colden, Jeremiah Randolph, and Hector Craig, *Observations on the Intended Application of the North American Coal and Mining Company, to the Legislature of the State of New York* (New York, 1814).

24. Abbott, *Rise of the Business Corporation*, 4; Tucker, *Notes of Lectures on Corporations*, 100–101. In 1820, the Lehigh Coal and the Lehigh Navigation companies "agreed to amalgamate their interests, and to unite themselves into one company." *A History of the Lehigh Coal and Navigation Company* (Philadelphia: William S. Young, 1840), 11. See also Howard Bodenhorn, "Banking and the Integration of Antebellum American Financial Markets, 1815–1859" (Ph.D. diss., Rutgers University, 1990), v.

25. Butler, quoted in Micklethwait and Wooldridge, *The Company*, xxi.

26. Wood, *The Long-Suffering Shareholder*, 5:283.

27. Charles Haddock, *Address of the Northern Railroad Company to the Friends of Internal Improvement in New Hampshire* (Hanover, N.H.: Hanover Press, 1845), 15. On early U.S. economic growth, see Walt W. Rostow, *The Stages of Economic Growth: A Non-Communist Manifesto* (New York: Cambridge University Press, 1960), 9; Walter B. Smith and Arthur Cole, *Fluctuations in American Business, 1790–1860* (New York: Russell & Russell, 1935), 3; Louis Johnston and Samuel H. Williamson, "What Was the U.S. GDP Then?," MeasuringWorth, 2010, www.measuringworth.org/usgdp; Joseph H. Davis, "An Annual Index of U.S. Industrial Production, 1790–1915," *Quarterly Journal of Economics* 119, 4 (November 2004): 1177–1215.

28. Wright, "Rise of the Corporation Nation," 248–52.

29. Lincoln, quoted in John L. Brooke, *The Heart of the Commonwealth: Society and Political Culture in Worcester County, Massachusetts, 1713–1861* (Amherst: University of Massachusetts Press, 1989), 307.

30. Abbot, quoted in J. M. Opal, *Beyond the Farm: National Ambitions in Rural New England* (Philadelphia: University of Pennsylvania Press, 2008), 157.

31. *Report of the Committee on Banks and Insurance Companies on the Several Petitions Presented to the Senate, Praying Acts of Incorporation with Banking Privileges* (Albany, N.Y.: Croswell, Barnum & Van Bethuysen, 1826), 11.

32. Littleton Teackle, *An Address to the Members of the Legislature of Maryland, Concerning the Establishment of a Loan Office for the Benefit of the Landowners of the State* (Annapolis, Md., 1817), 20.

33. Jonas Platt, *Mr. Platt's Speech on the Bill for Establishing the Western District Bank* (1811).

34. Francis Dodge, *First Annual Report of the President and Directors to the Stockholders of the Metropolitan Railroad Company* (Georgetown: A. L. Settle, 1854), 33.

35. Staten Island Railroad, *Reports of the Committee and Engineer to the President and Directors of the Staten Island Railroad Company Embracing Surveys and Estimates* (New York: Baker, Godwin, 1852), 13–14.

36. Thomas G. Cary, *Result of Manufactures at Lowell* (Boston: Charles C. Little & James Brown, 1845), 7–8, 18.

37. Butler, quoted in Richard Tedlow, *The Rise of the American Business Corporation* (Chur, Switzerland: Harwood Academic Publishers, 1991), v.

38. Abbott, *Rise of the Business Corporation*, 2.

39. "Manufacturing Corporations," *American Jurist* (July 1829): 94.

40. Gouverneur, *Remarks on the Life Insurance Laws of New York, and the Fallacy of Any System of Legislation Which Undertakes the Controll and Management of Life Insurance Companies* (New York, 1852), 7.

41. *Substance of Argument of Respondents' Counsel on the Application of the Seekonk Branch Rail Road Company to the Committee of the Legislature, to Run Locomotive Engines on the Providence and Worcester Rail Roads and through the Worcester Merchandize Depot* (Boston: John H. Eastburn, 1838), 7.

42. Seymour Dunbar, *A History of Travel in America* (Indianapolis: Bobbs-Merrill, 1915), 3:821 n. 2, 828, 835–39; *The North Branch Canal Company: Its Prospects, and Its Laws of Incorporation* (Philadelphia, 1845); Peter G. Stuyvesant, *Memorial of the New York and Erie Railroad Company to the Legislature of the State of New York* (New York: G. P. Scott, 1837), 6; Albert Fishlow, "Internal Transportation," in Lance Davis et al., *American Economic Growth: An Economist's History of the United States* (New York: Harper & Row, 1972), 478–81; Joseph Durrenberger, *Turnpikes: A Study of the Toll Road Movement in the Middle Atlantic States and Maryland* (Cos Cob, Conn.: John E. Edwards, 1931, 1968), 139.

43. *The Schuylkill Navigation Company* (Philadelphia: Crissy & Markley, 1852), 1–2.

44. Ronald Wilcox, *Whatever Happened to Thrift? Why Americans Don't Save and What to Do About It* (New Haven, Conn.: Yale University Press, 2008).

Chapter 2

1. A Citizen, *Observations on the Real, Relative and Market Value of the Turnpike Stock of the State of New York* (New York: S. Gould, 1806), 15–16.

2. J. David Lehman, "Explaining Hard Times: Political Economy and the Panic of 1819 in Philadelphia" (Ph.D. diss., University of California, Los Angeles, 1992), 319. It is important to note that, outside certain legal circles, contemporaries used the same basic definitions and made the same distinctions as I have here. See, e.g., John Cox, *On the Argument, in Reference to the Bridge Bill, Prepared by Judge Cranch and Doctor May* (1832?), 2–3; Pauline Maier, "The Revolutionary Origins of the American Corporation," *William and Mary Quarterly* 50 (January 1993): 53–55; Jason Kaufman, "Corporate Law and the Sovereignty of States," *American Sociological Review* 73 (2008): 402–25; Johann

N. Neem, *Creating a Nation of Joiners: Democracy and Civil Society in Early National Massachusetts* (Cambridge, Mass.: Harvard University Press, 2008); Ronald Seavoy, *The Origins of the American Business Corporation, 1784–1855: Broadening the Concept of Public Service During Industrialization* (Westport, Conn.: Greenwood, 1982), 9–38.

3. *Letter on the Use and Abuse of Incorporations, Addressed to the Delegation from the City of New York in the State Legislature by One of Their Constituents* (New York: G. & C. Carvill, 1827), 53.

4. Abbott, *Rise of the Business Corporation*, 6; Tucker, *Notes of Lectures on Corporations*, 5; "Manufacturing Corporations," 110.

5. Campbell, quoted in James O. Wettereau to N. S. B. Gras, January 29, 1941, Wettereau Papers, Folder 23, Columbia University Library, New York, N.Y. (hereafter CUL).

6. John A. Seitz to ?, June 22, 1796, Filson Historical Society, Louisville, Kentucky (hereafter FHS).

7. Ronald C. White, Jr., *A. Lincoln: A Biography* (New York: Random House, 2009), 65.

8. Abbott, *Rise of the Business Corporation*, 6–8.

9. For more on limited partnerships, see Susan Pace Hamill, "From Special Privilege to General Utility: A Continuation of Willard Hurst's Study of Corporations," *American University Law Review* 81 (1999–2000): 180; Seavoy, *Origins of the American Business Corporation*, 97–98; Roy, *Socializing Capital*, 69; "Manufacturing Corporations," 111–14; Gower, "Some Contrasts between British and American Corporation Law," 1373; Shaw Livermore, *Early American Land Companies: Their Influence on Corporate Development* (New York: Commonwealth Fund, 1939), 270; Citizen of Boston, *Remarks upon the Rights and Powers*, 7; Eric Hilt and Katharine O'Banion, "The Limited Partnership in New York, 1822–58: Partnerships Without Kinship," *Journal of Economic History* 69 (September 2009): 615–45.

10. *Report of the Committee on Banks and Insurance Companies*, 7.

11. *An Inquiry into the Nature and Utility of Corporations*, 4.

12. Marshall, quoted in Lamoreaux, "Partnerships, Corporations," in Lipartito and Sicilia, eds., *Constructing Corporate America*, 32

13. Wormser, *Frankenstein*, 84; William R. Scott, *The Constitution and Finance of English, Scottish and Irish Joint-Stock Companies to 1720* (Cambridge: Cambridge University Press, 1912), 1:442; Oscar Handlin and Mary Handlin, "Origins of the American Business Corporation," *Journal of Economic History* 5 (May 1945): 21; Miller, *Supreme Court*, 9; Smith and Dyer, "The Rise and Transformation of the American Corporation," in Kaysen, ed., *The American Corporation Today*, 38; Micklethwait and Wooldridge, *The Company*, xv; A Citizen of New York, *What Is a Monopoly?*, 11; Dodd, *American Business Corporations*, 114–20; *Association of Centenary Firms and Corporations of the United States*, 2nd issue (Philadelphia: Christopher Sower, 1916).

14. John McDiarmid, *Government Corporations and Federal Funds* (Chicago: University of Chicago Press, 1938), xii.

15. Nettels, *Emergence of a National Economy*, 290; Maier, "The Revolutionary

Origins of the American Corporation," 55; Handlin and Handlin, "Origins of the American Business Corporation," 8–17; Colleen Dunlavy, "Social Conceptions of the Corporation: Insights from the History of Shareholding Voting Rights," *Washington and Lee Review* 63, 4 (2006): 1347–88.

16. Robert E. Wright and Richard Sylla, "Corporate Governance and Stockholder/ Stakeholder Activism in the United States, 1790–1860: New Data and Perspectives," in Jonathan Koppell, ed., *Origins of Shareholder Advocacy* (New York: Palgrave Macmillan, 2011), 231–51; Wright, "Rise of the Corporation Nation," in Irwin and Sylla, eds., *Founding Choices*, 242–43.

17. Simeon Baldwin, "American Business Corporations before 1789," *Annual Report of the American Historical Association for the Year 1902* (Washington, D.C.: Government Printing Office, 1903), 1:256; Scott, *The Constitution and Finance*, 1:447; Roy, *Socializing Capital*, 159, 163; Herbert Hovenkamp, *Enterprise and American Law, 1836–1937* (Cambridge, Mass.: Harvard University Press, 1991), 49; Dodd, *American Business Corporations*, 85, 89–91; John Cadman, *The Corporation in New Jersey: Business and Politics, 1791–1875* (Cambridge, Mass.: Harvard University Press, 1949), 327–28.

18. In fact, almost all the statements made in this book draw support from Angell and Ames's treatise. Joseph K. Angell and Samuel Ames, *A Treatise on the Law of Private Corporations Aggregate* (Boston: Hilliard, Gray, Little & Wilkins, 1832). See also J. Van Fenstermaker, *The Development of American Commercial Banking: 1782–1837* (Kent, Ohio: Kent State University, 1965), 23; A Citizen of New York, *What Is a Monopoly?*, 11.

19. "Manufacturing Corporations," 94.

20. Seavoy, *Origins of the American Business Corporation*, 47.

21. Chapman, quoted in Livermore, *Early American Land Companies*, 274, 284–85.

22. Richard Sylla, "Early American Banking: The Significance of the Corporate Form," *Business and Economic History* 14 (1985): 111.

23. "Manufacturing Corporations," 103.

24. Bray Hammond, *Banks and Politics in America from the Revolution to the Civil War* (Princeton, N.J.: Princeton University Press, 1957), 654.

25. Handlin and Handlin, "Origins of the American Business Corporation," 16–17; Dodd, *American Business Corporations*, 6.

26. Edwin Perkins, *American Public Finance and Financial Services, 1700–1815* (Columbus: Ohio State University Press, 1994), 373–76; Robert A. East, *Business Enterprise in the American Revolutionary Era* (New York: Columbia University Press, 1938), 286.

27. James Sullivan as quoted in Robert E. Wright, *The First Wall Street: Chestnut Street, Philadelphia and the Birth of American Finance* (Chicago: University of Chicago Press, 2005), 171.

28. Tucker, *Notes of Lectures on Corporations*, 67–69, 107–9. See also Van Fenstermaker, *The Development of American Commercial Banking*, 23.

29. *Reasons for Repealing the Laws of Massachusetts, Which Render the Members of Manufacturing Companies Personally Liable for Their Debts* (Boston: Dutton and Wentworth, 1830), 3–5. Many others made the same point. "Capitalists unhesitatingly refuse

to participate in our undertaking. When applied to, they uniformly point to that prominent and unnecessary clause in our charter, which provides that if they take a single share in our corporation, their entire fortunes may be taken from them." *A Report of the Important Hearing on the Memorial of the New England Coal Mining Company* (New England, 1838), 138.

30. *Reasons for Repealing*, 4.

31. For more on these points, see Dodd, *American Business Corporations*, 91, 391–437; Stanley E. Howard, "Stockholders' Liability under the New York Act of March 22, 1811," *Journal of Political Economy* 46, 4 (1938): 499–514; Skeel, *Icarus in the Boardroom*, 23; A Citizen of New York, *What Is a Monopoly?*, 20; "Manufacturing Corporations," 95–100; Handlin and Handlin, "Origins of the American Business Corporation," 16; "Manufacturing Corporations," 102; Hovenkamp, *Enterprise and American Law*, 50; Brooke, *Heart of the Commonwealth*, 307; Winifred Rothenberg, *From Market-Places to a Market Economy: The Transformation of Rural Massachusetts, 1750–1850* (Chicago: University of Chicago Press, 1992), 121; William Kessler, "Incorporation in New England: A Statistical Study, 1800–1875," *Journal of Economic History* 8 (May 1948): 54, 56.

32. "Manufacturing Corporations," 101; Livermore, *Early American Land Companies*, 269; Van Fenstermaker, *The Development of American Commercial Banking*, 23; *Prospectus of the California and New York Steamship Company* (San Francisco: Town Talk Office, 1857), 7; Leonce Bargeron and Kenneth Lehn, "Does Limited Liability Matter: An Analysis of California Firms, 1920–1940" (working paper, July 2012); Cadman, *The Corporation in New Jersey*, 327–56, 426; Edward Crowder, "State Regulation of Commercial Banking in New York" (Ph.D. diss., New York University, 1942), 126–27; Seavoy, *Origins of the American Business Corporation*, 186.

33. Albert Gallatin, *Considerations of the Currency and Banking System of the United States* (Philadelphia: Carey and Lea, 1831), 40.

34. *In the Court for the Trial of Impeachments and Correction of Errors between the President, Directors and Company of the Bank of Columbia, Appellants vs. the Attorney-General of the State of New York, Respondent* (Hudson: S. Curtis, 1829), 5.

35. L. Ray Gunn, *The Decline of Authority: Public Economic Policy and Political Development in New York, 1800–1860* (Ithaca, N.Y.: Cornell University Press, 1988), 235. For additional support of the points made in this paragraph, see Sylla, "Early American Banking," 119; "Manufacturing Corporations," 101; *An Act to Incorporate the Stockholders of the Bank of the United States, by the State of Pennsylvania* (Philadelphia: Joseph and William Kite, 1836), 10; Cadman, *The Corporation in New Jersey*, 426; Wilbur Dreikorn, "The History and Development of Banking in New Jersey" (master's thesis, Rutgers University, 1949), 31.

36. *Reasons for Repealing the Laws of Massachusetts*, 7–8.

37. David A. Moss, *When All Else Fails: Government as the Ultimate Risk Manager* (Cambridge, Mass.: Harvard University Press, 2002), 25–26, 40, 74–80; Hovenkamp, *Enterprise and American Law*, 53; Wright, "Rise of the Corporation Nation," 244.

38. Paul H. Rubin, *Darwinian Politics: The Evolutionary Origin of Freedom* (New Brunswick, N.J.: Rutgers University Press, 2002), 174, 196 n. 5.

39. "Manufacturing Corporations," 106.

40. Ibid., 111.

41. Julius Goebel, "Editor's Introduction," in Livermore, *Early American Land Companies*, x.

42. Tucker, *Notes of Lectures on Corporations*, 21, 27.

43. Abbott, *Rise of the Business Corporation*, 2.

44. Tucker, *Notes of Lectures on Corporations*, 59–61.

45. Harvey Tuckett, *Practical Remarks on the Present State of Life Insurance in the United States* (Philadelphia: Smith & Peters, 1850), 4, 6–7, 22, 29.

46. Gouverneur, *Remarks on the Life Insurance Laws*, 2. Incentives, while important, can be flummoxed by reality. I have an incentive to be a major league baseball player, for example, but it will never happen. Similarly, Alexander Bryan Johnson owned $40,000 worth of stock in the bank over which he presided. Nevertheless, the bank failed due to the peculation of its cashier. Charles Todd and Robert Sonkin, *Alexander Bryan Johnson: Philosophical Banker* (Syracuse, N.Y.: Syracuse University Press, 1977), 341. Incentives are not destiny, but getting them correctly aligned will lead to much better outcomes than not. Robin Pearson, "Mutuality Tested: The Rise and Fall of Mutual Fire Insurance Offices in Eighteenth-Century London," *Business History* 44 (October 2002): 1–28; Robert E. Wright and George Smith, *Mutually Beneficial: The Guardian and Life Insurance in America* (New York: New York University Press, 2004).

47. Tuckett, *Practical Remarks on the Present State of Life Insurance*, 7.

48. Eric Lomazoff, "Reconstructing the Hydra-Headed Monster: The Bank of the United States, Institutional Change, and American Constitutional Development" (Ph.D. diss., Harvard University, 2010); Joanne Freeman, ed., *Alexander Hamilton: Writings* (New York: Library of America, 2001), 611–46; Dodd, *American Business Corporations*, 2; Hitchcock, *Annual Address*, 237; John Travers et al., *Bergen Port Company* (Bergen Port, N.J., 1837), 2; *Report and Opinions Respecting the Powers and Duration of the Farmers' Fire Insurance and Loan Company* (New York: J. Booth, 1836).

49. A Citizen of New York, *What Is a Monopoly?*, 9–10, 30; Gunn, *Decline of Authority*, 112, 224.

50. Livermore, *Early American Land Companies*, 4, 278–79; *The Doctrine of Anti-Monopoly in an Address to the Democracy of the City of New York* (New York, 1835), 2; Julius Goebel, "Editor's Introduction," in Livermore, *Early American Land Companies*, xi–xxi; Charles E. Brooks, *Frontier Settlement and Market Revolution: The Holland Land Purchase* (Ithaca, N.Y.: Cornell University Press, 1996); Wright, "Rise of the Corporation Nation," 224–26; *A Statement of the Correspondence between the Banks in the City of New York* (New York, 1805), 3, 13; *The Memorial of the Subscribers, Merchants, Tradesmen, and Inhabitants of the City of New-York, to the Honourable, the Legislature of the State of New York, in Senate and Assembly Convened* (New York?); Lemuel Simon, *A Century of the National Bank of the Northern Liberties of Philadelphia, Pennsylvania* (Philadelphia, 1910), 11–12.

51. Tucker, *Notes of Lectures on Corporations*, 6, 14; Abbott, *Rise of the Business Corporation*, 8–9; Livermore, *Early American Land Companies*, 215; Samuel Williston, "History of the Law of Business Corporations Before 1800," *Harvard Law Review* 2, 3 (October 1888): 114; Dodd, *American Business Corporations*, 2, 158; Berle and Means, *The Modern Corporation*, 120 n. 2. Berle and Means point out that nonconsensual liabilities, like tort damages, cannot be eliminated by contract, but such liabilities are not usually meant when discussing stockholder liability because such claims were usually rare and insubstantial. James H. Godman and W. Milnor Roberts, *First Annual Report of the President and Directors of the Bellefontaine and Indiana Rail Road Company* (Cleveland: Sanford and Hayward, 1851), 7, 16; A Freeman of Massachusetts, *Remarks and Documents Concerning the Location of the Boston and Providence Rail-Road through the Burying Ground in East Attleborough* (Boston: Light & Horton, 1834), 26–27.

52. "Providence Hat Manufacturing Company," *Boston Patriot* (May 5, 1810), 3.

53. Livermore, *Early American Land Companies*, 63–64, 74, 229–30, 233–34, quotation on 74.

54. Robin Pearson, "Shareholder Democracies?: English Stock Companies and the Politics of Corporate Governance During the Industrial Revolution," *English Historical Review* 117 (September 2002): 849; "At the Annual Meeting," *Providence Gazette* (February 10, 1810), 3; "The Co-partnership," *Providence Columbian Phenix* (July 23, 1808), 1; "Frink Roberts," *Boston Independent Chronicle* (January 14, 1811), 4; "New Store and New Goods," *Rhode Island American* (May 10, 1811), 1; "Providence Hat Store," *Providence Gazette* (July 6, 1811), 4. The Printing and Bookselling Company of the City of Washington, for example, established itself via articles of incorporation in August 1801 with a capital of $1,000. According to its published bylaws, the company protected the liability of its shareholders by forbidding itself to borrow money. Tucker, *Notes of Lectures on Corporations*, 10; Seavoy, *Origins of the American Business Corporation*, 223–24; James Karmel, "Banking on the People: Banks, Politics, and Market Evolution in Early National Pennsylvania, 1781–1824" (Ph.D. diss., State University of New York, Buffalo, 1999), 153.

55. *History of the Lehigh Coal and Navigation Company*, 13.

56. Nathan Appleton, *Introduction of the Power Loom and Origin of Lowell* (Lowell, Mass.: B. H. Penhallow, 1858), 19–20.

57. William Constable to ?, April 15, 1794, CUL; Livermore, *Early American Land Companies*, 6, 254, 272–74, 282–83, 289; Stuart Banner, *American Property: A History of How, Why, and What We Own* (Cambridge, Mass.: Harvard University Press, 2011); Dodd, *American Business Corporations*, 16;

58. "We Understand," *Newburyport Herald* (February 4, 1820), 3.

59. Hollywood Cemetery Minute Books (1847–68), 13–15, 39–40, 113–15, 149, 150–54, 161–65, Virginia Historical Society, Richmond, Va. (hereafter VHS).

60. Livermore, *Early American Land Companies*, 242; Abbott, *Rise of the Business Corporation*, 8.

61. Abbott, *Rise of the Business Corporation*, 38.

62. Ibid., 20; Vikramaditya S. Khanna, "The Economic History of the Corporate Form in Ancient India" (working paper, November 1, 2005); Timur Kuran, "The Scale of Entrepreneurship in Middle Eastern History: Inhibitive Roles of Islamic Institutions," in David Landes, Joel Mokyr, and William Baumol, eds., *The Invention of Enterprise: Entrepreneurship from Ancient Mesopotamia to Modern Times* (Princeton, N.J.: Princeton University Press, 2010), 69–70; Timur Kuran, *The Long Divergence: How Islamic Law Held Back the Middle East* (Princeton, N.J.: Princeton University Press, 2010); Micklethwait and Wooldridge, *The Company*, 5–6.

63. Arthur Kuhn, *A Comparative Study of the Law of Corporations, with Particular Reference to the Protection of Creditors and Shareholders* (New York: AMS, 1968), 25–28. For further discussion of the points raised in this paragraph, see Abbott, *Rise of the Business Corporation*, 20–22; Tedlow, *Rise of the American Business Corporation*, 6; Micklethwait and Wooldridge, *The Company*, 4–5; A Citizen of New York, *What Is a Monopoly?*, 10; Michael Hudson, "Entrepreneurs: From the Near Eastern Takeoff to the Roman Collapse," in Landes, Mokyr, and Baumol, eds., *The Invention of Enterprise*, 28, 35; Handlin and Handlin, "Origins of the American Business Corporation," 1; Wormser, *Frankenstein*, 8; Tucker, *Notes of Lectures on Corporations*, 4–5.

64. Jonathan Baskin and Paul Miranti, *A History of Corporate Finance* (New York: Cambridge University Press, 1997), 38; Abbott, *Rise of the Business Corporation*, 30; Kuhn, *A Comparative Study of the Law of Corporations*, 34–36; Scott, *The Constitution and Finance*, 1:1–2, 12.

65. Baskin and Miranti, *A History of Corporate Finance*, 39–48; James Murray, "Entrepreneurs and Entrepreneurship in Medieval Europe," in Landes, Mokyr, and Baumol, eds., *The Invention of Enterprise*, 94–95; Abbott, *Rise of the Business Corporation*, 30; Scott, *The Constitution and Finance*, 1:1; Livermore, *Early American Land Companies*, 2–3; Kuhn, *A Comparative Study of the Law of Corporations*, 33.

66. Tedlow, *Rise of the American Business Corporation*, 6; Micklethwait and Wooldridge, *The Company*, 20; Oscar Gelderblom, Abe de Jong, and Joost Jonker, "An Admiralty for Asia: Business Organization and the Evolution of Corporate Governance in the Dutch Republic, 1590-1640," in Koppell, ed., *Origins of Shareholder Advocacy*, 29; Kuhn, *A Comparative Study of the Law of Corporations*, 38–42; Adam Smith, *An Inquiry into the Nature and Causes of the Wealth of Nations*, 5th ed. (London: Methuen, 1904), bk. 5, chap. 1, part 3, article 1.

67. Kuhn, *A Comparative Study of the Law of Corporations*, 43, 47; A Citizen of New York, *What Is a Monopoly?*, 10; Micklethwait and Wooldridge, *The Company*, 1–143; Williston, "History of the Law of Business Corporations Before 1800," 109, 118; Scott, *The Constitution and Finance*, 1:3, 10, 17, 443; Abbott, *Rise of the Business Corporation*, 23–30.

68. Abbott, *Rise of the Business Corporation*, 30–31; Micklethwait and Wooldridge, *The Company*, 18; Scott, *The Constitution and Finance*, 1:21–22.

69. John Munro, "Tawney's Century, 1540-1640: The Roots of Modern Capitalist Entrepreneurship," in Landes, Mokyr, and Baumol, eds., *The Invention of Enterprise*,

128–34. The most detailed study of early proto-corporations and pre–Bubble Act corporations and joint-stock companies in the U.K. is still Scott, *The Constitution and Finance*. See also Abbott, *Rise of the Business Corporation*, 32; Anne L. Murphy, *The Origins of English Financial Markets: Investment and Speculation before the South Sea Bubble* (New York: Cambridge University Press, 2009), 142; Steve Pincus, *1688: The First Modern Revolution* (New Haven, Conn.: Yale University Press, 2009), 157–61, 184, 202, 230, 257.

70. Murphy, *The Origins of English Financial Markets*, 1–2, 220; Abbott, *Rise of the Business Corporation*, 33; Scott, *The Constitution and Finance*, 1:439–41.

71. Steuart, quoted in A Citizen of New York, *Remarks on That Part of the Speech of His Excellency the Governor to the Legislature of the State of New York Relative to the Banking System* (1812), 5.

72. Gower, "Some Contrasts Between British and American Corporation Law," 1370.

73. Sykes, *The Amalgamation Movement in English Banking*, ix–29; Gallatin, *Considerations of the Currency and Banking System*, 35; George Heberton Evans, *British Corporation Finance, 1775–1850: A Study of Preference Shares* (Baltimore: Johns Hopkins University Press, 1936), 1; Williston, "History of the Law of Business Corporations Before 1800," 112–13; Munro, "Tawney's Century," in Landes, Mokyr, and Baumol, eds., *The Invention of Enterprise*, 134; Mark Freeman, Robin Pearson, and James Taylor, *Shareholder Democracies?: Corporate Governance in Britain and Ireland before 1850* (Chicago: University of Chicago Press, 2012), 8, 22–32.

74. Livermore, *Early American Land Companies*, 64, 67, 73; Wright, "Rise of the Corporation Nation," in Irwin and Sylla, eds., *Founding Choices*, 229–31; Abbott, *Rise of the Business Corporation*, 8.

75. Gower, "Some Contrasts Between British and American Corporation Law," 1370.

76. Abbott, *Rise of the Business Corporation*, 39–40; Julius Goebel, "Editor's Introduction," in Livermore, *Early American Land Companies*, xxii; Livermore, *Early American Land Companies*, 42–62; Baldwin, "American Business Corporations before 1789," 258; East, *Business Enterprise*, 20, 23, 25; Paskoff, *Industrial Evolution*, 65–66, 92.

77. Maier, "The Revolutionary Origins of the American Corporation," 56; Abbott, *Rise of the Business Corporation*, 38–39; Tedlow, *Rise of the American Business Corporation*, 6–7; Evans, *British Corporation Finance*, 3; Baldwin, "American Business Corporations before 1789," 257–59, 263; *New Hampshire Gazette* (December 26, 1766); Harold West, *Two Hundred Years, 1764–1964: The Story of Yarnall, Biddle & Co. Investment Bankers* (Philadelphia: Yarnall, Biddle, 1965), 16; East, *Business Enterprise*, 18; Calomiris and Ramirez, "Financing the American Corporation," in Kaysen, ed., *The American Corporation Today*, 141; Gower, "Some Contrasts Between British and American Corporation Law," 1372; Kuhn, *A Comparative Study of the Law of Corporations*, 55; Julius Goebel, "Editor's Introduction," in Livermore, *Early American Land Companies*, xxii; Tedlow, *Rise of the American Business Corporation*, 7; Freeman, Pearson, and Taylor, *Shareholder Democracies?*, 24.

78. Baldwin, "American Business Corporations before 1789," 256–65.

79. Ibid. See also Wormser, *Frankenstein*, 29; Nicholas Wainwright, *A Philadelphia Story: The Philadelphia Contributionship for the Insurance of Houses from Loss by Fire* (Philadelphia: The Contributionship, 1952); Elisha Douglass, *The Coming of Age of American Business: Three Centuries of Enterprise, 1600–1900* (Chapel Hill: University of North Carolina Press, 1971), 45.

80. Gower, "Some Contrasts Between British and American Corporation Law," 1372; Lawrence Lewis, *A History of the Bank of North America, the First Bank Chartered in the United States* (Philadelphia: J. B. Lippincott, 1882), 24, 33–35, 37, 43, 46; Baldwin, "American Business Corporations before 1789," 266–67.

81. Baldwin, "American Business Corporations before 1789," 267–70; Douglas Littlefield, "The Potomac Company: A Misadventure in Financing an Early American Internal Improvement Project," *Business History Review* 53 (1984): 562–85.

82. "This lag in the financial organization of colonial business was not due to an inadequacy of capital." East, *Business Enterprise*, 25. Durrenberger, *Turnpikes*, 97–99; Baldwin, "American Business Corporations before 1789," 271–72; Alice Hanson Jones, *Wealth of a Nation to Be: The American Colonies on the Eve of the Revolution* (New York: Columbia University Press, 1980), 51; East, *Business Enterprise*, 26.

Chapter 3

1. "Manufacturing Corporations," 92–93.

2. Seventy-Six, *Cause of, and Cure for, Hard Times* (New York, 1818), 55.

3. "Manufacturing Corporations," 93.

4. Brian P. Murphy, "Empire State Building: Interests, Institutions, and the Formation of States and Parties in New York, 1783–1845" (Ph.D. diss., University of Virginia, 2008), 225 n. 95; Abbott, *Rise of the Business Corporation*, 40–41; Freeman, ed., *Alexander Hamilton: Writings*, 624–26; Baldwin, "American Business Corporations before 1789," 272–73.

5. Thomas Doerflinger, *"A Vigorous Spirit of Enterprise": Merchants and Economic Development in Revolutionary Philadelphia* (Chapel Hill: University of North Carolina Press, 1986); Wright, *First Wall Street*; Robert E. Wright, *Hamilton Unbound: Finance and the Creation of the American Republic* (Westport, Conn.: Praeger, 2002); Robert E. Wright, *One Nation Under Debt: Hamilton, Jefferson, and the History of What We Owe* (New York: McGraw-Hill, 2008); Robert E. Wright and David J. Cowen, *Financial Founding Fathers: The Men Who Made America Rich* (Chicago: University of Chicago Press, 2006).

6. Tench Coxe, *A View of the United States of America: In a Series of Papers Written at Various Times, in the Years between 1787 and 1794* (New York: Augustus M. Kelley, 1965), 287, 364–65.

7. Hitchcock, quoted in Opal, *Beyond the Farm*, 50.

8. Gallatin, *Considerations of the Currency and Banking System*, 67.

9. *Report of the Committee on Banks and Insurance Companies*, 10–11.

10. Daniel Klein and John Majewski, "Economy, Community, and Law: The Turnpike Movement in New York, 1797–1845," *Law and Society Review* 26, 3 (1992): 469–512; Allan Kulikoff, *The Agrarian Origins of American Capitalism* (Charlottesville: University Press of Virginia, 1992); Rothenberg, *From Market-Places to a Market Economy*.

11. Thomas Hobbes, *Leviathan: Or the Matter, Forme, & Power of a Common-Wealth Ecclesiasticall and Civill*, ed. Ian Shapiro (New Haven, Conn.: Yale University Press, 2010), 200.

12. A Citizen of New York, *What Is a Monopoly?*.

13. Seventy-Six, *Cause of, and Cure for, Hard Times*, 27; East, *Business Enterprise*, 27.

14. Smith, quoted in Andreas Ortmann, "The Nature and Cause of Corporate Negligence, Sham Lectures, and Ecclesiastical Indolence: Adam Smith on Joint-Stock Companies, Teachers, and Preachers," *History of Political Economy* 31, 2 (1999): 297–315, at 297.

15. Smith, *An Inquiry Into the Nature and Causes of the Wealth of Nations*, bk. 5, chap. 1, part 3, article 1.

16. Scott, *The Constitution and Finance*, 1:451–52, 460–61.

17. Sidney Pollard, *The Genesis of Modern Management* (Baltimore: Penguin, 1965), 24; Steuart, *Inquiry into the Principles of Political Oeconomy*, 389–90. Smith allowed that temporary monopolies to trading companies and for patents and copyrights were acceptable ways of rewarding enterprising firms or individuals for assuming large risks.

18. Burke, quoted in David Bromwich, ed., *On Empire, Liberty, and Reform: Speeches and Letters of Edmund Burke* (New Haven, Conn.: Yale University Press, 2000), 260, 290.

19. Quoted in Wright, "Rise of the Corporation Nation," in Irwin and Sylla, eds., *Founding Choices*, 226–27.

20. Logan, quoted in Maier, "The Revolutionary Origins of the American Corporation," 72.

21. *Letter on the Use and Abuse of Incorporations*, 4.

22. "Manufacturing Corporations," 116.

23. Charles Sigourney, *To the Stockholders of the Phoenix Bank* (Hartford, Conn., 1837), 8.

24. *Report of the Committee on Banks and Insurance Companies*, 15.

25. Dunbar, *A History of Travel*, 3:1100–1101.

26. ? to Alexander Hamilton, September–October 1791, in Harold Syrett, ed., *The Papers of Alexander Hamilton* (New York: Columbia University Press, 1965), 9:250–52; Wright and Cowen, *Financial Founding Fathers*, 54–58, 76–80.

27. *Letter on the Use and Abuse of Incorporations*, 10, 53.

28. Seventy-Six, *Cause of, and Cure for, Hard Times*, 46.

29. Toby Ditz, "Shipwrecked; Or, Masculinity Imperiled: Mercantile Representations of Failure and the Gendered Self in Eighteenth-Century Philadelphia," *Journal of American History* 81 (June 1994): 51–80.

30. *Letter on the Use and Abuse of Incorporations*, 11.

31. *Report of the Committee on Banks and Insurance Companies*, 15.

32. Herman Krooss, "Financial Institutions," in David Gilchrist, ed., *The Growth of Seaport Cities, 1790–1825* (Charlottesville: University Press of Virginia, 1967), 133.

33. Stuart Banner, *Anglo-American Securities Regulation: Cultural and Political Roots, 1690–1860* (New York: Cambridge University Press, 1998); D. Morier Evans, *Fortune's Epitome of the Stocks and Public Funds, English, Foreign and American*, 15th ed. (London: Letts, Son, and Steer, 1850), 228.

34. A Citizen of Burlington, *Letters to the People of New Jersey on the Frauds Extortions, and Oppressions of the Railroad Monopoly* (Philadelphia: Carey and Hart, 1848), 2, 8.

35. Freeman, ed., *Alexander Hamilton: Writings*, 624–25.

36. Seventy-Six, *Cause of, and Cure for, Hard Times*, 26n.

37. Joseph R. Ingersoll, *Argument of Joseph R. Ingersoll, Esq. Before the General Assembly of New Jersey on the Memorial of the Trenton and New Brunswick Turnpike Company for the Amendment of Their Charter* (Philadelphia, 1834), 17.

38. *An Inquiry into the Nature and Utility of Corporations*, 1.

39. Albert Gallatin, *Suggestions on the Banks and Currency of the Several United States: In Reference Principally to the Suspension of Specie Payments* (New York: Wiley and Putnam, 1841), 68; Platt, *Mr. Platt's Speech*.

40. John Majewski, "Toward a Social History of the Corporation: Shareholding in Pennsylvania, 1800–1840," in Cathy Matson, ed., *The Economy of Early America: Historical Perspectives and New Directions* (Philadelphia: University of Pennsylvania Press, 2006), 311; Micklethwait and Wooldridge, *The Company*, xviii; Maier, "The Revolutionary Origins of the American Corporation," 67.

41. Logan, quoted in Wright, "Rise of the Corporation Nation," in Irwin and Sylla, eds., *Founding Choices*, 232–33. See also Freyer, "Business Law," in Engerman and Gallman, eds., *The Cambridge Economic History of the United States*, 436–37.

42. *Letter on the Use and Abuse of Incorporations*, 36.

43. Quoted in John Stealey, ed., *Kanawhan Prelude to Nineteenth-Century Monopoly in the United States* (Richmond: Virginia Historical Society, 2000), 60.

44. Vroom, quoted in Roy, *Socializing Capital*, 69.

45. Quoted in Maier, "The Revolutionary Origins of the American Corporation," 73.

46. Micklethwait and Wooldridge, *The Company*, 27.

47. Ingersoll, *Argument of Joseph R. Ingersoll, Esq. Before the General Assembly*, 18.

48. *An Inquiry into the Nature and Utility of Corporations*, 2.

49. Ditz, "Shipwrecked," 51–80; Majewski, "Toward a Social History of the Corporation," 312.

50. "South Carolina Rail Road Company," *Richmond Enquirer* (February 2, 1830), 4.

51. *Letter on the Use and Abuse of Incorporations*, 7.

52. *The Doctrine of Anti-Monopoly*, 2; Cadman, *The Corporation in New Jersey*, 390–91.

53. *Letter on the Use and Abuse of Incorporations*, 7.

54. Ibid., 8.

55. Ibid., 9.

56. Bryan, quoted in Gunn, *Decline of Authority*, 112.

57. Robert E. Wright, "Banking and Politics in New York, 1784–1829" (Ph.D. diss., State University of New York, Buffalo, 1996), 290–519.

58. Ferris Pell, *Review of the Administration and Civil Police of the State of New York* (New York: E. Conrad, 1819), 33.

59. J. W. Stevenson to Norvin Green, [May] 1848, Norvin Green Papers, Correspondence, FHS.

60. *Letter on the Use and Abuse of Incorporations*, 10.

61. A Citizen of Lowell, *Corporations and Operatives* (Lowell: Samuel J. Varney, 1843), 65; Norman Ware, *The Industrial Worker, 1840–1860: The Reaction of American Industrial Society to the Advance of the Industrial Revolution* (Boston: Houghton Mifflin, 1924), 23, 85, 97, 101–2, 106–8, 139, 152; Majewski, "Toward a Social History of the Corporation," 312; Lawrence A. Peskin, *Manufacturing Revolution: The Intellectual Origins of Early American Industry* (Baltimore: Johns Hopkins University Press, 2003), 186.

62. Quoted in Wright, "Rise of the Corporation Nation," in Irwin and Sylla, eds., *Founding Choices*, 234.

63. A Citizen of Burlington, *Letters to the People of New Jersey*, 4–5.

64. Diary of Blair Bolling, 1810–37, 1:261, VHS.

65. A Freeman of Massachusetts, *Remarks and Documents Concerning the Location*, 10.

66. Maier, "The Revolutionary Origins of the American Corporation," 71–72.

67. Seventy-Six, *Cause of, and Cure for, Hard Times*, 28, 44, 54–55.

68. Maryland, General Assembly, House of Delegates, Committee on Corporations, *Evidence Taken Before the Committee on Corporations* (1860).

69. A Freeman of Massachusetts, *Remarks and Documents Concerning the Location*, 28.

70. Ibid.

71. Shepherd Knapp, *Letter to the Stockholders of the Mechanics' Bank from Shepherd Knapp, in Replay to the Defence of Francis W. Edmonds, Their Late Cashier* (New York: H. Anstice, 1855), 6–7.

72. Seventy-Six, *Cause of, and Cure for, Hard Times*, 46.

73. Diary of Henry Van Der Lyn, 1:214, NYHS.

74. Samuel String and James Van Ingen, *A View of Certain Proceedings in the Two Houses of the Legislature, Respecting the Incorporation of the New State Bank* (Albany, N.Y.: Daniel and Samuel Whiting, 1803), 4, 15–16, 23–24, quotations at 4, 16.

75. A Citizen of New York, *Remarks on that Part of the Speech*, 5; *Substance of Argument of Respondents' Counsel*, 4.

76. *Substance of Argument of Respondents' Counsel on the Application of the Seekonk Branch Rail Road Company to the Committee of the Legislature, to Run Locomotive Engines on the Providence and Worcester Rail Roads and Through the Worcester*

Merchandize Depot (Boston: John H. Eastburn, 1838), 4. See also Songho Ha, *The Rise and Fall of the American System* (London: Pickering & Chatto, 2009).

77. Teackle, *An Address to the Members of the Legislature of Maryland*, 15.

78. Seventy-Six, *Cause of, and Cure for, Hard Times*, 15, 32 n., 37, 56.

79. See *Merchants' Bank* (New York?, 1805?), 1; Dreikorn, "History and Development of Banking in New Jersey," 31.

80. Maier, "The Revolutionary Origins of the American Corporation," 66–71, 76–77; James O. Wettereau to N. S. B. Gras, June 15, 1948, Wettereau Papers, CUL; Lewis, *A History of the Bank of North America*, 54–74; *In the Recent Report of the Board of Public Works* (1833), 1; Tucker, *Notes of Lectures on Corporations*, 9; Micklethwait and Wooldridge, *The Company*, 46; Cadman, *The Corporation in New Jersey*, 365–80.

81. Maier, "The Revolutionary Origins of the American Corporation," 60–64.

82. *An Inquiry into the Nature and Utility of Corporations*, 3.

83. A Freeman of Massachusetts, *Remarks and Documents Concerning the Location*, 9.

84. Seventy-Six, *Cause of, and Cure for, Hard Times*, 27.

85. Klein and Majewski, "Economy, Community, and Law," 486–91.

86. Meredith, quoted in Maier, "The Revolutionary Origins of the American Corporation," 74, 74 n. 67.

87. Maryland, *Evidence Taken before the Committee on Corporations*, 8–14, 133–36.

88. *Merchants' Bank*, 1.

89. Roland Baumann, "Philadelphia's Manufacturers and the Excise Taxes of 1794: The Forging of the Jeffersonian Coalition," *Pennsylvania Magazine of History and Biography* 106 (January 1982): 3–39; Lehman, "Explaining Hard Times," 89, 204–49, 294; Wright, "Banking and Politics in New York"; Frank Herriott, *An Introduction to the History of Corporation Taxes in Iowa* (Des Moines, Iowa: Plain Tale Printing House, 1902), 44.

90. Maier, "The Revolutionary Origins of the American Corporation," 68–69.

91. Charles G. Haines, *Arguments against the Justice and Policy of Taxing the Capital Stock of Banks and Insurance Companies in the State of New York* (New York: Franklin Law Press, 1824), 33–34.

92. Seventy-Six, *Cause of, and Cure for, Hard Times*, 38.

93. Murphy, "Empire State Building," 252–54.

94. Quoted in Alan Houston, *Benjamin Franklin and the Politics of Improvement* (New Haven, Conn.: Yale University Press, 2008), 60.

95. Teackle, *An Address to the Members of the Legislature of Maryland*, 16–17.

96. *Letter on the Use and Abuse of Incorporations*, 29.

97. *An Inquiry into the Nature and Utility of Corporations*, 2.

98. Citizen of Boston, *Remarks Upon the Rights and Powers*, 12.

99. Charles B. Haddock, *Address of the Northern Rail Road Company to the Friends of Internal Improvement in New Hampshire* (Hanover: Hanover Press, 1845), 4.

100. Freyer, "Business Law," in Engerman and Gallman, eds., *The Cambridge Economic History of the United States*, 440; Micklethwait and Wooldridge, *The Company*, 4.

101. Except where otherwise noted, this section is based on Asa Martin, "Lotteries in Pennsylvania Prior to 1833," *Pennsylvania Magazine of History and Biography* 47 (1923): 307–27, and 48 (1924): 66–93, 159–80; Harold Gillingham, "Lotteries in Philadelphia Prior to 1776," *Pennsylvania History* 5 (January 1938): 77–100; John Ezell, "The Lottery in Colonial America," *William and Mary Quarterly* 5 (April 1948): 185–200; Perkins, *American Public Finance and Financial Services*, 305–9.

102. John James and Richard Sylla, "The Changing Nature of American Public Debt," in *La dette publique aux XVIIe et XIXe siècles son developpement sur le plan local, regional et national* (Brussels: Credit Communal de Belgique, 1980), 243–73.

103. John F. Watson, *Annals of Philadelphia: Being a Collection of Memoirs, Anecdotes and Incidents of the City and Its Inhabitants* (Philadelphia: E. L. Carey and A. Hart, 1830), 219, 710–12; *Scheme of a Lottery for One Hundred Thousand Acres of Land in the Province of Pennsylvania* (1735); New York Province, *College Lottery Advertisement* (New York, 1748); New Brunswick Church Lottery, *A List of Numbers That Came Up Prizes in the New-Brunswick Church Lottery, Drawn April, 1749* (1749); Massachusetts General Assembly, *An Act to Enable the Precinct of Teticut in the County of Plymouth, to Raise a Sum by Lottery towards Building a Bridge over the Teticut River* (1755); *A List of the Numbers That Came Up Prizes in Biles'-Island Lottery, for the Benefit of a Place of Worship in Borden-Town* (1755); *Scheme of a Lottery to Raise £10,000 Old Tenor, for Carrying on the Fortification for the Defence of the Colony of Rhode-Island* (1756); "Scheme of a Lottery for Raising 3000 Pieces of Eight for the Use of the College and Academy of Philadelphia," *Pennsylvania Gazette* (May 5, 1757), 1; *Scheme of a Second Class of a Lottery Granted by the General Assembly of the Colony of Rhode-Island . . . for Raising Six Thousand Pounds Old Tenor, to Be Appropriated for the Building of a Wharf at a Place Called Church's Cove in Little Compton* (1764); *Faneuil-Hall Lottery* (Boston, January 1768); "A List of the Fortunate Numbers in the Plainfield Road Lottery," *Providence Gazette* (September 16, 1769), 4; Houston, *Benjamin Franklin*, 92–98.

104. *A Lottery, Set Forth by Bethiah Hughes, of Newport, Rhode-Island* (1733).

105. Quoted in Gillingham, "Lotteries in Philadelphia," 84.

106. Ibid.

107. *Newcastle Lottery, Instituted by the Friends of the American China Manufactory* (Christiana Bridge, Del., 1771).

108. *Supplement to the American Flint Glass Manufactory Pettie's Island Cash Lottery* (1774).

109. "A Lottery for Old Maids," *New York Evening Post* (April 10, 1749). See also "The Fortunate Numbers in the Pettey's Island Cash Lottery," *Pennsylvania Chronicle* (February 22, 1773), 231; "Whereas Some Enemies of the Lottery Scheme," *New York Gazette* (August 21, 1748), 1; *Pettey's Island Lottery, for the Effects to the Full Value of 10,000 Dollars, or £375 [sic] without any Deduction* (1761); *Scheme of a Lottery, Consisting of Three Classes* (New York, 1769); *New-Ark Land and Cash Lottery, in New Castle County on Delaware, for Disposing of a Furnace, Forge, and Gristmill* (1771); *Dover Land and Cash Lottery . . . for Disposing of Certain Valuable and Improved Farms and Tracts of*

Land (1771); "Managers of the Delaware Lottery," *Newport Mercury* (April 20, 1772), 4; *Scheme of a Lottery, for Disposing of the Following Houses, Plate, Furniture &c. &c.* (1773); *Delaware Lottery. for the Sale of Lands Belonging to the Earl of Stirling* (1774).

110. *The Lottery: A Dialogue between Mr. Thomas Trueman and Mr. Humphrey Dupe* (Germantown, 1758); Jeremiah Brown, "Christ's Example, and the Fashion of the World: Or, a Ticket Looking-Glass, Where Every One May See His Face" (1768). See also "An Account of a Person in London Being Likely Ruined by Means of His Having the Luck to Draw the £2,000 Prize in the Late State Lottery," *Newport Mercury* (August 10, 1762), 1.

111. *United States Lottery, 1776* (1776); *United States Lottery, 1778* (1778); Dunbar, *A History of Travel*, 1:323; *Laws, Documents and Judicial Decisions Relating to the Baltimore and Fredericktown, York and Reistertown, Cumberland and Boonsborough Turnpike Road Companies* (Baltimore: John D. Toy, 1841), 44–45; Massachusetts, State Lottery, *The General Assembly having passed a resolve for raising a sum of money . . . for the benefit of those officers and soldiers who inlisted into the fifteen Continental battalions raised by this state, appointed . . . directors of a lottery for that purpose* (1778); *A List of the Fortunate Members in the New-York Poor Lottery* (1779); *New-Haven Lottery for Building a Bridge over East-River* (New Haven, Conn., 1780); *Scheme of a lottery, granted by the Honorable General Assembly of the state of Rhode-Island, and Providence-Plantations, at their session in February, 1784, for raising 1500 dollars, to be appropriated towards repairing the meeting and parsonage houses of the Congregational Society in the town of Tiverton* (1785).

112. "Charleston Bridge Company," *Charleston Courier* (June 25, 1810), 3; "These May Inform the Publick," *New-London Summary* (May 30, 1760), 1; "The Tickets in the Faneuil Hall Lottery Number Nine," *Boston News-Letter* (May 28, 1767), 2; "Newmarket and Stratham Lottery," *New-Hampshire Gazette* (June 9, 1769), 2; Walter Sanderlin, *The Great National Project: A History of the Chesapeake and Ohio Canal* (Baltimore: Johns Hopkins University Press, 1946), 38–39; Littlefield, "The Potomac Company," 562–85.

113. *Philadelphia in 1824* (Philadelphia: H. C. Carey & I. Lea, 1824), 161.

114. Union Canal Company of Pennsylvania, *An Act to Incorporate the Union Canal Company of Pennsylvania* (Philadelphia: John Binns, 1811), 26.

115. See, e.g., Watson, *Annals of Philadelphia*, 219; *Society for the Prevention of Pauperism, Documents Relative to Savings Banks, Intemperance, and Lotteries* (New York, 1819); Job R. Tyson, *A Brief Survey of the Great and Evil Tendencies of the Lottery System, as Existing in the United States* (Philadelphia: William Brown, 1833); M. J. Heale, "Humanitarianism in the Early Republic: The Moral Reformers of New York, 1776–1825," *Journal of American Studies* 2 (1968): 161–75; Seventy-Six, *Cause of, and Cure for, Hard Times*, 67.

116. Colden, Randolph, and Craig, *Observations*, 8.

117. Seventy-Six, *Cause of, and Cure for, Hard Times*, 66–72.

118. A Citizen of Burlington, *Beauties of the Monopoly System of New Jersey* (Philadelphia: C. Sherman, 1848); C. Fraser Smith, *Here Lies Jim Crow: Civil Rights in*

Maryland (Baltimore: Johns Hopkins University Press, 2008), 118; Francis Wharton, *A Treatise on the Criminal Law of the United States*, 4th and rev. ed. (Philadelphia, 1857), 897–903; Mordecai M'Kinney, *Our Government: An Explanatory Statement of the System of Government of the Country, Presenting a View of the Government of the United States*, 2nd ed. (Philadelphia, 1856), 257; Benjamin Abbott Vaughan, *Judge and Jury: A Popular Explanation of Leading Topics in the Law of the Land* (New York, 1880), 225–31.

119. Pell, *Review of the Administration and Civil Police*, 32–33.

120. Tamara Thornton, "'A Great Machine' or a 'Beast of Prey': A Boston Corporation and Its Rural Debtors in an Age of Capitalist Transformation," *Journal of the Early Republic* 27, 4 (winter 2007): 567–97.

121. A Citizen of Burlington, *Beauties of the Monopoly System*, 4.

122. Opal, *Beyond the Farm*, 186–87; Micklethwait and Wooldridge, *The Company*, 77.

123. Lockwood, "How to Reform Business," 295; Herriott, *An Introduction to the History of Corporation Taxes*, 44–45.

124. Quoted in John A. Patterson, "Ten and One-Half Years of Commercial Banking in a New England Country Town: Concord, Massachusetts, 1832–1842" (working paper, Old Sturbridge Village, Mass., 1971), 16.

125. Maier, "The Revolutionary Origins of the American Corporation," 75.

126. Citizen of Boston, *Remarks Upon the Rights and Powers*, 3.

127. Quoted in Stealey, ed., *Kanawhan Prelude*, 58.

128. A Citizen of New York, *What Is a Monopoly?*, 9.

129. John Wallis, "Constitutions, Corporations, and Corruption: American States and Constitutional Change, 1842 to 1852," *Journal of Economic History* 65 (March 2005): 214–15.

130. "Manufacturing Corporations," 94.

131. Quoted in Stealey, ed., *Kanawhan Prelude*, 58.

132. Pell, *Review of the Administration and Civil Police*, 83.

133. *Federal Gazette & Baltimore Daily Advertiser*, February 6, 1804.

134. Maier, "The Revolutionary Origins of the American Corporation," 75; Tom Paine, *Dissertations on Government, the Affairs of the Bank, and Paper Money* (Charles Cist: Philadelphia, 1786); Seventy-Six, *Cause of, and Cure for, Hard Times*, 36; Howard Bodenhorn, "Free Banking and Financial Entrepreneurship in Nineteenth-Century New York: The Black River Bank of Watertown," *Business and Economic History* 27 (fall 1998): 102–14.

135. *Proceedings of a Meeting of Representatives of the Several Railroad Companies between New York, Boston, Philadelphia and Baltimore, Chicago, Cincinnati, and the Ohio and Mississippi Rivers, Held at Cleveland November 28th, 1854* (Cleveland, 1854), 16. See also Union Canal Company of Pennsylvania, *An Act to Incorporate*, 30; A Citizen of Lowell, *Corporations and Operatives*, 11.

136. Maier, "The Revolutionary Origins of the American Corporation," 66–67.

137. Majewski, "Toward a Social History of the Corporation," 296.

138. As quoted in Maier, "The Revolutionary Origins of the American Corporation," 75.

139. For examples of frauds perpetrated against corporations, see "Conspiracy to Defraud an Insurance Company," *Boston Daily Evening Transcript* (November 9, 1850), 1; Henry Ashmead, *History of the Delaware County National Bank* (Chester, Pa.: Press of the Chester Times, 1914), 55; Simon, *A Century of the National Bank of the Northern Liberties*, 18–19, 27; "Defrauding a Gas Company," *Philadelphia Public Ledger* (September 15, 1860), 1; Herman Haupt, *Documents Referring to the Controversy between the Canal Commissioners of the State of Pennsylvania and the Harrisburg and Lancaster and the Pennsylvania Railroad Companies with Remarks upon the Relative Position of the State Improvements and the Pennsylvania Railroad* (Philadelphia: T. K. and P. G. Collins, 1852), 28.

140. *Report of the Committee Appointed by the Directors of the Winnipiseogee Canal to Prepare a Statement of Such Facts and Circumstances, in Relation to the Proposed Canal, as They Might Deem Proper to Be Laid before the Publick* (Dover, N.H.: J. Dickman, 1826), 6.

141. Evans, quoted in Dunbar, *A History of Travel*, 3:886. .

142. "The Raft Company," *The Standard* (Clarksville, Tex.) (January 28, 1860), 2.

143. String and Van Ingen, *A View of Certain Proceedings*, 6.

144. Maier, "The Revolutionary Origins of the American Corporation," 51–84.

145. Wright, "Rise of the Corporation Nation," in Irwin and Sylla, eds., *Founding Choices*, 231–32.

146. Gerry, quoted in Neem, *Creating a Nation of Joiners*, 62.

147. "We Call Attention," *Tallahassee Floridian and Advocate* (April 25, 1840), 3.

148. Bodenhorn, "Banking," 30; Diary of Henry Van Der Lyn, 1:245, NYHS; Lewis, *A History of the Bank of North America*, 93–94.

149. Miller, *Supreme Court*, 24–26; Neem, *Creating a Nation of Joiners*, 140–51; *An Inquiry into the Nature and Utility of Corporations*, 1; Arthur Schlesinger, Jr., *The Age of Jackson* (Boston: Little, Brown, 1945), 337; Hammond, *Banks and Politics in America*, 275.

150. Tilden, quoted in Schlesinger, *Age of Jackson*, 339.

151. Coxe, *A View of the United States of America*, 337, 354.

152. Julius Goebel, "Editor's Introduction," in Livermore, *Early American Land Companies*, xxv.

153. Schlesinger, *Age of Jackson*, 337.

154. Ibid., 335.

155. Ware, *The Industrial Worker, 1840–1860*, 133–35, 157.

156. "Manufacturing Corporations," 94.

157. See, e.g., Wormser, *Frankenstein*; John Kenneth Galbraith, *The New Industrial State*, 2nd rev. ed. (Boston: Houghton Mifflin, 1971); Joel Bakan, *The Corporation: The Pathological Pursuit of Profit and Power* (New York: Free Press, 2004).

158. *Letter on the Use and Abuse of Incorporations*, 3.

Chapter 4

1. J. S. Robinson, *Annual Report of the Secretary of State, to the Governor of the State of Ohio* (Columbus, Ohio: Westbote, 1885).

2. Platt, *Mr. Platt's Speech.*

3. Achille Murat, *A Moral and Political Sketch of the United States of North America* (London: Effingham Wilson, 1833), 331.

4. For the GDP numbers, see Johnston and Williamson, "What Was the U.S. GDP Then?." For commentary on changing macroeconomic conditions, see Smith and Cole, *Fluctuations in American Business*, 12–21, 81–84, 87–92, 94, 98, 100, 104. As late as 1842, "every day" looked like "Sunday in the streets" of Louisville, Kentucky, and conditions were so "dull" that no one saw any "prospect for any improvement." Henry Gilpin to Mrs. H. A. Gilpin, June 12, 1842, FHS. See also Kessler, "Incorporation in New England," 57; *Report of the Grantees of the Nashua and Lowell Rail Road Corporation* (Nashua, N.H.: Alfred Beard, 1836), 6; Charles Huntington, *A History of Banking and Currency in Ohio before the Civil War* (Columbus, Ohio: F. J. Heer, 1915), 176–77.

5. James O. Wettereau to N. S. B. Gras, January 29, 1941, Wettereau Papers, Folder 23, CUL.

6. Philip Elbert Taylor, "The Turnpike Era in New England" (Ph.D. diss., Yale University, 1934), 215.

7. H. S. Tanner, *A Description of the Canals and Rail Roads of the United States, Comprehending Notices of All the Works of Internal Improvement throughout the Several States* (New York: T. R. Tanner and J. Disturnell, 1840), 23.

8. Robert G. Shaw, *Report of the Board of Directors of the Lewis Wharf Company to the Stockholders* (Boston: Beals & Greene, 1840), 8.

9. George Tibbits, Moses Warren, and William Roberts, *Report of the Troy Turnpike and Rail Road Company, June, 1838* (Troy, N.Y.: Tuttle, Belcher & Burton, 1838), 8–9.

10. Austin Hutcheson, "Philadelphia and the Panic of 1857," *Pennsylvania History* 3 (July 1936): 182–94; National City Bank of New York, *135 Years of Banking* (New York: National City Bank of New York, 1947); Ashmead, *History of the Delaware County National Bank*, 60; Huntington, *A History of Banking and Currency in Ohio*, 249.

11. Shaw, *Report of the Board of Directors of the Lewis Wharf Company*, 5.

12. *Annual Report of Messrs. A. J. Pleasonton, John Moss, Richard Ronaldson and John Sharp, Jr., Directors of the Affairs and Proceedings of the Harrisburg, Portsmouth, Mount Joy and Lancaster Railroad Company* (Philadelphia: T. K. & P. G. Collins, 1840), 9.

13. Quoted in Hutcheson, "Philadelphia and the Panic of 1857," 190.

14. Appleton, *Introduction of the Power Loom*, 29.

15. Paul Peel, "History of the Lancaster Bank: 1814–1856," *Journal of the Lancaster County Historical Society* (spring 1962): 72.

16. Frank Dobbin and Timothy Dowd, "How Policy Shapes Competition: Early Railroad Foundings in Massachusetts," *Administrative Science Quarterly* 42 (September 1997): 508, 515.

17. Ludwig von Mises, *Interventionism: An Economic Analysis* (Indianapolis: Liberty Fund, 1998), 43.

18. Quoted in Huntington, *A History of Banking and Currency in Ohio*, 141.

19. Tatham, quoted in Appleton, *Introduction of the Power Loom*, 31.

20. Appleton, *Introduction of the Power Loom*, 31.

21. Bruchey, *Roots of American Economic Growth*, 138–39.

22. Miller, *Supreme Court*, 46–48.

23. Stuart Bruchey and Eleanor Bruchey, *A Brief History of Commercial Banking in the Old Line State* (Baltimore: Maryland Historical Society, 1996), 23.

24. Ashmead, *History of the Delaware County National Bank*, 9; Miller, "A Note on the History of Business," 157; Peel, "History of the Lancaster Bank," 68.

25. T. G. Cary, *The Americans Defended* (London: John Chapman, 1844), 6.

26. Lehman, "Explaining Hard Times," 73–79.

27. "A Sketch of Mr. Markley's Remarks," *Franklin Gazette* (February 8, 1820), 2.

28. Dobbin and Dowd, "How Policy Shapes Competition," 501–29; James Ranger-Moore, Jane Banaszak-Holl, and Michael Hannan, "Density Dependent Dynamics in Regulated Industries: Founding Rates of Banks and Life Insurance Companies," *Administrative Science Quarterly* 36 (1991): 36–65.

29. William Boyd, *Communication from the President of the Union Canal Company, Accompanied with a Report of James D. Harris, Principal Engineer, Relative to Enlarging the Union Canal* (Harrisburg, Pa.: Boas & Copan, 1839), 5.

30. *Federal Gazette & Baltimore Daily Advertiser* (February 6, 1804).

31. Union Canal Company of Pennsylvania, *An Act to Incorporate*, 30.

32. Murat, *A Moral and Political Sketch of the United States*, 338.

33. Dobbin and Dowd, "How Policy Shapes Competition," 506.

34. Thomas Fernon, *Municipal Subscriptions Made by the City of Philadelphia and the Incorporated Districts of Spring Garden, Richmond, and the Northern Liberties in the County of Philadelphia to the Capital Stock of the North Pennsylvania Rail Road Company* (Philadelphia: Crissy & Markley, 1854), 8.

35. Ibid., 3–4; A Citizen of Philadelphia, *The Claims of the Delaware and Raritan Canal Company to a Repeal of the Law of Pennsylvania* (Philadelphia: Joseph R. A. Skerrett, 1826).

36. Tanner, *A Description of the Canals and Rail Roads of the United States*, 21.

37. Stuyvesant, *Memorial of the New York and Erie Railroad Company*, 8–10.

38. J. G. Hopkins, *The Northern Railroad in New York, with Remarks on the Western Trade* (Ogdensburgh, N.Y.: A. Tyler, 1849), 13–14.

39. Dunbar, *A History of Travel*, 3:829–30; J. L. Sullivan, *A Description of a Sub-Marine Aqueduct, to Supply New York with Water from New Jersey* (New York: G & C. & H. Carvill, 1830), 14–16.

40. *President and Directors of the Baltimore and Susquehanna Rail Road Company to the Stockholders* (Baltimore: Sands & Neilson, 1835), 4–5.

41. Sanderlin, *The Great National Project*, 49–54, 83–92.

42. Edwin F. Johnson, *Engineer's Report on the New York and Boston Railroad* (Middletown, Conn.: Charles Pelton, 1847), v.

43. Stephen N. Stockwell, *Argument of Hon. Chas. Theo. Russell in Behalf of the Boston and New York Central Railroad Co., Remonstrants* (Boston: Damrell & Moore, 1854).

44. Godman, quoted in Godman and Roberts, *First Annual Report*, 3.

45. Alexander Nisbet, *Annual Report from the President and Directors of the Baltimore and Susquehanna Rail Road* (Annapolis, Md.: William M'Neir, 1836); Matthew Newkirk, *The First Annual Report of the Philadelphia, Wilmington and Baltimore Rail Road Company since the Union of the Original Companies* (Philadelphia, 1839); *North Branch Canal Company*, 3; John P. Kennedy, *Address of the President and Directors of the Northern Central Railway Company to the Stockholders* (Baltimore: John Murphy, 1855), 40–44; *Circular Statement of the Condition and Prospects of the Northern Indiana Railroad Company* (New York: Van Norden & Amerman, 1851), 8; Nathaniel Marsh, *Address of the Directors of the New York and Erie Railroad Company to the Stockholders* (New York: Snowden's Printing Establishment, 1850), 3–5; Henry S. Durand, *Third Annual Report of the Racine and Mississippi Railroad Company* (New York: Baker & Godwin, 1856), 10; *Substance of Argument of Respondents' Counsel*, 21–23; J. G. Telford, *First Exhibit by the Dayton and Michigan Rail-Road Company of the Conditions and Prospects of Their Road* (New York: Van Norden & Amerman, 1852), 12; Minute of June 20, 1835, Board of Directors' Minutes, 1834–35, Richmond, Fredericksburg, and Petersburg Records, VHS.

46. Tanner, *A Description of the Canals and Rail Roads of the United States*, 15.

47. *Address of the Delaware and Raritan Canal and Camden and Amboy Railroad Companies to the People of New Jersey* (Trenton: Sherman and Harron, 1848), 14.

48. Ingersoll, *Argument of Joseph R. Ingersoll, Esq. before the General Assembly*, 11. See also "A charter of incorporation is therefore a grant of exclusive privilege, and every grant of exclusive privilege, strictly speaking, creates a monopoly": A Citizen of New York, *What Is a Monopoly?*, 12.

49. Rhode Island's penchant for chartering banks, and presumably other corporations, was noted by Lamoreaux and Glaisek. Naomi Lamoreaux and Christopher Glaisek, "Vehicles of Privilege or Mobility?: Banks in Providence, Rhode Island, During the Age of Jackson," *Business History Review* 65, 3 (autumn 1991): 504. See also Hamill, "From Special Privilege to General Utility," 179.

50. Diary of Blair Bolling, 1838–39, 3:49, VHS; A. Glenn Crothers, "Public Culture and Economic Liberalism in Post-Revolutionary Northern Virginia, 1780–1820," *Canadian Review of American Studies* 29, 3 (1999): 61–89.

51. "Manufacturing Corporations," 94.

52. "Virginia Life Insurance Company," *Macon (Ga.) Daily Telegraph* (April 3, 1860), 2.

53. Maier, "The Revolutionary Origins of the American Corporation," 56–57.

54. Robert E. Wright, *Fubarnomics: A Lighthearted, Serious Look at America's Economic Ills* (Buffalo, N.Y.: Prometheus, 2010), 83–115.

55. Dodd, *American Business Corporations*; Maier, "The Revolutionary Origins of the American Corporation," 53.

56. John Shirley, "The Fourth New Hampshire Turnpike," *Granite Monthly* 4 (October 1881): 220.

57. Opal, *Beyond the Farm*.

58. Livermore, *Early American Land Companies*, 258–60.

59. Kessler, "Incorporation in New England," 51.

60. Lehman, "Explaining Hard Times," 66–71.

61. Simeon Draper, *The Burns Ranche Gold Mining Company* (New York: Office of the Burns Ranche Gold Mining Company, 1851), 4.

62. Smith and Cole, *Fluctuations in American Business*, 3, 5, 20; Kessler, "Incorporation in New England," 53.

63. Appleton, *Introduction of the Power Loom*, 12–13.

64. Henry Livingston to [Samuel] Breese, December 2, 1816, Livingston Family Papers, NYHS.

65. *To the Honorable the Senate and House of Representatives of the United States, in Congress Assembled, the Petition of the Citizens of the United States, Engaged in Manufactories on the Brandywine, and in its Vicinity* (Wilmington, Del., 1815), 2–3.

66. On these points, see Appleton, *Introduction of the Power Loom*, 14; Haines, *Arguments against the Justice and Policy of Taxing*, 31–32; Robert Varnum Spalding, "The Boston Mercantile Community and the Promotion of the Textile Industry in New England, 1813–1860" (Ph.D. diss., Yale University, 1963), 125, 165–78.

67. "We Learn from Undoubted Authority," *Portsmouth, New Hampshire Gazette* (August 4, 1840), 2.

68. Appleton, *Introduction of the Power Loom*, 31; Elias Derby, *Boston: A Commercial Metropolis in 1850: Her Growth, Population, Wealth, and Prospects* (Boston: Redding, 1850), 8.

69. "The High Price of Raw Material," *Albany Evening Journal* (April 30, 1850), 2.

70. "The Granite Manufacturing Company," *Baltimore Sun* (May 20, 1850), 2.

71. "Charleston Cotton Manufacturing Company," *Baltimore Sun* (July 2, 1850), 1–2.

72. "The Pepperell Manufacturing Company," *Boston Daily Atlas* (December 28, 1850), 2.

73. Mary Furner, "From 'State Interference' to the 'Return of the Market': The Rhetoric of Economic Regulation from the Old Gilded Age to the New," in Edward J. Balleisen and David A. Moss, eds., *Government and Markets: Toward a New Theory of Regulation* (New York: Cambridge University Press, 2010), 97.

74. "Why did manufacturing remain institutionally separate from the corporate system for so long? And why was the corporate revolution so explosive when it finally occurred?" As shown here, manufacturing did not remain separate, and its late nineteenth-century explosion was not its first. Roy's claims that "the large, publicly traded manufacturing corporation was rare" until the very end of the nineteenth

century and that "if large corporations had been rational for manufacturing firms in 1850, they still would not have been created because those who controlled necessary resources would not have been willing to invest in them" are here exploded, unless, perhaps, one employs an ahistorical definition of "large." Roy, *Socializing Capital*, xiv, 3, 9.

75. Quoted in Stealey, ed., *Kanawhan Prelude*, 58.

76. Many others assume, wrongly, that antebellum manufacturing corporations were limited to the famous textile mills of New England. Berle and Means, *The Modern Corporation*, 13; Dodd, *American Business Corporations*, 9; Lamoreaux, "Partnerships, Corporations," in Lipartito and Sicilia, eds., *Constructing Corporate America*, 30; Naomi Lamoreaux, "Entrepreneurship, Business Organization, and Economic Concentration," in Engerman and Gallman, eds., *The Cambridge Economic History of the United States*, 404–14; Peskin, *Manufacturing Revolution*, 108–9, 182; Gilpin, "Journal of a Tour," 73; Baumann, "Philadelphia's Manufacturers," 3–39; Wilbur Plummer, "Consumer Credit in Colonial Philadelphia," *Pennsylvania Magazine of History and Biography* 66 (October 1942): 385–409.

77. Tucker, *Notes of Lectures on Corporations*, 14.

78. Milo L. Bennett, *The Opinion of the Chancellor, in the Case of Byron Stevens vs. the Rutland and Burlington Railroad Company and Others* (Burlington, Vt.: Chauncey Goodrich, 1851), 31.

79. *Letter on the Use and Abuse of Incorporations*, 46.

80. See also Seavoy, *Origins of the American Business Corporation*, 7, 73–76; Dodd, *American Business Corporations*, 25–29; Roy, *Socializing Capital*, 6, 41–50; Tedlow, *Rise of the American Business Corporation*, 12–13.

81. Many scholars have made the mistake of dismissing early corporations because of their small size compared with what came later. Such reasoning is ahistorical. The real comparison is with noncorporate businesses of the same epoch, not later corporate entities. Moreover, such scholars do not attempt to measure corporate size in real terms— that is, by adjusting for changes in the price level, the size of the economy, or the population. Scholars such as William Roy therefore ignore the antebellum corporation and fixate on the great merger movement and its aftermath. Roy, *Socializing Capital*, xiii–xiv. Berle and Means are much closer to the mark when they note that "small though these figures seem . . . they are none the less significant." Berle and Means, *The Modern Corporation*, 12. The best historical understanding of the relative nature of large may be Pollard, *Genesis of Modern Management*, 20–23.

82. Coxe, *A View of the United States of America*, 357.

83. Appleton, *Introduction of the Power Loom*, 30.

84. Thomas C. Cochran, "An Analytical View of Early American Business and Industry," in Joseph R. Frese and Jacob Judd, eds., *Business Enterprise in Early New York* (Tarrytown, N.Y.: Sleepy Hollow, 1979), 12–13.

85. Hopkins, *The Northern Railroad in New York*, 18.

86. "American Friction Match Company," *Boston Daily Courier* (February 17, 1840), 1.

87. A Citizen, *Observations*, 36.

88. Miller, "A Note on the History of Business," 160; Cadman, *The Corporation in New Jersey*, 209; Joseph Davis, *Essays in the Earlier History of American Corporations* (Cambridge, Mass.: Harvard University Press, 1917); Bruchey and Bruchey, *A Brief History of Commercial Banking*, 19.

89. Oneida County Commissioners to William L. Marcy, New York State Archives, Albany (hereafter NYSA).

90. Robert Cull, Lance Davis, Naomi Lamoreaux, and Jean-Laurent Rosenthal, "Historical Financing of Small- and Medium-Size Enterprises," *Journal of Banking and Finance* 30 (2006): 3034.

91. Durrenberger, *Turnpikes*, 55, 74, 107.

92. Taylor, "The Turnpike Era in New England," 164.

93. *President and Directors of the Baltimore and Susquehanna Rail Road*, 4.

94. Terrence Harper, *Historical Account of Vermont Paper Currency and Banks* (Numismatic Scrapbook Magazine), 14.

95. Frederick Whittlesey, David Scott, and Jonathan Child, *Report upon the Tonawanda Rail Road Company, Exhibiting Its Present Situation and Future Prospects* (Rochester, N.Y.: William Alling, 1837), 7.

96. Baldwin, "American Business Corporations Before 1789," 270–71; Tucker, *Notes of Lectures on Corporations*, 19; Dodd, *American Business Corporations*, 57, 170. Many mining companies chartered in the West maintained offices in Manhattan and London to help facilitate the sale of shares and bonds. See, e.g., Draper, *The Burns Ranche Gold Mining Company*, 15–16. Some coal-mining companies chartered in one state but operated in another. See, e.g., *A Brief Sketch of the Property Belonging to the North American Coal Company; With Some General Remarks on the Subject of Coal and Coal Mines* (New York: George F. Hopkins, 1827). See also Cadman, *The Corporation in New Jersey*, 216–17; Dodd, *American Business Corporations*, 53–56, 170–81; Paskoff, *Industrial Evolution*, 120; Bruchey and Bruchey, *A Brief History of Commercial Banking*, 26; Hammond, *Banks and Politics in America*, 625–26.

97. Platt, *Mr. Platt's Speech*; *Prospectus of the West Virginia Iron Mining and Manufacturing Company, Incorporated by the Legislature of Virginia, March 15, 1837* (1837), 4, 6.

98. *Letter on the Use and Abuse of Incorporations*, 48.

99. *Annual Report of the South-Carolina Canal and Rail Road Company, by the Direction* (Charleston, S.C.: Irishman & Democrat, 1831), 6.

100. Godman and Roberts, *First Annual Report*, 6.

101. Quoted in Appleton, *Introduction of the Power Loom*, 24.

102. Samuel Breck, *Sketch of the Internal Improvements Already Made by Pennsylvania* (Philadelphia: J. Maxwell, 1818), 47n.; *Speech of Mr. Keating in the House of Representatives of Pennsylvania* (Harrisburg, Pa.: Henry Welsh, 1834), 34.

103. J. Mauldin Lesesne, *The Bank of the State of South Carolina: A General and Political History* (Columbia: University of South Carolina Press, 1970), 22–25, 185–86.

104. Taylor, "The Turnpike Era in New England," 156–57.

105. Appleton, *Introduction of the Power Loom*, 23, 33.

106. One observer argued the converse: "One of the banks of this city is applying for *a reduction of its capital.* . . . Either the whole of the capital originally authorized by the charter has not been 'paid in, or secured to be paid'—or there is no profitable employment for it." *Letter on the Use and Abuse of Incorporations*, 48.

107. "Petitions Have Been Preferred," *Rhode-Island American* (January 19, 1830), 2.

108. Bruchey and Bruchey, *A Brief History of Commercial Banking*, 26.

109. Appleton, *Introduction of the Power Loom*, 7–8, 10–11, 24. Appleton refers to the company as the Waltham Company but clarifies the issue on p. 24.

110. Platt, *Mr. Platt's Speech.*

111. Lamoreaux and Glaisek, "Vehicles of Privilege or Mobility?," 512.

112. Huntington, *A History of Banking and Currency in Ohio*, 145, 147, 160.

113. Breck, *Sketch of the Internal Improvements*, 46–47; *A Statement of the Correspondence between the Banks*, 12.

114. *Charleston Mercury* (April 14, 1845, July 13, 1846). According to Platt, "The legal right or capacity of employing capital in banks or manufactories, is one thing; and the actual investment of that capital is another thing. . . . [It] well might it be contended that ten millions of dollars are actually employed by the manufacturing companies in this state because the acts for their incorporation authorize them to go to that extent." Platt, *Mr. Platt's Speech.*

115. *The Act of Incorporation, Constitution, and By-Laws of the Mutual Fire Insurance Company of Loudon County* (Virginia: Washingtonian Print, 1899), 1; Lewis, *A History of the Bank of North America*, 51–53; Breck, *Sketch of the Internal Improvements*, 13; Appleton, *Introduction of the Power Loom*, 19–23, 28, 34; *Address of the Delaware and Raritan Canal*, 11.

116. "Dissolution of the San Francisco and San Jose Railroad Company," *San Francisco Evening Bulletin* (June 16, 1860), 2. See also Karmel, "Banking on the People," 328–29.

117. Kessler, "Incorporation in New England," 45.

118. Huntington, *A History of Banking and Currency in Ohio*, 143–44.

119. "The Silk Company," *Philadelphia Public Ledger* (May 19, 1840), 4.

120. Seavoy, *Origins of the American Business Corporation*, 103.

121. J. L. Sullivan, *Refutation of Mr. Colden's "Answer" to Mr. Sullivan's Report to the Society for Establishing Useful Manufactories in New Jersey upon the Intended Encroachments of the Morris Canal Company in Diverting from Their Natural Course the Waters of the Passaic* (1828), 4.

122. Marine Insurance Company of Alexandria, "In Pursuance of Public Notice," January 15, 1846, Broadside Collection, VHS.

123. Oneida County Commissioners to William L. Marcy, NYSA.

124. Gallatin, *Considerations of the Currency and Banking System*, 50–51.

125. For more discussion of bank failures, see, e.g., Warren E. Weber, "Count of

Banks by State—Daily," Federal Reserve Bank of Minneapolis; Warren Weber, "Early State Banks in the United States: How Many Were There and When Did They Exist?" (working paper, December 2005); *Historical Statistics of the United States*, Table Cj251; Seventy-Six, *Cause of, and Cure for, Hard Times*, 24; Robert E. Wright, "Governance and the Success of U.S. Community Banks, 1790–2010: Mutual Savings Banks, Local Commercial Banks, and the Merchants (National) Bank of New Bedford, Massachusetts," *Business and Economic History Online* 9 (2011).

126. Harper, *Historical Account of Vermont Paper Currency*, 11.

127. Bruchey and Bruchey, *A Brief History of Commercial Banking*, 20.

128. *In the Court for the Trial of Impeachments and Correction of Errors*, 5–6.

129. L. Carroll Root, "New York Bank Currency: Safety Fund vs. Bond Security," *Sound Currency* 2 (February 1895): 287, 290–91, 303.

130. Dreikorn, "History and Development of Banking in New Jersey," 21–24, 34, 36, 69, 70, 73.

131. Alan Olmstead, "Investment Constraints and New York City Mutual Savings Bank Financing of Antebellum Development," *Journal of Economic History* 32 (December 1972): 812.

132. John Dix, *Sketch of the Resources of the City of New York* (New York: G. & C. Carvill, 1827), 44.

133. *Historical Statistics of the United States*.

134. "All the Property," *Boston Weekly Messenger* (October 21, 1830), 3.

135. Last two quotations in the paragraph are from Cary, *Result of Manufactures*, 6.

136. Citizen of Boston, *Remarks upon the Rights and Powers*, 7.

137. Murat, *A Moral and Political Sketch of the United States*, 338.

138. Alexis de Tocqueville, *Democracy in America*, trans. and ed. Harvey C. Mansfield and Delba Winthrop (Chicago: University of Chicago Press, 2000), 489.

139. Freeman, Pearson, and Taylor, *Shareholder Democracies?*, 9, 15–16, 19.

140. Dan Bogart, "Turnpike Trusts and the Transportation Revolution in Eighteenth Century England," *Explorations in Economic History* 42 (October 2005): 479–508; Robin Pearson, Mark Freeman, and James Taylor, "Constructing the Company: Governance and Procedures in British and Irish Joint Stock Companies, 1720–1844," UK Data Archive, SN 5622, 2007, www.esds.ac.uk/doi/?sn=5622#1, accessed March 2, 2012.

141. Evans, *Fortune's Epitome of the Stocks*, 226.

142. "Manufacturing Corporations," 94.

143. *At a General Meeting of the Company of Proprietors of the Lancaster Canal Navigation, Held at the Town Hall in Lancaster* (Lancaster: Jackson, 1800), 2; W. Wheelwright, *To the Directors and Proprietors of the Pacific Steam Navigation Company* (London, 1843); Freeman, Pearson, and Taylor, *Shareholder Democracies?*, 5–7; Pearson, "Shareholder Democracies?," 865–66.

144. *Report of the Committee on Banks and Insurance Companies*, 4.

145. Evans, *British Corporation Finance*, 5, 11–62, quotation at 5.

146. Joel Mokyr, *The Enlightened Economy: An Economic History of Britain, 1700–1850* (New Haven, Conn.: Yale University Press, 2009), 357–58.

147. The exact figures and generalizations in this paragraph are drawn from Dodd, *American Business Corporations*, 120; Evans, *British Corporation Finance*, 1; Armand Dubois, *The English Business Company after the Bubble Act, 1720–1800* (New York, 1938); Bishop Hunt, *The Development of the Business Corporation in England, 1800–1867* (Cambridge, Mass.: 1936); Pearson, "Shareholder Democracies?," 843–45; Ron Harris, *Industrializing English Law: Entrepreneurship and Business Organization, 1720–1844* (New York: Cambridge University Press, 2000), 170–92; Wright and Sylla, "Corporate Governance," in Koppell, ed., *Origins of Shareholder Advocacy*, 232; Micklethwait and Wooldridge, *The Company*, 51–52; Henry English, *A Complete View of the Joint Stock Companies Formed during the Years 1824 and 1825* (London: Boosey, 1827).

148. Lawrence Officer, *Between the Dollar-Sterling Gold Points: Exchange Rates, Parities and Market Behavior, 1791–1931* (New York: Cambridge University Press, 1996), 55.

149. Joseph Sykes, *The Amalgamation Movement in English Banking, 1825–1924* (London: P. S. King, 1926), ix–29, 95, 98, 101, 129; William Spackman, *Statistical Tables of the Agriculture, Shipping, Colonies, Manufactures, Commerce, and Population of the United Kingdom of Great Britain and Its Dependencies* (London: Longman and Col., 1842), 67.

150. John Reid, *A Manual of the Scottish Stocks and British Funds, with a List of the Joint Stock Companies in Scotland* (Edinburgh, 1841), 163–71; Spackman, *Statistical Tables*, 96–106.

151. Gower, "Some Contrasts Between British and American Corporation Law," 1371; Micklethwait and Wooldridge, *The Company*, 50.

152. Evans, *British Corporation Finance*, 83.

153. Tuckett, *Practical Remarks on the Present State of Life Insurance*, 7.

154. Robert Ward, *Notes on Joint-Stock Companies* (London: Effingham Wilson and Simpkin, Marshall, 1865), in Wright et al., eds., *History of Corporate Governance*, 4:317.

155. Micklethwait and Wooldridge, *The Company*, 52–53, 81–87.

156. William Z. Ripley, *Main Street and Wall Street* (Boston: Little, Brown, 1929), 16–17.

157. "Plan of the Loan Company at Hamburgh," *Philadelphia Universal Gazette* (January 2, 1800), 2; "A New Company," *Albany Centinel* (May 8, 1801), 3; "Mediterraneo-Transatlantic Company," *Charleston Southern Patriot* (April 9, 1840), 2; "A Joint Stock Farming Company," *Macon (Ga.) Daily Telegraph* (July 25, 1860), 2; Michael Pammer, "Economic Growth and Lower Class Investments in Nineteenth Century Austria," *Historical Social Research* 25, 1 (2000): 27.

158. The data and generalizations stated in this paragraph were drawn from Micklethwait and Wooldridge, *The Company*, 46–47, 53, 90–99; Handlin and Handlin, "Origins of the American Business Corporation," 4; Rondo Cameron, *France and the Economic Development of Europe, 1800–1914: Conquests of Peace and Sees of War*

(Chicago: Rand McNally, 1961), 26–28; Yi-Wen Yu, "Rethinking the Kirby Puzzle: A Reassessment of Chinese Companies' Incorporation from the Public and Corporate Finances Perspectives, 1860–1949," *Business and Economic History Online* 8 (2010): 1–28.

159. This paragraph is based on Stanley Engerman and Kenneth Sokoloff, "Factor Endowments, Institutions, and Differential Paths of Growth Among New World Economies: A View from Economic Historians of the United States," in Stephen Haber, ed., *How Latin America Fell Behind: Essays on the Economic Histories of Brazil and Mexico, 1800–1914* (Stanford, Calif.: Stanford University Press, 1997), 289–91; Haddock, *Address of the Northern Railroad Company*, 14; J. C. A. Stagg, "Between Black Rock and a Hard Place: Peter B. Porter's Plan for an American Invasion of Canada in 1812," *Journal of the Early Republic* 19 (fall 1999): 385–422.

160. Haddock, *Address of the Northern Railroad Company*, 14.

161. Ronald Rudin, "Banking on Quebec: The French Banks and the Mobilization of French Funds, 1835–1925," *Journal of Canadian Studies* 20 (fall 1985): 47–63.

162. See Hugh G. J. Aitken, "A New Way to Pay Old Debts," in William Miller, ed., *Men in Business: Essays on the Historical Role of the Entrepreneur*, 2nd ed. (New York: Harper & Row, 1962), 75; John F. Whiteside, "The Toronto Stock Exchange and the Development of the Share Market to 1885," *Journal of Canadian Studies* 20 (fall 1985): 64–81.

163. *Report of the Provisional Committee Appointed by the Stockholders of the Gas Light and Water Company, to Ascertain the Whole Cost of Erecting Gas Works for the Town of Halifax* (Halifax, N.S.: John Munro, 1840); Gower, "Some Contrasts Between British and American Corporation Law," 1370.

164. *By-Laws, Rules and Regulations, for the Management of the Affairs of the Montreal Mining Company, Confirmed by the Stockholders* (Montreal: J. C. Becket, 1847), 10–11.

165. A. W. Currie, "The First Dominion Companies Act," *Canadian Journal of Economics and Political Science* 28 (1962): 387–404.

166. Aldo Musacchio, *Experiments in Financial Democracy: Corporate Governance and Financial Development in Brazil, 1882–1950* (New York: Cambridge University Press, 2009), 28–39, 121.

167. Gonzalo Isla Rojas, "Does Regulation Matter? An Analysis of Corporate Charters in a Laissez-faire Environment" (working paper, September 2007); Michael Reid, *Forgotten Continent: The Battle for Latin America's Soul* (New Haven, Conn.: Yale University Press, 2007).

168. Tanner, *A Description of the Canals and Rail Roads of the United States*, 11–12.

Chapter 5

1. Tanner, *A Description of the Canals and Rail Roads of the United States*, 11–12.

2. "Manufacturing Corporations," 94.

3. Kent, quoted in Citizen of New York, *What Is a Monopoly?*, 12.

4. Ward, *Notes on Joint-Stock Companies*, 8.

5. Tocqueville, *Democracy in America*, 490.

6. John Travers, "Bergen Port Company" (1837), 3.

7. Lough, *Corporation Finance*, 13–14.

8. Hollywood Cemetery Minute Books, 1847–68, 160–61, VHS.

9. *An Act to Incorporate the Stockholders of the Bank of the United States*, 15; Perkins, *American Public Finance and Financial Services*, 278.

10. Livermore, *Early American Land Companies*, 224.

11. Hopkins, *The Northern Railroad in New York*, 12.

12. Wright, "Banking and Politics in New York," 290–313.

13. Livermore, *Early American Land Companies*, 258; Brooke, *Heart of the Commonwealth*, 280–90.

14. "The Two 'Learned Gentleman' Who Drew Up the Regulations," *Keene New Hampshire Sentinel* (November 14, 1850), 2.

15. Sigourney, *To the Stockholders of the Phoenix Bank*, 1–2.

16. Seavoy, *Origins of the American Business Corporation*, 5; Gunn, *Decline of Authority*, 227.

17. Quoted in Kessler, "Incorporation in New England," 44.

18. Dodd, *American Business Corporations*, 3.

19. Sullivan, *Refutation of Mr. Colden's "Answer" to Mr. Sullivan's Report*, 14; Henry N. Butler, "Nineteenth-Century Jurisdictional Competition in the Granting of Corporate Privileges," *Journal of Legal Studies* 14, 1 (January 1985): 150–51.

20. *The Memorial of the Subscribers, Merchants, Tradesmen, and Inhabitants*.

21. Cadman, *The Corporation in New Jersey*, 389–93; Dreikorn, "History and Development of Banking in New Jersey," 22.

22. Wright, "Corporate Entrepreneurship in the Antebellum South," in Delfino, Gillespie, and Kyriakoudes, eds., *Southern Society and Its Transformation*, 206.

23. Wright, "Rise of the Corporation Nation," in Irwin and Sylla, eds., *Founding Choices*, 225.

24. For evidence of the generalizations made in the text, see Wright, "Corporate Entrepreneurship in the Antebellum South," in Delfino, Gillespie, and Kyriakoudes, eds., *Southern Society and Its Transformation*, 205; Cadman, *The Corporation in New Jersey*, 389; Elias Hore Account Book, VHS; Faquier White Sulphur Spring Company Tax Receipt, 1856, Keith Family Papers, VHS; Auditor of Public Accounts, "Report on Taxes Due on Dividends, 1827–59," Library of Virginia, Richmond, Virginia; Eric Hilt, "When Did Ownership Separate from Control? Corporate Governance in the Early Nineteenth Century," *Journal of Economic History* 68, 3 (2008): 662.

25. For supporting documentation, see "Schedule of the names of the several Incorporated companies in the County of Oneida, liable to be taxed," NYSA; Livermore, *Early American Land Companies*, 260–61; Wright, "Rise of the Corporation Nation," in Irwin and Sylla, eds., *Founding Choices*, 222; Alabama State Auditor, Journal of Receipts, Alabama State Archives, Montgomery, Ala.

26. Haines, *Arguments against the Justice and Policy of Taxing*, 32.

27. Sigourney, *To the Stockholders of the Phoenix Bank*, 1.

28. The data from this paragraph were culled from Lewis, *A History of the Bank of North America*, 89; Minutes of the Board of Directors of the Farmers Bank of Virginia, April 15, 1824, VHS; *An Act to Incorporate the Stockholders of the Bank of the United States*, 15; Peel, "History of the Lancaster Bank," 72; Breck, *Sketch of the Internal Improvements*, 20; *Origins, Provisions and Effect of the Safety Fund Law of the State of New York* (Albany, N.Y.: Packard and Van Benthuysen, 1834), 12; James B. Congdon, "The Banking System of Massachusetts," *Bankers' Magazine and Statistical Register* (June 1851); Lamoreaux and Glaisek, "Vehicles of Privilege or Mobility?," 519; Bruchey and Bruchey, *A Brief History of Commercial Banking*, 20; *Address of the Delaware and Raritan Canal*, 10; Olmstead, "Investment Constraints," 818–21; Charles Scott, *Farmers National Bank of Bucks County: A Century's Record, 1814–1914* (Bristol, Pa., 1914), 27.

29. Seavoy, *Origins of the American Business Corporation*, 98–102; *The Memorial of the Subscribers, Merchants, Tradesmen, and Inhabitants*; Dreikorn, "History and Development of Banking in New Jersey," 22; Evans, *Fortune's Epitome of the Stocks*, 235.

30. Huntington, *A History of Banking and Currency in Ohio*, 174–75.

31. Haines, *Arguments against the Justice and Policy of Taxing*, 1.

32. Haines, *Arguments against the Justice and Policy of Taxing*, 21, 30.

33. A Citizen of Lowell, *Corporations and Operatives*, 20.

34. Bronson, quoted in Wright, "Banking and Politics in New York," 292.

35. Watson, quoted in Wright, "Banking and Politics in New York," 290.

36. Cox, *On the Argument, in Reference to the Bridge Bill*, 3. "Unless the individual investor tended to benefit on the whole," an early historian of corporations explained, "it would be idle to expect him to have continued adventuring his resources over a protracted period." Scott, *The Constitution and Finance*, 1:444.

37. Roy, *Socializing Capital*, 47; Eric Hilt and Jacqueline Valentine, "Democratic Dividends: Stockholding, Wealth and Politics in New York, 1791–1826" (NBER Working Paper No. 17147, June 2011).

38. Quoted in Wright, "Rise of the Corporation Nation," in Irwin and Sylla, eds., *Founding Choices*, 233.

39. *An Inquiry into the Nature and Utility of Corporations*, 2.

40. Caleb Cushing, *Speeches Delivered in the House of Representatives of Massachusetts, on the Subject of the Currency and Public Deposites* (Salem, Mass.: Register Press, 1834), 12.

41. *A Report of the Important Hearing on the Memorial of the New England Coal Mining Company*, 137.

42. Joseph Martin, *Martin's Twenty-One Years in the Boston Stock Market or Fluctuations Therein, from January 1835 to January 1856* (Boston: Redding, 1856), 6.

43. Majewski, "Toward a Social History of the Corporation," 302, 305.

44. Ingersoll, quoted in Lehman, "Explaining Hard Times," 25.

45. Letters Patent, 1814–74, Corporation Bureau, Department of State, RG 26, Pennsylvania State Archives, Harrisburg, Pennsylvania (hereafter PSA).

46. Derby, *Boston: A Commercial Metropolis*, 16.

47. Citizen of Boston, *Remarks upon the Rights and Powers*, 6.

48. Baldwin, "American Business Corporations Before 1789," 271.

49. Haines, *Arguments against the Justice and Policy of Taxing*, 14.

50. Robert E. Wright, *The Wealth of Nations Rediscovered: Integration and Expansion in American Financial Markets, 1780–1850* (New York: Cambridge University Press, 2002), 135–66.

51. Elizabeth Nuxoll, "Illegitimacy, Family Status, and Property in the Early Republic: The Morris-Croxall Family of New Jersey," *New Jersey History* 113 (fall/winter 1995): 3–21.

52. Teackle, *An Address to the Members of the Legislature of Maryland*, 5–6, 21.

53. William Duane, *Observations on the Principles and Operation of Banking* (Philadelphia: Helmbold, 1804), 18; Seventy-Six, *Cause of, and Cure for, Hard Times*, 36; A Citizen of New York, *Remarks on That Part of the Speech*; Lewis, *A History of the Bank of North America*, 58.

54. Haines, *Arguments against the Justice and Policy of Taxing*, 31.

55. A Citizen of New York, *Remarks on That Part of the Speech*, 7; Laura Croghan Kamoie, *Irons in the Fire: The Business History of the Tayloe Family and Virginia's Gentry, 1700–1860* (Charlottesville: University of Virginia Press, 2007), 138–39; Appleton, *Introduction of the Power Loom*, 8; Ashmead, *History of the Delaware County National Bank*, 13; Spalding, "The Boston Mercantile Community," 81; Alfred D. Chandler, "Patterns of American Railroad Finance, 1830–50," *Business History* 28 (1954): 259.

56. "Lexington and Ohio Rail Road Company," *Boston Weekly Messenger* (March 4, 1830), 3.

57. Moncure Robinson, *First Annual Report of the President and Managers of the Philipsburg and Juniata Rail Road Company to the Stockholders* (New York: G. F. Hopkins, 1833), 21.

58. Pryor Lea and Albert M. Lea, *Concerning the Aransas Road Company* (New Orleans: Picayune, 1858). See also Murphy, "Empire State Building," 178–79.

59. Lea and Lea, *Concerning the Aransas Road Company*, 6.

60. *Panama Rail Road Company* (New York: Van Norden & Amerman, 1849); G. M. Totten, *Communication of the Board of Directors of the Panama Railroad Company to the Stockholders, Together with the Report of the Chief Engineer to the Directors* (New York: John F. Trow, 1853).

61. *North Branch Canal Company*, 5.

62. Theodore Woolsey, "The Old New Haven Bank," *Papers of the New Haven Colony Historical Society* (New Haven, Conn.: New Haven Colony Historical Society, 1914), 8:310–14.

63. Sullivan, *Refutation of Mr. Colden's "Answer" to Mr. Sullivan's Report*, 12.

64. For more on these examples, see Robert Blackson, "Pennsylvania Banks and the Panic of 1819: A Reinterpretation," *Journal of the Early Republic* 9 (fall 1989): 338; Peel, "History of the Lancaster Bank," 68–69; Scott, *Farmers National Bank of Bucks County*, 11–12; Ashmead, *History of the Delaware County National Bank*, 13–15.

65. "Report of the Committee Appointed 21 June 1834 to Enquire into Expediency of Re-opening Books or Taking Other Measures," Minute of June 20, 1835, Board of Directors' Minutes, 1834–35, Richmond, Fredericksburg, and Petersburg Records, VHS.

66. *Address of the Delaware and Raritan Canal*, 10.

67. Wright, *Wealth of Nations Rediscovered*, 132–35.

68. "Proposals Having Been Made," *Providence Journal* (January 15, 1800), 2.

69. "A Letter from Schenectady," *New York American Citizen* (July 30, 1800), 3.

70. "At a Meeting," *Otsego (N.Y.) Herald* (August 13, 1801), 3.

71. J. H. Sloan, *To the President and Directors of the Camden and Amboy Rail Road and Transportation Company* (1831), 4, 6.

72. "A General Meeting," *New York Morning Herald* (July 9, 1830), 2.

73. "The Amount Subscribed," *Baltimore Patriot* (February 27, 1830), 2.

74. Whittlesey, Scott, and Child, *Report upon the Tonawanda Rail Road Company*, 3.

75. "The Subscription Books," *New York Mercantile Advertiser* (April 23, 1801), 2.

76. Francis Kimball, *Faithfully Serving Community, State, and Nation for 125 Years* (Albany, N.Y.: National Commercial Bank and Trust Company of Albany, 1950?), 11–13, 15.

77. Many early corporations had "so many small investors that they defy analysis as to sources of capital." East, *Business Enterprise*, 306. See also Hilt, "When Did Ownership Separate from Control?," 664, 668; Lance Davis, "Stock Ownership in the Early New England Textile Industry," *Business History Review* 32, 2 (summer 1958): 204–22; Perkins, *American Public Finance and Financial Services*, 291; Letters Patent, 1814–1874, Corporation Bureau, Department of State, RG 26, PSA; Durrenberger, *Turnpikes*, 102–4, 107–8; Francis Bloodgood, *Report of the President and Directors to the Stockholders of the Ithaca and Owego Rail Road Company* (Ithaca, N.Y.: Mack & Andrus, 1833).

78. See J. D. Forbes, *Israel Thorndike, Federalist Financier* (New York: Exposition, 1953), 142; Letters Patent, 1814–74, Corporation Bureau, Department of State, RG 26, PSA; John Denis Haeger, *The Investment Frontier: New York Businessmen and the Economic Development of the Old Northwest* (Albany: State University of New York Press, 1981), 51–54.

79. Cushing, *Speeches Delivered in the House of Representatives of Massachusetts*, 26. See also Taylor, "The Turnpike Era in New England," 165.

80. By-laws and stockholders of the Cleveland Gas Light & Coke Company, John Jeffrey Manuscripts, FHS.

81. Forbes, *Israel Thorndike*, 138–39.

82. "Manufacturing Corporations," 110.

83. Lamoreaux and Glaisek, "Vehicles of Privilege or Mobility?," 511–12.

84. Corporate Tax Records, NYSA; Hilt, "When Did Ownership Separate from Control?," 664.

85. W. Robinson to the President and Directors of the Richmond, Fredericksburg and Potomac Railroad Company, July 3, 1835, Board of Directors' Minutes, 1834–35, Richmond, Fredericksburg, and Petersburg Records, VHS.

86. Wright, *Wealth of Nations Rediscovered*, 99–121.

87. Diary of Henry Van Der Lyn, 1:43, NYHS.

88. Godman and Roberts, *First Annual Report*, 28.

89. A Citizen of Lowell, *Corporations and Operatives*, 3.

90. "Manufacturing Corporations," 107.

91. Chandler, "Patterns of American Railroad Finance," 260.

92. Quoted in Lehman, "Explaining Hard Times," 165–66. See also *Poulson's American Daily Advertiser* (April 1, 1818).

93. Rothenberg, *From Market-Places to a Market Economy*, 120–22, 141.

94. Kamoie, *Irons in the Fire*, 125–47, 156–60; "An Account Book of Evan Hall Plantation, Ascension Parish, La., Kept during the ownership of Henry McCall," original in the possession of Henry G. McCall, New Orleans, La.; Ralph Catterall, *The Second Bank of the United States* (Chicago: Chicago University Press, 1903), 508.

95. Wright, *Wealth of Nations Rediscovered*, 63–66, 83–97, 122–29, 137–47, 208; Wright, *Hamilton Unbound*, 89–124; Wright, *One Nation Under Debt*, 218, 287–92; James River Company Account Book, 1785–1790, VHS.

96. George Britton Journal, MS5:3B7787:1, VHS; Union Bank, Elizabethtown, Kentucky, Cash Book, 1819–20, FHS.

97. Karmel, "Banking on the People," 209–10; Patterson, "Ten and One-Half Years of Commercial Banking," 14, 18.

98. Number of Shares of Votes of Each Stockholder, Richmond, Fredericksburg & Potomac Railroad Company Records, Board of Directors, 1834–35, VHS.

99. *An Inquiry into the Nature and Utility of Corporations*, 2.

100. Cushing, *Speeches Delivered in the House of Representatives of Massachusetts*, 25–26.

101. *Report of the Troy Turnpike and Rail Road Company* (Troy, N.Y.: Tuttle, Belcher & Buron, 1838), 16–21.

102. Cary, *Result of Manufactures*, 13.

103. Vicksburg Gas Light Company Papers, 1853–60, List of stockholders of the Covington Gas Light Co. Jan[uar]y 10th 1859, John Jeffrey Papers, FHS.

104. Bank of the Commonwealth Dividends, 1859–61, VHS.

105. Davis, "Stock Ownership in the Early New England Textile Industry," 215–16, 218–22.

106. Ashmead, *History of the Delaware County National Bank*, 26, 60.

107. Patricia Cleary, "'She Will Be in the Shop': Women's Sphere of Trade in Eighteenth-Century Philadelphia and New York," *Pennsylvania Magazine of History and Biography* 119 (July 1995): 181–202; Lisa Wilson Waciega, "A 'Man of Business': The Widow of Means in Southeastern Pennsylvania, 1750–1850," *William and Mary Quarterly* 44 (January 1987): 40–64; Wright, *Hamilton Unbound*, 173–94; Wright, *One Nation Under Debt*, 213–14, 306–7, 317; Karmel, "Banking on the People," 209–10; Naaman Keyser, "Early Transportation to Germantown," *Germantown History* (1902): 42–43; Ashmead, *History of the Delaware County National Bank*, 62.

108. *Executive Communication to the General Assembly of Maryland . . . on the Subject of Turnpike Roads* (Annapolis, Md.: Jehu Chandler, 1819), 17.

109. J. C. Ayer, *Some of the Usages and Abuses in the Management of Our Manufacturing Corporations* (1863), 20.

110. Woody Holton, *Abigail Adams* (New York: Free Press, 2009); Waciega, "A 'Man of Business,'" 53–54.

111. Ayer, *Some of the Usages and Abuses*, 4.

112. Quoted in Pearson, "Shareholder Democracies?," 851.

113. For governments as investors, see Dreikorn, "History and Development of Banking in New Jersey," 27; Robert Clark, Lee Craig, and Jack Wilson, "Privatization of Public-Sector Pensions: The U.S. Navy Pension Fund, 1800–1842," *Independent Review* 3 (spring 1999): 549–64; Carl Lane, "For 'A Positive Profit': The Federal Investment in the First Bank of the United States, 1792–1802," *William and Mary Quarterly* 54 (July 1997): 601–12.

114. String and Van Ingen, *A View of Certain Proceedings*, 11–13, 22.

115. *In the Court for the Trial of Impeachments and Correction of Errors*, 3; A Citizen of New York, *Remarks on That Part of the Speech*, 7; Upper Appomattox Company Minute Book, 1842–72, 5, VHS.

116. Samuel Bryan, *Report of the Register-General of the State of the Finances of Pennsylvania for the Year MDCCXCVII* (Philadelphia: Francis and Robert Bailey, 1798); Breck, *Sketch of the Internal Improvements*, 20; Richard Blow to Thomas Newton, November 21, 1807, Richard Blow Letterbook, 254–57, VHS.

117. Harper, *Historical Account of Vermont Paper Currency*, 6–10.

118. Sylla, "Early American Banking," 111.

119. Benjamin Nead, *A Brief Review of the Financial History of Pennsylvania* (Harrisburg, Pa.: Lane S. Hart, 1881), 22.

120. Tench Tilghman, *Report of the State's Agents in Joint Stock Companies* (Annapolis, Md.: House of Delegates, February 12, 1842).

121. "An Act to Sell the State's Interest in the Internal Improvement Companies, and to Pay the Debts of the State," March 11, 1843, Broadside Collection, VHS.

122. Evans, *Fortune's Epitome of the Stocks*, 235, 243.

123. T. Fortune, *An Epitome of the Stocks and Publick Funds, Containing Every Thing Necessary to Be Known for Perfectly Understanding the Nature of Those Securities*, 2nd ed. (London: T. Boosey, 1796), iii, 56–71.

124. Seventy-Six, *Cause of, and Cure for, Hard Times*, 44.

125. Haines, *Arguments against the Justice and Policy of Taxing*, 21. See also Dix, *Sketch of the Resources of the City of New York*, 41.

126. Evans, *Fortune's Epitome of the Stocks*, 242.

127. Spackman, *Statistical Tables*, 72. For additional support for the generalizations made in this paragraph, see Simon, *A Century of the National Bank of the Northern Liberties*, 31; Gallatin, *Considerations of the Currency and Banking System*, 41; Patterson, "Ten and One-Half Years of Commercial Banking," 20; James C. Riley, "Foreign Credit and Fiscal Stability: Dutch Investment in the United States, 1781–1794," *Journal of American*

History 65 (December 1978): 654–78; Ferguson, "The American Public Debt," 18–19; Lewis, *A History of the Bank of North America*, 67; A Citizen of New York, *Remarks on That Part of the Speech*, 8; Smith and Cole, *Fluctuations in American Business*, 6; Albert Gallatin, *Report of the Secretary of the Treasury to Whom Was Referred the Memorial of the Stockholders of the Bank of the United States Praying a Renewal of Their Charter* (Washington, D.C.: R. C. Weightman, 1809), 4, 9; Catterall, *Second Bank of the United States*, 508; Spackman, *Statistical Tables*, 71–72; John Davis, Robert Schuyler, Amos Binney, and W. Raymond Lee, *Report of a Committee of Investigation into the Affairs of the Philadelphia and Reading Rail Road Company* (Boston: Eastburn's, 1846), 10, 12–13.

128. Haines, *Arguments against the Justice and Policy of Taxing*, 20–21.

129. Dix, *Sketch of the Resources of the City of New York*, 41n.

130. *Speech of Mr. Keating in the House of Representatives of Pennsylvania*, 7–8.

131. Dreikorn, "History and Development of Banking in New Jersey," 26–27.

132. Seventy-Six, *Cause of, and Cure for, Hard Times*, 44.

133. Evans, *Fortune's Epitome of the Stocks*, 255–56.

134. Hilt, "When Did Ownership Separate from Control?"; Letters Patent, 1814–74, Corporation Bureau, Department of State, RG 26, PSA; Cadman, *The Corporation in New Jersey*, 247; Galbraith, *New Industrial State*, 78.

135. Platt, *Mr. Platt's Speech*; Ayer, *Some of the Usages and Abuses*, 3.

136. Ayer, *Some of the Usages and Abuses*, 3.

137. "Most Lowell corporations by the 1830s were owned by more than a hundred proprietors and the individual holdings were small." Some corporations in other textile cities remained closely held but many followed in the footsteps of Lowell by the late 1830s and 1840s. Spalding, "The Boston Mercantile Community," 35, 54–55, 69, 86–88, 111. See also Berle and Means, *The Modern Corporation*, 11–12.

138. Brooke, *Heart of the Commonwealth*, 305.

139. Ware, *The Industrial Worker, 1840–1860*, 103–6. Evelyn Knowlton, *Pepperell's Progress: History of a Cotton Textile Company, 1844–1945* (Cambridge, Mass.: Harvard University Press, 1948), 385–88.

140. Wright, *Wealth of Nations Rediscovered*, 185–86; Wood, *The Long-Suffering Shareholder*, in Wright et al., eds., *History of Corporate Governance*, 5:284.

141. F. H. Stow, *The Capitalist's Guide and Railway Annual for 1859* (New York: Samuel T. Callahan, 1859), 18–19.

142. Appleton, *Introduction of the Power Loom*, 14.

143. Steuart, *Inquiry into the Principles of Political Oeconomy*, 395.

144. See Stealey, ed., *Kanawhan Prelude*, 5; Baskin and Miranti, *A History of Corporate Finance*, 61.

145. *By Laws of the North Wayne Scythe Company, with an Appendix, Giving a Description of Its Locality and Importance* (Boston: Beals & Greene, 1849), 26.

146. "The New England Glass Company," *Boston Emancipator and Republican* (August 29, 1850), 3.

147. "William L. Gilbert," *Lowell Daily Citizen and News* (May 23, 1860), 2.

148. Brooke, *Heart of the Commonwealth*, 296.

149. N. P. Willis, "N. P. Willis' Visit to the Watch Factory of the American Watch Company," *Trenton Daily State Gazette and Republican* (May 30, 1860), 2; "American Watches Made by the American Watch Company, Waltham, Mass.," *Trenton Daily State Gazette and Republican* (June 26, 1860), 2.

150. Appleton, *Introduction of the Power Loom*, 14–16.

151. New York Superior Court, *The Amoskeag Manufacturing Company against Spear & Ripley* (New York: J. P. Wright, 1849).

152. Appleton, *Introduction of the Power Loom*, 30.

153. Stealey, ed., *Kanawhan Prelude*, 57–58; Lucius Ellsworth, "Craft to National Industry in the Nineteenth Century: A Case Study of the Transformation of the New York State Tanning Industry," *Journal of Economic History* 32 (March 1972): 399–402.

154. Diary of Blair Bolling, 1810–37, 1:235, 245, VHS.

155. See Paskoff, *Industrial Evolution*, 80–81, 91, 95–111, 115–18, 134–35; Joseph E. Walker, *Hopewell Village: A Social and Economic History of an Iron-Making Community* (Philadelphia: University of Pennsylvania Press, 1966), 165.

156. Joseph J. Gurney, *A Journey in North America Described in Familiar Letters to Amelia Opie* (Norwich: Josiah Fletcher, 1841), 135.

157. Ivan Steen, "Philadelphia in the 1850's," *Pennsylvania History* 33 (January 1966): 30–32; U.S. Hotel Accounts, Cabell Family Papers, VHS.

158. C. A. Weslager, *Brandywine Springs: The Rise and Fall of a Delaware Resort* (Wilmington, Del.: Hambleton, 1949).

159. Ibid., 12.

160. *Hallowell (Maine) Gazette* (July 5, 1826).

161. *Delaware Gazette and State Journal* (April 10, 1827).

162. Ibid. (June 26, 1827).

163. *Delaware Patriot and American Watchman* (July 8 and 18, 1828).

164. *Baltimore Gazette and Daily Advertiser* (May 14, 1829).

165. Bishop Davenport, *A New Gazetteer, or, Geographical Dictionary of North America and the West Indies* (Baltimore: G. M'Dowell, 1835), 441; *Baltimore Patriot* (August 7, 1830, and July 12, 1834).

166. *Baltimore Gazette and Daily Advertiser* (May 13, 1837).

167. *Phelps' Hundred Cities and Large Towns of America: With Railroad Distances throughout the United States, Maps of Thirteen Cities, and Other Embellishments* (New York: Phelps, Fanning, 1853), 44; John Disturnell, *Springs, Water-Falls, Sea-Bathing resorts, and Mountain Scenery of the United States and Canada* (New York: J. Disturnell, 1855), 122; Brandywine Springs Collection, 1830–1961, Historical Society of Delaware, Wilmington, Del.

168. Diary of Blair Bolling, 1838–39, 3:38.

169. George Peyton, White Sulphur Springs Company to ?, September 1, 1882, Greenbrier County Miscellaneous Documents, VHS.

170. Diary of Blair Bolling, 1838–39, 3:23–24.

171. Ibid., 3:25.

172. Ibid, 3: 27.

173. Diary of Blair Bolling, 1838–39, 3:26–30.

174. All quotations in paragraph are from ibid., 31–36.

175. A Freeman of Massachusetts, *Remarks and Documents concerning the Location*, 14–15.

176. All other quotations in this paragraph are from Hollywood Cemetery Minute Books, 1847–68, 2–28, 91–99, 101, 105, 114–15, VHS.

177. Steen, "Philadelphia in the 1850's," 39.

178. Diary of Blair Bolling, 1822, 2:8.

179. Durrenberger, *Turnpikes*, 98, 115.

180. Durand, *Third Annual Report of the Racine and Mississippi Railroad*, 9.

181. E. H. Derby, *Report of the Delegation to Albany to the Stockholders of the Western Railroad Corporation* (Boston: Dutton and Wentworth's Print, 1840).

182. *Circular Statement of the Condition and Prospects of the Northern Indiana Railroad*, 4.

183. W. P. Burrall, *Annual Report of the Board of Directors of the Housatonic Railroad Company to the Stockholders* (Bridgeport, Conn.: William S. Pomeroy, 1851), 13–23.

184. Tanner, *A Description of the Canals and Rail Roads of the United States*, 18.

185. Kennedy, *Address of the President and Directors of the Northern Central Railway*, 5–6, 8–9.

186. Newkirk, *First Annual Report of the Philadelphia, Wilmington and Baltimore Rail Road*, 4.

187. *Letter on the Use and Abuse of Incorporations*, 46–47.

188. Stealey, ed., *Kanawhan Prelude*, 5, 7, 14.

189. Ronald Coase, "The Nature of the Firm (1937)," in Oliver E. Williamson and Sidney G. Winter, eds., *The Nature of the Firm: Origins, Evolution, and Development* (New York: Oxford University Press, 1993), 18–33.

190. Winter, "On Coase," in Williamson and Winter, eds., *The Nature of the Firm*, 183; Tucker, *Notes of Lectures on Corporations*, 41; Spalding, "The Boston Mercantile Community," 40–41, 76, 138, 145–46; Forbes, *Israel Thorndike*, 140–41.

191. Appleton, *Introduction of the Power Loom*, 12, 27.

192. "Lowell Company," *Lowell Daily Citizen and News* (January 6, 1860), 2.

193. See Ayer, *Some of the Usages and Abuses*, 6–9; Spalding, "The Boston Mercantile Community," 74–76.

194. Paskoff, *Industrial Evolution*, 74, 76.

195. All the quotations in this paragraph are from William H. Swift and Nathan Hale, *Report on the Present State of the Chesapeake and Ohio Canal* (Boston: Dutton and Wentworth, 1846), 24–25.

196. Kennedy, *Address of the President and Directors of the Northern Central Railway*, 14–19.

197. *Annual Report of Messrs. A. J. Pleasonton, John Moss, Richard Ronaldson and John Sharp, Jr.*, 9–10, 34.

198. *Substance of Argument of Respondents' Counsel*, 6–7.

199. *Prospectus of the California and New York Steamship Company*, 6.

200. *Report of the Directors to the Stockholders of the Illinois Central Railroad Company* (New York: Geo. Scott Roe, 1854), 9.

201. *History of the Lehigh Coal and Navigation Company*, 8–9.

202. Joshua Lippincott, *Address to the Stock and Loan Holders of the Schuylkill Navigation Company* (Philadelphia: Joshua Lippincott, 1847), 6.

203. *The Schuylkill Navigation Company*, 16.

204. *The Sunbury Canal and Water-Power Company and Sunbury Lumber and Car Manufacturing Company* (Philadelphia: McLaughlin Brothers Book and Job Printing Office, 1854), 3–4.

205. *A Brief Sketch of the Peculiar Advantages of the Shamokin Coal and Iron Company Situate in Northumberland County, State of Pennsylvania* (Philadelphia: Brown, Bicking & Guilbert, 1841), 6.

206. String and Van Ingen, *A View of Certain Proceedings*; "Towsontown and Baltimore Road and Railway Company," *Baltimore Sun* (June 29, 1860), 2.

207. A Citizen of Lowell, *Corporations and Operatives*, 11, 20–28, 65–66, 69.

208. Ware, *The Industrial Worker, 1840–1860*, 23, 85, 97, 101–2, 106–8, 139, 152; Majewski, "Toward a Social History of the Corporation," 312; A Citizen of Lowell, *Corporations and Operatives*, 20.

209. Quoted in Ware, *Industrial Worker*, 45.

210. A Citizen of Lowell, *Corporations and Operatives*, 20.

211. Ibid., 21.

212. Ibid., 65–66.

213. Ibid., 69.

214. Wright, "Rise of the Corporation Nation," in Irwin and Sylla, eds., *Founding Choices*, 223.

215. *Substance of Argument of Respondents' Counsel*, 9; Sullivan, *Refutation of Mr. Colden's "Answer" to Mr. Sullivan's Report*, 4.

216. Seventy-Six, *Cause of, and Cure for, Hard Times*, 40. See also G.H.E., "To the Working Men of the United States," *Radical, in Continuation of Working Man's Advocate* (January 1841); circular letter of E. W. Capron, secretary of Auburn National Reform Association [to Julius Rockwell], Auburn, New York, July 15, 1848.

217. Seventy-Six, *Cause of, and Cure for, Hard Times*, 46. See also Jeremiah O'Callaghan, *Usury, Funds, and Banks* (Burlington, Vt.: For the Author, 1834), 156.

218. "Chenango Bank Stopped," Diary of Henry Van Der Lyn, 1:214, NYHS.

219. Platt, *Mr. Platt's Speech*, 2–4, 10; *Observations on the Principles and Operation of Banking with Strictures on the Opposition to the Bank of Philadelphia* (Philadelphia: Helmbold, 1804), 11.

220. Gallatin, *Suggestions on the Banks and Currency of the Several United States*, 67–68.

221. John L. Sullivan, *The Answer of Mr. Sullivan to the Letter and Mis-statements of*

the Hon. Cadwallader D. Colden (Troy, N.Y.: William S. Parker, 1823), 20. For more on the steamboat controversy, see William Alexander Duer, *A Reply to Mr. Colden's Vindication of the Steam-Boat Monopoly* (Albany: E. and E. Hosford, 1819), 15–16; Patterson, "Ten and One-Half Years of Commercial Banking," 8–9; Maurice Baxter, *The Steamboat Monopoly: Gibbons v. Ogden, 1824* (New York: Alfred Knopf, 1972); *Memorial and Petition of Robert Fulton and Edward P. Livingston, in Behalf of Themselves, and the Heirs of the Late Robert R. Livingston* (Albany, N.Y., 1814).

222. G. Edward White, *The Marshall Court and Cultural Change, 1815–1835*, abridged ed. (New York, 1991), 568–80.

223. Burton Folsom, *The Myth of the Robber Barons*, 3rd ed. (Herndon, Va.: Young America's Foundation, 1996), 3.

224. *A History of the Steam-Boat Case, Lately Discussed by Counsel before the Legislature of New Jersey* (Trenton, 1815), 27–28. See also Duer, *A Reply to Mr. Colden's Vindication of the Steam-Boat Monopoly*; John L. Sullivan, *Demonstration of the Right to the Navigation of the Waters of New York without the License of the Owners of the Monopoly of Steam and Fire Granted to Robert R. Livingston and Robert Fulton* (Cambridge, Mass.: Hilliard and Metcalf, 1821); Sullivan, *The Answer of Mr. Sullivan to the Letter; Facts and Considerations on the Question: Why Is Steam-Boat Navigation Interesting to Connecticut?* (Hartford, Conn.: George Goodwin, 1819), 4; *A History of the Steam-Boat Case*, 6–15, 26–27.

225. See Miller, *Supreme Court*, 35–41; Seavoy, *Origins of the American Business Corporation*, 44; *Letters to the People of New Jersey on the Frauds, Extortions, and Oppressions of the Railroad Monopoly* (Philadelphia: Carey and Hart, 1848), 3; *Can the Camden and Amboy Monopoly Be Lawfully Abolished?* (Burlington, N.J., 1855), 6; Cadman, *The Corporation in New Jersey*, 54–60, 400.

226. *Hoosac Tunnel: The Memorial of the Western Railroad Corporation* (Boston: Eastburn's, 1853); Ansel Phelps, *Hoosac Tunnel* (Boston: Eastburn's, 1853); Dunbar, *A History of Travel*, 3:995–98.

227. *Proceedings of a Meeting of Representatives of the Several Railroad Companies*, 16.

228. Stockwell, *Argument of Hon. Chas. Theo. Russell*, 10.

229. *Substance of Argument of Respondents' Counsel*, 17.

230. Stockwell, *Argument of Hon. Chas. Theo. Russell*, 23.

231. Ingersoll, *Argument of Joseph R. Ingersoll, Esq. before the General Assembly*, 18.

232. *Proceedings of a Meeting of Representatives of the Several Railroad Companies*, 17.

Chapter 6

1. Sigourney, *To the Stockholders of the Phoenix Bank*, 14.

2. Naomi Lamoreaux puts a negative spin on convergence, arguing that it limited "contractual freedom." I see convergence more as a regulatory issue: not allowing incorporators to repeat known mistakes. Lamoreaux, "Partnerships, Corporations," in Lipartito and Sicilia, eds., *Constructing Corporate America*, 34.

3. Abbott, *Rise of the Business Corporation*, 4. A similar case can be made for Great Britain. Freeman, Pearson, and Taylor, *Shareholder Democracies?*, 9–10.

4. Adams, MSS1 Ad198a, VHS.

5. Lieber, quoted in Wright, *Hamilton Unbound*, 67.

6. Roy, *Socializing Capital*, 83–84; Tucker, *Notes of Lectures on Corporations*, 38.

7. Richard K. Matthews, *If Men Were Angels: James Madison and the Heartless Empire of Reason* (Lawrence: University Press of Kansas, 1995).

8. Berle and Means, *The Modern Corporation*, 12, 122; Mitchell, *Speculation Economy*, 43.

9. *An Inquiry into the Nature and Utility of Corporations*, 2.

10. Maier, "The Revolutionary Origins of the American Corporation," 79; Dodd, *American Business Corporations*, 104–7, 188–90; Morton Horwitz, *The Transformation of America Law, 1870–1960: The Crisis of Legal Orthodoxy* (New York: Oxford University Press, 1992), 77; Freyer, "Business Law," in Engerman and Gallman, eds., *The Cambridge Economic History of the United States*, 460, 471; Seward Brice and Ashabel Green, *A Treatise on the Doctrine of Ultra Vires*, 2nd American ed. (New York: Baker, Voorhis, 1880), 28–33. Confusingly, ultra vires also, erroneously, sometimes referred to the inability of a corporation to bind dissident shareholders and several other matters. Brice and Green, *Treatise*, 34–36.

11. William Wright, *A Reply of the Board of Managers to a Report of a Committee of Stockholders of the Columbia, Pa. Bridge Company* (Columbia, Pa.: William Greer, 1820), 19.

12. Hovenkamp, *Enterprise and American Law*, 59.

13. *Opinion of Isaac H. Williams, Esq. and Garret D. Wall, Esq. in Relation to the Corporate Powers of "The Trenton and New-Brunswick Turnpike Company"* (Trenton, N.J.: Joseph Justice, 1835), 3–5.

14. *Louisiana State Statutes*, 1848.

15. *The Annual Report of the President and Directors of the Canton Company of Baltimore Made to the Stockholders at Their Annual Meeting* (Baltimore: John Murphy, 1850), 6. See also Tucker, *Notes of Lectures on Corporations*, 25–26, 40; *Proceedings of the First Meeting of the Stockholders of the Manassas Gap R. R. Company* (Alexandria, Va.: Alexandria Gazette Office, 1850), 14–37.

16. Bennett, *The Opinion of the Chancellor in the Case of Byron Stevens vs. the Rutland and Burlington Railroad Company and Others*, 36.

17. Tucker, *Notes of Lectures on Corporations*, 40.

18. Wright, *A Reply of the Board of Managers*.

19. Tucker, *Notes of Lectures on Corporations*, 39; Livermore, *Early American Land Companies*, 257.

20. *Documents Relating to the Potomac and Alleghany Coal and Iron Manufacturing Company* (New York: David Felt, 1841), 35.

21. *City of Sonora Tunnel Company* (Sonora, Calif.: Herald Office, 1853), 8.

22. *Documents Relating to the Phoenix Mining and Manufacturing Company:*

Comprising Extracts from Various Official Reports, Made under Direction of Government Officers and Others (New York: Sibell & Mott, 1847), in Wright et al., eds., *History of Corporate Governance*, 4:68; *Proceedings of the First Meeting of the Stockholders of the Manassas Gap R. R.*, 8–10; Knowlton, *Pepperell's Progress*, 380–84.

23. Scott, *Farmers National Bank of Bucks County*, 15.

24. *Act of Incorporation and By-Laws of the Eastern Railroad Company* (Salem, Mass.: Palfray and Chapman, 1836), 34. See also *The Bank of Baltimore: An Important Factor in the Financial History of the State of Maryland and the City of Baltimore in the Past Century* (1895), 10.

25. *Federal Gazette & Baltimore Daily Advertiser*, February 6, 1804.

26. Minutes of the Board of Directors of the Farmers Bank of Virginia, January 18, 1821, VHS; Wright, *First Wall Street*, 173.

27. *Proceedings of the First Meeting of the Stockholders of the Manassas Gap R. R.*, 5.

28. Berle and Means, *The Modern Corporation*, 123–24.

29. George Newton to John Allman, Aaron Milhado, W. J. Hardy, December 24, 1834, Allmand Family Papers, VHS.

30. *Address of Mr. McLane, President, to the Stockholders of the Baltimore & Ohio R. Road Company at Their Meeting on the 5th of April, 1847* (Baltimore: James Lucas, 1847), 6.

31. A. C. Page, *Award of the Commissioners under the Act in Relation to Rail-Road Corporations, in the Matter between the Schenectady and Troy Rail-Road Company and the Utica and Schenectady Rail-Road Company, and the Albany and Schenectady Rail-Road Company* (Troy, N.Y.: J. C. Kneeland, 1847), 11.

32. Minutes of the Board of Directors of the Farmers Bank of Virginia, January 22, 1846, VHS.

33. Simon, *A Century of the National Bank of the Northern Liberties*, 13.

34. Quoted in Bennett, *The Opinion of the Chancellor, in the Case of Byron Stevens*, 8–17, quotation on 17. See also Robert Hessen, "The Modern Corporation and Private Property: A Reappraisal," *Journal of Law and Economics* 26 (June 1983): 288; A Citizen of Lowell, *Corporations and Operatives*, 46; Woolsey, "The Old New Haven Bank," 320; Hamilton Brewer, *Address of the Board of Directors of the New York and Boston Railroad Company to the Stockholders and Friends of the Road* (1850), 3.

35. Tucker, *Notes of Lectures on Corporations*, 39.

36. Minute of June 20, 1835, Board of Directors' Minutes, 1834–35, Richmond, Fredericksburg, and Petersburg Records.

37. Upper Appomattox Company Minute Book, 1842–72, 17, VHS.

38. *Proposals of the Pennsylvania Company for Insurance on Lives and Granting Annuities* (Philadelphia: James Kay Jun. & Brother, 1837), 15–16.

39. Cadman, *The Corporation in New Jersey*, 257, 288–89, 318–19; A. E. Belknap, *Report of the Directors of the Boston Exchange Company* (Boston: S. N. Dickinson, 1843), 19; Dodd, *American Business Corporations*, 71–74.

40. *Act of Incorporation and By-Laws of the Boston and Barre Company* (Boston: Perkins & Marvin, 1832), 7.

41. *Annual Report of the President and Directors of the Canton Company of Baltimore Made to the Stockholders at Their Annual Meeting* (Baltimore: John Murphy, 1853), 10.

42. Charles C. Bonney, *Speech of Charles C. Bonney of Peoria against an Act Entitled an Act to Incorporate the Illinois River Improvement Company Delivered on Behalf of the Common Council and Citizens of Peoria at St. Louis, June 23rd, 1857* (Peoria, Ill.: B. Foster, 1857), 6.

43. Wormser, *Frankenstein*, 91.

44. Seventy-Six, *Cause of, and Cure for, Hard Times*, 44.

45. *Executive Communication to the General Assembly of Maryland*, 16.

46. H. D. Bird, *Comparison of the Petersburg and Roanoke Railroad Company with the Richmond, Fredericksburg and Potomac Railroad Company* (Petersburg, Va., 1845).

47. Shirley, "The Fourth New Hampshire Turnpike," 428.

48. Forbes, *Israel Thorndike*, 134–48.

49. Harry Stevens, "Bank Enterprises in a Western Town, 1815–1822," *Business History Review* 29, 2 (1955): 139–56.

50. *Annual Report of the South-Carolina Canal and Rail Road*, 6.

51. Quoted in Ashmead, *History of the Delaware County National Bank*, 64.

52. See, e.g., *Annual Report of the South-Carolina Canal and Rail Road*; *An Address to the Stockholders of the Schuylkill Navigation Company*, 9.

53. *Address of Mr. McLane, President, to the Stockholders*, 29.

54. Tucker, *Notes of Lectures on Corporations*, 38.

55. *An Act to Incorporate the Stockholders of the Bank of the United States*, 13; Thomas H. De Witt, Secretary of the Board of Public Works, Circular to State Proxies and Directors, Taylor Family Papers, Section 3, VHS; *Annual Report of the President and Directors of the Canton Company of Baltimore Made to the Stockholders at Their Annual Meeting* (Baltimore: John Murphy, 1855), 4; John W. Rice Account Books, 1857–66, VHS.

56. "The New Bedford Standard," *Trenton State Gazette* (July 8, 1850), 2.

57. Appleton, *Introduction of the Power Loom*, 29–30.

58. Lamoreaux and Glaisek, "Vehicles of Privilege or Mobility?," 515–19; Hilt, "When Did Ownership Separate from Control?," 667.

59. Ward, *Notes on Joint-Stock Companies*, 11.

60. John Taylor to Joseph Ellicott, February 5, 1819, John Taylor Papers, Rutgers University Special Collections and Archives, New Brunswick, N.J.

61. Joseph Saltar, "U.S. Bank at Buffalo," July 1862, University of Rochester, Rochester, N.Y.

62. *Jenk's Portland Gazette* (June 30, 1800), 2.

63. Appleton, *Introduction of the Power Loom*, 30.

64. "A letter was received from Mr. Bernard Peyton, stating his acceptance of the appointment of a Director of the Office of the Bank of the United States and containing his resignation as a member of this Board." February 3, 1820, Minutes of the Board of Directors of the Farmers Bank of Virginia, 1820–27, VHS. An exception was the unusually poorly governed New York and Erie Railroad. Murphy, "Empire State Building,"

250. See also Minutes of the Board of Directors of the Farmers Bank of Virginia, April 27, August 3, 1820, VHS; *An Act to Incorporate the Stockholders of the Bank of the United States*, 7; *Prospectus of the West Virginia Iron Mining and Manufacturing Company*, 11.

65. *An Act to Incorporate the Stockholders of the Bank of the United States*, 7.

66. Zephaniah Pease, *The Centenary of the Merchants National Bank* (New Bedford, Mass., 1925), 51.

67. Elihu Bunker, *A Reply to "The Proceedings and Minutes of New-York and Boston Steam-Boat Company"* (New York: George F. Nesbitt, 1831), 8–9, 13.

68. "At an Election," *New York Columbian* (May 5, 1810), 2.

69. Richard Blow Commonplace Book, 12–15, passim, VHS.

70. Harper, *Historical Account of Vermont Paper Currency*, 29.

71. Cadman, *The Corporation in New Jersey*, 317; Gower, "Some Contrasts Between British and American Corporation Law," 1389–90.

72. Sigourney, *To the Stockholders of the Phoenix Bank*, 1; Knapp, *Letter to the Stockholders of the Mechanics' Bank*, 4; Ashmead, *History of the Delaware County National Bank*, 65, 104–8, 114–15; *The Bank of Baltimore*, 15; Lewis, *A History of the Bank of North America*, 119; Kimball, *Faithfully Serving Community, State, and Nation*, 15; National City Bank of New York, *135 Years of Banking*; Woolsey, "The Old New Haven Bank," 315, 321; Pease, *Centenary of the Merchants National*, 53, 84.

73. Thomas H. De Witt, Secretary of the Board of Public Works, Circular to State Proxies and Directors, Taylor Family Papers, Section 3, VHS; Ashmead, *History of the Delaware County National Bank*, 10, 44; Knapp, *Letter to the Stockholders of the Mechanics' Bank*, 5; *An Act to Incorporate the Stockholders of the Bank of the United States*, 13; *Prospectus of the West Virginia Iron Mining and Manufacturing Company*, 16; Tilghman, *Report of the State's Agents in Joint Stock Companies*, 11; Scott, *Farmers National Bank of Bucks County*, 14.

74. Union Canal Company of Pennsylvania, *An Act to Incorporate*, 7.

75. Ashmead, *History of the Delaware County National Bank*, 34–35.

76. James Boorman, *Communications from James Boorman to the Stockholders of the Hudson River Railroad Company in Reply to Mr. A. C. Flagg, Late President of That Company* (New York: Wm. C. Bryant, 1849), 3.

77. Ibid, 7.

78. "At a Very Numerous Special General Meeting," *Providence Columbian Phenix* (April 14, 1810), 4.

79. Shirley, "The Fourth New Hampshire Turnpike," 291; "Resolution of July 6, 1835," Board of Directors' Minutes, 1834–1835, Richmond, Fredericksburg, and Petersburg Records, VHS; Joseph Lawrence, "To the Providence Mutual Fire-Insurance Company," *Providence Gazette* (March 17, 1810), 3.

80. *Prospectus of the West Virginia Iron Mining and Manufacturing Company*, 15.

81. Appleton, *Introduction of the Power Loom*, 29.

82. Minute of June 20, 1835, Board of Directors' Minutes, 1834–35, Richmond, Fredericksburg, and Petersburg Records, VHS. See also Hollywood Cemetery Minute

Books, 1847–68, 13, VHS; *Prospectus of the West Virginia Iron Mining and Manufacturing Company*, 15.

83. Sigourney, *To the Stockholders of the Phoenix Bank*, 2–3, 7. See also Ashmead, *History of the Delaware County National Bank*, 10.

84. Woolsey, "The Old New Haven Bank," 320.

85. Shirley, "The Fourth New Hampshire Turnpike," 291; Tucker, *Notes of Lectures on Corporations*, 18.

86. *Prospectus of the West Virginia Iron Mining and Manufacturing Company*, 14; Bank of Kentucky, Greensburg Branch, Minute Book, 1835–61, June 27, 1835, FHS.

87. Washington Mutual Assurance Company, *The Charter, Bye-Laws, and Rates* (New York: T and J. Swords, 1809), 12.

88. Minutes of the Board of Directors of the Farmers Bank of Virginia, January 22, 1846, VHS. And see Ashmead, *History of the Delaware County National Bank*, 25.

89. Knapp, *Letter to the Stockholders of the Mechanics' Bank*, 3–4.

90. Ward, *Notes on Joint-Stock Companies*, 8–9.

91. Appleton, *Introduction of the Power Loom*, 26; Forbes, *Israel Thorndike*, 140.

92. Appleton, *Introduction of the Power Loom*, 8, 26.

93. *Prospectus of the West Virginia Iron Mining and Manufacturing Company*, 8; Ashmead, *History of the Delaware County National Bank*, 25.

94. *Annual Report of Messrs. A. J. Pleasonton, John Moss, Richard Ronaldson and John Sharp, Jr.*, 23.

95. Pease, *Centenary of the Merchants National*, 58–59.

96. Appleton, *Introduction of the Power Loom*, 3, 15–16.

97. Patrick Macaulay, *Proposals and Plan of the American Life Insurance and Trust Company* (London: Charles Skipper and East, 1836), 9. See also Dodd, *American Business Corporations*, 70–74.

98. John Jeffrey to James Lawton, June 23, 1852, John Jeffrey Manuscripts, FHS.

99. Regulations for Gas Co., John Jeffrey Manuscripts, FHS.

100. Bye Laws Convington Gas Light Co., John Jeffrey Manuscripts, FHS.

101. Stow, *Capitalist's Guide and Railway Annual*, 18.

102. *Annual Report of the President and Directors of the Canton Company of Baltimore Made to the Stockholders at Their Annual Meeting* (Baltimore: John Murphy, 1851), 4.

103. Lippincott, *Address to the Stock and Loan Holders of the Schuylkill Navigation Company*, 10.

104. Vicksburg Gas Light Company Papers, 1853–60, John Jeffrey Collection, FHS.

105. *Proceedings of the Stockholders of the Canton Company of Baltimore and the Annual Report on Their Affairs, June 11, 1846* (Baltimore: Publication Rooms, 1846), 6; *The Annual Report of the President and Directors of the Canton Company*, 3.

106. *Proceedings of the First Meeting of the Stockholders of the Manassas Gap R. R.*, 7. See also "At a Meeting of the Stockholders of the Insurance Company of North America," *Claypoole's American Daily Advertiser* (January 16, 1800), 3; "The Following

Gentlemen Were Elected Directors of the New-York Insurance Company," *New York Spectator* (January 18, 1800), 4; "At an Election Held on Monday for President, Directors, and Treasurer of the Schuylkill Permanent Bridge," *Philadelphia Gazette of the United States* (January 7, 1801), 2; "At a Meeting of the Directors," *Boston Patriot* (October 6, 1810), 2; Tilghman, *Report of the State's Agents in Joint Stock Companies*, 11; "Portland Gas-Light Company," *Portland Daily Advertiser* (January 3, 1850), 2; "Fitchburg Railroad Company," *Boston Evening Transcript* (January 30, 1850), 2; "Vt. & Mass. Railroad Company," *Brattleboro (Vt.) Weekly Eagle* (February 18, 1850), 2.

107. Scott, *The Constitution and Finance*, 1:461; Graeme G. Acheson and John D. Turner, "Investor Behaviour in a Nascent Capital Market: Scottish Bank Shareholders in the Nineteenth Century," *Economic History Review* 64 (2011): 188–213.

108. "Baltimore and Southern Steam Packet Company," *Baltimore Sun* (March 5, 1850), 2.

109. Bunker, *A Reply*, 12.

110. "The Following Gentlemen," *New York Daily Advertiser* (January 11, 1800), 3.

111. *Federal Gazette and Baltimore Daily Advertiser* (August 23, 1796).

112. Peskin, *Manufacturing Revolution*, 171.

113. *New York Herald* clipping in Wo* 99 v. 6, Historical Society of Pennsylvania, Philadelphia, Pa.

114. Hollywood Cemetery Minute Books, 1847–68, 12–15, VHS.

115. Hiram Sibley to Norvin Green, April 3, 7, 1858, Norvin Green Papers, Correspondence, FHS. See also Dodd, *American Business Corporations*, 67–70; Cadman, *The Corporation in New Jersey*, 302–18; Bank of the United States, Mss4 B22586, VHS; Berle and Means, *The Modern Corporation*, 6. A similar phenomenon occurred in Britain. Freeman, Pearson, and Taylor, *Shareholder Democracies?*, 241; Dalia Tsuk Mitchell, "Shareholders as Proxies: The Contours of Shareholder Democracy," *Washington and Lee Law Review* 63, 4 (fall 2006): 1508.

116. Usha Rodrigues, "The Seductive Comparison of Shareholder and Civic Democracy," *Washington and Lee Law Review* 63, 4 (fall 2006): 1390–91, 1406.

117. Livermore, *Early American Land Companies*, 227–28; Washington Mutual Assurance Company, *The Charter*, 11. Colleen Dunlavy's claim that the absence of a voting rule in a charter meant that each stockholder received one vote, regardless of his or her shareholdings, must be rejected. Colleen Dunlavy, "From Citizens to Plutocrats: Nineteenth-Century Shareholders Voting Rights and Theories of the Corporation," in Lipartito and Sicilia, eds., *Constructing Corporate America*, 67, 72–79. See Wright, "Rise of the Corporation Nation," in Irwin and Sylla, eds., *Founding Choices*, 234–35; Hilt, "When Did Ownership Separate from Control?," 659. Ratner set the record straight. David L. Ratner, "The Government of Business Corporations: Critical Reflections on the Rule of 'One Share, One Vote,'" *Cornell Law Review* 56, 1 (November 1970): 1–56. See also Freeman, ed., *Alexander Hamilton: Writings*, 598.

118. Hilt, "When Did Ownership Separate from Control?," 645–85.

119. Tucker, *Notes of Lectures on Corporations*, 114.

120. Quoted in Stealey, ed., *Kanawhan Prelude*, 61. See also Lamoreaux, "Partnerships, Corporations," in Lipartito and Sicilia, eds., *Constructing Corporate America*, 38.

121. Jeffrey Kerbel, "An Examination of Nonvoting and Limited Voting Common Shares—Their History, Legality, and Validity," *Securities Regulation Law Journal* 15 (1987): 48–49; Livermore, *Early American Land Companies*, 229; Dunlavy, "From Citizens to Plutocrats," 79–84; Tucker, *Notes of Lectures on Corporations*, 38; Timothy Jacobson et al., *Knowledge for Generations: Wiley and the Global Publishing Industry* (Hoboken, N.J.: John Wiley, 2007), 325.

122. Ayer, *Some of the Usages and Abuses*, 20; *A Statement of the Correspondence Between the Banks*, 25–27.

123. Tilghman, *Report of the State's Agents in Joint Stock Companies*, 5.

124. Tucker, *Notes of Lectures on Corporations*, 70.

125. Quoted in Bennett, *The Opinion of the Chancellor, in the Case of Byron Stevens*, 7.

126. *An Act to Incorporate the Stockholders of the Bank of the United States*, 8.

127. *City of Sonora Tunnel Company*, 8.

128. Shirley, "The Fourth New Hampshire Turnpike," 293, 347–48.

129. A Stockholder, "To the Directors of the Congaree and Santee Steam Boat Company," *Charleston Courier* (July 14, 1820), 2.

130. Charles W. Ashby to Joseph Holt, August 29, 1849, Charles William Ashby Papers, VHS. See also Dunbar, *A History of Travel*, 3:941–42.

131. Joseph Stiglitz, "Government Failure vs. Market Failure: Principles of Regulation," in Balleisen and Moss, eds., *Governments and Markets*, 26.

132. Gallatin, *Considerations of the Currency and Banking System*, 70–71.

133. Wright, *Wealth of Nations Rediscovered*, 171; Cadman, *The Corporation in New Jersey*, 320.

134. Quoted in Wright, "Corporate Entrepreneurship in the Antebellum South," in Delfino, Gillespie, and Kyriakoudes, eds., *Southern Society and Its Transformation*, 198.

135. Minute of June 20, 1835, Board of Directors' Minutes, 1834–35, Richmond, Fredericksburg, and Petersburg Records.

136. Diary of Blair Bolling, 1810–37, 1:233, VHS.

137. Bylaws and stockholders of the Cleveland Gas Light & Coke Company, John Jeffrey Manuscripts, FHS.

138. Knapp, *Letter to the Stockholders of the Mechanics' Bank*, 4.

139. Spalding, "The Boston Mercantile Community," 52.

140. *Report on the Affairs of the Mohawk and Hudson Railroad: Submitted to the Stockholders by the Executive Committee* (Schenectady, N.Y.: Riggs & Norris, 1840), 3.

141. Swift and Hale, *Report on the Present State of the Chesapeake and Ohio Canal*, 6.

142. *Report of the Directors to the Stockholders of the Illinois Central Railroad*, 7.

143. Dale Flesher, Gary Previts, and William Samson, "Early American Corporate Reporting and European Capital Markets: The Case of the Illinois Central Railroad, 1851–1861," *Accounting Historians Journal* 33 (June 2006): 3–24.

144. Franklin Fell, *Report of the Board of Directors of the Buck Mountain Coal Company* (Philadelphia: T. K. & P. G. Collins, 1846), 5.

145. *Proceedings of the Stockholders of the Canton Company of Baltimore*, 3.

146. Cary, *Result of Manufactures*, 12; *Report of the Committee Appointed by the Directors of the Winnipiseogee Canal*, 15–16.

147. Somerville Pinkney, *The First Annual Report of the Directors of the Annapolis and Elk-Ridge Rail Road Company* (Annapolis, Md.: William M'Neir, 1839).

148. *Annual Report of the President and Directors of the Canton Company 1851*, 3–4.

149. Boorman, *Communications from James Boorman*, 2.

150. Fernon, *Municipal Subscriptions Made by the City of Philadelphia*, 18.

151. Bunker, *A Reply*, 4.

152. Brewer, *Address of the Board of Directors*; Flesher, Previts, and Samson, "Early American Corporate Reporting," 3–24.

153. Haddock, *Address of the Northern Railroad Company*, 5.

154. *Proceedings of the First Meeting of the Stockholders of the Manassas Gap R. R.*, 6.

155. Godman and Roberts, *First Annual Report*, 28.

156. See, e.g., "Terms of Subscription, and Plan of the S. Carolina Steam Navigation Company," *Camden Gazette* (February 3, 1820), 3; *Report of the Committee Appointed by the Directors of the Winnipiseogee Canal*, 4; Telford, *First Exhibit by the Dayton and Michigan Rail-Road.*

157. *The Commissioners and Directors Appointed by the Act Incorporating the Hudson River Rail Road Company Submit to the Consideration of the Public, the Following Statement, Showing the Prospects of Business and the Importance of the Proposed Rail Road* (New York: E. B. Clayton, 1846), 2.

158. *Petition of the Stockholders of the Spot Pond Aqueduct Company Circular* (Boston, 1845).

159. *Prospectus of the West Virginia Iron Mining and Manufacturing Company*, 3.

160. Haddock, *Address of the Northern Railroad Company*, 10–12.

161. Brewer, *Address of the Board of Directors*, 7.

162. Bloodgood, *Report of the President and Directors to the Stockholders*, 9–10.

163. "We Understand the Directors," *Raleigh Star* (December 6, 1810), 196.

164. Louisville Hotel Company, Cash Book, 1832–36, FHS. And see Dodd, *American Business Corporations*, 74. For explicit discussion of subscriptions as options, see Mark Casson and Andrew Godley, "Entrepreneurship in Britain, 1830–1900," in Landes, Mokyr, and Baumol, eds., *The Invention of Enterprise*, 233.

165. Plummer, "Consumer Credit in Colonial Philadelphia," 385–409; Sullivan, *Refutation of Mr. Colden's "Answer" to Mr. Sullivan's Report*, 42; Knowlton, *Pepperell's Progress*, 103–4; *Documents Relating to the Potomac and Alleghany Coal and Iron Manufacturing Company*, 39; Godman and Roberts, *First Annual Report*, 6.

166. Dodd, *American Business Corporations*, 74–84; Cadman, *The Corporation in New Jersey*, 250–52; Livermore, *Early American Land Companies*, 279–82.

167. "Resolution," Minute of June 20, 1835, Treasurer's Report and Board Resolution,

July 10, 1835, Board of Directors' Minutes, 1834–35, Richmond, Fredericksburg, and Petersburg Records, VHS.

168. A. D. Murphey, "State of North-Carolina: Yadkin Navigation Company," *Raleigh Star and North-Carolina State Gazette* (July 28, 1820), 4.

169. Taylor, "The Turnpike Era in New England," 155.

170. "Onondaga Gypsum Company," *Albany Register* (February 20, 1810), 2.

171. Shaw, *Report of the Board of Directors of the Lewis Wharf Company*, 12.

172. Patterson, "Ten and One-Half Years of Commercial Banking," 36–37.

173. *The North Branch Canal Company; Its Prospects, and Its Laws of Incorporation* (Philadelphia, 1845), 31–32.

174. Robert Smith to George Salmon, May 23, 1798, Richard C. Sharp Collection, Maryland Historical Society, Baltimore, Md.

175. Tucker, *Notes of Lectures on Corporations*, 63–64.

176. "The Property Owners," *Trenton State Gazette* (May 8, 1850), 3.

177. Cornelius Glen Peebles, *Exposé of the Atlantic & Pacific Railroad Company* (New York, 1854), 14.

178. Wright, *A Reply of the Board of Managers*, 12–13.

179. *Hoosac Tunnel: The Memorial of the Western Railroad*, 4.

180. Sullivan, *A Description of a Sub-Marine Aqueduct*, 27–28.

181. "To the Petitioners for the Incorporation of a Company to Supply Charleston with Pure, Wholesome, Fresh Water," *Charleston City Gazette* (February 15, 1800), 3.

182. J. Ant. Teissier, *Projected Salt Works in Boston Bay* (Boston: James Loring, 1828), 1.

183. Godman and Roberts, *First Annual Report*, 6, 10.

184. "Massachusetts Mutual Fire Insurance Company," *Salem (Mass.) Gazette* (March 11, 1800), 3.

185. *Proposals of the Pennsylvania Company for Insurance on Lives*, 5.

186. *Act of Incorporation, Articles of Association, and By-Laws of the Brooklyn Female Academy; Together with a List of Stockholders* (Brooklyn, N.Y.: Lees & Foulkes, 1847), 22–29.

187. *Proceedings of the First Meeting of the Stockholders of the Manassas Gap R. R.*, 6.

188. *The Adirondack Iron and Steel Company, New York* (New York: W. E. & J. Sibell, 1854), 3–4.

189. *Documents Relating to the Potomac and Alleghany Coal and Iron Manufacturing Company*, 3.

190. Draper, *The Burns Ranche Gold Mining Company*, 14.

191. "Insurance," *Milwaukee Sentinel* (February 2, 1860), 2; *Address of the Delaware and Raritan Canal*, 22; Godman and Roberts, *First Annual Report*, 8, 16, 29.

192. Burrall, *Annual Report of the Board of Directors of the Housatonic Railroad* (Bridgeport, Conn.: William S. Pomeroy, 1851), 12.

193. Robert Lively, "The American System: A Review Article," *Business History Review* 29, 1 (1955): 90. The same conclusion about the gaming of financial statements was reached in Britain at about the same time. Freeman, Pearson, and Taylor, *Shareholder*

Democracies?, 211–39. See also Tuckett, *Practical Remarks on the Present State of Life Insurance*, 23; *Speech of Mr. Keating in the House of Representatives of Pennsylvania*, 22.

194. *Origins, Provisions and Effect of the Safety Fund Law*, 4.

195. "The Statement of the President of the Pennsylvania Railroad Company," *Philadelphia Public Ledger* (January 21, 1860), 4.

196. "A Subscriber," "Illinois Coal Company," *Daily Missouri Republican* (St. Louis) (March 23, 1850), 3.

197. "Lexington and Ohio Rail Road Company," *Boston Weekly Messenger* (March 4, 1830), 3.

198. Knowlton, *Pepperell's Progress*, 114–17; Berle and Means, *The Modern Corporation*, 135.

199. *Origins, Provisions and Effect of the Safety Fund Law*, 4.

200. *Prospectus of the West Virginia Iron Mining and Manufacturing Company*, 11.

201. Cadman, *The Corporation in New Jersey*, 320–24.

202. Ashmead, *History of the Delaware County National Bank*, 23; *An Act to Incorporate the Stockholders of the Bank of the United States*, 12.

203. Cary, *Result of Manufactures*, 13.

204. Fell, *Report of the Board of Directors of Buck Mountain Coal*, 5.

205. *An Address to the Stockholders of the Schuylkill Navigation Company in Reply to a Pamphlet Circulated by the Reading Rail Road Company* (Philadelphia: For the Author, 1844), 10.

206. William Constable to ?, April 15, 1794, Wettereau Papers, CUL; Cary, *Result of Manufactures*, 11–12.

207. Patterson, "Ten and One-Half Years of Commercial Banking," 55.

208. Scott, *Farmers National Bank of Bucks County*, 22–26.

209. "Manufacturing Corporations," 117–18; Banner, *Anglo-American Securities Regulation*, 200–201, 241.

210. Minutes of the Board of Directors of the Farmers Bank of Virginia, January 23, 1823, VHS.

211. Arnold Bodin, *Minority Report, Submitted to the Stockholders of the Citizens' Bank of Louisiana* (New Orleans, 1847), in Wright et al., eds., *History of Corporate Governance*, 4:75–81.

212. Gelderblom, Jong, and Jonker, "An Admiralty for Asia," in Koppell, ed., *Origins of Shareholder Advocacy*, 29–60.

213. *Annual Report of Messrs. A. J. Pleasonton, John Moss, Richard Ronaldson and John Sharp, Jr.*

214. Upper Appomattox Company Minute Book, 1842–72, 25, VHS.

215. Ward, *Notes on Joint-Stock Companies*, 4.

216. Ayer, *Some of the Usages and Abuses*, 4.

217. Cary, *Result of Manufactures*, 12.

218. Minute of June 20, 1835, Board of Directors' Minutes, 1834–35, Richmond, Fredericksburg, and Petersburg Records, VHS.

219. *Prospectus of the West Virginia Iron Mining and Manufacturing Company*, 12.

220. See James C. Fisher, *Communication from the Chesapeake and Delaware Canal Company and a Report and Estimate of William Strickland to the President and Directors* (Philadelphia: Joseph R. A. Skerrett, 1823), 4; Lucy Newton, "The Birth of Joint-Stock Banking: England and New England Compared," *Business History Review* 84 (spring 2010): 41–42.

221. "The Pacific Knitting Company," *Trenton Daily State Gazette and Republican* (November 13, 1860), 2; "Manufacturing Corporations," 105–6.

222. The mathematics of portfolio diversification dates from the 1960s, but the concept is much older. For the classic technical discussion, see Harry Markowitz, *Portfolio Selection: Efficient Diversification of Investments* (New York: John Wiley, 1959). "There is one admirable rule," an investment guru noted in 1910, "and that is to put your eggs in as many baskets as possible." Carl Snyder, "Railroad Stocks as Investments," *Annals of the American Academy of Political and Social Science* 35 (May 1910): 173. For the effect of portfolio diversification on investors' monitoring incentives, see James P. Hawley, Shyam J. Kamath, and Andrew T. Williams, "Introduction," in James P. Hawley, Shyam J. Kamath, and Andrew T. Williams, eds., *Corporate Governance Failures: The Role of Institutional Investors in the Global Financial Crisis* (Philadelphia: University of Pennsylvania Press, 2011), 10.

223. Gerald Berk, *Alternative Tracks: The Constitution of American Industrial Order, 1865–1917* (Baltimore: Johns Hopkins University Press, 1994), 65.

224. "We Call the Attention," *Trenton Daily State Gazette and Republican* (November 14, 1860), 3.

225. "A Few Suggestions," *Milwaukee Sentinel and Gazette* (September 9, 1850), 2; *Address to the Stockholders of the Schuylkill Navigation Company*.

226. Pease, *Centenary of the Merchants National*, 26.

227. U.S.-style preferred shares (as opposed to British preference shares) may have stemmed from the insurance or guarantee of dividends idea in A Citizen, *Observations*, 18. See "A Bondholder," "First Mortgage Debt of the Union Canal Company," *Philadelphia Public Ledger* (April 25, 1860), 1; "Affairs of the Milwaukee and Mississippi Railroad Company," *Milwaukee Sentinel* (May 1, 1860), 2; Tibbits, Warren, and Roberts, *Report of the Troy Turnpike and Rail Road*, 16–22.

228. Stow, *Capitalist's Guide and Railway Annual*, 16.

229. Davis et al., *Report of a Committee of Investigation*, 2–4, 21, 36–42.

Chapter 7

1. *Report of the Committee on Banks and Insurance Companies*, 18–19.

2. Upper Appomattox Company Minute Book, 1842–72, 26, VHS.

3. Cadman, *The Corporation in New Jersey*, 301.

4. Spalding, "The Boston Mercantile Community," 77.

5. Although less common and smaller than today, malfeasance occurred in antebellum corporate America, claims to the contrary notwithstanding. Skeel, *Icarus in the Boardroom*, 24.

6. Eric Hilt, "Rogue Finance: The Life and Fire Insurance Company and the Panic of 1826," *Business History Review* 83 (spring 2009): 89.

7. "Manufacturing Corporations," 116–17.

8. "Arrest of Hoffman, the Alleged Defaulter of the Pacific Steamship Company," *New York Herald* (July 7, 1860), 7. See also Dunbar, *A History of Travel*, 2:664; Scott, *The Constitution and Finance*, 1:451, 463.

9. Ward, *Notes on Joint-Stock Companies*, 10.

10. Ibid., 11.

11. Tuckett, *Practical Remarks on the Present State of Life Insurance*, 18–20.

12. *Letter on the Use and Abuse of Incorporations*, 11.

13. *President and Directors of the Baltimore and Susquehanna Rail Road*, 3. And see Spalding, "The Boston Mercantile Community," 22–23.

14. *Richmond Enquirer* (June 30, 1835), 3; (July 25, 1837), 4; (April 13, 1840), 3; (March 3, 1838), 4.

15. *The Richmond City Directory, 1866: Containing a Business Directory, of All the Persons Engaged in Business, Classified according to the Business, and a City Register, Containing Much Useful Information* (Richmond, Va.: E. P. Townsend, 1866), 113; *Report of the Investigating Committee on the Affairs of the Manchester Cotton and Wool Manufacturing Company, at a Meeting of Stockholders Held Dec. 6, 1855* (Richmond, Va.: Chas. H. Wynne, 1855).

16. *Report of the Investigating Committee on the Affairs of Manchester Cotton and Wool*.

17. *Proceedings of the Stockholders of the Canton Company of Baltimore*; *The Annual Report of the President and Directors of the Canton Company*, 3–4; *Annual Report of the President and Directors of the Canton Company 1851*; *Annual Report of the President and Directors of the Canton Company of Baltimore Made to the Stockholders at Their Annual Meeting* (Baltimore: John Murphy, 1852); *Annual Report of the President and Directors of the Canton Company*; *Annual Report of the President and Directors of the Canton Company of Baltimore Made to the Stockholders*, 8; *Annual Report of the President and Directors of the Canton Company of Baltimore Made to the Stockholders at Their Annual Meeting* (Baltimore: Lucas Brothers, 1859); *Annual Report of the President and Directors of the Canton Company of Baltimore Made to the Stockholders at Their Annual Meeting* (Baltimore: John Murphy, 1864); *Annual Report of the President and Directors of the Canton Company of Baltimore Made to the Stockholders at Their Annual Meeting* (Baltimore: John Murphy, 1867), 3.

18. Fell, *Report of the Board of Directors of Buck Mountain Coal*, 6.

19. Morton, quoted in Bunker, *A Reply*, 21.

20. Knowlton, *Pepperell's Progress*, 64.

21. "An Observer," "Chesapeake and Ohio Canal Company," *Richmond Enquirer* (February 4, 1830), 3. For more discussion of early management, see Pollard, *Genesis of Modern Management*, 37–77.

22. *Communication of the Board of Directors of the Panama Railroad Company to the Stockholders* (New York: John F. Trown, 1853), 17–18.

23. Stealey, ed., *Kanawhan Prelude*, 56.

24. W. D. Reid (New Orleans) to Dr. Green, March 4, 1855, Norvin Green Papers, Correspondence, FHS.

25. *Exposition of the Baltimore and Cuba Smelting & Mining Company* (Baltimore: Robert Neilson, 1845); Cadman, *The Corporation in New Jersey*, 216; John Jeffrey Manuscripts, FHS; Robert E. Wright, "Corporations and the Economic Growth and Development of the Antebellum Ohio River Valley," *Ohio Valley History* (winter 2009): 47–70.

26. Benjamin Silliman, *Report of the Board of Examiners Appointed by the Connecticut River Steam Boat Company to Inquire into the Causes of the Explosion of the Steam Boat New England* (New Haven, Conn.: Hezekiah Howe, 1833); Paul Paskoff, *Troubled Waters: Steamboat Disasters, River Improvements, and American Public Policy, 1821–1860* (Baton Rouge: Louisiana State University Press, 2007), 19–20, 171–73, 214–15; "The Powder Mill," *Portsmouth Journal of Literature and Politics* (January 4, 1840), 2; "Melancholy Occurrence," *Portsmouth, New Hampshire Gazette* (August 18, 1840), 1.

27. Cary, *Result of Manufactures*, 15.

28. Gouverneur, *Remarks on the Life Insurance Laws*, 1.

29. "Scheme, for the Improvement of the South-Carolina Homespun Company," *Charleston City Gazette* (September 5, 1810), 2.

30. *Address of Mr. McLane, President, to the Stockholders*, 8.

31. *Report of the Directors to the Stockholders of the Illinois Central Railroad*, 7–8.

32. *Substantial Facts Relating to the Great Richness of the Coal Hill and Union Mines, about to Be Extensively Worked by the Northern Lead Company of New York* (New York: James D. Torrey, 1852), 16, 19.

33. Jackson, quoted in Spalding, "The Boston Mercantile Community," 177.

34. "Defrauding a Railroad Company," *Baltimore Sun* (September 10, 1860), 1; "Heavy Embezzlement in a Railroad Company," *Washington, D.C. Constitution* (September 11, 1860), 3.

35. "The Troubles of the Great Eastern," *New York Herald* (August 26, 1860), 2.

36. Gallatin, *Report of the Secretary of the Treasury*, 13.

37. Ibid, 81.

38. Gallatin, *Suggestions on the Banks and Currency of the Several United States*, 69.

39. Quoted in Todd and Sonkin, *Alexander Bryan Johnson*, 337.

40. Huntington, *A History of Banking and Currency in Ohio*, 119.

41. Wright, *A Reply of the Board of Managers*, 28–29.

42. Simon, *A Century of the National Bank of the Northern Liberties*, 26–27.

43. *In the Court for the Trial of Impeachments and Correction of Errors*, 3.

44. Ibid., 10–11.

45. Bodin, *Minority Report*, 11–12

46. Harper, *Historical Account of Vermont Paper Currency*, 25–26.

47. Simon, *A Century of the National Bank of the Northern Liberties*, 20–22.

48. Woolsey, "The Old New Haven Bank," 324.

49. Peel, "History of the Lancaster Bank," 76–77.

50. Todd and Sonkin, *Alexander Bryan Johnson*, 338–40; Alexander Bryan Johnson, "Eulogy on a Body Corporate," *Bankers' Magazine and Statistical Register* (June 1855), 925.

51. Lehman, "Explaining Hard Times," 206, 215, 224, 227, 249–60.

52. *An Act to Incorporate the Stockholders of the Bank of the United States*, 19. See also Chandler, "Patterns of American Railroad Finance," 253.

53. Cary, *Americans Defended*, 5–8.

54. Sigourney, *To the Stockholders of the Phoenix Bank*, 14.

55. Stow, *Capitalist's Guide and Railway Annual*, 18.

56. Patterson, "Ten and One-Half Years of Commercial Banking," 24, 35; String and Van Ingen, *A View of Certain Proceedings*, 6, 10, 12, 19–20.

57. New York Assembly, *Mr. Crafts, from the Committee to Whom Was Referred the Petition of John Sanders and Others* (New York, 1814).

58. Tuckett, *Practical Remarks on the Present State of Life Insurance*, 28.

59. *Proceedings of the First Meeting of the Stockholders of the Manassas Gap R. R.*, 22.

60. Mutual corporations were also sometimes run by rogues. In the 1840s and 1850s, many mutual life insurers in Maryland, Pennsylvania, and elsewhere promised "a glorious profit for the members" by assuming in their sales illustrations (examples) "that each person would live out his expectation, at a full rate of compound interest on his whole amount of premiums," which were wildly unrealistic assumptions bordering on fraudulent. Tuckett, *Practical Remarks on the Present State of Life Insurance*, 11, 14. See also Cadman, *The Corporation in New Jersey*, 246–50; Peskin, *Manufacturing Revolution*, 172–73; Banner, *Anglo-American Securities Regulation*, 226.

61. Platt, *Mr. Platt's Speech*.

62. *Prospectus of the California and New York Steamship Company*, 5.

63. Brewer, *Address of the Board of Directors*, 12.

64. *Report of the Committee on Banks and Insurance Companies*, 18.

65. *Executive Communication to the General Assembly of Maryland*, 18.

66. Bodin, *Minority Report*, 1.

67. Asa Dickinson to William Dickinson, October 21, 1859, VHS.

68. Murphy, *The Origins of English Financial Markets*, 222.

69. Carla Tighe and Ron Michener, "The Political Economy of Insider-Trading Laws," *American Economic Review* 84, 2 (May 1994): 164–68.

70. Manne, "Out Two Corporation Systems," 266–67.

71. Wright, "Banking and Politics in New York," 315–16.

72. A Stockholder of the Morris Canal, *A Review by a Stockholder of the Morris Canal of the "Views of a Stockholder, in Relation to the Delaware and Hudson Canal Company"* (Jersey City, N.J.: E. B. Spooner, 1831), 3; Sullivan, *Refutation of Mr. Colden's "Answer" to Mr. Sullivan's Report*.

73. Cary, *Result of Manufactures*, 12–13.

74. Ayer, *Some of the Usages and Abuses*, 12.

75. "To the Stockholders of the Hope Insurance Company," J. Wills to John O'Connor, January 31, 1824, John Michael O'Connor Papers, 1792–1825, NYHS.

76. North River Bank, Proceedings in Chancery, 1824, NYHS.

77. That dividends provided useful signals has been proved econometrically for 1880s Britain. Gareth Campbell and John D. Turner, "Substitutes for Legal Protection: Corporate Governance and Dividends in Victorian Britain," *Economic History Review* 64, 2 (2011): 571–97.

78. Wright, *A Reply of the Board of Managers*, 38.

79. *Annual Report of Messrs. A. J. Pleasonton, John Moss, Richard Ronaldson and John Sharp, Jr.*, 18.

80. *The Annual Report of the President and Directors of the Canton Company*, 4–5.

81. Davis et al., *Report of a Committee of Investigation*, 4.

82. Tuckett, *Practical Remarks on the Present State of Life Insurance*, 26.

83. Boorman, *Communications from James Boorman*, 8.

84. The expectation was that they were large stockholders who would be amply rewarded for their efforts with higher dividends and stock prices. Wright, *First Wall Street*, 174.

85. Gallatin, *Suggestions on the Banks and Currency of the Several United States*, 20.

86. Knapp, *Letter to the Stockholders of the Mechanics' Bank*, 8.

87. *Annual Report of Messrs. A. J. Pleasonton, John Moss, Richard Ronaldson and John Sharp, Jr.*, 6.

88. A Freeman of Massachusetts, *Remarks and Documents Concerning the Location*, 21.

89. Ayer, *Some of the Usages and Abuses*, 11–12.

90. "We the Subscribers," *New York Columbian* (June 8, 1810), 3.

91. *Federal Gazette & Baltimore Daily Advertiser* (February 15, 1797).

92. Ayer, *Some of the Usages and Abuses*, 15–18.

93. Livermore, *Early American Land Companies*, 229; Lamoreaux, "Partnerships, Corporations," in Lipartito and Sicilia, eds., *Constructing Corporate America*, 40.

94. Berryville and Charleston Turnpike Company Records, VHS.

95. Ayer, *Some of the Usages and Abuses*, 15; Bunker, *A Reply*, 13. Large percentages of a bank's funds could be lent to insiders without fraud or failure if the borrowers repaid their loans as they did at many institutions. Andrew Beveridge, "Local Lending Practice: Borrowers in a Small Northeastern Industrial City, 1832–1915," *Journal of Economic History* 45 (June 1985): 393–403; Naomi Lamoreaux, *Insider Lending: Banks, Personal Connections, and Economic Development in Industrial New England* (New York: Cambridge University Press, 1994). Sigourney, *To the Stockholders of the Phoenix Bank*, 3.

96. Ayer, *Some of the Usages and Abuses*, 15.

97. Peebles, *Exposé of the Atlantic & Pacific Railroad Company*, 7; *Circular to the Stockholders of the Atlantic and Pacific Railroad Company* (New York: George F. Nesbitt, 1855), 5, 14.

98. Wright, *A Reply of the Board of Managers*, 38.

99. Congdon, "The Banking System of Massachusetts."

100. Seventy-Six, *Cause of, and Cure for, Hard Times*, 59–62.

101. Mark W. Geiger, *Financial Fraud and Guerrilla Violence in Missouri's Civil War, 1861–1865* (New Haven, Conn.: Yale University Press, 2010).

102. Harper, *Historical Account of Vermont Paper Currency*, 21.

103. Stephen Allen, *An Examination of Some of the Provisions of the Act . . . Passed April, 1829* (New York: Ludwig & Tolefree, 1829), 13; Hilt, "Rogue Finance," 87–112.

104. Teackle, *An Address to the Members of the Legislature of Maryland*, 8; Jesse Hunt, "No. 10," *Baltimore Patriot* (August 8, 1834); Robert E. Shalhope, *The Baltimore Bank Riot: Political Upheaval in Antebellum Maryland* (Chicago: University of Illinois Press, 2009); Bernard C. Steiner, *Life of Reverdy Johnson* (Baltimore: Norman, Remington, 1914), 11–14; Bruchey and Bruchey, *A Brief History of Commercial Banking*, 23–24; Reverdy Johnson and John Glenn, *Reply to a Pamphlet Entitled "A Brief Exposition of Matters Relating to the Bank of Maryland," with an Examination into Some of the Causes of the Bankruptcy of That Institution* (Baltimore: Jas. Lucas & E. K. Deaver, 1834), 3–5.

105. "From Niles' Register," *Portsmouth Journal of Literature and Politics* (April 19, 1834)

106. Ibid.

107. Samuel Jones et al., "Merchants and Traders' Meeting," *Baltimore Patriot* (July 25, 1834).

108. "The City of Baltimore," *Hagerstown Torch Light* (July 24, 1834).

109. "Bank of Maryland," *Vermont Gazette* (June 10, 1834); "Prices of Stocks, Exchange &c," *Baltimore Gazette and Daily Advertiser* (March 29, 1834); "Bank of Maryland," *Richmond Enquirer* (April 8, 1834); "From the Harrisburgh Chronicle of Monday," *Baltimore Patriot* (April 9, 1834); "Patriotic Bank, Washington" *Baltimore Gazette and Daily Advertiser* (July 11, 1834).

110. Hutcheson, "Philadelphia and the Panic of 1857," 182–94.

Chapter 8

1. *Substance of Argument of Respondents' Counsel*, 9.

2. Douglass, *The Coming of Age of American Business*, 157–58; Ayer, *Some of the Usages and Abuses*, 20.

3. When the Trenton Iron Company slowed production, for example, "South Trenton and Trenton too, feel sensibly now the bad effects of its partial suspension." "The Trenton Iron Company," *Trenton State Gazette* (June 27, 1850), 3. See also R. W. Conrad and L. W. [?] To E. Stanton, Secretary of War, May 1, 1862, Conrad Family Papers, VHS; "A Movement," *New Albany (Ind.) Daily Ledger* (January 14, 1860), 2; Ware, *The Industrial Worker, 1840–1860*, 126.

4. Shirley, "The Fourth New Hampshire Turnpike," 430; *An Act to Incorporate the Stockholders of the Bank of the United States*, 13; Sullivan, *Refutation of Mr. Colden's "Answer" to Mr. Sullivan's Report*, 41–45.

5. Dodd, *American Business Corporations*, 57–61, 145, 181–83; *Can the Camden & Amboy Monopoly Lawfully Be Abolished?* (Burlington, N.J., 1855); A Citizen of New York, *What Is a Monopoly?*, 11; Hovenkamp, *Enterprise and American Law*, 63–64; Wright, *A*

Reply of the Board of Managers, 25–26; Neem, *Creating a Nation of Joiners*, 79; Livermore, *Early American Land Companies*, 260; Seavoy, *Origins of the American Business Corporation*, 242; Charles Warren, *History of the Harvard Law School and of Early Legal Conditions in America* (New York: Lewis, 1908), 148; Dodd, *American Business Corporations*, 140; Citizen of Boston, *Remarks upon the Rights and Powers*; Cadman, *The Corporation in New Jersey*, 424; Lewis, *A History of the Bank of North America*, 89–91.

6. Platt, *Mr. Platt's Speech*; *Report of the Committee on Banks and Insurance Companies*, 14.

7. "Manufacturing Corporations," 118.

8. Hovenkamp, *Enterprise and American Law*, 126; Bonney, *Speech of Charles C. Bonney of Peoria*, 7.

9. *An Act to Incorporate the Stockholders of the Bank of the United States*, 7.

10. Ashmead, *History of the Delaware County National Bank*, 9.

11. A Citizen of Burlington, *Beauties of the Monopoly System*.

12. "The Commissioners," *Trenton State Gazette* (February 18, 1850), 2.

13. Roger Stuart White, "State Regulation of Commercial Banks, 1781–1843" (Ph.D. diss., University of Illinois at Urbana-Champaign, 1971), 55–56.

14. Congdon, "The Banking System of Massachusetts."

15. Davis et al., *American Economic Growth*, 356.

16. Gallatin, *Considerations of the Currency and Banking System*, 69–70.

17. *In the Court for the Trial of Impeachments and Correction of Errors*, 11.

18. *Origins, Provisions and Effect of the Safety Fund Law*, 11.

19. Allen, *An Examination of Some of the Provisions of the Act*.

20. For a more detailed discussion of the Safety Fund's origins and operations, see Wright, *Wealth of Nations Rediscovered*, 177–92; *Origins, Provisions and Effect of the Safety Fund Law*, 3, 5, 8.

21. All quotations in this paragraph are from *Origins, Provisions and Effect of the Safety Fund Law*, 7.

22. Ibid., 3–4, 6.

23. Wright, *Wealth of Nations Rediscovered*, 191; David J. Cowen, "The First Bank of the United States and the Securities Market Crash of 1792," *Journal of Economic History* 60 (December 2000): 1047; "List of Balances from Ledger Commencing April 9th 1798 and ending May 13th 1799," Bank of New York Archives, Bank of New York, New York, New York; Hilt, "Rogue Finance," 87–112.

24. Gallatin, *Considerations of the Currency and Banking System*, 65. See also Sigourney, *To the Stockholders of the Phoenix Bank*, 9–11.

25. *Origins, Provisions and Effect of the Safety Fund Law*, 3, 5, 9, 12; Allen, *An Examination of Some of the Provisions of the Act*, 21; Crowder, "State Regulation of Commercial Banking," 104–5; Wright, *Wealth of Nations Rediscovered*, 187.

26. Gallatin, *Considerations of the Currency and Banking System*, 70; A Citizen of New York, *What Is a Monopoly?*, 27; Allen, *An Examination of Some of the Provisions of the Act*, 4.

27. All quotations in this paragraph are from *Origins, Provisions and Effect of the Safety Fund Law*, 11, 13.

28. Allen, *An Examination of Some of the Provisions of the Act*, 10.

29. Diary of Henry Van Der Lyn, 1:213–14, NYHS.

30. Warren E. Weber, "Bank Liability Insurance Schemes Before 1865" (Federal Reserve Bank of Minneapolis Working Paper No. 679, April 22, 2010).

31. Smith and Cole, *Fluctuations in American Business*, 89; Livermore, *Early American Land Companies*, 5; Sylla, "Early American Banking," 105–23; Hugh Rockoff, "The Free Banking Era: A Reexamination," *Journal of Money, Credit and Banking* 6, 2 (May 1974): 141–67.

32. Evans, *Fortune's Epitome of the Stocks*, 256.

33. Gunn, *Decline of Authority*, 229; Hitchcock, *Annual Address*, 242.

34. Davis et al., *American Economic Growth*, 357.

35. Quoted in Bodenhorn, "Free Banking and Financial Entrepreneurship," 108.

36. Pease, *Centenary of the Merchants National*, 45–46.

37. Gallatin, *Suggestions on the Banks and Currency of the Several United States*, 71, 77, 82.

38. Gary Gorton, "Reputation Formation in Early Bank Note Markets," *Journal of Political Economy* 104 (April 1996): 346–97; Davis et al., *American Economic Growth*, 357; Kessler, "Incorporation in New England," 49.

39. "A General Gas Company Law," *New York Herald-Tribune* (March 19, 1860), 4. See also Hovenkamp, *Enterprise and American Law*, 52; Lively, "The American System," 91; Steuart, *Inquiry into the Principles of Political Oeconomy*, 395–96;

40. Sharon Ann Murphy, "Securing Human Property: Slavery, Life Insurance, and Industrialization in the Upper South," *Journal of the Early Republic* 25 (winter 2005): 645.

41. A Citizen of Lowell, *Corporations and Operatives*, 2, 4, 10, 46, 69.

42. "General incorporation laws had always had a one-size-fits-all character." Lamoreaux, "Partnerships, Corporations," in Lipartito and Sicilia, eds., *Constructing Corporate America*, 51. See also Gunn, *Decline of Authority*, 235; Bruchey, *Roots of American Economic Growth*, 136.

43. Butler, "Nineteenth-Century Jurisdictional Competition in the Granting of Corporate Privileges," 143–50; Kessler, "Incorporation in New England," 48.

44. Quoted in Huntington, *A History of Banking and Currency in Ohio*, 178.

45. Ibid., 179–201, 210, 216–19, 228–34, 253–54, 279–82; Van Fenstermaker, *The Development of American Commercial Banking*, 22.

46. Abbott, *Rise of the Business Corporation*, 43–45; Maier, "The Revolutionary Origins of the American Corporation," 57; Gunn, *Decline of Authority*, 225; Yale Law School, *Two Centuries' Growth of American Law, 1701–1901* (1901), 247; Baldwin, "American Business Corporations Before 1789," 274.

47. Sullivan, *A Description of a Sub-Marine Aqueduct*, 5.

48. Handlin and Handlin, "Origins of the American Business Corporation," 4, 15;

Abbott, *Rise of the Business Corporation*, 45; *General Laws of Massachusetts*, 1823, 1:571; Neem, *Creating a Nation of Joiners*, 77; Seavoy, *Origins of the American Business Corporation*, 43; Brooke, *Heart of the Commonwealth*, 285; Peskin, *Manufacturing Revolution*, 172, 185.

49. "Manufacturing Corporations," 101; W. C. Kessler, "A Statistical Study of the New York General Incorporation Act of 1811," *Journal of Political Economy* 48 (December 1940): 877–82; Peskin, *Manufacturing Revolution*, 185; Seavoy, *Origins of the American Business Corporation*, 65–72; Howard, "Stockholders' Liability," 499–514.

50. Abbott, *Rise of the Business Corporation*, 45; Kessler, "Incorporation in New England," 44; Schlesinger, *The Age of Jackson*, 337. Berle and Means called the statute "the first really modern type" of general incorporation law. Berle and Means, *The Modern Corporation*, 126. See also Kessler, "Incorporation in New England," 57.

51. Hovenkamp, *Enterprise and American Law*, 52; Gunn, *Decline of Authority*, 238–39; Sylla, "Early American Banking," 113; Seavoy, *Origins of the American Business Corporation*, 191–93; Hitchcock, *Annual Address*, 239; Miller, "A Note on the History of Business," 153 n. 1; Warren, *History of the Harvard Law School*, 148.

52. Dreikorn, "History and Development of Banking in New Jersey," 45–53, 62.

53. Yale Law School, *Two Centuries' Growth of American Law*, 247–48.

54. Abbott, *Rise of the Business Corporation*, 45; Hamill, "From Special Privilege to General Utility," 81–180; Cadman, *The Corporation in New Jersey*, xi–xii; Butler, "Nineteenth-Century Jurisdictional Competition in the Granting of Corporate Privileges," 129–66; Samuel Curtis, *Engineer's Report No. 1 to the Directors of the Navigation and Hydraulic Company of the Mississippi Rapids* (Cincinnati: George W. Tagart, 1849), 18–21; Lively, "The American System," 91; Hitchcock, *Annual Address*, 236–38; Hamill, "From Special Privilege to General Utility," 179.

55. Steuart, *Inquiry into the Principles of Political Oeconomy*, 392.

56. Neem, *Creating a Nation of Joiners*, 135; Ayer, *Some of the Usages and Abuses*, 23.

57. Hovenkamp, *Enterprise and American Law*, 105.

58. *Report of the Committee on Banks and Insurance Companies*, 5.

59. *Substance of Argument of Respondents' Counsel*, 9.

60. Wright, *Wealth of Nations Rediscovered*, 167–92.

61. *Report of the Committee on Banks and Insurance Companies*, 14–15.

62. Gallatin, *Suggestions on the Banks and Currency of the Several United States*, 81.

63. "At a Recent Meeting," *Trenton Daily State Gazette and Republican* (April 25, 1860), 3.

64. Stow, *Capitalist's Guide and Railway Annual*, 19.

65. Dunbar, *A History of Travel*, 3:1073.

66. Seavoy, *Origins of the American Business Corporation*, 244.

67. Tuckett, *Practical Remarks on the Present State of Life Insurance*, 21.

68. Gouverneur, *Remarks on the Life Insurance Laws*, 1.

69. George J. Benston, *Regulating Financial Markets: A Critique and Some Proposals* (Washington, D.C.: AEI, 1999), 7.

70. *Speech of Mr. Keating in the House of Representatives of Pennsylvania*, 9.

71. Ibid., 10–11, 20–21, 30–33.

72. Galbraith, *New Industrial State*, 77.

73. Tuckett, *Practical Remarks on the Present State of Life Insurance*, 15, 27.

74. Bakan, *The Corporation*, 156–58; *Answer and Remonstrance of the American Telegraphy Company to the Memorial of the Magnetic Telegraph Company and the New England Union Telegraph Company* (1858); A Citizen of Burlington, *Beauties of the Monopoly System*; Cadman, *The Corporation in New Jersey*, 394.

75. Hayes, quoted in Micklethwait and Wooldridge, *The Company*, xiv.

76. Ibid., 75.

77. Berk, *Alternative Tracks*, 101.

78. Thomas L. Green, *Corporation Finance: A Study of the Principles and Methods of the Management of the Finances of Corporations in the United States* (1898), in Robert E. Wright and Richard E. Sylla, eds., *The History of Corporate Finance: Development of Anglo-American Securities Markets, Financial Practices, Theories and Laws* (London: Pickering & Chatto, 2003), 6:207.

79. Bakan, *The Corporation*, 159.

Chapter 9

1. Hitchcock, *Annual Address*, 258.

2. Smith and Dyer, "The Rise and Transformation of the American Corporation," in Kaysen, ed., *The American Corporation Today*, 45–47.

3. Garfield, quoted in Dunbar, *A History of Travel*, 4:1395, 1397.

4. Hitchcock, *Annual Address*, 255.

5. See, e.g., *Trial: Boston Gas Light Company versus William Gault, Containing the Arguments of Counsel and the Charge of the Judge* (Boston: Eastburn's, 1848); Pell, *Review of the Administration and Civil Police*, 83. But see also Thornton, who notes that one insurer was reluctant to sue until it was absolutely necessary to do so. Thornton, "'A Great Machine' or a 'Beast of Prey,'" 585.

6. McCalmont Brothers, *Mr. Gowen's Defence: Speeches of Mr. Franklin B. Gowen (ex-President) and Others concerning the Philadelphia and Reading Railroad Company* (London, 1881), in Wright et al., eds., *History of Corporate Governance*, 5:4.

7. "Topics in Wall Street," *New York Times* (March 8, 1907), 11.

8. Bryce, quoted in Gerald D. Nash, "Government and Business: A Case Study of State Regulation of Corporate Securities, 1850–1933," *Business History Review* 38, 2 (summer 1964): 144–62.

9. See also Knowlton, *Pepperell's Progress*, 117, 124; Wood, *The Long-Suffering Shareholder*, in Wright et al., eds., *History of Corporate Governance*, 5:287. Wood spoke of general opinion here as he doubted the ability of "the real, not the ideal government" to regulate intelligently given that it was composed of "unexpert and unconscientious politicians." Hovenkamp, *Enterprise and American Law*, 105, 114; New York Cheap Transportation Association, *Arguments of the New York Cheap Transportation*

Association (Albany, N.Y., 1874), in Wright et al., eds., *History of Corporate Governance*, 4:366–67.

10. Berle and Means, *The Modern Corporation*, 6–7.

11. Nash, "Government and Business," 145–47.

12. Hitchcock, *Annual Address*, 252–53, 255.

13. *Objects and Advantages of Life Insurance, as Presented by the Charter Oak Life Insurance Company, Hartford, Conn.* (Springfield, Ohio: David Cooper, 1852), 12–13.

14. New York Cheap Transportation Association, *Arguments of*, in Wright et al., eds., *History of Corporate Governance*, 4:366.

15. "The Contest Against Corporations," *New York Times* (August 14, 1878), 4.

16. Wood, *The Long-Suffering Shareholder*, in Wright et al., eds., *History of Corporate Governance*, 5:283.

17. William W. Cook, *A Treatise on the Law of Corporations Having a Capital Stock*, 4th ed. (New York: Callaghan, 1898).

18. Horwitz, *Transformation of America Law, 1870–1960*, 77–78.

19. As quoted in Lamoreaux, "Partnerships, Corporations," in Lipartito and Sicilia, eds., *Constructing Corporate America*, 47–48.

20. See also Freyer, "Business Law," in Engerman and Gallman, eds., *The Cambridge Economic History of the United States*, 471; Ripley, *Main Street and Wall Street*, 63; Berle and Means, *The Modern Corporation*, 127; Abbott, *Rise of the Business Corporation*, 47–48.

21. Mitchell, *Speculation Economy*, 107–8; Basil M. Manly et al., *Final Report of the Commission on Industrial Relations* (Washington, D.C., 1915), 21 n. 1, which notes that U.S. Steel executives questioned whether it was worth "a few thousand dollars" to mail annual reports to stockholders.

22. Ripley, *Main Street and Wall Street*, 161–62.

23. Ibid., 162.

24. Janette Rutterford, "The Shareholder Voice: British and American Accents, 1890–1965," *Enterprise and Society* 13, 1 (March 2012): 122, 132–33, 138–39.

25. Quoted in ibid., 138–39.

26. Ripley, *Main Street and Wall Street*, 164–65, 177, 185.

27. Lough, *Corporation Finance*, 370.

28. Lockwood, "How to Reform Business," 295. See also Herriott, *An Introduction to the History of Corporation Taxes*, 299.

29. Wood, *The Long-Suffering Shareholder*, in Wright et al., eds., *History of Corporate Governance*, 5:284.

30. Berle and Means, *The Modern Corporation*, 182.

31. Jonathan Macey and Geoffrey Miller, "Origin of the Blue Sky Laws," *Texas Law Review* 70 (December 1991): 347–98; Gower, "Some Contrasts Between British and American Corporation Law," 1373–74; Lough, *Corporation Finance*, 316–24.

32. Kuhn, *A Comparative Study of the Law of Corporations*, 146–47; Banner, *Anglo-American Securities Regulation*, 281–89; Nash, "Government and Business," 151–52; Manne, "Out Two Corporation Systems," 266 n. 15.

33. Quoted in Dunlavy, "From Citizens to Plutocrats," 86.

34. Ibid., 87.

35. Berle and Means, *The Modern Corporation*, 6.

36. Wood, *The Long-Suffering Shareholder*, in Wright et al., eds., *History of Corporate Governance*, 5:284.

37. Minnesota Electoral Reform Association, *Minority Representation*, in Wright et al., eds., *History of Corporate Governance*, 4:351–60.

38. Berle and Means, *The Modern Corporation*, 6.

39. Ayer, *Some of the Usages and Abuses*, 4. See also Roy, *Socializing Capital*, 84.

40. Ripley, *Main Street and Wall Street*, 139; Berle and Means, *The Modern Corporation*, 210; Manne, "Out Two Corporation Systems," 268; Lough, *Corporation Finance*, 44–45.

41. Micklethwait and Wooldridge, *The Company*, xix.

42. Gould, quoted in Wormser, *Frankenstein*, 127.

43. Lockwood, "How to Reform Business," 294.

44. Manly et al., *Final Report of the Commission on Industrial Relations*, 18–19.

45. Veblen, quoted in Mitchell, *Speculation Economy*, 15.

46. Minnesota Electoral Reform Association, *Minority Representation*, in Wright et al., eds., *History of Corporate Governance*, 4:351–60; New York Cheap Transportation Association, *Arguments of*, in Wright et al., eds., *History of Corporate Governance*, 4:363–84; Wormser, *Frankenstein*, 157.

47. Wood, *The Long-Suffering Shareholder*, in Wright et al., eds., *History of Corporate Governance*, 5:289.

48. Woodrow Wilson, "Before the War: How Things Looked Then," in Ripley, *Main Street and Wall Street*, 13.

49. "The Contest Against Corporations," *New York Times* (August 14, 1878), 4. See also Horwitz, *Transformation of America Law, 1870–1960*, 73–74.

50. Ratner, "The Government of Business Corporations," 54.

51. New York Cheap Transportation Association, *Arguments of*, in Wright et al., eds., *History of Corporate Governance*, 4:365.

52. Hitchcock, *Annual Address*, 240. See also Lockwood, "How to Reform Business," 302.

53. Minnesota Electoral Reform Association, *Minority Representation*, in Wright et al., eds., *History of Corporate Governance*, 4:354. See also John S. Parker, *Where and How: A Hand Book of Incorporation* (New York: Broun-Green, 1903), 152–53.

54. Ripley, *Main Street and Wall Street*, 104–5, 146. See also Mitchell, "Shareholders as Proxies," 1508.

55. Berle and Means, *The Modern Corporation*, liv, 71–72.

56. Ripley, *Main Street and Wall Street*, 86–88, 122. See also Berk, *Alternative Tracks*, 69.

57. Wormser, *Frankenstein*, 91.

58. Galbraith, *New Industrial State*, 80.

59. For further discussion of voting rights, see Kerbel, "An Examination of Nonvoting and Limited Voting Common Shares," 37–68; Mike Burkart and Samuel Lee, "One Share-One Vote: The Theory," *Review of Finance* 12, 1 (2008): 1–49; Renee Adams and Daniel Ferreira, "One Share-One Vote: The Empirical Evidence," *Review of Finance* 12, 1 (2008): 51–91.

60. Freyer, "Business Law," in Engerman and Gallman, eds., *The Cambridge Economic History of the United States*, 470–71; Dunlavy, "From Citizens to Plutocrats," 71.

61. Mary A. O'Sullivan, "What Opportunity Is Knocking? Regulating Corporate Governance in the United States," in Balleisen and Moss, eds., *Governments and Markets*, 348; Manne, "Out Two Corporation Systems," 270–72.

62. Hovenkamp, *Enterprise and American Law*, 62.

63. Jennifer Carpenter, Thomas Cooley, and Ingo Walter, "Reforming Compensation and Corporate Governance," in Viral Acharya, Thomas Cooley, Matthew Richardson, and Ingo Walter, eds., *Regulating Wall Street: The Dodd-Frank Act and the New Architecture of Global Finance* (Hoboken, N.J.: John Wiley, 2011), 499; Ripley, *Main Street and Wall Street*, 38, 56.

64. Hovenkamp, *Enterprise and American Law*, 62.

65. Wood, *The Long-Suffering Shareholder*, in Wright et al., eds., *History of Corporate Governance*, 5:284; Berle and Means, *The Modern Corporation*, 115; Skeel, *Icarus in the Boardroom*, 24.

66. Berle and Means, *The Modern Corporation*, 83.

67. Alfred Chandler, *The Visible Hand: The Managerial Revolution in American Business* (Cambridge, Mass.: Harvard University Press, 1977), 415–16, 451–52; Wormser, *Frankenstein*, 126; Crowder, "State Regulation of Commercial Banking," 284–86.

68. Mitchell, *Speculation Economy*, 28–32, 41; Chandler, *The Visible Hand*, 319–36.

69. Roy, *Socializing Capital*, 19, 70, 151, 164–72.

70. Hovenkamp, *Enterprise and American Law*, 257–63.

71. I do not mean to imply that a race *to* the bottom was inevitable or that one, in fact, occurred, but merely that competition induced some pressure for pro-management rules. Clearly, it was possible to frighten away stockholders by giving too much power to executives. Various pundits tried to induce states to improve their corporate laws so as to attract capital at the expense of other states. Also, states with the laxest laws suffered because investors eschewed the shares of corporations chartered within them. See Minnesota Electoral Reform Association, *Minority Representation*, in Wright et al., eds., *History of Corporate Governance*, 4:355; Manne, "Out Two Corporation Systems," 269–70 n. 20; Robert E. Wright, "Chartermongering by South Dakota in the Early Twentieth Century," in Jon Lauck, John Miller, and Donald Simmons, Jr., eds., *Political Culture of South Dakota* (Pierre: South Dakota State Historical Society Press, forthcoming).

72. Wormser, *Frankenstein*, 89–91; Mitchell, *Speculation Economy*, 42; Lough, *Corporation Finance*, 53–64; Rutterford, "The Shareholder Voice," 122, 147.

73. Ripley, *Main Street and Wall Street*, 74.

74. Quoted in Horwitz, *Transformation of America Law, 1870–1960*, 77.

75. A useful summary of Colorado's corporate laws, which included many of the checks and balances developed in the antebellum era, is Luther S. Kauffman, *Kauffman's Manual for Stock Companies, Organized under the Laws of Colorado* (Denver, 1882), in Wright et al., eds., *History of Corporate Governance*, 5:75–278.

76. Mitchell, *Speculation Economy*, 54–56; Ripley, *Main Street and Wall Street*, 34–35.

77. Quoted in Ripley, *Main Street and Wall Street*, 29–30.

78. Ibid., 16.

79. Wormser, *Frankenstein*, 88.

80. Berle and Means, *The Modern Corporation*, 136, 152–53.

81. Micklethwait and Wooldridge, *The Company*, 141.

82. Wormser, *Frankenstein*, 93.

83. Rutterford, "The Shareholder Voice," 127.

84. Berle and Means, *The Modern Corporation*, 6.

85. Hovenkamp, *Enterprise and American Law*, 59–61; Manne, "Out Two Corporation Systems," 271; Mitchell, *Speculation Economy*, 42–48; Naomi Lamoreaux, *The Great Merger Movement in American Business, 1895–1904* (New York: Cambridge University Press, 1985), 162–69; Hovenkamp, *Enterprise and American Law*, 241–44; Roy, *Socializing Capital*, 151–58; Smith and Dyer, "The Rise and Transformation of the American Corporation," in Kaysen, ed., *The American Corporation Today*, 39–49; Alfred Marshall, *Industry and Trade: A Study of Industrial Technique and Business Organization* (1919), in Wright and Sylla, eds., *History of Corporate Finance*, 6:368.

86. Roy, *Socializing Capital*, 5–6.

87. Ripley, *Main Street and Wall Street*, 178.

88. Berk, *Alternative Tracks*, 69.

89. Smith and Dyer, "The Rise and Transformation of the American Corporation," in Kaysen, ed., *The American Corporation Today*, 44; Micklethwait and Wooldridge, *The Company*, 117.

90. Ripley, *Main Street and Wall Street*, 196.

91. Roy, *Socializing Capital*, 11, 108–9.

92. Wollman, quoted in Berk, *Alternative Tracks*, 56–58.

93. Berk, *Alternative Tracks*, 70.

94. Banner, *Anglo-American Securities Regulation*, 250–80; Mitchell, *Speculation Economy*, 108–12.

95. Calomiris and Ramirez, "Financing the American Corporation," in Kaysen, ed., *The American Corporation Today*, 153.

96. Pujo, quoted in Bakan, *The Corporation*, 15.

97. Lippman, quoted in Smith and Dyer, "The Rise and Transformation of the American Corporation," in Kaysen, ed., *The American Corporation Today*, 48.

98. Jeffrey Fear and Christopher Kobrak, "Banks on Board: German and American Corporate Governance, 1870–1914," *Business History Review* 84 (winter 2010): 703–36;

Smith and Dyer, "The Rise and Transformation of the American Corporation," in Kaysen, ed., *The American Corporation Today*, 44, 47; Calomiris and Ramirez, "Financing the American Corporation," in Kaysen, ed., *The American Corporation Today*, 139, 153; Eugene White, "Regulation and Governance: A Secular Perspective on the Development of the American Financial System," in Stefano Battilossi and Jaime Reis, eds., *State and Financial Systems in Europe and the USA: Historical Perspectives on Regulation and Supervision in the Nineteenth and Twentieth Centuries* (Burlington, Vt.: Ashgate, 2010), 71–73; Benston, *Regulating Financial Markets*, 67–68.

99. Harwell Wells, "U.S. Executive Compensation in Historical Perspective," in Jennifer Hill and Randall Thomas, eds., *Research Handbook on Executive Compensation* (Northampton, Mass.: Edward Elgar, 2012), 5.

100. Ripley, *Main Street and Wall Street*, 37, 119–22.

101. Wiley B. Rutledge, "Significant Trends in Modern Corporation Statutes," *Washington University Law Quarterly* 22 (1937): 305, 337, quoted in John Armour and Brian Cheffins, "Origins of 'Offensive' Shareholder Activism in the United States," in Koppell, ed., *Origins of Shareholder Advocacy*, 262.

102. Wormser, *Frankenstein*, 87.

103. Berle and Means, *The Modern Corporation*, liii.

104. Wormser, *Frankenstein*, 118, 121, 156–57. See also Calomiris and Ramirez, "Financing the American Corporation," in Kaysen, ed., *The American Corporation Today*, 154.

105. Snyder, "Railroad Stocks as Investments," 164–74.

106. Chandler, *The Visible Hand*, 464–500.

107. Lough, *Corporation Finance*, 316.

108. Berle and Means, *The Modern Corporation*, 49, 66–111; Thomas Nixon Carter, *The Present Economic Revolution in the United States* (Boston: Little, Brown, 1925), 103–4; Knowlton, *Pepperell's Progress*, 356.

109. Snyder, "Railroad Stocks as Investments," 165.

110. Wormser, *Frankenstein*, 49–50.

111. Carter, *The Present Economic Revolution*, 99–104.

112. See also Lough, *Corporation Finance*, 7; Mitchell, *Speculation Economy*, 99–103, 200; Berle and Means, *The Modern Corporation*, 52; Ripley, *Main Street and Wall Street*, 95.

113. Carter, *The Present Economic Revolution*, 107; Mitchell, *Speculation Economy*, 103; Berle and Means, *The Modern Corporation*, 56; Berle, "Property, Production and Revolution," in Berle and Means, *The Modern Corporation*, xxi, xxxii.

114. Manly et al., *Final Report of the Commission on Industrial Relations*, 17–18.

115. Mitchell, *Speculation Economy*, 13, 48–49, 65.

116. Cadman, *The Corporation in New Jersey*, 252–55; Hovenkamp, *Enterprise and American Law*, 52–53; Freyer, "Business Law," in Engerman and Gallman, eds., *The Cambridge Economic History of the United States*, 471.

117. Tucker, *Notes of Lectures on Corporations*, 62.

118. Marshall, *Industry and Trade*, in Wright and Sylla, eds., *History of Corporate Finance*, 6:365.

119. Wormser, *Frankenstein*, 14.

120. Ibid., 142.

121. Ibid., 148.

122. Ibid., 149.

123. Ripley, *Main Street and Wall Street*, 192.

124. Mitchell, *Speculation Economy*, 30–32, 74–75, 88.

125. Marshall, *Industry and Trade*, in Wright and Sylla, eds., *History of Corporate Finance*, 6:365–66.

126. Green, *Corporation Finance*, in Wright and Sylla, eds., *History of Corporate Finance*, 6:263–70.

127. Lockwood, "How to Reform Business," 294; Mitchell, *Speculation Economy*, 1, 60–61, 81–85.

128. Fear and Kobrak, "Banks on Board," 703.

129. Smith and Dyer, "The Rise and Transformation of the American Corporation," in Kaysen, ed., *The American Corporation Today*, 51–52; Calomiris and Ramirez, "Financing the American Corporation," in Kaysen, ed., *The American Corporation Today*, 158–59.

130. Berle, "Property, Production and Revolution," in Berle and Means, *The Modern Corporation*, xxii.

131. Gardiner Means, "Implications of the Corporate Revolution in Economic Theory," in Berle and Means, *The Modern Corporation*, xlii, xlvii. See also Armour and Cheffins, "Origins of 'Offensive' Shareholder Activism," in Koppell, ed., *Origins of Shareholder Advocacy*, 263; Galbraith, *New Industrial State*, 79; O'Sullivan, "What Opportunity Is Knocking?" in Balleisen and Moss, eds., *Governments and Markets*, 347; Chandler, *The Visible Hand*, 493.

132. Wormser, *Frankenstein*, 129–30; O'Sullivan, "What Opportunity Is Knocking?," in Balleisen and Moss, eds., *Governments and Markets*, 348; Smith and Dyer, "The Rise and Transformation of the American Corporation," in Kaysen, ed., *The American Corporation Today*, 43–44; Freeman, Pearson, and Taylor, *Shareholder Democracies?*, 5.

133. Chandler, *The Visible Hand*, 492.

134. Galbraith, *New Industrial State*, 84.

135. Ibid., 85.

136. Ibid., 397.

137. Ibid., xix, 2.

138. Quoted in O'Sullivan, "What Opportunity Is Knocking?," in Balleisen and Moss, eds., *Governments and Markets*, 348. See also Tedlow, *Rise of the American Business Corporation*, 4–5; Mitchell, *Speculation Economy*, 274–75; Calomiris and Ramirez, "Financing the American Corporation," in Kaysen, ed., *The American Corporation Today*, 162; Hovenkamp, *Enterprise and American Law*, 55.

139. Galbraith, *New Industrial State*, 1.

140. Mark Roe, "From Antitrust to Corporation Governance? The Corporation and

the Law, 1959–1994," in Kaysen, ed., *The American Corporation Today*, 104; Rutterford, "The Shareholder Voice," 134, 144–45.

141. Calomiris and Ramirez, "Financing the American Corporation," in Kaysen, ed., *The American Corporation Today*, 163–65.

142. Galbraith, *New Industrial State*, 81. See also Roe, "From Antitrust to Corporation Governance?," in Kaysen, ed., *The American Corporation Today*, 105–9; Smith and Dyer, "The Rise and Transformation of the American Corporation," in Kaysen, ed., *The American Corporation Today*, 52–57; Roe, "From Antitrust to Corporation Governance?," in Kaysen, ed., *The American Corporation Today*, 106.

143. Berle and Means, *The Modern Corporation*, 82.

144. Galbraith, *New Industrial State*, 80. The loser must still pay up. Mitchell, "Shareholders as Proxies," 1507. See also Armour and Cheffins, "Origins of 'Offensive' Shareholder Activism," in Koppell, ed., *Origins of Shareholder Advocacy*, 253–76; Micklethwait and Wooldridge, *The Company*, 139–40; Roe, "From Antitrust to Corporation Governance?," in Kaysen, ed., *The American Corporation Today*, 110.

145. Manne, "Out Two Corporation Systems," 265–66; Smith and Dyer, "The Rise and Transformation of the American Corporation," in Kaysen, ed., *The American Corporation Today*, 32, 54–57; Calomiris and Ramirez, "Financing the American Corporation," in Kaysen, ed., *The American Corporation Today*, 164; Baskin and Miranti, *A History of Corporate Finance*, 326.

146. Macey, *Corporate Governance*, 10–11.

147. O'Sullivan, "What Opportunity Is Knocking?," in Balleisen and Moss, eds., *Governments and Markets*, 350; Roe, "From Antitrust to Corporation Governance?," in Kaysen, ed., *The American Corporation Today*, 104; Ratner, "The Government of Business Corporations," 23–25; Skeel, *Icarus in the Boardroom*, 124–27.

148. Mitchell, *Speculation Economy*. Occasionally, investors will pay more for a stock than they believe it is worth in order to retain control. For example, "several of the defendants" in the Jacob Barker governance fiasco purchased stock "although they knew it could not be obtained but at a price exceeding its intrinsic value." North River Bank, Proceedings in Chancery, 1824, NYHS. "If the market perceives that a company is *undervalued* because of poor managerial talent, a successful takeover can replace management and increase the market value of the targeted firm [emphasis added]." Calomiris and Ramirez, "Financing the American Corporation," in Kaysen, ed., *The American Corporation Today*, 164–65.

149. Baskin and Miranti, *A History of Corporate Finance*, 197–99, 201.

150. Wormser, *Frankenstein*, 149.

151. Benston, *Regulating Financial Markets*, 62.

152. Quoted in Wormser, *Frankenstein*, 113.

153. David Einhorn, *Fooling Some of the People All of the Time: A Long Short Story* (Hoboken, N.J.: John Wiley, 2008); Robert Sloan, *Don't Blame the Shorts: Why Short Sellers Are Always Blamed for Market Crashes and How History Is Repeating Itself* (New York: McGraw-Hill, 2009).

154. Veblen, quoted in Mitchell, *Speculation Economy*, 15.

155. F. W. Taussig and W. S. Barker, "American Corporations and Their Executives: A Statistical Inquiry," *Quarterly Journal of Economics* 40 (November 1925): 11–18, 22–23. See also Carola Frydman and Raven Molloy, "Pay Cuts for the Boss: Executive Compensation in the 1940s," *Journal of Economic History* 72, 1 (March 2012): 225–51.

156. Wormser, *Frankenstein*, 115–21; Roy, *Socializing Capital*, 84; Skeel, *Icarus in the Boardroom*, 154.

157. Michael Jensen and Kevin Murphy, "CEO Incentives—It's Not How Much You Pay, But How," *Harvard Business Review* 68 (May/June 1990): 138–49.

158. Mill, quoted in Sidney G. Winter, "On Coase, Competence, and the Corporation," in Williamson and Winter, eds., *The Nature of the Firm*, 182. See also Wells, "U.S. Executive Compensation in Historical Perspective"; Skeel, *Icarus in the Boardroom*, 152–54; John Naisbitt and Patricia Aburdene, *Re-Inventing the Corporation: Transforming Your Job and Your Company for the New Information Society* (New York: Warner, 1985), 54–59.

159. Wells, "U.S. Executive Compensation in Historical Perspective"; Avinash Arya and Huey-Lian Sun, "Stock Option Repricing: Heads I Win, Tails You Lose," *Journal of Business Ethics* 50 (April 2004): 297–312.

Chapter 10

1. *Report of the Committee on Banks and Insurance Companies*, 7.

2. Tucker, *Notes of Lectures on Corporations*, 15.

3. The data presented in this paragraph can be found in Thomas Navin and Marian Sears, "The Rise of a Market for Industrial Securities, 1887–1902," *Business History* 29 (1955): 105–38; Hitchcock, *Annual Address*, 245; Lamoreaux, "Partnerships, Corporations," in Lipartito and Sicilia, eds., *Constructing Corporate America*, 34; Roy, *Socializing Capital*, 5; Micklethwait and Wooldridge, *The Company*, xx.

4. See Tedlow, *Rise of the American Business Corporation*, 5. Galbraith argued that there were in the postwar period several different types of corporations—most broadly, older, smaller, more traditional ones akin to Manhattan brownstones and new behemoths analogous to skyscrapers. Galbraith, *New Industrial State*, 73–75. See also Berle, "Property, Production and Revolution," in Berle and Means, *The Modern Corporation*, xxi.

5. Bigelow, quoted in Spalding, "The Boston Mercantile Community," 178.

6. Wormser, *Frankenstein*, v–viii, 53–54. For a more detailed treatment of corporate governance since the Civil War (but a very truncated discussion of governance before it), see Skeel, *Icarus in the Boardroom*.

7. June 10, 2011.

8. Quoted in Todd and Sonkin, *Alexander Bryan Johnson*, 339.

9. "Each Icarus Effect scandal has prompted this kind of 'tit-for-tat' response." Skeel, *Icarus in the Boardroom*, 43, 194. The same back-and-forth dynamic occurred in Britain. Freeman, Pearson, and Taylor, *Shareholder Democracies?*, 248–50; *Report of the Committee on Banks and Insurance Companies*, 15.

10. Bakan, *The Corporation*, 28–59; Rutterford, "The Shareholder Voice," 122.

11. Ripley, *Main Street and Wall Street*, 116.

12. Baskin and Miranti, *A History of Corporate Finance*, 322.

13. Ibid.

14. See also Macey, *Corporate Governance*, 15; O'Sullivan, "What Opportunity Is Knocking?," 342–43; Micklethwait and Wooldridge, *The Company*, 153.

15. Benston, *Regulating Financial Markets*, 62–64.

16. Robert E. Wright, ed. *Bailouts: Public Money, Private Profit* (New York: Columbia University Press, 2010).

17. Skeel, *Icarus in the Boardroom*, 161–70.

18. Micklethwait and Wooldridge, *The Company*, 154.

19. For a more general review of managerial incentives and corporate fraud, see Shane A. Johnson, Harley E. Ryan, Jr., and Yisong S. Tian, "Managerial Incentives and Corporate Fraud: The Sources of Incentives Matter," *Review of Finance* 13, 1 (2009): 115–45.

20. Susan Pulliam and Deborah Solomon, "Uncooking the Books: How Three Unlikely Sleuths Discovered Fraud at WorldCom," *Wall Street Journal* (October 30, 2002), as reprinted in Lipman and Lipman, *Corporate Governance Best Practices*, 256–64.

21. Minnesota Electoral Reform Association, *Minority Representation*, in Wright et al., eds., *History of Corporate Governance*, 4:354.

22. Micklethwait and Wooldridge, *The Company*, 153; Lough, *Corporation Finance*, 370–71.

23. Derek Laing, *Labor Economics: Introduction to Classic and the New Labor Economics* (New York: W. W. Norton, 2011), 613–16.

24. Lucian Bebchuk and Jesse Fried, *Pay without Performance: The Unfulfilled Promise of Executive Compensation* (Cambridge, Mass.: Harvard University Press, 2004), ix.

25. Quoted in O'Sullivan, "What Opportunity Is Knocking?," 352.

26. Bebchuk and Fried, *Pay without Performance*, 11.

27. Ripley, *Main Street and Wall Street*, 75.

28. See Laing, *Labor Economics*, 620–21; Clifford Holderness, "Blockholders Are More Common in the United States than You Might Think," *Journal of Applied Corporate Finance* 22, 4 (2010): 75–85. "The owners of most large, publicly held American enterprises have little or no influence over the election and removal of directors. The nomination process for directors is typically controlled by incumbent directors and, in some cases, even by senior corporate executives. . . . And, because most companies had plurality (rather than majority) voting for director elections until recently, only one favorable vote was required to elect a director." O'Sullivan, "What Opportunity Is Knocking?," 345. See also Michael Bednar, "Watchdog or Lapdog?: A Behavioral View of the Media as a Corporate Governance Mechanism," *Academy of Management Journal* 55, 1 (2012): 131–50; Wells, "U.S. Executive Compensation in Historical Perspective"; Skeel, *Icarus in the Boardroom*, 154, 201–4; Berle and Means, *The Modern Corporation*, 9.

29. See Kaysen, "Introduction," in Kaysen, ed., *The American Corporation Today*, 5;

O'Sullivan, "What Opportunity Is Knocking?," 343–44; Mark Roe, *Strong Managers, Weak Owners: The Political Roots of American Corporate Finance* (Princeton, N.J.: Princeton University Press, 1994), 260–62.

30. Xavier Giroud and Holder M. Mueller, "Does Corporate Governance Matter in Competitive Industries?" (working paper, August 2007).

31. O'Sullivan, "What Opportunity Is Knocking?," 336.

32. Helmut Dietl, Tobias Duschl, and Markus Lang, "Executive Pay Regulation: What Regulators, Shareholders, and Managers Can Learn from Major Sports Leagues," *Business and Politics* 13, 2 (2011): 1–30.

33. Naisbitt and Aburdene, *Re-Inventing the Corporation*, 1.

34. In their classic study, Berle and Means noted that "if the community is to save, . . . it will, in large measure, be obliged to invest in corporate securities." If individuals distrust the "corporate system," therefore, they will have little incentive to save. Such, then, may be a leading reason for Americans' recent lack of thrift. Berle and Means, *The Modern Corporation*, 64.

35. Wilcox, *Whatever Happened to Thrift?*

36. Minnesota Electoral Reform Association, *Minority Representation*, in Wright et al., eds., *History of Corporate Governance*, 4:355.

37. Ripley, *Main Street and Wall Street*, 228.

38. Benston, *Regulating Financial Markets*, 72–83; Crowder, "State Regulation of Commercial Banking," 287; O'Sullivan, "What Opportunity Is Knocking?," 337; Micklethwait and Wooldridge, *The Company*, 156; Hawley, Kamath, and Williams, "Introduction," in Hawley, Kamath, and Williams, eds., *Corporate Governance Failures*, 6.

39. White, "Regulation and Governance," in Battilossi and Reis, eds., *State and Financial Systems*, 78. And see O'Sullivan, "What Opportunity Is Knocking?," 337–39.

40. Bebchuk and Fried, *Pay without Performance*, 2–3.

41. Ripley, *Main Street and Wall Street*, 133.

42. White, "Regulation and Governance," 77.

43. Einhorn, *Fooling Some of the People All of the Time*.

44. Bakan, *The Corporation*, 161; Coglianese and Kagan, *Regulation*; David Skeel, William Cohan, and Harvey Miller, *The New Financial Deal: Understanding the Dodd-Frank Act and Its (Unintended) Consequences* (Hoboken, N.J.: Wiley, 2010); Acharya et al., eds., *Regulating Wall Street*; Vern McKinley, *Financing Failure: A Century of Bailouts* (Oakland, Calif.: Independent Institute, 2011).

45. Thurlow, quoted in Micklethwait and Wooldridge, *The Company*, 33.

46. Dodd, *American Business Corporations*, 70–71.

47. Bakan also got this wrong. Bakan, *The Corporation*, 161.

48. Wilson, "Before the War," in Ripley, *Main Street and Wall Street*, 4.

49. Wood, *The Long-Suffering Shareholder*, in Wright et al., eds., *History of Corporate Governance*, 5:286.

50. Lockwood, "How to Reform Business," 299.

51. "Kansas Beats Stock Swindling," *Wall Street Journal* (March 2, 1912), 6.

52. Carpenter, Cooley, and Walter, "Reforming Compensation and Corporate Governance," in Acharya et al., eds., *Regulating Wall Street*, 499; William Hamilton, *A Manual of Company Law for the Use of Directors and Promoters* (London: Sevens, 1891), in Wright et al., eds., *History of Corporate Governance*, 6:272–346; Hitchcock, *Annual Address*, 258.

53. Wollman, quoted in Berk, *Alternative Tracks*, 57.

54. Wells, "U.S. Executive Compensation in Historical Perspective," 24–25.

55. Ripley, *Main Street and Wall Street*, 76.

56. Wilson, "Before the War," 7.

57. Galbraith, *New Industrial State*, 77.

58. Roe, *Strong Managers, Weak Owners*, 286, quotation on x.

59. Macey, *Corporate Governance*, viii, 10.

60. Ripley, *Main Street and Wall Street*, 129.

61. For the widespread acceptance of Ripley's views, see Mitchell, "Shareholders as Proxies," 1509.

62. Roe, "From Antitrust to Corporation Governance?," in Kaysen, ed., *The American Corporation Today*, 103.

63. Ripley, *Main Street and Wall Street*, 130.

64. Berle and Means, *The Modern Corporation*, 83.

65. Ripley, *Main Street and Wall Street*, 106.

66. Macey, *Corporate Governance*, 16.

67. Roe, *Strong Managers, Weak Owners*, x, 103, 278–80. See also O'Sullivan, "What Opportunity Is Knocking?," 345–46. By law, directors and executives are supposed to work fairly, diligently, honestly, and intelligently on behalf of stockholders. Berle and Means, *The Modern Corporation*, 197. See also Daniel Greenwood, "Democracy and Delaware: The Mysterious Race to the Bottom/Top," *Yale Law & Policy Review* 23 (spring 2005): 382–83.

68. O'Sullivan, "What Opportunity Is Knocking?," 341, 353, 358; Hawley, Kamath, and Williams, "Introduction," 21.

69. See Calomiris and Ramirez, "Financing the American Corporation," in Kaysen, ed., *The American Corporation Today*, 165; O'Sullivan, "What Opportunity Is Knocking?," 344; Macey, *Corporate Governance*, 14.

70. Bebchuk and Fried, *Pay without Performance*, 11–12, 189–216. See also Rudiger Fahlenbrach, "Shareholder Rights, Boards, and CEO Compensation," *Review of Finance* 13, 1 (2009): 81–113.

71. Ripley, *Main Street and Wall Street*, 134–40.

72. Frederick D. Lipman and L. Keith Lipman, *Corporate Governance Best Practices: Strategies for Public, Private, and Not-for-Profit Organizations* (Hoboken, N.J.: John Wiley, 2006), 3, 9–11.

73. Murray Weidenbaum and Mark Jensen, "Introduction to the Transaction Edition," in Berle and Means, *The Modern Corporation*, xvii.

74. Bednar, "Watchdog or Lapdog?," 131–50.

75. Macey, *Corporate Governance*, 14–15.

76. Roe, *Strong Managers, Weak Owners*, xi; Macey, *Corporate Governance*, 1, 14.

77. Ripley, *Main Street and Wall Street*, 130.

78. Quoted in Mitchell, *Speculation Economy*, 98.

79. Ripley, *Main Street and Wall Street*, 130. See also Wood, *The Long-Suffering Shareholder*, in Wright et al., eds., *History of Corporate Governance*, 5:290.

80. Ripley, *Main Street and Wall Street*, 107–9.

81. Roe, *Strong Managers, Weak Owners*, 268–69.

82. Mark Roe, "Some Differences in Corporate Structure in Germany, Japan, and the United States," *Yale Law Journal* 102 (June 1993): 1929.

83. See Hawley, Kamath, and Williams, "Introduction," 2, 6, 24–25; Micklethwait and Wooldridge, *The Company*, 137; O'Sullivan, "What Opportunity Is Knocking?," 349; Roe, "From Antitrust to Corporation Governance?," 117.

84. Hawley, Kamath, and Williams, eds., *Corporate Governance Failures*.

85. Micklethwait and Wooldridge, *The Company*, 137–38.

86. Quoted in Ratner, "The Government of Business Corporations," 26.

87. O'Sullivan, "What Opportunity Is Knocking?," 353–54.

88. Roe, *Strong Managers, Weak Owners*, 269. See also 270–78.

89. See Hawley, Kamath, and Williams, "Introduction," 25.

90. Carpenter, Cooley, and Walter, "Reforming Compensation and Corporate Governance," 498.

91. Ibid., 497–98; Claudine Mangen and Michel Magnan, "'Say on Pay': A Wolf in Sheep's Clothing?," *Academy of Management Perspectives* 26, 2 (May 2012): 86–104.

92. Carpenter, Cooley, and Walter, "Reforming Compensation and Corporate Governance," 498.

93. Ibid., 502.

94. Hawley, Kamath, and Williams, "Introduction," 23.

Index

For the names of individual persons, companies, and corporations mentioned in the text, see the following main headings: commentators (historical, mostly pre-twentieth-century individuals who commented on or influenced any aspect of corporations and their development); companies (historical and contemporary, incorporated and not); practitioners and scholars (contemporary scholars and businesspeople, mostly twentieth century, but classical economists like Adam Smith are also included).

companies (*cont.*)

    Company, 67, 140, 148; Whitesboro Cotton Company, 61; White Sulphur Springs Company, 106; Worldcom, 215–20; Wrightsville Canal Company, 159; Yadkin Navigation Company, 142; York Factory, 63; York Manufacturing Company, 73. *See also* Bank of the United States (1791–1811); Bank of the United States (1816–1836); United States Bank of Pennsylvania

Companies Act of 1867 (Great Britain), 222

company. *See* corporations; joint-stock companies; unchartered joint-stock companies

competition. *See* market power

Connecticut: corporation taxation in, 83–84; early corporations in, 24; general incorporation laws of, 185; limited partnership law of, 10; opposition of to New York's steamship monopoly, 113; ownership of equities by government of, 93; sale of shares of delinquent stockholders in, 142

corpora, 19

corporate entrepreneurs. *See* entrepreneurs

corporate governance. *See* governance

corporate laws. *See* corporations

corporate seal, 4, 20–21, 127

corporation, sole, 14–15

corporations: Adam Smith on, 28–30; agency costs within, 28–29, 81–82, 152–72, 205, 214, 219; alignment of incentives within, 128–32, 138, 152, 173, 179, 187–88, 227–29; Americanization of, 19; angst against, 4, 31; annual meetings of, 136; annual reports of, 138–39; apologists for, 215–16, 222, 225; assets of, 73; attraction of shysters by, 166; attributes of modern form of, 48; attrition rates of, 66, 69, 72–74; bankruptcies of, 2, 5, 12, 31, 71, 73, 170, 202; benefits of relatively large size of, 80–115; board of directors of, 119–20; body of lacking, 48, 222; bonding policies of, 127–28; British, 1; business cycle and, 52–54, 63; business types and, 61–63; bylaws of, 118, 127; capital calls of, 69, 141–44; capital management by, 68; capitalization of by business sector, 62–63; capitalization of checked by charters, legislators, and stockholders, 120–21; capital of, 4, 49–53, 57–63, 67–69, 73, 60, 75–76, 102–3, 106–7, 154, 171, 179–80, 185–86, 194, 215; capital

of as a percentage of aggregate output, 49, 51–52, 57–58; caveats concerning, 66–74; change in legal status of, 67; as characterized by John Kenneth Galbraith, 300 n.4; charter applications of, 60; chartering costs of, 81–82; chartering of, 48, 67, 82–83; checks and balances of, 120, 135; Chinese, 19; closely held, 3; colonial, 23; commercial rivalries between states and, 55–56; compensation of employees by, 128; competition between for charters, 56; Confederation era, 24; coordination of social cooperation by, 7; costs and benefits of, 183; criticism of, 27–38, 48; criticism of rebutted, 38–48; critics of described, 37; decision of to incorporate, 102; defend themselves from fraud and attack, 45, 173; delayed formation of, 66; democracy analogy of examined, 134–35; derivatives use by, 158; development of, 1; direct public offerings of, 99; dissolution (voluntary) of, 71; dividends paid out by, 146–47; economic effects of, 2, 3, 6–7, 44, 46, 55; economic importance of, 2–9, 215–16, 219–20; economies of scale and, 65, 80–81; efficiency of, 32; elections held by, 122, 132; equities of owned by foreigners, 97–98; equities of owned by governments, 96–97; equities of owned by other corporations, 97; exercise of market power by in Lowell, Mass., 112; exit of from business, 5, 71; factors influencing the formation of, 61; failure of to form, 66–67; farmers aided by, 6; female stockholders in, 93–94; financial bubbles and, 53–54; financial panics and, 72; foreign investors in, 193; formation of by entrepreneurs, 122; general incorporation laws and, 61, 185–86; geographical dispersion of stockholders in, 91, 133; goals of, 217; governance costs of, 81, 128–29, 163, 191, 201–2; governance of compared to political governance, 116–17, 121; governments and, 95–97, 173–74; Greek, 19; inactivity of, 71–72; incentives of directors of, 123; Indian (Asia), 19; influence of on government, 38–39, 45, 81, 183, 191; information content in prices of equities of, 207; information disclosure by, 137–41; interest rates and, 52–53; interstate 67, 108; investment in facilitated by

Acknowledgments

Funding for this project was received from the National Science Foundation (SES-0751577, administered by the National Bureau for Economic Research); the Berkley Center for Entrepreneurial Studies at the Stern School of Business, New York University; the Virginia Historical Society in Richmond, Virginia; the Filson Historical Society in Louisville, Kentucky; and the Nef Family Foundation in Sioux Falls, South Dakota.

Brian Cheffins, Cambridge University; Timothy Guinanne, Yale University; Perry Hanavan, Augustana College (South Dakota); Leslie Hannah, London School of Economics and Political Science; Eric Hilt, Wellesley College; Dan Holt, Federal Judicial Center; Doug Irwin, Dartmouth College; Christopher Kingston, Amherst College; Jonathan Koppell, Arizona State University; Naomi Lamoreaux, Yale University; Pauline Maier, MIT; Brian Murphy, Baruch College; Johann Neem, Western Washington University; Robin Pearson, Hull University; Richard Sylla, Stern School of Business, NYU; and John Wallis, University of Maryland all provided valuable comments on the manuscript or related cognates such as conference papers and book chapters. Two anonymous reviewers procured by the publisher also deserve thanks for improving the book with their extensive comments. Any remaining errors remain the author's sole responsibility.